Heidegger, Dilthey, and the Crisis of Historicism

Heidegger, Dilthey, and the Crisis of Historicism

Charles R. Bambach

CORNELL UNIVERSITY PRESS   *Ithaca and London*

First published 1995 by Cornell University Press.
First printing, Cornell Paperbacks, 1995.

Printed in the United States of America

Library of Congress Cataloging-in-Publication Data

Bambach, Charles R.
      Heidegger, Dilthey, and the crisis of historicism / Charles R. Bambach.
          p. cm.
      Includes bibliographical references (p.) and index.
      ISBN 0-8014-3079-8 (cloth: alk. paper)
      ISBN 0-8014-8260-7 (pbk.: alk. paper)
        1. Historicism. 2. Heidegger, Martin, 1889–1976—Views on historicism.
    3. Dilthey, Wilhelm, 1833–1911—Views on historicism. 4. Philosophy,
    German—19th century. 5. Philosophy, German—20th century I. Title.
B3184.5B35 1995
149—dc20   95-3392

Cloth printing   10 9 8 7 6 5 4 3 2 1

Paperback printing   10 9 8 7 6 5 4 3 2

For Joanne La Riccia, John Scanlan, and Catherine Bambach

Contents

Acknowledgments

During my work on this book I was generously supported by grants from the Earhart Foundation and the University of Texas at Dallas, School of Arts and Humanities, which enabled me to pursue my writing in Chicago, Baltimore, and New York. Earlier, I was aided by grants from the Deutscher Akademischer Austauschdienst at the Universität Tübingen and Universität Heidelberg.

A book of this nature depends on primary sources. For their help and generosity in providing me with copies of transcripts from Heidegger's early writings I thank Professor Frithjof Rodi, Director of the Dilthey Forschungsstelle and Dr. Friedrich Hogemann of the Hegel-Archiv, both at the Ruhr Universität Bochum. I also thank Theodore Kisiel for helping me track down Heidegger's Kassel lectures. John van Buren graciously provided me with a draft of his own forthcoming book on the young Heidegger, which proved extremely helpful in tracing Heidegger's connections to Luther and Christian theology.

Work on the book began in Tübingen, in the seminars of Walter Schulz and Dieter Jähnig, and in conversations with my friends Joseph Lawrence, Steven Kaplan, John Macken, and Rolf Maier. I also owe an important debt to my former teachers, Michael Geyer and Graves F. Ray, for their help and advice, and especially to Stephen

Tonsor, who gave more than was asked. For their comments on the original manuscript I thank Hans Kellner, Ernst Breisach, Georg Iggers, David Pellauer, Richard Palmer, Thomas Sheehan, Robert Mugerauer, Frederick Hotz, and Ashley Carr. Closer to home, I thank my colleagues Tim Redman, Gerald Soliday, Victor Worsfold, and Frederick Turner for their comments on the manuscript, and I thank my graduate students for keeping the conversation alive. I am also grateful to the late Robert W. Corrigan. Peggy Eckelkamp rendered technical assistance, and Holda Borcherts and Vicki Bullock helped track down obscure titles. I also thank my editor at Cornell, John Ackerman, for his patience and balance, and Teresa Jesionowski and Nancy Malone for their scrupulous copyediting.

Rod Coltman and Candace Uhlmeyer offered support, painstaking criticisms, and timely suggestions, which helped me complete the book smoothly. I thank them for their generous friendship. I also thank my friends Garth Montgomery, Gertrud Rath-Montgomery, Thomas J. Bowes, and especially Theresa Biggs for her judicious eye and sympathetic ear. Finally, Joanne La Riccia, John Scanlan, and Catherine Bambach provided advice, criticism, irony, and humor. Without them the journey would have been harder to sustain.

CHARLES R. BAMBACH

Richardson, Texas

Heidegger, Dilthey, and the Crisis of Historicism

Introduction:
Modernity and Crisis

> It seems to be a fundamental trait of philosophical
> consciousness in the nineteenth century that it is no longer
> conceivable apart from historical consciousness.
> —Hans-Georg Gadamer, *Hegel's Dialectic*

> Every mere "-ism" is a misunderstanding and the death of
> history.
> —Martin Heidegger, *What Is a Thing?*

A t the beginning of the summer semester in 1939, the Freiburg philosopher Martin Heidegger opened his lecture course by identifying "the history of the era of modern times, of the end of the West" with the history of metaphysics. As Heidegger explained: "The whole of Western thinking from the Greeks through Nietzsche is metaphysical thinking. Each age of Western history is grounded in its respective metaphysics." Heidegger focused his attention during the semester especially on Nietzsche, whom he viewed as "the *last metaphysician* of the West"— the philosopher who, in precipitating the crisis of Western metaphysics, had heralded the modern epoch of nihilism.[1] Nietzsche's work represented to Heidegger the clearest expression of modernist metaphysics in its crisis state, a metaphysics whose historical legitimacy had been undermined as much by its own technological-scientific will to power as by historical experience itself. History and metaphysics—when thought together—posed a crisis for Western philosophy, Heidegger maintained, precisely insofar as they pre-

---

[1] Martin Heidegger, *Nietzsche*, vol. 3, trans. David Farrell Krell (New York: Harper and Row, 1987), 7–8; *Nietzsche*, vol. 1 (Pfullingen: Neske, 1961), 479–480. Unless indicated otherwise, all translations are mine.

sented the inner logic of modernity as an epoch preoccupied by thoughts of an "end." In philosophical terms, Heidegger understood modernity as the "final age"—an era of decline, apocalypse, and eschatological desperation—that would bring about the conclusion of Western culture. And for Heidegger, this nihilistic collapse was symbolized by the name "Nietzsche": "The age whose consummation unfolds in his thought, the modern age, is a final age. This means an age in which at some point and in some way the historical decision arises as to whether this final age is the conclusion of Western history or the counterpart to another beginning."[2]

Perhaps one could designate Heidegger's "historical decision" about "end" and "beginning" in the Nietzsche lectures as the inauguration of a postmodern attitude toward history or, rather, of a postmodern preoccupation with the "end of history." In his effort in these lectures to locate "the metaphysical character of history" within a discourse about the history of modernity, Heidegger provided a devastating critique of the grand narrative tradition of German historicism.[3] But he also succeeded in dismantling and deconstructing the optimistic *Geschichtsphilosophie* of Friedrich Meinecke's *Historism* (1936) and its latent metaphysical assumptions about progress, meaning, and rationality. As he lectured on the history of metaphysics, Heidegger no longer approached history in traditional historicist terms as the source of all creative value or as a model for the continuity of cultural tradition (*Bildungsgeschichte*). Instead, he interpreted historicism as a world view that was dead and obsolete—a mere remnant of the *Weltanschauungsphilosophie* that had dominated the consciousness of nineteenth-century Europe. But for Heidegger the death of historicism signified more than the collapse of a scholarly tradition within German historical thought. It also represented the awareness of an epochal transition for European thinking as a whole and provided the sense of an ending for the metaphysical tradition begun with the early Greeks. The collapse of historicism was intimately connected in Heidegger's critique with "the final age" of metaphysics, an age which had become surfeited with the insights of history and which had grown weary of the nihilistic tendencies of tradition itself. Coming at the end of a long generational debate about the meaning of historical consciousness, Heidegger's Nietzsche lectures offered to his

---

[2] Ibid.
[3] Martin Heidegger, *Nietzsche*, vol. 4, trans. David Farrell Krell (New York: Harper and Row, 1982), 241; *Nietzsche*, vol. 2 (Pfullingen: Neske, 1961), 386.

listeners the final word on historicism, or at least an interpretation that understood it as something "final." Considered as another expression of "the end of history," for Heidegger, historicism embodied the metaphysics of Western thought and its exhausted categories of temporality, linearity, and totality which reinforced the perception of a crisis of modernity.

Historicism was synonymous, in Heidegger's view, with the logic of linear narrative and diachronic succession which authorized the humanistic reading of the past from the position of a transcendental subject: the self-conscious, autonomous *cogito* of Cartesian metaphysics. In its crisis mode, however, historicism implied more than the appearance of doubts about a narrowly historiographical tradition: it ultimately expressed the bankruptcy of a whole metaphysical epoch constructed on the universal-rational principles of historicist metaphysics and anthropology. Insofar as Heidegger's work accounts for the end of the modern age and its relationship to the metaphysical principles of historicism, it serves as an important transition between the slippery categories of modernity and postmodernity. The ironic, playful awareness in contemporary literary criticism and philosophy concerning "the end of history" and "the end of philosophy" follows upon the collapse and implosion of traditional historicist categories.[4] Heidegger's critique was decisive in transforming the historiographical meaning of this collapse into a philosophical confrontation with the legacy of modernism. But his work was not the autochthonic expression of an isolated temperament; it took the form of a careful and pointed response to the actual debates about historical knowledge and meaning within contemporary German philosophy. To understand the full significance of Heidegger's critique, we will need to consider the specific context from which it developed.

In what follows I propose a kind of genealogy of historicist metaphysics which situates it within the crisis-consciousness that emerged out of German philosophical thinking in the era from 1880 to 1930. By looking at the work of four university philosophers intimately connected with the "crisis of historicism"—Wilhelm Windelband (1848–1915), Heinrich Rickert (1863–1936), Wilhelm Dilthey (1833–1911), and Martin Heidegger (1889–1976)—I endeavor to provide an ac-

---

[4] For a discussion of the "end of history" debate, there are several important sources: Lutz Niethammer, *Posthistoire*, trans. Patrick Camiller (London: Verso, 1992); Wolfgang Welsch, *Unsere postmoderne Moderne* (Weinheim: VCH, Acta Humaniora, 1991); Francis Fukuyama, *The End of History and the Last Man* (New York: Free Press, 1992); and Michael S. Roth, *Knowing and History* (Ithaca, N.Y.: Cornell University Press, 1988).

count of the aporias and contradictions within early-twentieth-century German philosophy which helped define it as a discipline in crisis.[5] I have chosen this group of philosophers because it seems to me that their work represents an important shift in modern German

[5] One of the peculiar ironies about the complex usage of the term *historicism* is that it does not become accepted until it reaches the end of its vital phase in the years after the Great War in Germany. As Herbert Schnädelbach explains in *Philosophy in Germany, 1831–1933* (Cambridge: Cambridge University Press, 1984), 34: "Although the term historicism may be traced back to very early in the nineteenth century, it first came into general use around the beginning of our own century: like many '-isms,' it was first used to denounce—it signified something to be overcome, something which was in crisis, something outmoded."

The characterization of a "crisis of historicism" gained wide acceptance through the early work of Ernst Troeltsch, *Der Historismus und seine Probleme* (Tübingen: Mohr, 1922) and *Der Historismus und seine Überwindung* (Berlin: Heise, 1924), as well as his essay "Die Krisis des Historismus," *Die Neue Rundschau* 33 (June 22): 572–590; see also the essays of Friedrich Meinecke in *Zur Theorie und Philosophie der Geschichte* (Stuttgart: Koehler, 1959) and the full-length study of the subject by Karl Heussi, *Die Krisis des Historismus* (Tübingen: Mohr, 1932). From its early beginnings, the term *historicism* has been the subject of much debate and confusion. With the recent development of a so-called new historicism among literary scholars such as Stephen Greenblatt (*Power of Forms in the English Renaissance* [Norman: University of Oklahoma Press, 1982]), Wesley Morris (*Towards a New Historicism* [Princeton, N.J.: Princeton University Press, 1972]), and others, the confusion has been compounded. I choose *historicism* (rather than the term *historism* adopted by J. E. Anderson in his translation of Friedrich Meinecke's *Historism* [London: Routledge, 1972]) as the English equivalent for the German term *Historismus*. In using this label I wish to avoid all association with the work of Karl Popper, who in *The Poverty of Historicism* (London: Routledge, 1957) uses the term to designate "an approach to the social sciences which assumes that historical prediction is their principal aim" (3) and which attempts to discover "patterns" or "laws" of historical evolution.

There is really no universally agreed-upon movement that can be called "historicism." As Terrence Tice and Thomas Slavens have argued, the term refers to "a diverse set of interests, problems and solutions"; nonetheless, they offer a working definition of historicism as "a tendency among several eminent German philosophers and historians in the nineteenth century: (1) to view human events especially in their singularity, (2) to try to understand the diverse relationships of these events to general but changing patterns or to evolutionary trends but in a dynamic and concrete manner, (3) to examine all human products in this historical fashion, and (4) to affirm for such inquiry—sometimes for the social sciences generally, on this basis—a scientific status distinctly different from that of the natural sciences." See Tice and Slavens, *Research Guide to Philosophy* (Chicago: American Library Association, 1983), 428–429.

Walter Schulz, in his magisterial work *Philosophie in der veränderten Welt* (Pfullingen: Neske, 1972), offers a general account of historicism as "the radical breakdown of supra-temporal systems of norms *and* the increasing knowledge that we must understand ourselves as historical beings right to the inner core of our humanity." He goes on to say that historicism is the comprehension "of history as the fundamental principle in human knowledge and in the understanding of the human world. This means—fundamentally—that all being can and must only be understood in terms of its 'historicity'" (492–493). For a linguistic history of the term, see Erich Rothacker, "Das Wort Historismus," *Zeitschrift für deutsche Wortforschung* 16 (1960): 3–6; and Gunter Scholz, "Historismus," in *Historisches Wörterbuch der Philosophie*, vol. 3 (Basel: Schwabe, 1974), 1141–1147. Also helpful are Georg Iggers, "Historicism," in *The Dictionary of the History of Ideas* (New York: Scribners, 1973), 456–464; Hans-Georg Gadamer, "Historismus," in

philosophy which coincides with the generational perception of a "crisis in the sciences." Both Windelband and Rickert, for example, offered Neo-Kantian solutions to the crisis, solutions that seem today to be limited by their own historical assumptions. But it is precisely in grasping these limits, I believe, that we can begin to understand and more clearly define our own postmodern predicament, caught as we are in our metaphysical attitudes toward science and historical definitions of time. The insights of Dilthey and Heidegger go far toward helping us transcend the narrowly epistemological focus of Neo-Kantianism, providing a way of reconceiving the project of modernity from within the horizon of historical life experience. In their work, the limits of historicist thinking are confronted by the productive possibilities of a new kind of crisis-consciousness, possibilities that go beyond traditional historicist questions about scientific objectivity, cultural relativism, the autonomy of the human sciences, and the meaning of historical value to engage the whole problem of philosophical modernity.

By focusing on the explicitly *philosophical* meaning of crisis and crisis-consciousness in Windelband's and Rickert's epistemology of historical science, Dilthey's critique of historical reason, and Heidegger's destruction of the history of ontology, I want to show how the crisis of historicism can be read as an expression of the philosophical contradictions within modernity itself. As I see it, historicism represents not only the development of a cultural world view or a process of professionalization within a specific academic discipline; it also authorizes a metaphysical reading of history which both determines and undermines modern and postmodern thought. Modernism and postmodernism, I will argue, are essentially reactive in character; that is, both constitute responses to a previously established historical narrative, even where this narrative threatens the stability of modern or

Religion in Geschichte und Gesellschaft, vol. 3 (Tübingen: Mohr, 1959), 369–370; Waldemar Besson, "Historismus," in *Das Fischer Lexikon: Geschichte* (Frankfurt: Fischer, 1961), 102–116; Harry Ritter, "Historicism, Historism," in *Dictionary of Concepts in History* (Westport, Conn.: Greenwood, 1986), 183–187; Guntolf Herzberg, "Historismus: Wort, Begriff, Problem, und die philosophische Begründung durch Wilhelm Dilthey," *Jahrbuch für Geschichte* 25 (1982): 259–304; Wolfgang Hardtwig, *Geschichtsschreibung zwischen Alteuropa und moderner Welt: Jacob Burckhardt in seiner Zeit* (Göttingen: Vandenhoeck & Ruprecht, 1974), esp. 201–243; Arie Nabrings, "Historismus als Paralyse der Geschichte," *Archiv für Kulturgeschichte* 65 (1983): 157–212; Otto G. Oexle, "'Historismus': Überlegungen zur Geschichte des Phänomens und des Begriffs," *Jahrbuch der Braunschweigischen Wissenschaftlichen Gesellschaft* (1986): 119–155; and Volker Steenblock, *Transformationen des Historismus* (Munich: Fink, 1991).

postmodern interpretations. Thus, for example, when Joyce's Stephen Dedalus experiences history as a nightmare from which he is trying to awake or when Yeats's pilgrim in "The Second Coming" understands it as a narrative whose center cannot hold, they are both reacting to a tradition whose meaning and relevance have radically been called into question. Modern and postmodern visions of history share this sense of anxiety and instability, that the past is a lost whole that threatens to break apart into anarchic fragments at any moment. Both are constituted as responses to a historicist reading of history which first establishes a unidirectional metaphysics of time as the basis of historical progress. Thus, for example, if modernism tautologically reaffirms the highest cultural value as "modern"—namely, that which is new—it can do so only on the basis of *overcoming* what is past, what precedes the modern. Only after one has already established a narrative of unity, meaning, and totality can one begin to speak of fragmentation, crisis, or rupture. The historicist reading of history offered just such a narrative of directionality and purpose, a kind of secularized theology of cause and effect which presumed the coherence of all events. For philosophical historicists such as Hegel, historical meaning was achieved through the cunning of reason, whereas for theological historicists such as Ranke, universal history was organized according to providential design. In this affirmation of the past as something teleologically or even eschatologically directed, traditional historicism justified the agonistic logic of events as a narrative of the victors and the defeated. With the collapse of the historicist vision during the period from 1880 to 1930, however—with Nietzsche's proclamation of the "death of God," Spengler's "*Menschendämmerung*" ("twilight of humanity"), Husserl's *Crisis of the European Sciences*, Troeltsch's "Crisis of Historicism," and the postwar academic manifestos outlining the collapse of Western civilization—this linear narrative of meaning and progress was decisively broken. What predominated in its stead was a radical skepticism about the ultimate meaning of history and a new crisis-rhetoric and crisis-consciousness.

Crisis, in its original Greek sense, denotes a sifting or separating that leads one to a judgment or point of decision.[6] In Hippocrates and Galen the term is used to denote the turning point in a disease. By

---

[6] Charles S. Halsey, *Etymology of Latin and Greek* (New Rochelle, N.Y.: Caratzas, 1983), 57; and Alois Vanicek, *Griechisch-Lateinisches Etymologisches Wörterbuch* (Leipzig: Teubner, 1887), 1088.

contrast, the crisis of historicism represents a judgment about a different matter: that is, a turning away from or break with the dominant nineteenth-century philosophy of historical progress, with its expectations of meaning and order. One could argue that this crisis in German historical thinking dates from the publication in 1874 of Nietzsche's second essay from *Untimely Meditations*, "On the Uses and Disadvantages of History for Life." But no one text can serve as the point of origin; the perception of crisis emerged as a reaction to a complex set of assumptions, values, traditions, and cultural clichés that predominated in late-nineteenth-century Germany. And yet Nietzsche captured more perfectly than his contemporaries the mood of senescence and passivity in historicist ideology. For Nietzsche, historicism was a disease of modern consciousness which fostered a contemplative, research-oriented personality. Drawn by the alexandrine pleasures of textual study, Nietzsche's historian became a passive observer immersed in the archives, unable to act or create, having been reduced to a mere "eunuch in the harem of history."[7] But even as Nietzsche fulminated against the "historical sickness" of the nineteenth century, the institutional power of historicist ideas grew, extending their influence to every branch of the *Geisteswissenschaften*, or "human sciences," in Germany. It was not until after the Great War, when the carnage brought on by the new technologies had resulted in widespread political chaos, economic collapse, and social dislocation, that there occurred a wholesale dissolution of historicist thinking. Following the "catastrophe of 1918" in Germany, Oswald Spengler's *Decline of the West* (1918) and Theodor Lessing's *History as the Bestowal of Meaning on the Meaningless* (1919) echoed the generational mood of lost faith and expressed in exemplary fashion the crisis-mentality of modernism.

As a historical category, modernism represents this heightened awareness that crisis can serve as a model for cultural perception. It suggests, however, far more than an aesthetic preference for images of fragmentation and dispersal. Modernism also signifies a new understanding of time and narrative. In modernist time, events no longer cohere; their unity is disrupted by a break in the line of history. As the chain of events is severed by the perception of crisis, the idea of crisis itself substitutes as the new source of historical interpretation.

[7] Friedrich Nietzsche, *Untimely Meditations*, trans. R. J. Hollingdale (Cambridge: Cambridge University Press, 1983).

By undermining the logic of succession and continuity, it challenges the historicist narrative of progressive and unitary time. Hence, if by the term *historicism* we understand a preoccupation with and devotion to the past, and with everything old and antiquarian, then the idea of modernism can be best described, as Gianni Vattimo explains, "as an era of overcoming and of the new which rapidly grows old and is immediately replaced by something still newer."[8] Vattimo persuasively argues in *The End of Modernity* that Nietzsche's narrative of nihilism serves as an important catalyst for modern and postmodern attempts to think of history in terms of crisis. For Vattimo, the collapse of all transcendent and suprahistorical values brings with it a nihilistic, posthistorical form of thinking: "Since the notion of truth no longer exists, and foundation no longer functions (insofar as there is no longer a foundation for the belief in foundation . . .) there can be no way out of modernity through a critical overcoming, for the latter is a part of modernity itself. It thus becomes clear that an alternative means must be sought and this is the moment that could be designated as the moment of the birth of postmodernity in philosophy."[9]

In the avant-garde movements at the turn of the century, the modernist preoccupation with overcoming tradition and fetishizing the new appears as a bold rejection of the past. And yet even as modernism attempts to overcome the basic historicist position, we can see that it is still tied to the fundamental tenets of historicism, if only negatively. "Historicism characterizes modernity," in Vattimo's words, because in establishing a metaphysical vision of time as pure temporal succession, it persistently undergirds, and reinforces, the modernist logic of overcoming.[10] In so doing it inscribes the history of modernity as the history of metaphysics and opens the path for the dissolution of metaphysics and the "end of history." Modernist thought is punctuated by a peculiarly historicist understanding of time as a linear, rosary bead sequence of cause and effect. This way of thinking about the past produces a kind of "neutral time," a time in which all events are measured objectively, much as cartography measures space according to empirical canons of distance and location. "Empty, homogeneous time," as Walter Benjamin calls it, the time of cartography and mathematics, provides the ultimate context for sus-

[8] Gianni Vattimo, *The End of Modernity*, trans. Jon Snyder (Baltimore: Johns Hopkins University Press, 1988), 166.
[9] Ibid., 167.
[10] Gianni Vattimo, "The End of History," *Chicago Review* 35, no. 4 (1987): 25.

taining the value of neutrality; it creates the illusion of a historical continuum with equally measured intervals where one can, as Leopold von Ranke expressed it, "see with unbiased eyes the progress of universal history."[11] Classical historicism was committed to the ideas of value-free judgment and neutral perspective as the very essence of historical objectivity. But these values were themselves possible only on the basis of a neutral temporality that allowed for another illusion: a causally demonstrable continuum of historical effects. Modernism breaks with classical historicism in that the modern experience of history is acausal, discontinuous, and ironic. For the modernist, the text of history reads more like a newspaper divided into unrelated columns than like a unitary narrative. In a chapter from his book *Essere, storia, e linguaggio in Heidegger*, "The Destruction of Historicism," Gianni Vattimo tries to show the close connection between the dissolution of historicist categories—categories established by a metaphysics that understands time as something inherently directional—and the crisis of modernity. For Vattimo, Heidegger's destruction of a historicist notion of time constitutes an eschatological break with the "predominance of the past."[12] This break—or crisis—in Heidegger's thinking is not merely "the appearance of a different stage of history," writes Vattimo, but the end of history itself: postmodern destruction offers "not only something new in relation to the modern, but also a dissolution of the category of the new . . . as an experience of 'the end of history.'"[13] As Vattimo interprets it, postmodernism is complicitous in the dissolution of historicism because it marks the end of the Hegelian pageant of world history. Hence, Vattimo concludes, "the postmodern meditation on history can only be a sort of 'revised,' distorted form of historicism."[14]

Vattimo's work is exemplary in showing the kind of connections one can make between the modern/postmodern reading of crisis and the dissolution of historicism. But his is only one voice among many. Thinkers such as Jean-François Lyotard and Jacques Derrida have also seized on the problems of crisis and dissolution as ways of interpret-

[11] Walter Benjamin, *Illuminations*, trans. Harry Zohn (New York: Schocken, 1969), 261; and Leopold von Ranke, *The Secret of World History*, trans. Roger Wines (New York: Fordham University Press, 1981), 259.
[12] Gianni Vattimo, *Essere, storia, e linguaggio in Heidegger* (Genoa: Marietti, 1989), quoted in Daniel Barbiero, "A Weakness for Heidegger: The German Root of *Il Pensiero Debole*," *New German Critique* 55 (1992): 160–161.
[13] Vattimo, *End of Modernity*, 4.
[14] Ibid., 176. Compare the translation in Barbiero, "Weakness for Heidegger," 162.

ing "the postmodern condition." Lyotard, for example, describes postmodernism as an "incredulity toward metanarrative" which he links to the obsolescence of Enlightenment-idealist philosophy of history and the "crisis of metaphysical philosophy."[15] Derrida, too, pursues the underlying connection between the linear scheme of time in modernist thinking and the metaphysical narrative of history, themes that he finds in Heidegger and Nietzsche. In *Positions*, Derrida writes, "The metaphysical character of the concept of history is not only linked to linearity, but to an entire *system* of implications (teleology, eschatology, elevating and interiorizing accumulation of meaning . . . a certain concept of continuity, of truth, etc.)."[16] In his deconstruction of "history," Derrida shows how linear temporality and the discourse it produces—the "archeo-teleological program of all European discourse about Europe"—is intimately bound up with crisis-thinking. In *The Other Heading*, he explicitly links the consciousness of "direction" (*sens*) to "the tradition of modernity at the moment and as the very moment of what was called *crisis* . . . 'the crisis of the European sciences' or 'the crisis of European humanity': the teleology that guides the analysis of history and the very history of this crisis, of the recovery of the transcendental theme in (and since) Descartes."[17] In deconstructing the explicit categories of a totalizing, metaphysical vision of history, Derrida displaces history with a plurality of histories and inscribes on the palimpsest of the past the heterogeneous discourses of the future.

Like Derrida and Lyotard, many other postmodern thinkers have become preoccupied by problems connected with the perceived dissolution or dismantling of the historicist *Fragestellung*.[18] From a post-

[15] Jean-François Lyotard, *The Postmodern Condition*, trans. Geoff Bennington (Minneapolis: University of Minnesota Press, 1984), xxiv.

[16] Jacques Derrida, *Positions*, trans. Alan Bass (Chicago: University of Chicago Press, 1971), 56–57.

[17] Jacques Derrida, *The Other Heading*, trans. Michael Naas and Pascale-Ann Brault (Bloomington: Indiana University Press, 1992), 27 and 33.

[18] Throughout this book I use the term *Fragestellung* to denote a particular way of "posing a question" which determines a basic path of inquiry and mode of questioning. But it involves much more. A philosophical term used often in German scholarship, it means "the way one approaches the question," "the way one structures the inquiry," "the paradigm one employs," and the like. Of course, the way one asks a question often determines the way one answers it, and so when I use this specific German term, I am attempting to show that the *way* one poses a question is indeed not only a personal or subjective problem but also involves a whole way of thinking, a whole set of (sometimes unspoken) generational assumptions, and often reflects the cultural limits, biases, and prejudices of a specific form of inquiry. I wish to emphasize that the very posing of a question can structure the path of inquiry and determine its

modern perspective, historicism implies far more than a research methodology for the study of the past. It signifies a metaphysical reading of history which is founded on the history of metaphysics; in other words, it represents a privileging of metaphysical concepts of time, narrative, order, succession, continuity, and totality which derive from the single-point perspective of Cartesian and Kantian subjectivity and its corresponding insistence on the values of objectivity, methodological clarity, and scientific truth. These postmodernist thinkers understand that the crisis of modernism from which they are trying to recover (in Heidegger's sense of *Verwindung*) is intimately bound up with the metaphysical assumptions of historicism.[19] In his study *The New Historicism*, which focuses on postmodern literary theory, Brook Thomas has tried "to show to what extent poststructuralism, and especially deconstruction, is a historical response to a crisis in historicism from which Western thought has not yet recovered."[20] On Thomas's reading, the crisis of historicism confronts the postmodern critic as an occasion for rethinking the basic categories of philosophical modernity, categories that underlay the model of scientific certainty fostered in the early modern era.

In my interpretation of the work of Rickert, Windelband, Dilthey, and Heidegger, I propose to explore the kinds of philosophical connections between historicist thinking and the crisis of modernity which Thomas's work alludes to. I have chosen the specific period in German academic philosophy between 1880 and 1930 because it seems to me that in the epistemological projects of the Neo-Kantians and Dilthey, and their subsequent dismantling in the early work of Heidegger, one can clearly trace the formation of a crisis-thinking that undergirds and determines the basic *Fragestellung* of modern and postmodern discourse.

Most scholarship detailing the historicist tradition has been historiographically focused. It has concentrated largely on the political, ideological, and nationalist presuppositions of German historians and

---

basic approach. For example, the seventeenth-century tradition of early modern science adopted a specific truth model based on method, verification, certitude, causality, and Cartesian doubt. Later-nineteenth-century thinkers, critical of Descartes and the early modern philosophy of science, rejected many of their findings but still adopted their *Fragestellung*. It is, I believe, the *Fragestellung* that unifies a tradition and *not* the answers at which it arrives.

[19] For a postmodern approach to the problem of *Verwindung*, see Gianni Vattimo, "Optimistic Nihilism," *Common Knowledge* 1, no. 3 (1992): 37–44.

[20] Brook Thomas, *The New Historicism* (Princeton, N.J.: Princeton University Press, 1991), 35.

their attempts to develop a more professionalized method of research within the "disciplinary matrix" of a historical *Fachwissenschaft*. Historians such as Georg Iggers and Jörn Rüsen have masterfully analyzed the social and institutional character of historicist thinking, attempting to locate its scientific and rational elements in its research methods and interpretive principles. Rüsen, in fact, argues that an excessive focus on method led to the establishment of a "paradigmatic, disciplinary form" of historical science.[21] He finds that historicist thinkers were motivated by the promise of a new logic of research (*Historik*) which functioned as the standard of scholarly excellence within academic historiography. More recently, scholars such as Peter Reill, Michael Ermarth, Horst Walter Blanke, and Friedrich Jaeger have built on the work of Rüsen and Iggers and have tried to make connections between historicism and the scientific aims of the Enlightenment. Part of their achievement has been to show "how deeply historicism is rooted in the Enlightenment notwithstanding its own disavowal of this relationship."[22] As a result of their careful work, contemporary historians have finally been able to challenge Troeltsch's and Meinecke's problematic claims about the deep-rooted opposition between Enlightenment and historicist thinking. Their efforts have done much to show how historicism was completely dependent on ideals of scientific thinking from the early modern era, ideals dominated by Cartesian-Kantian notions of rationality, consciousness, methodological access to truth, and philosophical certitude. These historians have previously demonstrated that as the historicist tradition took root in the early-nineteenth-century German

[21] Horst Walter Blanke and Jörn Rüsen, eds. *Von der Aufklärung zum Historismus* (Paderborn: Schöningh, 1984), 15–57. See also Georg Iggers, *The German Conception of History* (Middletown, Conn.: Wesleyan University Press, 1986); and Friedrich Jaeger and Jörn Rüsen, *Geschichte des Historismus* (Munich: Beck, 1992).
[22] Georg Iggers, "Review of *Von der Aufklärung zum Historismus*," *History and Theory* 1 (1987): 114–121. Some of the best sources for a critique of the Troeltsch-Meinecke thesis of historicism include Hans-Erich Bödeker et al., eds., *Aufklärung und Geschichte* (Göttingen: Vandenhoeck & Ruprecht, 1986); Herbert Schnädelbach, *Vernunft und Geschichte* (Frankfurt: Suhrkamp, 1987); Peter Reill, *The German Enlightenment and the Rise of Historicism* (Berkeley: University of California Press, 1975); Reill, "Narration and Structure in Late Eighteenth-Century Historical Thought," *History and Theory* 25 (1986): 286–298; and Reill, "Die Geschichtswissenschaft um die Mitte des 18. Jahrhunderts," in Rudolf Vierhaus, ed., *Wissenschaften im Zeitalter der Aufklärung* (Göttingen: Vandenhoeck & Ruprecht, 1985), 163–193. See also the essays collected in Georg Iggers and James Powell, eds., *Leopold von Ranke and the Shaping of the Historical Discipline* (Syracuse, N.Y.: Syracuse University Press, 1990); Hans Schleier, "Leistungen und Grenzen des idealistischen deutschen Historismus," *Zeitschrift für Geschichtswissenschaft* 35 (1987): 955–970; and Georg Iggers, "The University of Göttingen, 1760–1800, and the Transformation of Historical Scholarship," *Storia della Storiografia* 2 (1982): 11–37.

university, with the dominance of Humboldt, Ranke, Niebuhr, and, later, Droysen, its methodological imperative toward objective research—the basic theme of Rüsen's work—was wedded to a fundamentally metaphysical faith in the meaning and purpose of historical development as something individual, unique, and unrepeatable.

Classical historicism in this sense knew no value relativism but rather was committed to the ethical unfolding of God's ultimate plan which manifested itself in Ranke's divinatory *Weltgeschichte*, Humboldt's spiritual *Ideen*, Droysen's "moral powers" (*sittliche Mächte*), and Hegel's Christological revelation of *Geist*. In the later period after 1880, however, with the challenge of new positivist models of research fashioned on the epistemological principles of the natural sciences, there emerged contradictions between methodological objectivity and metaphysical faith which called into question the scientific foundations of historicist scholarship.

Part of my effort in this book is to show how the work of Windelband, Rickert, and Dilthey can be interpreted as self-conscious attempts to reclaim the objectivity of historical research against these metaphysical incursions of idealist *Geschichtstheologie*. These turn-of-the-century philosophers adopted a fundamentally Kantian perspective from which to consider the controversies concerning historical relativism, the anarchy of values, the classification of the natural and human sciences, and the criteria of historical judgment. From their epistemological standpoint, they succeeded in bringing to self-awareness the metaphysical contradictions within classical historicism, even if, as I try to indicate, they ultimately succumbed to a more fundamental, deep-rooted metaphysical thinking in their own work. On my reading, their logical-methodological-epistemological attempts to overcome metaphysics and to establish an autonomous science of history, culture, and *Geist*, were different from the conceptual model of the natural sciences. Their effort was aimed at broadening the basic *Fragestellung* of the earlier historicists and establishing a new epistemological-metaphysical version of historicism. Yet unlike many of the early historicists, none of the four thinkers whom I discuss here—Windelband, Rickert, Dilthey, or Heidegger—were professional historians. They each approached the basic problems of historicism from a decisively philosophical perspective, convinced that by philosophically engaging questions of historical knowledge, historical consciousness, and historicity, they could redefine the fundamental meaning of philosophy in the modern tradition. In their attempts to "overcome" metaphysics, these philosophers thematized history in such a way as to open up the very contradictions that established the basic agenda of modern and postmodern thinking: Cartesian-Kantian presuppositions about absolute time; the single-point perspective of the cogito; the commitment to scientific rationality; the belief in rigorously methodological access to truth—ideas that, by embodying the universal validity of scientific consciousness, seemed to contradict the lived experience and historicity of finite, historical consciousness.

My interest in the crisis of historicism is connected to the kind of crisis-thinking generated by the historicist debate. What is at stake in these academic controversies about value judgments, objectivity, and scientific truth in the work of the Neo-Kantians, Dilthey, and especially the early Heidegger seems to me nothing less than the viability of the modernist project of European philosophy. What spurs my reading is the belief that the fundamental contradictions of modernist thinking can be located in the epistemological and methodological debates at the turn of the century. In the work of Spengler, Barth, Weber, Bloch, Meinecke, Troeltsch, and others, there was a generational preoccupation with the themes of loss, destruction, apocalypse, and decline. The crisis notion of historical consciousness was transformed in this postwar epoch and converted into a cliché of modern life—a banal and degraded form of Nietzsche's axiological nihilism. *Weltanschauungsphilosophie* of the Weimar period was replete with examples of this type of fashionable crisis-consciousness.[23] But out of these superficial and modish discussions of crisis *in* history, science, theology, and philosophy emerged a genuine philosophy *of* crisis in the early work of Heidegger. Heidegger rejected the interpretations of his contemporaries and sought instead to redefine crisis as the very turning that initiates the course of history, particularly the history of Western metaphysics. Rather than denying the instability and anxiety of the crisis-condition or attempting to overcome it by substituting a new, more secure foundation for metaphysics, Heidegger affirmed

---

[23] For examples of crisis-consciousness and crisis-rhetoric, see Paul Forman, "Weimar Culture, Causality, and Quantum Theory," *Historical Studies in the Physical Sciences* 3 (1971): 1–116; Fritz Ringer, *The Decline of the German Mandarins* (Cambridge: Harvard University Press, 1969); Andras Gedo, *Crisis Consciousness in Contemporary Philosophy*, trans. Salomea Genin (Minneapolis: Marxist Educational Press, 1982); and Allan Megill, *Prophets of Extremity: Nietzsche, Heidegger, Foucault, Derrida* (Berkeley: University of California Press, 1985). I discuss the impact of crisis-consciousness in more detail in Chap. 1.

crisis as the originary state of all genuine science and philosophy. As he wrote in *Being and Time*, "The level which a science has reached is determined by how far it is capable of a crisis in its basic concepts."[24]

Heidegger discovered that historicist assumptions about truth, objectivity, research practices, temporal distance, and scholarly judgment were derived from the early modern definition of the sciences, which, in turn, were grounded in the static ontology of Greek metaphysics. By refusing to grasp history simply as a process of sequential development (*Geschichte*) or as a *Fachwissenschaft* committed to historicoscientific observation (*Historie*), Heidegger came to understand history in a new sense as historicity (*Geschichtlichkeit*), as the temporal-historical happening that we ourselves are.[25] As he explained it in his lecture "The Concept of Time" (1924): "Philosophy will never discover what history is as long as it analyzes it as an object, in terms of a method. The enigma of history lies in what it means to *be* historical."[26] Rickert's and Windelband's taxonomical approach to history had wholly obscured the historicity of human being which Dilthey's work had tried to open up. Against this Neo-Kantian influence, Heidegger reclaimed Dilthey's hermeneutics of historical experience and offered an ontological reading of historicity which altered the basic terms of the historicist *Fragestellung*.

Heidegger's work of the early twenties proceeded from the same aporia of subject/object thinking which lay at the heart of the historicist tradition, but he never succumbed to a cultural reading of the contemporary crisis of science and philosophy. Instead, he rethought this aporia as a way of dismantling the metaphysical structure that first made historicism possible. By viewing the problem of history as a phenomenon of human existence rather than as a case study for epistemological analysis, Heidegger offered a path of thinking which rendered the traditional "crisis" of historicism antiquated and irrelevant. By the time of his Nietzsche lectures in the 1930s, historicism had ceased to be a viable cultural force; it persisted only in an attenuated form as the cultural ideology of a privileged mandarinate embittered by the nihilistic tendencies of the modern world. One can see

---

[24] Martin Heidegger, *Being and Time*, trans. John Macquarrie and Edward Robinson (New York: Harper and Row, 1962), 29; *Sein und Zeit* (Tübingen: Niemeyer, 1976), 9.

[25] Heidegger, *Being and Time*, 434–455; *Sein und Zeit*, 382–404. See Chap. 5 for a fuller treatment of this whole issue.

[26] Martin Heidegger, *Der Begriff der Zeit* (Tübingen: Niemeyer, 1989), 26.

this kind of epigonic consciousness at work in Meinecke's classic study *Historism* (1936), which reads more like an elegy for a passing tradition than a work of critical engagement.

Historicism represented a dead end in twentieth-century German thinking, Heidegger claimed, precisely because it failed to grasp the very contradictions that made it possible. Still tied to scientific criteria of objectivity and epistemological certitude, historicist thinkers tried to grasp the reality of historical experience by either denying or attempting to overcome the idea of subjectivity. Their crisis rhetoric during the Weimar period was marked by a persistent uneasiness about historical relativism, which, they believed, threatened to level all cultural values. But even as his contemporaries saw a clear opposition between subjective values and objective truth, Heidegger understood that they belonged together. For him, historical relativism was really only the complement of a covert objectivism masked by an idealist discourse about cultural diversity, individual freedom, unique processes of development, and the like. Heidegger understood that the crisis-rhetoric of Spengler and his contemporaries was unable to account for the underlying contradictions in historicist discourse between epistemological objectivity and the historicity of the human subject. By attempting to fit history within the recalcitrant frame of science, historicists had denied the hermeneutic experience that first made history possible. These problems were hardly unique to the postwar generation. They originated with the romantic hermeneutics of Ranke, whose understanding of historicity was focused primarily on the object of research within the stream of historical time. Following Ranke, Droysen attempted to overcome the pure objectivism of traditional scholarship by establishing "not the laws of history [*Geschichte*] but the laws of historical research and knowledge [*Historie*]." And yet Droysen still conceived of historicity in fundamentally epistemological terms.[27] Like most others in the historicist tradition, he always understood "history" in a twofold sense according to a subject/object metaphysics: either as the name for the totality of events (*res gestae*) or as the interpretive account of those events in themselves (*historia rerum gestarum*). At the end of the nineteenth century, the Neo-Kantians accepted this basic subject/object framework as the starting point for their inquiry. Although they rejected the relativistic

---

[27] Johan Gustav Droysen, *Historik* (Darmstadt: Wissenschaftliche Buchgesellschaft, 1977), 424. For a shorter, English version of Droysen's basic *Grundriß der Historik*, see *Outline of the Principles of History* trans. E. Benjamin Andrews (Boston: Ginn, 1893).

implications of historicity and affirmed a universal theory of values, their critique still focused on the historicity of the object as something "there to be known." Dilthey tried to break with this Neo-Kantian approach by emphasizing the historicity of the subject, coming to understand that human life is not simply something that occurs *in* history; instead, historicity is a fundamental category of human life. As Gadamer explains, "The fundamental character of historicity does not depend on the fact that the human being has a history; rather, all history depends on the originary temporality and historicity of human being."[28] And yet even as Dilthey sought to overcome the contradictions within historicist thinking, his work was still determined by an overall theory of the human sciences which was incompatible with his insight into the historicity of life.

As Heidegger began to reframe the insights of Dilthey and the Neo-Kantians, he noticed that they led to the same impasse: subjective historicity could never really be reconciled with objective science. What was needed, he believed, was a radical destruction of the subject/object form of thinking which made historicism possible. Although he ultimately rejected historicism as an expression of metaphysical thinking, Heidegger did, nonetheless, view the crisis of historicism as an occasion for coming to grips with the bankruptcy of the modernist tradition. He understood that despite their apparent antipathy, scientism and historicism belonged together, for each represented a complementary side of the same fundamental position. Rather than choosing between them, as if they were alternatives, he felt that one should try to rethink their relationship in a new and more originary way. This he found in a reappropriation and simultaneous destruction of the history of ontology. By grasping the

---

[28] Hans-Georg Gadamer, "Geschichtlichkeit," in *Religion in Geschichte und Gesellschaft*, 3 (Tübingen: Mohr, 1959), 1496–1498. For a historical treatment of the term *historicity*, see Leonhard Renthe-Fink, "Geschichtlichkeit," in *Historisches Wörterbuch der Philosophie* (Basel: Schwabe, 1971), 3: 404–408; Renthe-Fink, "Zur Herkunft des Wortes 'Geschichtlichkeit,'" *Archiv für Begriffsgeschichte* 15 (1971): 306–312; and Renthe-Fink, *Geschichtlichkeit: Ihr terminologischer und begrifflicher Ursprung bei Hegel, Haym, Dilthey, und Yorck* (Göttingen: Vandenhoeck & Ruprecht, 1964). For a broader approach, see Gerhard Bauer, *Geschichtlichkeit* (Berlin: de Gruyter, 1963); David Linge, "Historicity and Hermeneutic," Ph.D. diss., Vanderbilt University, 1969; Herbert Boeder, "Dilthey 'und' Heidegger: Zur Geschichtlichkeit des Menschen," in E. W. Orth, ed., *Dilthey und der Wandel des Philosophiebegriffs* (Freiburg: Alber, 1984), 161–177; David Hoy, "History, Historicity, and Historiography," in Michael Murray, ed., *Heidegger and Modern Philosophy* (New Haven, Conn.: Yale University Press, 1978); Otto Pöggeler, "Historicity in Heidegger's Late Work," *Southwestern Journal of Philosophy* 4 (1973): 53–73; and Jeffrey Barash, *Heidegger and the Problem of Historical Meaning* (Dordrecht: Martinus Nijhoff, 1988).

essence of history not as a science but as an expression of human historicity, Heidegger managed to transform the cultural and historiographical crisis of historicism into a crisis of philosophy and metaphysics. The crisis of historicism signified for Heidegger the realization that modernist thought was at an impasse. No longer able to resolve its questions within the terms of its own discourse, historicism was forced to confront its inherent contradictions in the form of a historical crisis. But it is precisely these contradictions that proved to be philosophically fruitful in Heidegger's work.

My reading of Heidegger helps to determine in any number of ways this book's emphasis on crisis and crisis-consciousness in modern German philosophy. It also helps to explain why I have chosen to focus on a philosophical reading of historicism (particularly in the work of Windelband, Rickert, and Dilthey) rather than to explore the historiographical or methodological writings of historians themselves. The usual interpretations of historicism (and here the works of Iggers and Rüsen come readily to mind) hardly mention Heidegger or else conceive of his work within the selfsame subject/object framework that he sought to dissolve. Iggers, for example, interprets Heidegger as a "philosophical irrationalist" committed to a peculiar kind of existential subjectivity, someone for whom "the hard world of real objective Being seemed to dissolve."[29] Moreover, these historiographically focused treatments of historicism invariably place the thought of Dilthey and the Neo-Kantians within the same *Fragestellung* as the work of traditional historians such as Ranke, Droysen, and Lamprecht. In so doing, they miss the explicitly philosophical confrontation with the Cartesian-Kantian tradition of the sciences at work in the philosophy of Dilthey, Rickert, and Windelband. By including Heidegger in my discussion and concentrating especially on his early work (between 1919 and 1927), which has been largely ignored by most interpreters of historicism, I try to reconfigure the crisis of historicism along new lines.

In the next few chapters I want to explore the implications of this crisis in order to understand more fully the connections between historicist thinking and the development of modern philosophy in Ger-

[29] In their book *Geschichte des Historismus*, Jaeger and Rüsen wholly avoid any discussion of Heidegger's work or his influence, and in *The German Conception of History*, Iggers mentions Heidegger only in the most marginal way, preferring to treat him as an irrationalist and existentialist. No real connections are made to the philosophical theme of crisis or to Heidegger's relation to Rickert, Windelband, or Dilthey.

many. I find that a reading of historicism makes sense only as part of an overall understanding of crisis and that crisis itself has philosophical implications for grasping modernist thought. As part of this project, I develop in my first chapter a sense of the basic crisis within German philosophy at the turn of the century. In the following four chapters I offer separate readings of the thinkers whose work helped define the fundamental crisis of historicism: Windelband, Rickert, Dilthey, and Heidegger. These are by no means, however, intended to be isolated studies; rather, I try to build on each previous chapter, showing each thinker's underlying connection to the problem of history as a form of metaphysics. My intention is to offer a reading not only of the crisis of historicism but also of crisis itself as one of the dominant themes in modern thought.

CHAPTER ONE

German Philosophy between Scientism and Historicism

Genuine crises are rare.
—Jacob Burckhardt, *Reflections on History*

Crisis sells well.
—Umberto Eco, *Travels in Hyperreality*

i. The Legitimation Crisis in Post-Hegelian Philosophy

The near half-century that extends from the publication of Dilthey's *Introduction to the Human Sciences* in 1883 to the appearance of Heidegger's *Being and Time* in 1927 represents a remarkable period in the history of German philosophy. From the vantage point of our own age, we can look back and discern an important intellectual shift during this era from an epistemological approach concerned with questions of "scientific foundations" to a new hermeneutical ontology that stressed the temporality and historicity of human being-in-the-world.[1] In the work of different philosophers ranging from Rickert and Windelband to Vaihinger, Simmel, Troeltsch, and Cassirer, one notices the same rigorous focus on developing a critical theory of knowledge divided by the dual spheres of subject and object, mind and nature, *Geist* and *Natur*. These philosophers turned to epistemology as a way of providing foundations for both the human and the natural sciences; in so doing, they

[1] Richard Rorty, *Philosophy and the Mirror of Nature* (Princeton, N.J.: Princeton University Press, 1979), for example, tries to show the development "from epistemology to hermeneutics," esp. in chap. 7, 315–356.

aimed to establish philosophy itself as the science of science. And yet despite their best efforts at effecting this kind of consensus, by 1927 most university philosophers had been confronted by a sense of impending "crisis" in their discipline.

This crisis-mentality was, in some respects, the product of a long-standing tradition in German thinking which went back to the decline of idealist metaphysics. For almost a century the void created by the collapse of the Hegelian system and its subsequent debunking by the empirical sciences had forced philosophers to reconsider their proper role vis-à-vis other branches of learning. Hegel's magisterial proclamation that the goal of philosophy was "the scientific knowledge of truth" was met with mocking resistance by a generation of research scientists trained in the laboratory methods of physiology, optics, mechanics, dynamics, and other applied sciences.[2] Whereas Hegel had declared that there was only one absolute science—the science of philosophy—which included both the philosophy of nature and the philosophy of spirit, by the time of the *Materialismusstreit* in Göttingen in 1854, naturalists such as Ludwig Büchner, Karl Vogt, and Jacob Moleschott argued for the end of philosophical dominance over the natural sciences. Instead, they called for the universal validity of scientific method as the only legitimate path to truth.[3] The discrediting of Hegel's system led to a rejection of philosophy in general by the practitioners of the specialized sciences, except in the form of scientism (or positivism), which asserted that science itself satisfied all the requirements of rigorous philosophy.[4] One spoke, in Marx's phrase, of "the poverty of philosophy" and contrasted its metaphysical presumptions with the empirical facts gleaned from hard wrought research.

Specialized scientific knowledge had usurped many of the former areas of speculative philosophy of nature and had (with its unflagging emphasis on methodological procedure and empirical research)

---

[2] G. W. F. Hegel, *Die Enzyklopädie der philosophischen Wissenschaften* (Hamburg: Meiner, 1955), 3. See also the excellent discussion in Herbert Schnädelbach's *Philosophy in Germany, 1831–1933* (Cambridge: Cambridge University Press, 1984), chap. 3.

[3] Klaus Christian Köhnke, *Entstehung und Aufstieg des Neukantianismus: Die deutsche Universitätsphilosophie zwischen Idealismus und Positivismus* (Frankfurt: Suhrkamp, 1986), esp. 157–159, 242, 273.

[4] On the topic of "scientism," see Schnädelbach, *Philosophy in Germany*, 93–100; Wladyslaw Tatarkiewicz, *Nineteenth Century Philosophy* (Belmont, Calif.: Wadsworth, 1973); Walter M. Simon, *European Positivism in the Nineteenth Century* (Ithaca, N.Y.: Cornell University Press, 1963); Jürgen Habermas, *Knowledge and Human Interests*, trans. Jeremy Shapiro (Boston: Beacon, 1971), 4; and Leszek Kolakowski, *The Alienation of Reason*, trans. Norbert Guterman (New York: Anchor, 1968).

destroyed the basis of romantic metaphysics. Consequently, German philosophy in the post-Hegel era was confronted by what Herbert Schnädelbach has aptly termed a "philosophical identity-crisis."[5] Both within and without the philosophical profession, questions were raised concerning the function of philosophy in an age committed to the ideal of positivist research in the sciences: How could philosophy assure its own scientific character in relation to the spectacular technical and material achievements of the special sciences? More fundamentally, what was, in the end, genuinely "scientific" about philosophical discourse? Was it subject matter? Method? A rigorous adherence to internal rules of scientific logic? In an era of post-Hegelian crisis, one asked: What was the principal relationship of philosophy to science (as a model) and to the sciences (as specific forms of research)?

Writing about this period of German philosophy after the death of Hegel, Martin Heidegger called attention to its basic "perplexity over the proper task of philosophy."[6] And Hans-Georg Gadamer, Heidegger's student, remarked that by the mid-nineteenth century, "philosophy as a whole had gone bankrupt and the breakdown of the Hegelian domination of the world by spirit was only a consequence of the bankruptcy of philosophy in general."[7] In his survey *The Problem of Knowledge*, Ernst Cassirer reinforced the judgment that "in the domain of science, Hegel's system led him and his disciples and successors to everlasting blundering and pretensions that necessarily deprived speculative philosophy of any credit among empirical investigators."[8] Among philosophers themselves as well as practitioners in the human and natural sciences, philosophy's traditional role as *scientia scientiarum* (the organon of scientific knowledge, or the science of science) was challenged by a new generation of thinkers.[9]

In an effort to reestablish philosophy's credibility as "the science [that offers] the totality of the highest and most essential knowledge," professional philosophers pursued various strategies of making their

[5] Schnädelbach, *Philosophy in Germany*, 5–11.
[6] Martin Heidegger, *Hegels Phänomenologie des Geistes. Gesamtausgabe 32.* (Frankfurt: Klostermann, 1980), 15.
[7] Hans-Georg Gadamer, *Reason in the Age of Science*, trans. Frederick G. Lawrence (Cambridge: MIT Press, 1981), 24. For a similar view, see Max Müller, *Existenzphilosophie im geistigen Leben der Gegenwart* (Heidelberg: Kerle, 1949), 35.
[8] Ernst Cassirer, *The Problem of Knowledge*, trans. W. H. Woglom (New Haven, Conn.: Yale University Press, 1950), 3.
[9] For a fuller discussion on this topic, see Robert Flint, *Philosophy as Scientia Scientiarum* (New York: Arno, 1975).

discipline more scientific.[10] This process of "scientization" (*Verwissenschaftlichung*), which was really an attempt to legitimate philosophy's position within the newly professionalized nineteenth-century university, took a number of forms.[11] In what follows I will classify these attempts under three general categories: historical-hermeneutic research, the philosophy of world views, and scientism. Many classically trained German academics sought to resolve philosophy's generational identity crisis by bringing their historical-hermeneutical skills to bear on a philological critique of selected primary texts or on the history of philosophical systems. Thus, one finds in nineteenth-century scholarship a penchant for multivolume histories of philosophy as well as individual studies of Bacon, Descartes, Kant, Plato, and Fichte. Under the guise of this new professional model, philosophy denounced its quondam role as the science of the sciences and became instead a science of interpretation based on the critical reading of texts. Speculative excess was held to a minimum, and the scientific quality of work was secured through an emphasis on technical training, historical erudition, and the sober regard for method. For these philosophers, such as Kuno Fischer, Friedrich Überweg, and Rudolf Haym, the historicization (*Vergeschichtlichung*) of philosophy constituted a legitimate strategy for making philosophy, or the history of philosophy, one of the premier human sciences. Through professionalization, philological skills, and an awareness of the methods of the *Quellenkritik* (critique of original sources), they hoped to make philosophy a bona fide science by abjuring the Hegelian model of a speculative science of metaphysics and emphasizing instead a new understanding of science as "research."[12] One of the problems arising from

[10] Heidegger, *Hegels Phänomenologie*, 13.

[11] The process of "scientization" which I am discussing here affected both the natural and the human sciences. For an excellent discussion of its philosophical implications, see Walter Schulz, *Philosophie in der veränderten Welt* (Pfullingen: Neske, 1972), 11–245. But the process of *Verwissenschaftlichung* also affected philological, historical, and hermeneutical practices in all the human sciences as well, as Ulrich Muhlack has pointed out in "Zum Verhältnis von klassischer Philologie und Geschichtswissenschaft im 19. Jahrhundert," in *Philologie und Hermeneutik*, ed. Helmut Flashar et al. (Göttingen: Vandenhoeck & Ruprecht, 1979). See also Julius Kraft, *Philosophie als Wissenschaft und als Weltanschauung* (Hamburg: Meiner, 1977).

[12] Lutz Geldsetzer, *Die Philosophie der Philosophiegeschichte im 19. Jahrhundert: Zur Wissenschaftstheorie der Philosophiegeschichtsschreibung und Betrachtung* (Meisenheim am Glan: Anton Hain, 1968), provides a history of the historiography involved in nineteenth-century attempts at writing a history of philosophy. For a model of the research practices and strategies of nineteenth-century German science, see Alwin Diemer, ed., *Konzeption und Begriff der Forschung in den Wissenschaften des 19. Jahrhunderts* (Meisenheim am Glan: Anton Hain, 1978); and Diemer, ed., *Beiträge zur Entwicklung der Wissenschaftstheorie im 19. Jahrhundert* (Meisenheim am Glan: Anton Hain, 1968).

such an approach, however, was that sheer restoration of philosophical ideas from the past—in the form of Neo-Kantianism, Neo-Hegelianism, Neo-Thomism, Neo-Aristotelianism, Neo-Fichteanism, and other resurrected movements—did not encourage innovative or energetic solutions to philosophy's perceived identity crisis. In this sense, the professional philosopher's fondness for reviving antiquated philosophical systems during the nineteenth century might best be compared to the flourishing of historicist art forms during the same period. Just as the revival of classical, Gothic, baroque, and mannerist styles confirmed a generation's inability to fashion its own unique style, so, too, the renaissance of various philosophical systems in the late nineteenth century revealed the shortcomings of post-Hegelian philosophy in Germany.

Ultimately, the historical-hermeneutic turn within philosophy not only affected the industry of writing dissertations, publishing articles, professionalizing the university curriculum, and apprenticing *Dozenten* (university lecturers) and other lower-level academics; it also influenced important thinkers such as Windelband, Dilthey, Husserl, and Heidegger. Even if these thinkers did not see themselves primarily as historians of thought, each wrote an important book on the history of Western philosophy, addressing in different ways the question of philosophy's role as a legitimate science. Dilthey's project of providing a foundation for the *Geisteswissenschaften*, for example, sought to address the problem of philosophy's relationship to the human sciences by undertaking a hermeneutic history of the idea of science itself. This led him to offer a theory of world views (*Weltanschauungslehre*) which tried to reconcile the limited historical insights of individual epochs with the demand for a scientific history of thought. Windelband, Husserl, and Heidegger all rejected Dilthey's philosophy of world views, however, and attempted to resolve the crisis in philosophy in their own unique ways. Following a Neo-Kantian theory of values, Windelband sought a transcendental science that would overcome the relativism he perceived in Dilthey; Husserl aimed at a phenomenological revolution in German thinking which would avoid the subjectivism of world views and which instead would steer philosophy on the rigorous path of science. Heidegger, too, was unsympathetic to the theory of world views; he perceived the choice itself between philosophy as world view or as science (*Weltanschauung* versus *Wissenschaft*) to be one of the major reasons for the so-called crisis in philosophy. In his early lectures at the University of Freiburg in 1919, titled "The Idea of Philosophy and the

Problem of the World View," Heidegger called for a rethinking of the essence of philosophy, which he now considered a "primordial science" (*Urwissenschaft*), something more originary than mere *Wissenschaft*.[13] But even here Heidegger's own hermeneutical project was defined in and against the reigning notion of a crisis in the sciences which philosophy needed to address.

Given this situation of conflict, the strategy behind the philosophy of world views was to overcome the demands of science by synthesizing knowledge into a personalized system of wisdom, relating all experience of the world to the subjective life-conditions of the individual.[14] By stressing the lived, relative, and historical character of truth, world-view philosophy (in its most popular forms as *Lebensphilosophie*, fictionalism, monism, voluntarism, theosophy) tried to offer meaning for the self in a world threatened by the depersonalizing forces of modernity. Friedrich Paulsen, a professor at the University of Berlin at the turn of the century and a classic representative of the academic mandarin mentality, captured the mood of his generation perfectly when he bemoaned the inability of science to confront the intimate questions of life: "Everyone now works harder than ever before, but the inner necessity and rationale of the enterprise is not there; one has the feeling that the result for inner, personal life does not correspond to the expenditure of energy; the burden of a hundred camels that one tows along does not increase wisdom, it does not make one richer in the knowledge of human and divine things."[15] Paulsen's elegiac lament was fairly typical in an age in which *Wissenschaft* and *Weltanschauung* were seen as antipodes and object was set against subject, knowledge against life, and natural science against human science. Of course, there were those, like Dilthey, who wished to bridge the distance between these realms; more typically, however, philosophers migrated to either one group or the other. There were many world-view philosophers who claimed that it was the model of traditional science which was responsible for the crisis within philosophy in the first place. Abandoning the pretense of rigorous science,

[13] Martin Heidegger, *Zur Bestimmung der Philosophie*, Gesamtausgabe 56/57 (Frankfurt: Klostermann, 1987), 13–17.

[14] For a fuller discussion of the problem of *Weltanschauungsphilosophie*, see Walter Betz, "Zur Geschichte des Wortes 'Weltanschauung,'" in *Kursbuch der Weltanschauungen* (Frankfurt: Ullstein, 1981), 18–28; Theodor Litt, *Wissenschaft, Bildung, und Weltanschauung* (Leipzig: Teubner, 1928); and Helmut Meier, "Weltanschauung: Studien zu einer Geschichte und Theorie des Begriffs," diss., University of Munich, 1967.

[15] Theobald Ziegler, *Die geistigen und sozialen Strömungen des 19. Jahrhunderts* (Berlin: Bondi, 1901), 672.

these philosophers hoped to integrate human experience and under-standing into their philosophical approach. And yet despite this vital-ist critique of science, world-view philosophy did not really provide a satisfactory answer to the perceived crisis of the sciences, its success among the educated, genteel *Bildungsbürgertum* notwithstanding. During the 1920s frequent polemics were still marked by a crisis-con-sciousness within philosophy.

Besides the legitimation strategies of world-view philosophy and historical-hermeneutic research, there were also many other at-tempts—in the form of positivism, materialism, Darwinism, psychol-ogism, empiriocriticism, naturalism, and others—to make philosophy more scientific by modeling it on the methods of the natural sciences. This new turn toward scientism in philosophy posited the unity of all science and the universality of scientific truth as its foundational prin-ciple. Writing about this period of German philosophy, in his book *Knowledge and Human Interests*, Jürgen Habermas focuses on scientism as a response to what he calls "the crisis of the critique of knowl-edge." In Habermas's words, "Scientism means science's belief in it-self: that is, the conviction that we can no longer understand science as *one* form of possible knowledge, but must rather identify knowl-edge with science."[16] Scientism, of course, took many forms, and it would be irresponsible to assume that all partisans of scientism advo-cated one form of scientific thinking. Still, *scientism* functions as a use-ful term to describe those movements within philosophy and the nat-ural and human sciences which identify reliable knowledge with the idea of science itself. With respect to the historical situation within philosophy-at-large, proponents of scientism felt that metaphysical questions should be handled empirically or not at all, because most questions concerning truth were simply improperly phrased ques-tions of method. For those committed to such a vision, scientism meant a moratorium on all romantico-poetic speculation about free-dom, the soul, eternity, metaphysics, and the like. In the eyes of these thinkers, were it to survive at all, philosophy would have to deny itself the luxury of wisdom for the sobriety of method.

By virtue of its logic, objectivity, and methodological rigor, scien-tism came to dominate a variety of disciplines in late-nineteenth-cen-tury Germany, even as its adherents failed in their attempts to over-come the crisis within German philosophy. As we shall see, Neo-

[16] Habermas, *Knowledge and Human Interests*, 4.

Kantianism, *Lebensphilosophie*, hermeneutics, and historicism all challenged, in a variety of ways, the very form of scientistic or positivist inquiry. Thinkers such as Rickert and Windelband rejected positivism for denying the importance of values; Dilthey despaired at its ahistorical approach and its denial of perspectivity. Husserl complained that the positivistic method had reduced "the idea of science to mere factual science" and went on to ask whether "the world and human existence in it, truthfully have a meaning if the sciences recognize as true only what is objectively established?"[17] All these philosophers could agree that the meaning of science was not something inherently scientistic but rather had to do with life, values, history, and the human world; in this sense, one could clearly label them antipositivists. But despite their contentious rhetoric, these philosophers shared many traits with their professed opponents. Like the positivists, they were virulently antimetaphysical, expressing a deep concern about questions of epistemology and methodological foundations. Moreover, they also sought to establish their truths in the name of science, which they perceived as the guarantor of certitude. Although they might argue about the proper emphasis within scientific philosophy on vitalistic, transcendental, empirical, or phenomenological elements, they could all agree that science itself yielded the only legitimate form of truth.

Among academic philosophers in the latter half of the nineteenth century, the turn toward scientific philosophy was carried out through a critical revival of Cartesian-Kantian epistemology. Neo-Kantianism, for example, though antipositivist in tone and character, still tried to overcome the crisis in philosophy by focusing on the problem of the "proper" scientific method. In place of Hegel's magisterial definition of philosophy as a science of metaphysics, the Neo-Kantians underscored the limits of their craft, defining philosophy as a science of knowledge. Beginning in the 1860s with Otto Liebmann's *Kant und die Epigonen* and the work of Eduard Zeller, Neo-Kantianism "rehabilitated philosophy as a whole in the form of a theory of knowledge by attributing to this discipline the function of a basis for philosophy and science."[18] If philosophy could no longer serve as scientia scientiarum, it might at least, under the name "epistemology,"

[17] Edmund Husserl, *The Crisis of the European Sciences*, trans. David Carr (Evanston, Ill.: Northwestern University Press, 1970), 6–7.
[18] Schnädelbach, *Philosophy in Germany*, 106.

still function as the methodological foundation of all scientific knowledge.[19] In fact, Zeller argued that this epistemological question served as "the formal basis of all philosophy; from here the final decision concerning the proper method for philosophy and for science was to find its starting point."[20] In his essay of 1862, "Über Bedeutung und Aufgabe der Erkenntnistheorie," Zeller claimed that epistemology could serve as a way of healing the crisis between science and philosophy:

> The relationship of philosophy to the special sciences has so altered that philosophy in general has actually more to learn from them now than it has had for some decades, while on the other hand it has more and more confirmed in them the prejudice against any need of philosophy for their purposes, and even made them feel that they should not be troubled by it in their work. No proof is required to show that this is not a healthy condition. In general where there is a continuous development the need appears from time to time of a return to the starting point, of recalling the original problems and again attempting a solution in the original spirit, though perhaps by other means. For German philosophy such a moment now appears to have arrived. The beginning of the period of evolution reached by modern philosophy is Kant, and the scientific achievement with which he broke the new way in his theory of knowledge. Everyone who wishes to improve the bases of our philosophy will have to go back to this inquiry first of all and must investigate the questions which Kant presented to us in the spirit of his own *Critique*, in order to avoid the errors Kant made—and to do so from the riches of scientific experience in our century.[21]

A generation later, Rickert extended Zeller's program to offer a way out of the crisis that he perceived between *Wissenschaft* and *Weltanschauung*, writing that "every problem of world views or of life is transformed for us into a problem of logic and epistemology."[22] Following Fichte's notion that "as the science of all sciences, the sci-

---

[19] Johannes Berger, in his perceptive dissertation on Heinrich Rickert, "Gegenstandskonstitution und geschichtliche Welt," University of Munich, 1967, traces the development of epistemology in Neo-Kantian thought. See also Köhnke, *Entstehung und Aufstieg des Neukantianismus*, and Hans-Georg Gadamer, "Neukantianismus," *Philosophisches Lesebuch*, vol. 3 (Frankfurt: Fischer, 1988), 215–218.

[20] Eduard Zeller, *Kleine Schriften*, vol. 1 (Berlin: Reimers, 1910), 240.

[21] Eduard Zeller, "Über Bedeutung und Aufgabe der Erkenntnistheorie," in *Vorträge und Aufsätze* (Leipzig: Fues, 1887), 489–490, cited in Cassirer, *Problem of Knowledge*, 4.

[22] Heinrich Rickert, *Die Grenzen der naturwissenschaftlichen Begriffsbildung: Eine logische Einleitung in die historischen Wissenschaften* (Tübingen: Mohr, 1929), 10.

ence of knowledge is to furnish all the sciences with fundamental principles," Rickert believed that he had found in epistemology a tenable solution to philosophy's crisis.

In his work Rickert, like Dilthey, intended to offer a unifying theory of knowledge which, though accepting a division between science and history or *Natur* and *Geist*, overcame this division in a new philosophical method. For Dilthey, the new method was wedded to hermeneutics; for Rickert, it followed the transcendental method of Kant. Each believed, however, that philosophical method could solve the fundamental problems of science and history, even if this meant the acceptance of different values for each sphere. Even Heidegger, in *Being and Time*, could argue that "the expression 'phenomenology' signifies primarily a *methodological conception*."[23] Throughout the late nineteenth and the early twentieth centuries, there was a widespread generational awareness that the solution to the crisis of philosophy lay in the development of a new philosophical method (whether epistemology, hermeneutics, positivism, or phenomenology) that would secure the possibility of rigorous scientific truth. In this sense the new philosophical consciousness echoed the old appeal made by Descartes three centuries earlier in his *Discourse on Method*: "We need a method if we are to investigate the truth of things."[24]

ii. The Cartesian Anxiety of Modern Philosophy

Part of my argument about the underlying contradictions within the historicist tradition depends on my reading of modernity as an era of crisis. By looking at the development of German philosophy from the 1880s to the 1930s, especially as it became more self-consciously concerned with questions of epistemology, methodology, and scientific certitude, I hope to draw some parallels between the latter stages of modernity in the postwar consciousness of crisis and the origins of modernity in the Cartesian project of scientific certitude. Heidegger's work becomes so important in this context because he recognized the patrimony of Cartesian metaphysics in the meth-

[23] Martin Heidegger, *Being and Time*, trans. John Macquarrie and Edward Robinson (New York: Harper and Row, 1962), 50; *Sein und Zeit* (Tübingen: Niemeyer, 1976), 27.
[24] René Descartes, *Philosophical Writings*, vol. 1, trans. John Cottingham (Cambridge: Cambridge University Press, 1985), 15.

odological debates about nature and history dominant at the turn of the century. Heidegger provided a genealogy of modernist thought, a kind of metaphysics of modernity which he believed had determined the crisis-thinking of his own age.

When considered within its own context, one can see how *Being and Time* represented a radical new beginning in German thinking. With its hermeneutic phenomenology, it offered a new ontology of *Dasein* grounded in historicity, facticity, and temporality. Its curious language of "fallenness," "disclosedness," "worldhood," "being-with" bordered on the neologistic and arcane. The very spirit of the book was stamped with an imprint of originality and freshness. Yet it is easy to forget that in many ways, the work was a curious refashioning of the old Neo-Kantian genre of history of philosophy. One of Heidegger's main tasks in this work was to achieve what he called "a destruction of the history of ontology."[25] More precisely, the work sought a destruction of the Greek ontological tradition of Plato and Aristotle transformed in the early modern period by Descartes and, later, Kant. As Heidegger put it: "In taking over Descartes' ontological position Kant made an essential omission: he failed to provide an ontology of Dasein. This omission was a decisive one in the spirit of Descartes' ownmost tendencies. With the '*cogito sum*' Descartes had claimed that he was putting philosophy on a new and firm footing. But what he left undetermined when he began in this 'radical' way, was the kind of being which belongs to the *res cogitans*, or—more precisely—the *meaning of the being of the 'sum.'*"[26]

For Heidegger, the Cartesian method of scientific knowledge—with its emphasis on proof, certitude, indubitability, clarity, and distinctness—was hardly "radical" at all. It proceeded from purely epistemological premises founded on belief in a knowing subject (the cogito) riven from history, language, and culture and serving as a kind of Archimedean foundation for scientific truth. What was taken as "radical" in Descartes's philosophy proved, through Heidegger's ontological analysis, to be nothing but a chimera of modernist metaphysics. In his task of *Destruktion*, Heidegger viewed the work of both Descartes and Kant as "inappropriate way[s] of approaching the problem" of being. Focused as it was on the demand for proof and

---

[25] Heidegger, *Being and Time*, 41–49; *Sein und Zeit*, 19–28.
[26] Heidegger, *Being and Time*, 46; *Sein und Zeit*, 24.

demonstration, their work attempted an objectivist critique of the flux of everyday life, of those unscientific and refractory elements in experience which Kant termed "the dark, confused and unserviceable."[27] By leading philosophy on "the secure path of a science," they hoped to overcome fundamental doubts about what Descartes, in his *Meditations*, termed "any firm and permanent structure in the sciences."[28] In *Beyond Objectivism and Relativism*, his critical study of the roots of modern philosophy, Richard Bernstein focuses on the patrimony of Cartesian and Kantian philosophy which has shaped so much of modern thought. The origins of the objectivist/relativist split derive, Bernstein argues, from the legacy of the Cartesian project which he sees at work in the whole crisis-mentality of modern and postmodern thought. Offering variations on a Heideggerian theme, Bernstein tries to show that problems of relativism, subjectivism, historicism, and nihilism are merely consequences of what he playfully calls a "Cartesian anxiety." Looking back over three centuries of Western philosophy, Bernstein seizes on the metaphor of "foundation" as the guiding trope for the modernist project:

It is the quest for some fixed point, some stable rock upon which we can secure our lives against the vicissitudes that constantly threaten us. The specter that hovers in the background of this journey is not just radical epistemological skepticism but the dread of madness and chaos where nothing is fixed, where we can neither touch bottom nor support ourselves on the surface. With a chilling clarity Descartes leads us with an apparent and ineluctable necessity to a grand and seductive Either/Or. Either there is some support for our being, a fixed foundation for our knowledge, or we cannot escape the forces of darkness that envelop us with madness, with intellectual and moral chaos.[29]

"We may," Bernstein writes, "purge ourselves of the quest for certainty and indubitability. But at the heart of the objectivist's vision . . . is the belief that there are or must be some fixed permanent constraints to which we can appeal and which are secure and stable." Part of my effort in this book is to show that what Bernstein, follow-

[27] Heidegger, *Being and Time*, 249; *Sein und Zeit*, 205. Immanuel Kant, *Critique of Pure Reason*, trans. Norman Kemp Smith (London: Macmillan, 1929), 8.
[28] René Descartes, *Philosophical Works*, vol. 1, trans. Elizabeth S. Haldane and G. R. Ross (Cambridge: Cambridge University Press, 1969), 144.
[29] Richard Bernstein, *Beyond Objectivism and Relativism* (Philadelphia: University of Pennsylvania Press, 1983), 18.

ing Heidegger, identifies as the "Cartesian anxiety" in modern philosophy is at work in the whole crisis-consciousness of the period from 1880 to 1930. What marks the epoch of modernity as a period of crisis, I argue, is its generational belief in the fundamental polarity between objectivism and relativism. Caught in the epistemological dilemma of this either/or, philosophers and historians defined the meaning of historicism in terms of their own contradictory metaphysical positions. What emerged from their methodological and epistemological debates about the scientific value of historical understanding was, of course, an awareness of the unworkability of the old approaches. But the lessons were not immediately understood, because many philosophers were unwilling to abandon their own traditional approaches. What did develop, however, was an awareness of crisis itself and of the necessity to resolve the crisis. For Windelband, Rickert, and Dilthey, the crisis of historicism offered a challenge to their own faith in philosophy's scientific character. In this sense, the crisis provided an occasion for rethinking the fundamental relation of history to science and of reconciling the contradictions between values and methods. For Heidegger, however, the situation appeared very different. As he saw it, the crisis of historicism was not a narrowly generational debate about the meaning of historical method; rather, it represented a coming to terms with the basic aporia of nineteenth-century thought: the legacy of classical science and the new insight into human historicity. What Heidegger succeeded in doing in his project of *Destruktion* was to dismantle the presuppositions of Cartesian-Kantian thinking which dominated the approach of both the Neo-Kantians and Dilthey. Moreover, he recognized that their debates about the proper method for securing historical truth were bound to a certain epistemological structure that decided in advance the very contours of any inquiry into nature or history.

Going back to the early modern division of the sciences, Heidegger argued, philosophers had distinguished between two domains of objects—nature and history—which were investigated by the two main groups of empirical sciences: the natural sciences and the human sciences. The basis of this highly schematized ordering of knowledge could be traced back to a demand for a clear and distinct method of scientific inquiry, the desideratum of Descartes's *Discourse on Method*. According to Heidegger, Cartesian method, in its approach to nature, focused more on the constitution of nature in and through human consciousness than on nature itself. As a result, it rendered explicit only that kind of truth already implicit in the method.[30] In his own phenomenological analysis of nature and history in *Being and Time*, Heidegger attempted to uncover "the ontologically inadequate way of starting" which characterized this whole tradition. This "scandal of philosophy," as Heidegger called it, was the continued expectation of a Cartesian demand for proof, objectivity, and certitude.[31] In Descartes, Kant, the Neo-Kantians, and the German academic tradition, Heidegger located a peculiar tendency to privilege epistemology as a way of establishing the objectivity of truth claims in the sciences of nature and the sciences of spirit.

Yet for Heidegger the very demand for objectivity was incompatible with an originary experience of the human world. If history or nature were to have any meaning at all, they could not be defined solely as objects of epistemological certitude but needed also to be understood as ways of phenomenological disclosure to human beings within the horizon of time. In applying the static time concept of mathematics and geometry to culture and history, academic epistemology had succeeded in hypostatizing the dynamic processes of truth in order to grasp them scientifically. But the experience, or rather the ontological condition, of historicity undermined the status of epistemological truth. In his lectures of 1925, "History of the Concept of Time," Heidegger explained why the epistemological *Fragestellung* of academic philosophy remained trapped in its own presuppositions, closing off any originary access to the phenomena it attempted to study. He opened by remarking:

> We tend to understand history and nature by way of the sciences which investigate them. But then history and nature would be accessible only insofar as they are objects thematized in these sciences. But it is not certain whether a domain of objects necessarily also gives us the actual area of subject matter out of which the thematic of the sciences is first carved. To say that the science of history deals with history does not necessarily mean that history as this science understands it is as such also the authentic reality of history. Above all, no claim is made as to whether historiographical knowledge of historical reality ever enables us to see history in its histori-

[30] For a critique of modern scientific practice and the problem of method, see Hans-Georg Gadamer, "Das Faktum der Wissenschaft," in *Das Erbe Europas* (Frankfurt: Suhrkamp, 1989), 87–105; and Rüdiger Bubner, "Das Faktum der Wissenschaft und Paradigmenwechsel," *Studia Leibnitiana*, Sonderheft 6 (1974): 78–94.
[31] Heidegger, *Being and Time*, 249; *Sein und Zeit*, 205.

city. It might well be that something essential necessarily remains closed to the potentially scientific way of disclosing a particular field of subject matter; indeed, must remain closed if the science wishes to perform its proper function. In the case before us, the separation of the two domains may well indicate that an original and undivided context of subject matter remains hidden and that it cannot be restored by a subsequent effort to bring the two, nature and spirit, together within the whole of human Dasein.

The separation comes first from the sciences, which reduce history and nature to the level of domains of objects. But the phenomenology of history and nature promises to disclose reality precisely as it shows itself *before* scientific inquiry, as the reality which is already given to it. Here it is not a matter of a phenomenology of the sciences of history and nature, or even of a phenomenology of history and nature as objects of these sciences, but of a phenomenological disclosure of the original kind of being and constitution of both.[32]

Within the Cartesian-Kantian tradition, Heidegger saw that distinctions between nature and history were epistemologically secured. Philosophy's aim in such a situation was to provide a scientific foundation for the study of the human and natural world. Yet Heidegger believed that science was not radical enough. To disclose "the original kind of being" of nature and history "*before* scientific inquiry," Heidegger acknowledged a need to dismantle the whole metaphysical structure of Cartesian-Kantian science. He offered in its stead not a new philosophical foundation but a way of approaching these phenomena which obviated the need for foundations as such. The very goal of seeking a foundational science was, for him, an essential contradiction because foundations themselves could never be secured, either logically or methodologically, in a spurious Archimedean beginning. The genuine origin of scientific knowledge, Heidegger insisted, was the experience of nature and history as phenomena before any scientific treatment.

In the context of this discussion, Heidegger raised the problem of what he called "the crisis of the sciences."[33] Questions of objectivity and relativism, of *Weltanschauung* versus *Wissenschaft*, and of nature and history were part of the essential crisis facing the European sciences in the modern era. Heidegger wrote:

---

[32] Martin Heidegger, *History of the Concept of Time*, trans. Theodore Kisiel (Bloomington: Indiana University Press, 1985), 1–2; *Prolegomena zur Geschichte des Zeitbegriffs*, *Gesamtausgabe* 20 (Frankfurt: Klostermann, 1988), 1–2.

[33] Heidegger, *History of the Concept of Time*, 2; *Prolegomena zur Geschichte des Zeitbegriffs*, 3.

Nowadays we speak of a crisis of the sciences in a twofold sense. First, there is the sense in which contemporary man, especially among the young, feels that he has lost an original relationship to the sciences. Recall the discussion evoked by Max Weber's lecture on this subject, which was so despairing over the sciences and their meaning. Taking Weber's standpoint to be that of despair and helplessness, one wanted to restore meaning to science and scientific work and sought to do so by cultivating a world view of science and constructing from it a mythical conception of the sciences.

But the real crisis is internal to the sciences themselves, wherein their basic relationship to the subject matter which each of them investigates has become questionable. . . . The crisis can be directed in ways which are fruitful and secure for the sciences only if we are clear about its scientific and methodological sense and see that the exposition of the primary field of subject matter calls for a mode of experience and interpretation in principle different from those which prevail in the concrete sciences themselves. In crisis, scientific research assumes a philosophical cast. Sciences thus say that they are in need of an original interpretation which they themselves are incapable of carrying out.[34]

In Heidegger's reading, the crisis within post-Hegelian philosophy extended beyond the intradisciplinary debates among Neo-Kantians and hermeneutically trained scholars to affect the very foundations of science itself. He understood this crisis-consciousness within philosophy less as a specific reaction to disciplinary themes and problems than as a part of a generational mood that defined postwar German thinking at all levels. What proved decisive for Heidegger was to understand science hermeneutically as a "concrete possibility of human *Dasein*" and not as a calcified tradition of rules and directives. By "bringing the subject matters under investigation to an original experience," that is, to an original interpretation of *Dasein*'s possibilities, Heidegger hoped to transform the meaning of "crisis" from a state of emergency or personal anxiety to a fundamental confrontation with the whole Western tradition. In so doing, he seized on the crisis in philosophy to refigure history and science themselves. If we are to understand Heidegger's singular deployment of the crisis-concept, especially as a way of dissolving the historicist *Fragestellung*, we will need to place it within the generational framework of the Weimar era, when the idea of a crisis-consciousness first develops. For Heidegger was especially sensitive to the popular tradition of German crisis-

[34] Heidegger, *History of the Concept of Time*, 2–3; *Prolegomena zur Geschichte des Zeitbegriffs*, 3–4.

thinking and tried to account for the generational interest in crisis on metaphysical grounds. What seemed to others a mere sociological reaction to the postwar collapse appeared to Heidegger as an epochal confrontation with the meaning of modernity. If the crisis of historicism confirmed the precarious state of epistemological and historiographical inquiry, it also revealed, in metaphysical terms, the collapse of the self-confident modernist vision that science could effectively circumscribe the realms of both nature and history.

iii. The Cultural Crisis of the German Mandarinate

Part of the "legitimation crisis" in German philosophy between 1880 and 1930 was the prevalence of epistemological and methodological "crises" that appeared to threaten the very status of philosophical inquiry. But after the Great War, the tone and urgency of crisis rhetoric changed. In the works of prominent German postwar writers such as Oswald Spengler, Ernst Troeltsch, Friedrich Meinecke, Karl Barth, and Ernst Bloch, there developed a new kind of rhetorical discourse sensitive to the collapse and dissolution of the old order. In these writers the catastrophe of 1918 touched off a crisis-consciousness which threatened the academic order of the Wilhelmine establishment.[35] Even in the now-forgotten polemical treatises of such mandarin thinkers as Erich von Kahler, Eduard Spranger, Erich Becher, Erich Rothacker, Theodor Litt, and others, one notices the same penchant for crisis-thinking.[36] It was in this climate that Rudolf Pannwitz wrote *Die Krisis der europäischen Kultur*, which was soon followed by Troeltsch's "Krisis des Historismus" and Arthur Liebert's *Die geistige*

[35] The "crisis-mentality" of Weimar was marked by the style and signature of apocalypse. Ernst Bloch's *Geist der Utopie* appeared in 1918, as did the first volume of Oswald Spengler's *Untergang des Abendlandes*. In his essay "Heidegger, Again" (*Salmagundi* 82–83 [1989]: 3–23), George Steiner draws some remarkable parallels between Karl Barth's *Epistle to the Romans* of 1919 and Franz Rosenzweig's *Stern der Erlösung* of 1921 and suggests that the postwar era in Germany fluctuated between messianic redemption and catastrophic figuration. I would argue that the academic debates concerning historicism were but another generational expression of underlying cultural crisis, albeit in a more traditional form.
[36] Fritz Ringer, *Decline of the German Mandarins* (Cambridge: Harvard University Press, 1969), traces the development of mandarin thinking about the *Krisis der Wissenschaft*, especially among those pedagogues who, like Erich Kahler in his *Beruf der Wissenschaft* (Berlin: Bondi, 1920), responded to the powerful address by Max Weber, "Wissenschaft als Beruf," in *Gesammelte Aufsätze zur Wissenschaftslehre* (Tübingen: Mohr, 1922). Ringer speaks of a "crisis of pedagogy" in the 1920s (407–410).

Krisis der Gegenwart.[37] *Crisis* became a catchword. Some spoke of the crisis of historicism and the relativity it brought to the world of cultural values; others remarked on the crisis of science and the loss of science's meaning for life. These thinkers might disagree about the genuine causes of the crisis—whether the roots lay in scientific or historical issues—but they could all agree on one generational platitude: that crisis itself was at the heart of learning and scholarship in the postwar world. Writing about his youth in the 1920s, Hans-Georg Gadamer explained: "We who were young then sought a new orientation in a disoriented world. . . . In those areas of literature and science affected by world views, there was truly a mood of catastrophe which gained ground and led to the break with the old traditions. The collapse of German idealism was only the academic side of the new generational mood. The other, more predominant side was expressed in the sensational success of Oswald Spengler's *Decline of the West*. . . . For the first time my entire outlook, my origins, education, school, and world all were relativized."[38]

For Gadamer and his contemporaries, the experience of disorientation was part of a widespread cultural phenomenon. The political threats, the economic insecurity, the social upheaval—all became part of a generational consciousness that defined itself in and through its precarious moral and intellectual identity. For the *Bildungsbürgertum* and the university elite, the threat of relativism at the heart of their world led to various attempts to solve the crisis that they perceived in the realms of life and learning. In his important work *The Decline of the German Mandarins*, Fritz Ringer captures the basic mood:

> Throughout the Weimar period, it was often said in academic circles that a crisis was in progress. No one felt the need to define the exact nature of this crisis, to ask where it came from or what it involved. "Sometimes [the educator Aloys Fischer wrote in 1924], the present situation is represented as a crisis of the . . . economic system only, sometimes as one of politics and of the idea of the state, or as a crisis of the social order. At other times it is conceived more deeply and inclusively as a crisis of the entire intellec-

[37] Rudolf Pannwitz, *Die Krisis der europäischen Kultur* (Nuremberg: Carl, 1917); Ernst Troeltsch, "Die Krisis des Historismus," *Die neue Rundschau* 33 (June 1922): 572–590; and Arthur Liebert, *Die geistige Krisis der Gegenwart* (Berlin: Pan-Verlag Rolf Heise, 1924).

[38] Hans-Georg Gadamer, "Selbstdarstellung," *Gesammelte Werke*, vol. 2 (Tübingen: Mohr, 1986), 479.

tual and spiritual culture. . . ." In any case, the crisis existed, if only by virtue of the fact that almost every educated German believed in its reality.[39]

Among philosophers, the reasons for such a crisis were debated back and forth. Liebert's *Geistige Krisis der Gegenwart*, whose popularity was reflected in the publication of three editions within five years, asserted that every epoch and every historical situation was determined by a sense of crisis. "A time without crisis," Liebert insisted, "is a dead time, as a man without crisis is a dead man."[40] What determined the crisis in Germany during the 1920s was its sense of historical relativism and its loss of cultural foundations. "The task of my work," Liebert professed, "is not to substantiate or present any one of the arbitrary crises of contemporary life, no matter how staggering a force it may possess. Rather, it is to expose *the* crisis of our time and of the whole contemporary world view and life-mood, i.e., the concept and meaning of all the individual crises and the common intellectual and metaphysical source by which they are conditioned and from which they are nourished." This consummate crisis of all crises lay, for Liebert, in "the fatal historical skepticism and relativism nourished by historicism."[41]

Other prominent philosophers such as Edmund Husserl and Karl Jaspers understood the genuine cause of cultural upheaval as the crisis of science itself. Both Husserl and Jaspers spoke of the incompatibility between the objective claims of science and the subjective element of the life-world, or between facts and values. Husserl claimed that "the positivistic reduction of the idea of science to mere factual science" had led to "the loss of science's meaning for life."[42] And Jaspers believed that the crisis of science "really depends upon the human beings who are affected by the scientific situation."[43] Even for the proponents of *Lebensphilosophie*, the crisis could be reduced to a conflict of life versus science. The choice was presented of defining philosophy either as subjective *Weltanschauung* or as objective *Wissenschaft*. In his essay, "Philosophy as Rigorous Science" (1911), Husserl saw the only legitimate solution to the identity crisis within phi-

[39] Ringer, *Decline of the German Mandarins*, 245.
[40] Liebert, *Die geistige Krisis der Gegenwart*, 5.
[41] Ibid., 7–9.
[42] Husserl, *Crisis of the European Sciences*, 5.
[43] Karl Jaspers, *Man in the Modern Age*, trans. Eden Paul and Cedar Paul (Garden City, N.Y.: Doubleday, 1957), 147.

losophy as a denial of historicism (which he felt had led to the rise of *Weltanschauung*-philosophy) and a renewed commitment to philosophy as a rigorous *Wissenschaft*.[44] In the same year, Dilthey wrote to Husserl suggesting that this was a falsely posed dichotomy. One could, Dilthey argued, maintain belief in a "universally valid theory of knowledge" while still offering a coherent theory of *Weltanschauungen*.[45] For the generation that followed, the resulting tension between *Weltanschauung* and *Wissenschaft* led to some critical questions: Was philosophy to follow the path of historicism and wind up, as Dilthey feared, prisoner "to a philosophically engendered anxiety caused by seeing philosophy divided and torn in three or even more directions"?[46] Or would it revive itself from its post-Hegelian trauma by following the tenets of scientism? And by what criteria might philosophy judge which alternative was to be followed?

In the university philosophy of the early twentieth century, the choice seemed decisive. Heinrich Rickert, for example, had no doubts as to why philosophy was in crisis; the *Weltanschauungspathos* (as Rickert sardonically termed it) had placed questions of value in the realm of subjective experience.[47] The answer to the crisis in philosophy lay in establishing a science of values, grounded in epistemology and the transcendental method, which would overcome the unsystematic, intuitive excesses of irrational *Lebensphilosophie* and the philosophy of *Weltanschauungen*.[48] For Rickert, there was a clear choice: philosophy was a science and had to reject the popular impulses of romantic-vitalist dilettantes such as Ludwig Klages, Rudolf Steiner, the George Circle, and the followers of Nietzsche. Others, including Eduard Spranger and Paul Natorp, also turned to a scientific definition of philosophy for an objective solution to the crisis. But even within the tradition of science, many academics perceived that the old foundations were in turmoil, and physicists, mathematicians, and biologists joined their colleagues in philosophy, history, and soci-

[44] Edmund Husserl, "Philosophy as Rigorous Science," in *Phenomenology and the Crisis of Philosophy*, trans. Quentin Lauer (New York: Harper Torchbooks, 1965), 71–148.
[45] Walter Biemel, ed., "The Dilthey-Husserl Correspondence," in Peter McCormick and Frederick Elliston, eds., *Husserl: Shorter Works* (South Bend, Ind.: University of Notre Dame Press, 1981), 203–208.
[46] Wilhelm Dilthey, "The Dream," in Hans Mayerhoff, ed., *The Philosophy of History in Our Time* (Garden City, N.Y.: Doubleday, 1959), 40.
[47] Heinrich Rickert, "Psychologie der Weltanschauung und Philosophie der Werte," *Logos* 10 (1920): 1–42.
[48] Heinrich Rickert, *Die Philosophie des Lebens* (Tübingen: Mohr, 1922).

ology in acknowledging the tenuous position of science in the crisis of the modern world. Science, too, was thought of in terms of a theory of *Weltanschauungen*: in biology, one spoke of vitalism; in physics, of mechanism and relativism; and in mathematics, of formalism and intuitionism.[49] Whether in the natural or the human sciences, the academic mandarin elite of the Weimar era saw themselves as being involved in a similar struggle: to find ways of solving the problems and conflicts that divided the sciences from life and separated *Wissenschaft* from *Weltanschauung*. The whole period in German thought from 1880 to 1930 is almost incomprehensible without an awareness of this crisis-mentality afflicting both the natural and the human sciences.

In mathematics, for example, Hermann Weyl wrote an essay in 1921 titled "The New Crisis in the Foundations of Mathematics." In the same year, in the field of physics, Richard von Mises delivered "On the Present Crisis in Mechanics," which was followed in 1922 by Johannes Stark's *The Present Crisis in German Physics*, Joseph Petzold's "Concerning the Crisis of the Causality Concept," and Albert Einstein's popular article "On the Present Crisis in Theoretical Physics."[50] Even Spengler, in his iconoclastic style, spoke of the crisis of physics, although he explained it in terms of a cultural *Weltanschauung*.[51] As historian of science Paul Forman, in his insightful study, "Weimar Culture, Causality, and Quantum Theory," has argued, "In this period . . . all German mathematicians and physicists went through deep and far-reaching crises, whose very definitions showed the most intimate relation with the principal currents of the Weimar intellectual milieu."[52] As the crisis-mentality developed, many failed to see that the choice between either scientism or historicism was itself a falsely posed

[49] Heidegger, *Prolegomena zur Geschichte des Zeitbegriffs*, 3–6; *History of the Concept of Time*, 3–5. For a thorough discussion of the crisis in 1920s Weimar physics and quantum theory, see Paul Forman, "Weimar Culture, Causality, and Quantum Theory," *Historical Studies in the Physical Sciences* 3 (1971): 1–116.
[50] Hermann Weyl, "Über die neue Grundlagenkrise der Mathematik," *Mathematische Zeitschrift* 10 (1921): 39–79; Richard von Mises, "Über die gegenwärtige Krise der Mechanik," *Zeitschrift für angewandte Mathematik und Mechanik* 1 (1921): 425–431; Johannes Stark, *Die gegenwärtige Krise in der deutschen Physik* (Leipzig: J. A. Barth, 1922); Joseph Petzold, "Zur Krisis des Kausalitätsbegriffs," *Naturwissenschaften* 10 (1922): 693–695; and Albert Einstein, "Über die gegenwärtige Krise der theoretischen Physik," *Kaizo* (Tokyo) 4 (December 1922): 1–8. See also Forman, "Weimar Culture," 62–67.
[51] Oswald Spengler, *The Decline of the West*, trans. C. F. Atkinson (New York: Knopf, 1926), 377–381.
[52] Forman, "Weimar Culture," 60. For a fictional treatment of the cultural crisis in German physics, see Russell McCormmach, *Night Thoughts of a Classical Physicist* (Cambridge: Harvard University Press, 1982).

question. Scientism did not offer universal validity; historicism was not simply a belief in historical relativity. Each implied the other in some originary sense.

If, in the spirit of the time, we can understand that history, philology, sociology, philosophy, jurisprudence, and linguistics were all favorably influenced by the process of scientization (*Verwissenschaftlichung*)—so that by the end of the nineteenth century one could speak of the new human sciences—then we must also recognize that the natural sciences (such as biology, physics, and mechanics) and mathematics were, conversely, historicized. As Herbert Schnädelbach reminds us, "Nineteenth-century consciousness as a whole achieved its emancipation from idealism in the name of science and history."[53]

[53] Schnädelbach, *Philosophy in Germany*, 33. By the end of the eighteenth century, history was free of the guardianship of theology, philology, and jurisprudence. No longer an ancillary science on the model of numismatics, heraldry, or genealogy, history achieved a status as a bona fide science during the nineteenth century. With the rigorous scholarship of Niebuhr, Ranke, the Göttingen school, and Theodor Mommsen, German historical science achieved a measure of legitimacy which (as Otto G. Oexle argued in "Die Geschichtswissenschaft im Zeichen des Historismus" *Historische Zeitschrift* 238 (1984): 18), established it as one of "the greatest forces in the modern era." With this "rise of historical consciousness," there developed for the first time a widespread movement to interpret human phenomena—in the realms of art, culture, language, politics, law, and economics—in boldfacedly historical terms. As a result, the traditional humanistic fields of research underwent a profound transformation in style, method, scope, and self-understanding. This "historicization" of reality, which began as a new approach to things human, radically challenged many Enlightenment theories on human nature, the natural world, civil society, and the ideal of reason. Yet, at the same time, the process of historicization occurred within the very categories of Enlightenment thought and led to a tension within historicism between its romantic-hermeneutic roots in the classical humanities and its enlightened aims of achieving scientifically objective truth, a tension that marks the whole history of the *Geisteswissenschaften* in Germany.

Even as history (*Geschichte*) or the historical profession (*Geschichtswissenschaft*) achieved a certain scientific status in German thought, however, it still held fast to the ideals of metaphysics. Reinhart Koselleck, in his article "Geschichte, Historie" [in *Geschichtliche Grundbegriffe*, vol. 4, ed. Otto Brunner, Werner Conze, and Reinhart Koselleck (Stuttgart: Klett, 1975), 647–653], has studied the history of the term *Geschichte* among European scholars since the middle of the eighteenth century and has noticed that it underwent significant revision. By 1800, the word no longer stood for a specific historical process, as, for example, in Winckelmann's *Geschichte der Kunst des Altertums* (1764), but began to be used apart from its *genitivus objectivus* as the history of the specific theme that it discusses. For the first time, *die Geschichte* is used in an abstract sense as a collective singular: history as such. Linguistically, *Geschichte* no longer refers merely to "the history of 'x'" but to the process of all histories unified together as "the" history of, for instance, the world (*Weltgeschichte*). With this shift in meaning, human reality begins to be grasped as part of an all-encompassing narrative process or pageant of teleological development. Ranke, Hegel, and the German romantics, for example, understood history as a unity and saw it as inherently meaningful. For most nineteenth-century German scholars, both within and without the historical profession,

Certainly, the notion that the nineteenth century was "the century of natural science as well as the century of historical consciousness" is a common perception.[54] And yet the prevailing model of a world split into nature *and* history (developed in the writings of Descartes, Kant, and Hegel) is misleading. The new critical approach to knowledge developed in the post-Hegel era involved a rethinking of history's relation to science but also of science's relation to history. Archival criticism, the new philology, critical hermeneutics, Rankean "self-extinguishment"—all attested to a new scientific element in historical thought. But the influence went both ways. With the new insight into the historicity of truth, science, too, became historicized or relativized, so much so that, as Dietrich von Engelhardt argues in *Historisches Bewußtsein in der Naturwissenschaft*, "an understanding of modern natural science is tied to its relation to history."[55]

---

history was understood developmentally as the unity of spiritual forces and ideas that constitute the meaning of the living cosmos.

Ranke's faith in history combined a pantheistic devotion to the divine process of becoming with an empiricist's appreciation of historical method (see Leopold von Ranke, *The Theory and Practice of History*, ed. Konrad Moltke and Georg Iggers [New York: Bobbs-Merrill, 1973], 100). Like Humboldt and Droysen, he believed that the very structure of history is meaningful because it rests on a precarious balance between ethical-spiritual forces and the world of human volition. Order prevails in Ranke's cosmos because all values stand in a meaningful relationship to a providential will. In this sense Ranke, like most early historicists, knew no value relativism; his world of historical facts was always anchored by the certainty of objective truth. Ranke's methods of inquiry might differ from those of his contemporaries, but they could all agree that there was a unity and meaning to the manifold developments in human history, a kind of eschatological narrative of human freedom. Even as they insisted on the inviolability of the scientific approach, however, it was their metaphysical prejudices about objectivity and unity that helped to define their methods. For a scholarly discussion of these issues, see Arie Nabrings, "Historismus als Paralyse der Geschichte," *Archiv für Kulturgeschichte* 65 (1983): 157–212; Gangolf Schrimpf, "Zum Begriff der geschichtlichen Tatsache," *Dilthey Jahrbuch für Philosophie und Geschichte der Geisteswissenschaften* 5 (1988): 100–140; and Friedrich Jaeger and Jörn Rüsen, *Geschichte des Historismus* (Munich: Beck, 1992).

[54] Ernst Wolfgang Orth, ed., *Dilthey und der Wandel des Philosophiebegriffs seit dem 19. Jahrhundert* (Freiburg: Alber, 1984), 7.

[55] Dietrich von Engelhardt, *Historisches Bewußtsein in der Naturwissenschaft: Von der Aufklärung bis zum Positivismus* (Freiburg: Alber, 1979), 9. Engelhardt's book is marked by an acute awareness of the reciprocal influence of the *Natur-* and *Geisteswissenschaften*. He argues that "in the nineteenth century the natural and human sciences diverged from each other more and more so that by the end of the century their classic opposition had become a reality. At the same time, one cannot overlook the fact that they shared a common fate; the turn away from idealism and romanticism intensified this opposition. Positivism and historicism are labels for this whole epoch, for all the sciences as well as for art and literature. One can detect many reciprocal influences, however; cultural history is pursued by natural scientists while historical research is oriented on the logic of the natural sciences" (166–167). Engelhardt clearly recognized

Among philosophers such as Dilthey, Rickert, Windelband, Husserl, Jaspers, and others, the separation of natural science from historical science was an uncritically assumed first principle. Indeed, the new epistemology sought to offer universally valid foundations for this split based on formal, material, methodological, and psychologistic principles, depending on the approach. But even as these thinkers attempted to distinguish the 'idiographic' from the 'nomothetic' and the 'sciences of law' (*Gesetzeswissenschaften*) from the 'sciences of experience' (*Erfahrungswissenschaften*), they often failed to notice the reciprocatory influence of historical and natural scientific concepts. Instead, they accepted the inherited structure of the sciences defined in the Cartesian-Kantian tradition of thought. Through the mathematization of nature, Descartes hoped to offer a model of truth for all the sciences, one that would destroy doubt and achieve genuine objectivity. Almost one hundred and fifty years later, this dream of a systematically achievable science was just as fundamental to Kant's project in the *Critique of Pure Reason*. As Kant explained in the preface: "In this enquiry I have made completeness my chief aim, and I venture to assert that there is not a single metaphysical problem which has not been solved, or for the solution of which the key at least has not been supplied. Pure reason is, indeed, so perfect a unity that if its principle were insufficient for the solution of even a single one of all the questions to which it itself gives birth we would have no alternative but to reject the principle, since we should then no longer be able to place implicit reliance upon it in dealing with any one of the other questions."[56] But as philosophy's relationship to science changed, with the decline of the Newtonian-mechanical world view in the nineteenth century and the development of a new institutionalized understanding of science as "research," the certitude of scientific truth was challenged.[57] In the seventeenth century, Descartes's program of a

---

that "the historicization of nature paralleled the history of knowledge concerning nature and in part was also immediately tied to it" (225). Engelhardt's book is important for demonstrating the shared epistemological presuppositions of both the natural and the human sciences.

[56] Kant, *Critique of Pure Reason*, trans. Norman Kemp Smith (London: Macmillan, 1929), 10.

[57] Martin Heidegger, in "The Age of the World Picture" (in *The Question concerning Technology*, trans. William Lovitt [New York: Harper and Row, 1977], 115–154), offers a sustained reading of the shift in scientific consciousness. See also the first three essays from Manfred Riedel's *Für eine zweite Philosophie* (Frankfurt: Suhrkamp, 1988), 7–91; and Hans-Michael Baumgartner, "Wissenschaft," in Hermann Krings and H.-M. Baumgartner, eds., *Handbuch philosophischer Grundbegriffe*, vol. 6 (Munich: Kösel, 1974), 1740–1764.

mathematization of nature offered objectivity in science; some three hundred years later, Spengler's ambitious design for a historicization of mathematics revealed only the relative truth of a *Weltanschauung*.[58] As easy as it is, however, to distinguish the historical relativism of Spengler from the objectivist dreams of Descartes, in some fundamental sense they represent the beginning and end of the same classical tradition that Bernstein outlines in *Beyond Objectivism and Relativism*. Both belong together as products of a philosophical search for ultimate foundations, expressions of the same epistemological vision within post-Hegelian German philosophy.[59] The crisis situation that I have tried to outline in this chapter represents in a certain sense the coming to self-consciousness of the instability of these foundations.

In his extraordinary study of contemporary science, *Crossroads in the Labyrinth*, Cornelius Castoriadis offers a penetrating account of the crisis-temperament in the modern period. For him, "crisis" is no mere historical phase in the evolution and progressive development of science but is, he suggests, "its permanent state."[60] Crisis itself, Castoriadis argues, is tied to "the historicity of science," revealing

> the uncertainty which has arisen in the course of scientific activity itself and which has . . . come to call in question and represent a crisis for the entire categorical framework of science. . . . For what is at stake here is not only the metaphysics that have underpinned three centuries of Western science and that have provided it with its implicit and unconscious conception of the ontological status of mathematical, physical, biological, psychical and social-historical objects. It is also and equally the logical framework within which these objects have been considered; it is the accepted model of the kind of knowledge to be pursued, the criteria of the presumed demarcation between science and philosophy, and the social-historical situation and function of science and of the organizations and people who sustain it.[61]

Scientific truth, in Castoriadis's narrative, is less the result of empirical research than the product of a metaphysical understanding of knowledge itself. That there can be no "pure" scientific standpoint but that science itself is inseparably linked to the historicity of the human world follows from the fact that Cartesian foundationalism

---

[58] Spengler, *Decline of the West*, 1:51–90.
[59] Rorty, *Philosophy and the Mirror of Nature*, 315.
[60] Cornelius Castoriadis, *Crossroads in the Labyrinth* (Cambridge: MIT Press, 1984), xiv.
[61] Ibid., 151.

has shown itself to be philosophically bankrupt. Castoriadis's aim is to rethink the bifurcation of objectivism/relativism and scientism/historicism by first dismantling epistemological concepts inherited from the early modern philosophical tradition.

Whereas Cartesian science advocated "an approach to knowledge which constitutes its object as a process evolving independently of the subject which can be located within a spatio-temporal framework of universal validity and utter transparency," Castoriadis, like Maurice Merleau-Ponty, maintains that the new science and philosophy of quantum mechanics and phenomenology offer a "set of questions wherein he who questions is himself implicated by the questions."[62] With the breakdown of Cartesian certitude and the insight into the historicity of knowledge, truth is understood not as propositional but as interpretive. In the wake of a post-Hegelian foundationalism in the state of collapse, Castoriadis's "philosophical interrogation" carries on Heidegger's task of challenging the subject/object metaphysics of scientific thinking in the modern era. By resituating science within the historicity and facticity of human existence, Castoriadis, like Heidegger, succeeds in making science something questionable—undermining in the process the very foundations of the Cartesian tradition that made modern science possible. In challenging the standard definition of science, Castoriadis helps to show that "scientific knowledge itself is undergoing a profound crisis with deep-lying roots and far-reaching consequences." But his critique is itself a historical response to the kind of crisis-consciousness generated in the postwar era, especially in the work of Heidegger. Heidegger's *Destruktion* of the Cartesian ontology that supported science led to a renewed reflection on crisis as the essential characteristic of scientific thinking in the late modern period. What Heidegger initiated in his work of the early twenties was a critique of science which functioned as a confrontation with modernity, defined as the era of scientific-metaphysical thinking. This becomes important within the context of the crisis of historicism because it shows how Heidegger was able to transform the customary rhetoric of crisis into a confrontation with the history of modernity itself, a history whose narrative was guided by underlying Cartesian assumptions.

[62] Ibid., 150; and Maurice Merleau-Ponty, *The Visible and the Invisible*, trans. Alphonso Lingis (Evanston, Ill.: Northwestern University Press, 1968), 27.

iv. Crisis-Consciousness and Cartesian Science

If one were to pick up any of the academic tracts in philosophy, science, or history which were written during the Weimar era, one would almost unavoidably come upon the word *crisis*. Even in the critical scholarly work on this period written since the 1960s, the term *crisis* survives as a convenient way of describing the turbulence of the era. Fritz Ringer speaks of the "crisis of learning" in the German academy; Robert Sullivan, in his account of the early Gadamer, alludes to "the crisis of the German philological movement"; Thomas Kuhn, in his studies of early-twentieth-century physics, investigates "the crisis of the old quantum theory"; and in *The German Conception of History*, Georg Iggers explores "the crisis of historicism."[63] The term *crisis* becomes so familiar in these and other studies that it functions as part scholarly explanation and part cliché. Paul Forman goes so far as to speak of a "craving for crises" among the natural scientists during this period. As he describes it: "It is worthwhile to emphasize how ready the mathematicians and physicists of this era were to serve themselves with the crisis rhetoric when addressing a general academic audience. For as the notion of crisis became a cliché, it also became an entrée, a ploy to achieve instant 'relevance.' . . . By applying the word 'crisis' to his own discipline the scientist has not only made contact with his audience, but has *ipso facto* shown that his field—and he himself—is 'with it,' sharing the spirit of the times."[64]

The question remains, however, of whether the idea of a crisis in postwar German thought can help us to make sense of the position of philosophy as it attempts to find its place between the crisis of the sciences and the crisis of historicism. Obviously, there is a peculiar tone to the language of this problem, a kind of rhetoric of crisis which determined the generational reception and interpretation of both the narrowly cultural world of Weimar and the larger meaning of the Western tradition. In the lectures of the physicists and philosophers— whether they spoke as did Hermann Weyl of "the inner untenability

[63] Ringer, *Decline of the German Mandarins*, 305–366; Robert Sullivan, *Political Hermeneutics* (University Park: Pennsylvania State University Press, 1989), 162–164; Thomas Kuhn, "The Crisis of the Old Quantum Theory, 1922–1925," address delivered to the American Philosophical Society, April 1966; and Georg Iggers, *The German Conception of History* (Middletown, Conn.: Wesleyan University Press, 1968), 124–228.
[64] Forman, "Weimar Culture," 58–59.

of the foundations of mathematics" or as did Dilthey of "the trembling of human society and all its concepts, which have not been seen since the days of the declining Greco-Roman world"—the same tone of urgency, haste, and fervor predominated.[65] In an age during which space was redefined as "curved," the principles of Euclidean geometry were overthrown, quanta replaced monads, and vitalist models supplanted mechanism, the rhetoric of crisis became pronounced. One could merely write this off as a special breed of academic insecurity in an age of upheaval, pointing for evidence to the crisis-consciousness of Liebert, Troeltsch, or Carl Schmitt. One might, conversely, broaden the discussion to include the whole crisis of Western European culture which animates Eliot's *The Waste Land* and Yeats's "The Second Coming." Each example conveys a sense of the pervasiveness of a generational crisis-consciousness attuned to the somber chords of a death knell for the Western tradition. One hears its echoes in Nietzsche's narrative of decline and disintegration under the heading of a "devaluation of the highest values" and "nihilism." By the 1920s, however, this narrative of decline was no mere academic problem; Spengler's work readily attested to the widespread awareness of a loss of meaning in history. The idea that history had a purpose, goal, or telos was brutally undermined by the very facts of historical experience. In our own generation, the name Auschwitz signifies the loss of hope in historical humanity. But in an earlier time, Passchendaele, the Somme, and Ypres came to signify the senselessness and irrationality of the Hegelian pageant of world history. The crisis in physics was not, however, bred in the trenches, and perceptive contemporaries understood that it was foolhardy to assume that problems of philosophy or science might be captured in the wayward struggles of infantrymen implacably slaughtering their fellows in a makeshift swamp in Flanders. They recognized, however, that although the most recent events were not responsible for the crisis in scientific circles, there was a sense that history—or rather its perceived loss of meaning—helped in forming a crisis-consciousness.

In the nineteenth century, Jacob Burckhardt defined crises as "accelerations of the historical process"; in a crisis, he explained, "the historical process is suddenly accelerated in terrifying fashion." Burck-

---

[65] Weyl and Dilthey, quoted in Forman, "Weimar Culture," 60; and Wilhelm Dilthey, *Gesammelte Schriften*, vol. 6 (Göttingen: Vandenhoeck & Ruprecht, 1958), 246.

hardt went back to the original meaning of the Greek term *krisis*, which referred to "an epidemic" or a "fever," as in Thucydides' remarkable description of the Athenian plague in the *Peloponnesian War*. For Burckhardt, *krisis* alludes to a turning point in a disease which could result in either recovery or death: when the "hour and real cause has come, the infection flashes like an electric spark over hundreds of miles. . . . The message goes through the air. . . . *Things must change*."[66] The Great War functioned as just this sort of crisis in modern European culture. As Harry Ritter argues, "The experience of World War I . . . pushed the notion of crisis into the forefront of Western consciousness, both popular and scholarly."[67] In England, France, and elsewhere on the Continent, one spoke of the "economic crisis," the "world crisis," the "crisis of liberalism," the "crisis of Western civilization," and other popular conceptions. In Germany, crisis-consciousness also flourished; but we need to ask whether we can explain intellectual changes in mathematics, physics, philosophy, sociology, and other fields in the human sciences in terms of a generational mood of crisis.

If crises do function as "accelerations of the historical process," then we might begin to see the experience of World War I less as a cause of crisis-consciousness than as a force of acceleration. I will argue in what follows that what comes to crisis in the period from 1880 to 1930 is nothing less than the project of modernity itself. In philosophical and scientific terms, this project signifies a break with the Cartesian philosophy of foundations and the mechanical world view of seventeenth-century science. In his *History of Modern Science: A Guide to the Second Scientific Revolution, 1800–1950*, Stephen Brush offers a lucid account of the modern era's revolutionary break with classical science, arguing that the classical science of Galileo, Kepler, and Newton was based on the themata "that the world consists of independent pieces of matter whose motion in absolute space is precisely determined by mathematical laws; that events occurring in different parts of the universe can be said to happen at the same time; that humans are qualitatively different from all other biological species and can, if they wish, liberate themselves from the influence of

[66] Jacob Burckhardt, *Force and Freedom*, trans. James Nichols (New York: Pantheon, 1943), 267–269.
[67] Harry Ritter, *Dictionary of Concepts in History* (Westport, Conn.: Greenwood, 1986), 82.

animal passions; and that the physical world has an objective existence independent of our observation of it."[68] The early modern sciences of nature and mathematics were at one with philosophy in wishing to guarantee a methodological certitude that would not be shaken by the vicissitudes of human error and judgment. As Galileo put it in his *Dialogue on the Great World Systems*: "If this point of which we dispute were some point of law, or other part of the studies called the humanities, wherein there is neither truth nor falsehood, we might give sufficient credit to the acuteness of wit, readiness of answers, and the greater accomplishment of writers, and hope that he who is most proficient in these will make his reason more probable and plausible. But the conclusions of natural science are true and necessary, and the judgment of man has nothing to do with them."[69] In keeping with this Galilean injunction, Brush maintains that classical science sought to guarantee objectivity and certitude as part of its belief in achieving a universal foundation for scientific thought. But, as Brush's history of the second scientific revolution suggests, the nineteenth and early twentieth centuries witnessed a fissure in these foundations.

The revolution that occurred with the theory of relativity and quantum mechanics transformed the paradigm of classical science. In *The Structure of Scientific Revolutions* Thomas Kuhn explains this paradigm shift in terms of a theory of crisis within science itself. Science, according to Kuhn, follows a cyclical pattern of normal science, crisis, revolution, normal science.[70] The role of crisis, as he sees it, is to shake the foundations of disciplinary certitude by placing in doubt the soundness of normal research practices. In this way, crisis functions as a creative force that challenges the old paradigm and opens up venues for new inquiry and reflection. To use Burckhardt's metaphor, crises accelerate the changes in scientific practice.

[68] Stephen G. Brush, *The History of Modern Science: A Guide to the Second Scientific Revolution* (Ames: Iowa State University Press, 1988), 5–6. See also Harry Redner, *The Ends of Philosophy* (Totowa, N.J.: Rowman and Allanheld, 1986). On the limits of classical science, see Ilya Prigogine, *Order out of Chaos: Man's New Dialogue with Nature* (Boulder, Colo.: New Science Library, 1984), and Harry Redner, *The Ends of Science* (Boulder, Colo.: Westview, 1987).

[69] Galileo Galilei, *Dialogue on the Great World Systems*, trans. Thomas Salusbury (Chicago: University of Chicago Press, 1953), 63.

[70] Thomas Kuhn, *The Structure of Scientific Revolutions* (Chicago: University of Chicago Press, 1962), 66–76. See also Joseph Rouse, *Knowledge and Power: Toward a Political Philosophy of Science* (Ithaca, N.Y.: Cornell University Press, 1987), for a discussion of natural science and hermeneutics.

As a new physics developed with the work of Einstein, Planck, Heisenberg, and Bohr, the certitude of classical science was challenged, and concepts such as indeterminacy and relativity began to shape the new research practices of scientists. Kuhn's thesis about crisis explores the meaning of this shift for science and philosophy. What emerges from the shift in paradigms, he argues, is not a movement from incoherence to truth or from failing certitude to a new and more foundational certitude. Rather, in Kuhn's interpretation, what is established is not a new metaphysics but a dynamic process of securing a workable model of scientific practice. Kuhnian theory challenges the idea of certitude and truth in science and focuses instead on its character as a form of praxis. Consequently, the movement from one paradigm to another is not to be construed as the introduction of a new truth; as John Caputo writes on Kuhn's crisis notion, "There is no meta-theory to which the advocates of both paradigms can appeal," for the very idea of transcendent or absolute truth has been abandoned.[71] Kuhn's example might help us to understand the changes in twentieth-century physics as part of a complex system of historical developments that are not traceable to the laboratory alone. His account shows that to achieve a measure of acceptance, new paradigms are forced to depend on the whole structure of persuasion, argumentation, and interpretation within a disciplinary matrix; in other words, their historical efficacy is determined by rhetorical and hermeneutical influences within science itself. By understanding scientific crisis as a response to the collapse of traditional paradigms, Kuhn comes to stress the historicity of scientific thought, a theme he shares with the early Heidegger. In the 1920s, Heidegger forged a connection between the crisis of historicism and the crisis of the sciences in an effort to dismantle the epistemological approach to science and history fashionable among Weimar academics. At stake in this crisis-rhetoric was not merely the research program of a few German physicists or historians but also the whole project of Cartesian metaphysics as a way of grasping modern European thought. Heidegger seized on the notion of crisis as essential to an understanding of "modernity" (which Heidegger defined as the Western tradition of philosophical-scientific discourse initiated by Descartes, carried out by the Enlightenment, and dominant in the contemporary

[71] John Caputo, *Radical Hermeneutics* (Bloomington: Indiana University Press, 1987), 218.

crises of scientism and historicism). Like Kuhn, Heidegger understood *crisis* as another name for revealing the essence of modernity.

Clearly, if we follow the thread of Heidegger's narrative, the logic of crisis proves to be somewhat curious. Essentially, crisis is about a perceived loss of meaning or at least a threat to the possibility of meaning. Whether such meaning is defined as absolute truth, scientific certainty, epistemological objectivity, historical progress, or the like, the expectation is that science, epistemology, history, and so on *should* have meaning, even as our practical experience teaches us that they do not. Ideas of crisis bring to consciousness this incommensurability between expectation and experience, offering a "turning point" or "point of decision" which either reaffirms the meaning of what is in crisis *or* undermines its viability. What remains unspoken in crisis-consciousness, however, is a recurrent tension between the expectation of historical meaning and the experience of cultural collapse where meaning is suspended or rather withdraws in an era marked by "the death of God" and nihilism. In a fundamental sense, then, crisis-consciousness lies at the heart of the modernist vision, for crisis signifies the rift between the modern and the traditional. With its logic of "the new" and its passion for always "overcoming" what precedes it, modernism is itself another name for a belief in crisis as the permanent state of things.

In his thoughtful study of another kind of crisis-consciousness, Allan Megill writes in *Prophets of Extremity* that "a precondition for the crisis view is the notion that history has directionality. Without the assumption that history is directional or linear in character, crisis would be inconceivable."[72] For Megill, both the modernist and the postmodernist movements make sense only within this crisis mentality, for each depends on the perception that history has lost its meaning and direction. With the collapse of historicism and the insight into the nihilistic character of all temporal narratives, there emerges a new kind of crisis-consciousness. Perhaps Nietzsche evoked the fundamental mood of both modernist and postmodernist crisis best when he underscored the discontinuity of history and the dissimulation of historiography. For Nietzsche, history and nihilism were inseparable;

[72] Allan Megill, *Prophets of Extremity: Nietzsche, Heidegger, Foucault, Derrida* (Berkeley: University of California Press, 1985), 294–298. Megill's book is exceptional, providing an insightful analysis into the crisis-consciousness of modernity. For a Marxist analysis of this period, see Andras Gedo, *Crisis Consciousness in Contemporary Philosophy*, trans. Salomea Genin (Minneapolis: Marxist Educational Press, 1982).

in lieu of the great Hegelian pageant of world-historical freedom, Nietzsche perceived a break in the line of progress. "What does nihilism mean?" he asked somewhat disingenuously, answering "that the highest values devaluate themselves. The aim is lacking; 'why' finds no answer."[73] But Nietzsche also understood that the awareness of a fissure in the line and direction of history was still tied to a metaphysical value structure predicated on the existence of meaning and direction.[74] Ironically, the crisis-consciousness that emerges out of the modernist perception of loss, destruction, scission, and discontinuity (what in the postmodern lexicon might be termed *alterity*) never really abandons its claims on such traditional values as meaning, direction, objectivity, and truth. On the contrary, the rhetorical trope of "crisis" is dependent on these same values, if only negatively. What becomes clearer as one critically engages the work of German philosophers in the period from 1880 to 1930 is how crisis-consciousness shapes the discourse of modernity and, more specifically, how the crisis of historicism serves as the precondition for crisis-consciousness.

All four thinkers in this study share a keen awareness of the crisis within the European tradition of the sciences. Each focuses his attention in a different way on the problems of epistemological nihilism, cultural dissolution, and historical relativism, attempting within his work to grasp the meaning of crisis for the history of European thought. Although none of them professed the fundamental faith of historicism, they all saw in the problems and contradictions of the historicist tradition an occasion and opportunity for redefining their own philosophical projects and, with them, the very meaning of modernity.

Especially in the work of Heidegger, one can detect a way of thinking through the contradictions in traditional historicist discourse. By dismantling the epistemological *Fragestellung* of Neo-Kantianism,

[73] Friedrich Nietzsche, *The Will to Power*, trans. Walter Kaufmann and R. J. Hollingdale (New York: Random House, 1968), 9.

[74] Within modern German historical thinking, for example, we can compare two very different thinkers—Hegel and Spengler. At first glance it might seem odd or unusual to link Spengler's narrative of decline to Hegel's progressive unfolding of world spirit, and yet both share a similar view: the idea that history itself, as process and as event, is guided by some narrative scheme. Each thinker also shares a peculiar sense of directionality and of meaning, even if they interpret these in very different ways. By introducing these examples, I want to show how historicism is grounded in the very ideas of narrativity, directionality, and purposiveness which mark modern historical consciousness.

Heidegger was able to show how conventional philosophical thinking had thwarted any genuine approach to problems of history and historical existence. His critique of Rickert's value-philosophy, much as his interpretation of both *Weltanschauungs-* and *Lebensphilosophie*, focused on the bankruptcy and naïveté of academic philosophy, especially its clichés about "crisis." Heidegger set about to practice a radical form of *Destruktion* which would deconstruct the logical-metaphysical edifice of nineteenth-century German thought. He believed that by undermining the viability of traditional Cartesian-Kantian categories in contemporary philosophy, he could bring philosophy itself to an impasse. Out of the failure and destruction of the old foundations, Heidegger hoped to bring about a new kind of philosophical self-reflection which would mean nothing less than "the end of philosophy."[75]

Heidegger understood "philosophy," in the traditional sense, to be synonymous with "modernity"—with that nihilistic movement of technological dominion over entities sanctioned and authorized by Cartesian, Baconian, and Newtonian physics and metaphysics. For him, the turn-of-the-century crisis of philosophy expressed the underlying crisis of modernity. Because historicist thinking dominated the debates by contemporary philosophers, Heidegger turned to a critique of historicism as a way of revealing the aporetic structures of modernist thought. If we are to make sense of Heidegger's interest in the academic "crisis of historicism," we will need to understand it against the background of these larger issues. The debates between the Neo-Kantians and Dilthey helped to define the historicist *Fragestellung*, framed as they were by philosophical issues about epistemology, logic, methodology, and axiology. In their reflections on the problems of science and history, the Neo-Kantians and Dilthey provided classic examples of the sort of Cartesian-Kantian metaphysics that Heidegger considered paradigmatic for modern philosophy. In the chapters that follow, I will offer an extended analysis of the work of Windelband, Rickert, and Dilthey organized around the themes of a crisis in philosophy and a crisis of historicism. By looking at these important figures in the history of German philosophy between 1880 and 1930, I want to raise questions about the tenability of modernist

[75] Martin Heidegger, "The End of Philosophy and the Task of Thinking," in *On Time and Being*, trans. Joan Stambaugh (New York: Harper and Row, 1972), 55–73; "Das Ende der Philosophie und die Aufgabe des Denkens," in *Zur Sache des Denkens* (Tübingen: Niemeyer, 1976), 61–80.

thinking and the philosophical contradictions that emerge from out of it. Part of my argument is that the philosophical attempts to resolve the crisis of historicism were in jeopardy from the outset, marked as they were by conflicting metaphysical and epistemological aims. By working through these debates, placing them in their own context, and attempting to follow their transcendental and hermeneutic logic, I hope to provide a way of thinking about historicism which links it to an explicitly *philosophical* reading of modernity and not merely an academic crisis about historiographical method.

Although Windelband, Rickert, and Dilthey reflected the Cartesian biases of historicist thought, it is really only in Heidegger's project of *Destruktion* that the philosophical contradictions of Neo-Kantianism and hermeneutics become manifest. Heidegger confronted the failure of historicism in the postwar generation by transforming its aporetic end into "another beginning" for thought. But in Heidegger's work, this "other" beginning was always tied to the history of philosophy itself, especially to the history of philosophical thinking about history, which Heidegger defined as an important characteristic of modernity. Since my argument concerning the philosophical project of modernity is tied to implicit assumptions about historicism—and to the crisis-consciousness it engendered—I will need to look more carefully at the four philosophers whose work raised questions about the meaning of crisis and, particularly, the crisis of historicism.

CHAPTER TWO

Wilhelm Windelband's Taxonomy of the Sciences

It is not the victory of science that distinguishes our
nineteenth century, but the victory of scientific method
over science.

—Friedrich Nietzsche, *Will to Power*

i. The Neo-Kantian Turn to Questions of Historical Method

We have seen how crisis-consciousness affected the
development of German philosophy in the period
from 1880 to 1930, helping to shape a path of inquiry that offered an alternative to the growing dominance of the
natural sciences. One finds, for example, in the work of philosophers
such as Ernst Cassirer, Rudolf Eucken, Erich Rothacker, Eduard
Spranger, Georg Simmel, Hermann Cohen, Paul Natorp, and others a
reframing of philosophical questions on the model of Kant's epistemology. These thinkers sought to revive the primacy of Kant's transcendental philosophy as a way of establishing and securing the scientific character of all the humanistic disciplines. Against the positivist attempt to explain all social, cultural, and historical phenomena on
the basis of natural scientific methods, these Neo-Kantian philosophers focused their attention on the different methods of study applicable to the sciences of nature and history, opting for a formal-logical
approach to the controversy over methods (*Methodenstreit*). In this
chapter I will focus on the development of the Baden, or southwest
German, school of Neo-Kantianism and in particular on the meth-

odological writings of Wilhelm Windelband. I do so for two reasons. First, Windelband's thought helped to determine the basic approach of his student Heinrich Rickert, whose more extensive writings on epistemology and value-philosophy shaped German academic philosophy during this period, especially in regard to questions of historical method. Dilthey, for example, expended great effort in trying to respond to Rickert's claims, and the younger Heidegger, who studied under Rickert at Freiburg, offered a series of lectures on Windelband and Rickert entitled "Phenomenology and Transcendental Value-Philosophy."[1] Second, Windelband's work provides a classic example of academic philosophy in its crisis mode: a return to Kantian-Cartesian questions of methodology and epistemology as a strategy for assuring the certitude of the sciences.

Windelband's distinction between natural-scientific and historical methods offered a new model of historical objectivity and helped to determine the *philosophical* approach to the older problems of historicism. For the earlier historicists such as Humboldt, Ranke, or Droysen, all threats of relativism were dissolved in the totality of the historical process itself. These classical historicists were committed to the idealist unity of "spirit," "idea," and "reason"; for them, history was a unified narrative of human progress and freedom in which contradictions, individual expressions, and cultural differences could be harmonized in one overarching scheme: the development of universal history. As this metaphysical edifice was being undermined by the new positivist critique of knowledge, however, the old foundations could no longer be secured. As part of an attempt to fend off positivist attacks and to establish the scientific character of philosophy itself as the definitive "science of knowledge," Neo-Kantianism offered a way of resolving problems of historical relativism by appealing to a universal concept of reason stripped of all metaphysical traces. But even as Windelband succeeded in making problems of history more genuinely "philosophical," that is, more epistemologically self-conscious, both he and Rickert ultimately contrived to alienate historical existence from its own vital origins through an almost blind concentration on the formal-logical definition of historical method. In their scheme of the sciences, history became a purely formal technique of research, a model for approaching the unique and individual devel-

[1] Martin Heidegger, *Zur Bestimmung der Philosophie*, Gesamtausgabe 56/57 (Frankfurt: Klostermann, 1987), 119–203.

opments of culture. Taxonomical purity aside, in attempting to re-solve the crisis within historicism, the Baden Neo-Kantians managed to rob history of its vital, experiential core, leaving only the desiccated husks of an abstract theory of method. There is a great paradox here, for despite the Baden school's preoccupation with the methods of his-tory, it was precisely in the natural-scientifically focused Marburg Neo-Kantians that significant historical interpretations of the philo-sophical tradition developed. One thinks of Cohen's three books on Kant, Natorp's work on Plato's theory of ideas, and Cassirer's studies on Leibniz, Kant, Renaissance cosmology, and the Enlightenment.[2] These works radically changed the historical understanding of philos-ophy within their given time. And yet Windelband's important text-books on the history of philosophy notwithstanding, there are no really important works in the Baden school which engage the history of philosophy in terms of genuine historical interpretation.

I would like to seize on this paradox as a way of reading the whole historicist tradition, finding in this separation between historical method and historical experience the aporia of the crisis in German thinking. As I will argue throughout this book, the crisis of histori-cism which emerged in Germany after 1900 was not grounded pri-marily in problems of historiographical practice. Crisis-thinking was not the result of a dysfunction within a specific academic discipline. Rather, as historical questions were transformed into questions of truth, value, certitude, verifiability, and objectivity, historians left to philosophers the task of securing epistemological foundations. Within the older historicist tradition, philosophical discussions of history had been mainly speculative, metaphysical accounts of the progress of na-tions, cultures, or races—what the Germans called *Geschichtsphiloso-phie*.[3] The new epistemological turn within the human sciences, how-

---

[2] Hermann Cohen, in his *Kants Theorie der Erfahrung* (Berlin: Dümmlers, 1871), *Kants Begründung der Ethik* (Berlin: Dümmlers, 1877), and *Kants Begründung der Aesthetik* (Ber-lin: Dümmlers, 1889), dealt with the three aspects of Kant's project: epistemology, ethics, and aesthetics. Paul Natorp's *Platons Ideenlehre* (Leipzig: Meiner, 1903), to which he added a metacritical supplement in 1921, was one of the most influential academic books of its generation. And Ernst Cassirer's historical studies, including *Leibniz' Sys-tem in seinen wissenschaftlichen Grundlagen* (Marburg: Elwert, 1902), *Kants Leben und Lehre* (Berlin: B. Cassirer, 1918), and *Individuum und Kosmos in der Philosophie der Renais-sance* (Leipzig: Teubner, 1927), all demonstrate the formidable historical erudition of the logically trained Marburg school.
[3] With the institutional and disciplinary changes within the German historical profes-sion during the nineteenth century, the tradition of speculative and metaphysical *Ges-chichtsphilosophie* was transformed. A new empirical emphasis on research practices,

ever, brought with it an emphasis on the logic of research rather than on the metaphysical meaning of cultural or intellectual developments. In the work of the Baden Neo-Kantians, we will observe an important shift in historicist thought away from the cultural meaning of history in favor of logical, methodological, and epistemological attempts at legitimizing historical research as a bona fide science. This shift signifies an important break with the older historicists, all of whom were active practitioners of the human sciences and, like Humboldt with his studies on the Kiwi language or Savigny in his research on Germanic law, had an intimate knowledge of the actual practice involved in historical research.

Baden Neo-Kantianism represents a kind of theoretical historicism—a historicism without history. Even as Windelband and Rickert sought to revive the historical philosophy of Kant, they did so in a way that denied the historicity of Kant's project and managed only to recover "problems" in a kind of atemporal-logical continuum. In what follows I would like to offer an account of Windelband's thought which places him squarely within the late nineteenth-century tradition of a systematic logic of the sciences; a fuller criticism of his work will be developed in subsequent chapters. Like other academic philosophers of his era, Windelband endeavored to rehabilitate philosophy in the name of epistemology and return to Kant's critique of metaphysics as a way of guaranteeing the scientific character of philosophic work. Seeking to avoid mere philological exegesis or dogmatic systematizing, Windelband aimed at an original reworking of Kant's critical method. As he explained in *Präludien*, an important collection of essays that were intended as "sketches for a systematic treatment of philosophy": "All we nineteenth-century philosophers are Kantians. Yet our contemporary 'Return to Kant' is not merely a renewal of a historically conditioned form of thought which presents the idea of a critical philosophy. The more thoroughly one grasps the antagonisms between the varying motifs in Kant's thought, the more readily one is able to find therein the means by which to solve those problems which Kant posed. To understand Kant is to go beyond him."[4]

---

scientific discourse, and professionalization replaced the theologically grounded idealist tradition of *Geschichtsphilosophie*. For a discussion of these changes, see Friedrich Jaeger and Jörn Rüsen, *Geschichte des Historismus* (Munich: Beck, 1992); for a discussion of the idealist sources for *Geschichtsphilosophie*, refer to the excellent book by Carl Hinrichs, *Ranke und die Geschichtstheologie der Goethezeit* (Göttingen: Musterschmidt, 1954), and to the article by Hans-Georg Gadamer, "Geschichtsphilosophie," in *Religion in Geschichte und Gegenwart*, 2 (Tübingen: Mohr, 1959), 1488–1493.

[4] Wilhelm Windelband, *Präludien* (Tübingen: Mohr, 1924), 1:iv.

Windelband's brand of Neo-Kantianism was a self-styled form of "*critical* science," an ongoing struggle against the excesses of uncritical scientism, positivism, and naturalism. Against these dogmatic approaches, Windelband believed that Kant offered philosophers formal rigor rather than any kind of catechetical certitude. By breaking with the dogmatic metaphysics of his predecessors, Kant brought epistemological order to the natural sciences and mathematics; Windelband's task was to bring this same methodological rigor to bear on the problems of the newly founded human sciences.

Despite his criticisms of Kant (which were many and varied), Windelband could still maintain that Kant had rendered philosophy an eternal service by formulating its one fundamental problem. In rigorously critical fashion, Kant asked, How, from the merely arbitrary and conditioned experience of individual perception, do we arrive at necessary, unconditioned, and universal truth? In an age dominated by scientific and technical progress, during which truth came to be understood in terms of facts and empirically verifiable conditions, Windelband tried to secure a purely logical, rather than psychological, foundation for philosophical inquiry. As he described it in his discussion of Kant from his *History of Philosophy*: "*A priori* is, with Kant, not a psychological but a purely epistemological mark; it means not a chronological priority to experience, but a universality and necessity of validity in principles of reason which really transcends all experience and is not capable of being proved by any experience (i.e. a logical not a chronological priority). No one who does not make this clear to himself has any hope of understanding Kant."[5] The Marburg Neo-Kantians had focused on Kant's transcendental logic as a way of securing the ideal, a priori legitimacy of *das Faktum der Wissenschaft* (the fact of science). According to Hermann Cohen, for example, any genuine science of knowledge had to begin with the logical structure of science itself rather than with the empirical sense data or psychological stimuli of human consciousness. While clinging to the necessity of this transcendental ideal, Windelband sought to grasp truth not merely as a logical condition but as a universal value as well. Hence, for Windelband, logic was linked to human history, culture, and anthropology and not only to natural science and mathematics. He found the basis for his conclusions in a reworking of Kant's own philosophy. In the *Logic*, Kant argued:

[5] Wilhelm Windelband, *A History of Philosophy* trans. James Tufts (New York: Macmillan, 1919), 534.

The whole field of philosophy in its widest cosmopolitan significance can be reduced to the following four questions:
1) What can I know?
2) What should I do?
3) What may I hope?
4) What is man?[6]

Drawing from Kant, Windelband maintained that all metaphysical, epistemological, ontological, and ethical questions of philosophy were, in the end, related to the problem of human values. Ultimately, he read Kant's *Logic* as the starting point for value theory. This reading marks Windelband's project as unique within his own time, because unlike most of his contemporaries who understood problems of value in terms of culture and *Weltanschauung*, Windelband wedded value to logic and *Wissenschaft*. In so doing he reframed the Kantian critique of science (which had focused on nature) to include the science of values with an emphasis on history.

Windelband's primary concern with history was the direct result of his own scholarly training and apprenticeship. As a young student at Jena, Berlin, and Göttingen in the 1860s and 1870s, he attended the lectures of Kuno Fischer and Hermann Lotze. From Fischer he developed a methodological sensitivity to issues of origin and context and an awareness that ideas do not originate in a vacuum but are the result of historical circumstance and cultural tradition. As he later wrote in *Präludien*, "He who wishes to engage in philosophical discourse concerning philosophical questions must at the same time have the courage to see everything in the context of its totality."[7] In methodological terms, this meant that all genuinely philosophical problems must be understood within their historical development. Fischer's ten-volume *History of Philosophy* served as a model of such an approach, even if, like the other great histories of philosophy written by Johann Erdmann and Eduard Zeller, it was too narrowly focused.[8] These authors organized the history of philosophy in a purely chronological fashion, narrating the development of the various systems of individual thinkers and stressing their historical character;

[6] Immanuel Kant, *Werke*, vol. 8, ed. Ernst Cassirer (Berlin: B. Cassirer, 1923), 342–343.
[7] Windelband, *Präludien*, 2:137.
[8] Eduard Zeller, *Geschichte der deutschen Philosophie seit Leibniz* (Munich: Oldenbourg, 1875), and Johann E. Erdmann, *Geschichte der Philosophie*, 3 vols. (Berlin: W. Hertz, 1866).

Windelband, on the other hand, sought to make the history of philosophy more philosophical than historical. In his famous *Lehrbuch der Geschichte der Philosophie* (1892) and *Geschichte der neueren Philosophie* (1880), he radically altered Fischer's methodological approach by conceiving of philosophy as a *Problemgeschichte* (history of specific problems) rather than as a series of great personalized systems.[9] In Windelband's account, philosophical problems developed as responses to the failure of disciplinary "paradigms": the great thinkers posed the leading questions that were then resolved and transformed by succeeding generations. Conceived in this way, the history of philosophy offered a model for self-reflection and critique rather than an extended narrative of human error and obfuscation. Moreover, Windelband believed that historical tradition, when used critically, did not have to be antiquarian but could serve as a catalyst for the development of new ideas.[10] This is part of what Windelband meant when he claimed that "to understand Kant is to go beyond him." History was never merely "historical" for Windelband but was always in the service of a philosophical system.

ii. Windelband's Definition of Philosophy as a Science of Values

Windelband's interpretation of Kant offered a model for the kind of critical history of philosophy which transformed the moribund philology of the older Neo-Kantians into a systematic and coherent new philosophy of values. Like his Marburg contemporary Hermann Cohen, Windelband stressed the primacy of epistemology, seeking to establish critical limits to our knowledge while securing its logical validity. Both men rejected the contingencies of the historical and psychological subject in favor of the timelessly valid, transcendental subject of logic. But where Cohen opted for a mathematical model of logic as the ground for a theory of the sciences, Windelband sought to demonstrate that science itself is not grounded in mathematical structures. If, in the *Critique of Pure Reason*, Kant had focused on these mathematical origins, Windelband argued that there was another

---

[9] Wilhelm Windelband's *Lehrbuch der Geschichte der Philosophie* (Tübingen: Mohr, 1949) has gone through several new editions and is still used in Germany today as a standard historical text.

[10] Windelband, *History of Philosophy*, 15–18.

Kant, one neglected by the Marburg school, who also focused on problems of morality, ethics, aesthetics, religion, history, and anthropology in his *Critique of Practical Reason, Critique of Judgement,* and lectures on anthropology and history. It was to this "other" Kant that Windelband turned for the principles of his new theory of values.

In his well-known essay "Was ist Philosophie?" (1882), Windelband defined philosophy as "the science of necessary and universally valid value judgments"; later, in the *Introduction to Philosophy,* he designated it as "the critical science of universal values."[11] Windelband interpreted this new definition of philosophy as a bold variation of the Kantian idea of "critical method," extending it beyond the realm of scientific facts to that of human values. Philosophy was now to be redefined not only as a science, or a strict form of *Wissenschaft,* but also as a *Weltanschauung,* or theory of life and value. In an openly self-conscious way, Windelband sought to use his own version of the "historical Kant" to help solve the old problem of philosophy's post-Hegelian identity crisis—whether philosophy is genuinely a form of *Wissenschaft* or *Weltanschauung.* Windelband had no doubt that philosophy is quintessentially a *Wissenschaft,* but he also realized that to have an effect in the late nineteenth century, it had to be a *Wissenschaft* that also spoke to problems of *Weltanschauung.* Philosophy's attention to problems of this kind would not compromise its scientific rigor, Windelband insisted, but rather would allow it to follow the very course that Kant himself had set. The origins of this generational debate could ultimately be traced to the monolithic conception of *Wissenschaft* which dominated late-nineteenth-century German academic life. Unlike the materialists, positivists, and other practitioners of the natural sciences who uncritically assumed that *Wissenschaft* was a form of knowledge focused on the problem of being or "what is" (*Sein*), Windelband tried to show that *Wissenschaft* also concerned the realm of value and "what ought to be" (*Sollen*). This kind of axiological revision of science and ontology characterized Windelband's entire approach.

On Windelband's reading, Kant's critical method of *Wissenschaft* was based on a new form of *transcendental logic,* a logic that inquired into the a priori conditions of our knowledge concerning being, the "is." The aim of Kant's *Critique of Pure Reason* had been to establish

---

[11] Windelband, *Präludien* 1:26; see also Wilhelm Windelband, *Introduction to Philosophy* trans. Joseph McCabe (London: Unwin, 1921).

the philosophical validity of rational-logical concepts that order the facts of being into a coherent theory of science. Windelband labeled this effort a "Tractatus on Method."[12] But where the Marburg school focused on the methodological side of Kant in order to establish the logical claims of *Wissenschaft*, Windelband stressed the axiological significance of Kant's project. He read Kant as a true Platonist, someone utterly convinced of the "reality" of the nonmaterial world, a philosopher for whom values were just as "real" as facts.

Windelband found the Marburg school's radical form of logical idealism to be too abstract and rational. The world-view philosophers had tried to rectify this approach by addressing problems of life, but in so doing they had sacrificed the rigor of logic. Windelband conceived his own "critical philosophy of values" as an attempt to steer between the Scylla and Charybdis of *Wissenschaft* or *Weltanschauung*. In his system, philosophy was still to be grounded in logic as an inquiry into the rational foundations of *Wissenschaft*, but it was also to be directed toward questions of existence: of religion, ethics, history, anthropology, aesthetics, and literature, in short, of *culture*. In this way, no difference existed in emphasis between the philosopher's relation to culture or nature. As Windelband conceived it, the purpose of philosophy was not to offer individual judgments on the scientific content of a fossil, an atom, a quasar, or an infinite set; rather, it was to provide a critique of the method of thinking and research used to deduce the actual properties of such "facts." Analogously, in matters of culture, the philosopher's aim was not to suggest rules of conduct, standards of beauty, or stratagems of history but to offer a critique of the methods used to study such life-related phenomena. As ever, the task of the philosopher was to pose a basic epistemological question: What are the valid principles of knowledge used to arrive at a definition of culture? Thus, where Cohen had set up a logic of research aimed at the study of nature, Windelband sought to offer a logic of culture based on a Kantian model of science. But whereas Cohen's logic intended a kind of Kantian alternative to the universal method of positivism, Windelband sought to secure the *autonomy* of two distinct methods of research—the genetic method of natural science and the critical method of cultural science. By demonstrating the worth of each, he hoped to complete Kant's aim of establishing a transcendental theory of being and value. Within Windelband's project, idealism

[12] Windelband, *Präludien*, 2:99.

would become a program of epistemology and axiology, one rooted in the rational claims of pure reason and the ethical demands of practical reason. In achieving such an extension of Kant's original program, Windelband hoped to connect knowledge (*Wissen*) of reality to its meaning and value (*Wert*). This categorical distinction between knowledge and values was to have a profound effect on Windelband's protégé Heinrich Rickert, who spent his career working out the methodological consequences of this position. A fuller, more critical discussion of the philosophical coherence of Rickert's view will have to wait until the next chapter. For the present, I will focus on the practical program that Windelband offered in his classic essay delivered on the occasion of his rectoral address at the University of Strassburg in 1894.

iii. The Rectoral Address: "History and Natural Science"

The issues addressed in Windelband's rectoral speech were in large measure a rehearsal of the fundamental themes of post-Hegelian German philosophy. In this ambitious lecture, Windelband tried to define the legitimate task of philosophy as a special form of knowledge, contrasting its proper sphere of activity with that of the other sciences. At the very outset he described the problem clearly:

> All scientific and scholarly work has the purpose of putting its special problems into a wider framework and resolving specific questions from the standpoint of a more general perspective. In this respect, there is no difference between philosophy and other disciplines. It is permissible for the other sciences to regard these more general perspectives and principles as given and established. This assumption is sufficiently reliable for the purpose of specialized research within the discipline in question. The essential feature of philosophy, however, is the following: its real object of investigation is actually these principles themselves.[13]

Windelband considered philosophy to be an autonomous branch of learning, independent of the empirical sciences and concerned more with the formal properties of knowledge than with their empirical manifestations as "objects" of research. The real link between philosophy and the specialized sciences was, however, logic, which Windel-

---

[13] Wilhelm Windelband, "History and Natural Science," trans. Guy Oakes, *History and Theory* 19, no. 2 (1980): 169.

band defined as "critical reflection upon the existing forms of knowledge that are actually employed in practice."[14]

For Windelband, the task of the logician did not lie in programmatic recommendations on practical matters within physics, history, mathematics, and so on but rather in defining "the general form of specific methods which have proven to be successful and to determine the significance, the epistemological value and the limits of the use of these methods."[15] Again, the proper domain of philosophy (according to its strict status as a form of logic and epistemology) was, he believed, to serve as a science of method with the primary goal of establishing the truth claims of conflicting methodological principles. This was hardly a new aim in the long history of philosophical writing. Descartes, in his *Discourse on Method* (1637), had attempted to define philosophy in terms of a new method of thinking which sought to go beyond the merely inductive methodology of Bacon. A century later, Giambattista Vico's *New Science* (1744) tried to modify the Cartesian method of philosophy by offering a "new science" of philological philosophy (hermeneutics). Kant, too, had set himself the task of writing a "Tractatus on Method" (1781) by formulating a critique of the limits of the scientific-mathematical method followed by Descartes, Newton, Kepler, and Galileo (especially as it related to the "science" of metaphysics).[16] Windelband's rectoral lecture was nothing less than a self-conscious renewal of this venerable philosophical tradition. He set as his task the establishment of a rigorous taxonomy of the various disciplines—a new organon of the sciences—with philosophy serving as a *Methodenlehre*, or methodological account, of "the system of knowledge."[17] Near the beginning of his lecture, Windelband sketched the history of this tradition and identified five different strands in modern thought which aimed at universalizing the particular method of one science by declaring its supremacy over all others.

Beginning in the seventeenth century with the mechanistic method of Newton and the geometric method of Descartes, there had been repeated attempts at supremacy on the part of the mathematical and natural sciences. By the nineteenth century, within the fields of philosophy, philology, history, and psychology, there were also claims to

[14] Ibid., 170.
[15] Ibid., 170–171.
[16] *Präludien*, 2:99.
[17] Windelband, "History and Natural Science," 171.

methodological preeminence: the dialectical method of Hegel greatly influenced Engels, Marx, Dühring, and others; the psychological method of Franz Brentano, Wilhelm Wundt, and Gustav Fechner (and later Wilhelm Dilthey) and the evolutionary-historical method of the Historical School, Droysen, Boeckh, and others also gained adherents. Each of these methods—which Windelband linked to the ideological programs of positivism, psychologism, and historicism—challenged the legitimate claim of philosophy as the science of knowledge and helped to spur a crisis in the foundations of post-Hegelian philosophy.[18] Yet each failed to gain predominance as the guiding science within "the entire circumference of human knowledge" because of their fundamental one-sidedness.[19] These older, more traditional systems of the sciences had dominated nineteenth-century logic, but, Windelband argued:

> The universalistic methodological tendency of this way of thinking was committed to a serious error: the failure to recognize the autonomy of individual provinces of knowledge. This methodological tendency subjected all phenomena to the constraints of one and the same method. . . . As the conflict between these different methodological tendencies appears to grow more pronounced, the crucial task is to provide a just evaluation of these conflicting claims and a balanced analysis of the legitimate domain of these various methodologies by means of the general premises of epistemology. At this point, the prospects for success of this enterprise do not seem to be unfavorable.[20]

Windelband was confident of the success of logical theory to solve the nineteenth-century debate on methods. By focusing on the form of knowledge rather than on its content, he hoped to develop a new taxonomy of the sciences which would render obsolete the academic division of labor within the nineteenth-century German university. This logical critique of methods would not be based on the actual practice of the various disciplines or on their specific historical development but would, rather, provide a coherent theory of knowledge that would supersede the technical questions of research. In the process, philosophy would establish itself as the most fundamental of all

[18] Wilhelm Windelband, *Die Philosophie im deutschen Geistesleben des 19. Jahrhunderts* (Tübingen: Mohr, 1927), esp. chap. 4.
[19] Windelband, "History and Natural Science," 171.
[20] Ibid. For a discussion of this whole tradition in European thought from the Greeks through Descartes and Kant to the twentieth century, see Robert Flint, *Philosophy as Scientia Scientiarum* (New York: Arno, 1975).

the sciences, the scientia scientiarum, not by its usurpation of the territory of the special sciences but by setting itself up as the science of those principles crucial to the establishment of any other science. In its reconstituted form, philosophy would both describe the methodological accomplishments of mathematics, physics, biology, philology, and history and offer a critique of their theoretical validity. The *Verwissenschaftlichungsprozess* (process of scientization) within the other sciences would thus be completed by philosophy, which would resume its former Kantian role as "the science of knowledge." As Windelband himself put it, "By science we understand that knowledge which knows itself as such, being conscious of its aim as well as its grounds, of the problem it has to solve as well as its manner of knowing."[21] Although the scope of the rectoral address offered only hints at a revolution within philosophical theory, its aim was extraordinarily ambitious: to complete the critique of natural-scientific and mathematical method initiated by Kant and to establish the philosophical value of the new human sciences.

Writing in 1781, Kant had taken mathematics to be the measure of science itself. This elevated appraisal of the mathematical-natural sciences was, according to Windelband, more than justified: it was necessary. For at that time, mathematics was far more established as a rigorous form of knowledge than were the other sciences, especially the fledgling disciplines of philology, anthropology, ethology, sociology, and history. During the course of the nineteenth century, however, the accomplishments of scholars such as Humboldt, Ranke, Droysen, Boeckh, Mommsen, Niebuhr, and Savigny had assured the scrupulous reliability of historicophilological research and had, in a certain sense, redressed the imbalance between the mathematical sciences and history. Because Kant had not been alive to experience the unprecedented flowering of German scholarship, he could not be blamed for failing to offer a rigorous epistemological critique of its limits, methods, and value. One hundred years later, however, philosophers could no longer ignore significant developments in this area. Defining the problem of knowledge in idealist terms, yet aware of Kant's myopia in regard to the new historical sciences, Windelband felt compelled to renew the Kantian program. He therefore applied Kant's epistemological critique of mathematics to the new science of history and developed a logic of both the *Naturwissenschaften* and the

---

[21] Wilhelm Windelband, *Theories in Logic* (New York: Philosophical Library, 1961), 18.

Geisteswissenschaften. The execution of Windelband's Neo-Kantian project thus went "beyond" and not merely "back" to Kant, also over-shadowing the mathematically oriented Neo-Kantianism of Cohen and Natorp. In his newly configured taxonomy, the old structures, boundaries, grounds, and principles of scientific classification needed to be redressed according to the new conditions of scientific research. And in the inaugural lecture "History and Natural Science," Windelband tried to draw the limits for conceiving this new approach to the sciences.

iv. The European Classification of the Sciences (Plato to Mill)

The starting point for Windelband's projected revision was a funda-mental criticism of the actual classification of the sciences within the traditional European system. At all major German universities, the disciplines were distinguished either as *Naturwissenschaften* (natural sciences) or as *Geisteswissenschaften* (sciences of the mind).[22] Yet char-acterized in this form, Windelband regarded the dichotomy as "unfor-tunate."[23] Historically, the philosophical problem of a division of the sciences had its origins in Greek philosophy with Plato's dialectics, physics, and ethics.[24] Aristotle, following Plato, had altered the classi-fication of knowledge through his own system of logic, and for centu-ries, formal logic and the classification of the sciences had gone hand in hand. Even into the early modern era, Leibniz, following Plato, divided the realm of science into "three great provinces": physics, moral sci-ences, and logic. By the nineteenth century, however, this classifica-tion had been abandoned in favor of the split between *Geistes-* and *Naturwissenschaften*, a division based primarily on the results of Carte-sian epistemic theory. Descartes sharply divided the realm of the cor-poreal from the realm of the intellectual-spiritual. The "inner" and "outer" identification with the mind and the body, based on the mechanistic researches of the natural sciences, was successfully trans-formed into a metaphysical foundation for all the sciences. In En-

[22] *Geisteswissenschaften* is a difficult term in English and has variously been translated as "human sciences," "sciences of spirit," "moral sciences," or simply "humanities." See the extensive bibliography in Hans-Georg Gadamer, "Geisteswissenschaften," in *Religion in Geschichte und Gegenwart*, and Theodor Bodammer, *Philosophie der Geistes-wissenschaften* (Freiburg: Alber, 1987).
[23] Windelband, "History and Natural Science," 173.
[24] Erich Becher, *Geisteswissenschaft und Naturwissenschaft* (Munich: Duncker and Hum-blot, 1921), chap. 1.

gland, Bentham divided the sciences of body-mind into the fields of somatology and pneumatology; in France, Ampère adopted the scheme of cosmology and noology; in Germany, Hegel's *Enzyklopaedie der Wissenschaften* classified the sciences into a philosophy of nature and a philosophy of spirit (*Naturphilosophie* and *Philosophie des Geistes*).[25] In 1843, John Stuart Mill published a two-volume work, *The System of Logic*, organized according to inductive and deductive categories, which affirmed this basic division. Mill's work was translated into German in 1849 and became extremely important in academic circles, serving as a logical justification for the split between the *Natur-* and *Geisteswissenschaften*.[26] By the time of Windelband's lecture in 1894, the systematic validity of this distinction between *Natur* and *Geist* had long been forgotten; its continuation depended more on custom and tradition than on rigorous conceptual scrutiny.

The point of the Strassburg lecture was to expose the tottering structure of this whole Cartesian tradition and to redefine the sciences according to more modern epistemological principles. Windelband argued that the traditional distinction between "*Natur* and *Geist* was a substantive dichotomy."[27] In other words, its principle of classification was based on the object being investigated—its content rather than its form. *Naturwissenschaften*, according to this model of the disciplines, were simply those sciences dealing with the objects of nature: physics, biology, chemistry, geology, meteorology, and the like. *Geisteswissenschaften* were, by contrast, those sciences dealing with the objects of human life: history, moral philosophy, economy, politics, and society. In this scheme, the *Naturwissenschaften* were concerned with the *external*, corporeal world of nature, and the *Geisteswissenschaften*, with the *internal*, reflexive world of mind. This whole system of classification could, Windelband maintained, be traced back to the thought of John Locke, who "reduced Cartesian dualism to the subjective formula: external and internal perception, sensation and reflection."[28] With the development of psychological research in the late nineteenth century, however, the logical foundation of Locke's epistemology was seriously challenged. The new science of psychology did not easily fit within the categories of this outmoded system of the sciences: "From

[25] Becher, *Geisteswissenschaft und Naturwissenschaft*, 2.
[26] Erich Rothacker, *Die Logik und Systematik der Geisteswissenschaften* (Bonn: Bouvier, 1948), 6.
[27] Windelband, "History and Natural Science," 173.
[28] Ibid.

the perspective of its subject matter, psychology can only be a science of the mind. In a certain sense, it may be described as the foundation of all the other sciences of the mind. From the perspective of psychology as an investigation, however, its entire methodological procedure is exclusively the method of the natural sciences."[29] Because of its singular status as a science of the mind which adopted natural scientific methods of inquiry, psychology defied the taxonomical structure of traditional academic disciplines. In the rectoral address, Windelband was intent on showing how "a classification which produces such difficulties has no systematic basis"; as he argued, what invariably separates the *Naturwissenschaften* from the *Geisteswissenschaften* is not their "substantive differences" but the aim of their research.[30]

Windelband went on to demonstrate that the sciences of nature, whatever their object of research—whether it concerned the motion of bodies, the transformation of matter, the development of organic life, or the process of imagination, emotion, and volition—invariably share a common aim: the discovery of *laws* of phenomena. The sciences of mind, on the other hand, have a distinctly different purpose, which is to "provide a complete and exhaustive description of a single, more or less extensive process which is located within a unique, temporally defined domain of reality."[31] They seek to uncover the unique (*einmalig*) element of reality: the biography of a single individual, the history of an entire nation, the definitive properties of language, a religion, a legal order, an artifact of literature, art, or science. The crucial difference between these two approaches, Windelband argued, is formal-logical rather than substantive-empirical. On this basis the traditional Cartesian dualism of the sciences can no longer stand, owing to its faulty epistemological premises. Windelband was careful to show that an object cannot be determined as an object merely because it is "external" to consciousness. Objects are not simply "given" as such but are the product of our rational consciousness. Hence, nature cannot be regarded as an ontological absolute but must be seen as the product of a constitutive faculty of mind. In this sense, there is never any ontological ground on which to divide experience into "inner" and "outer," or into perception and reflection. As Kant had argued in the *Critique of Pure Reason*: "Our knowledge springs

[29] Ibid.
[30] Ibid., 174. This is, in fact, the very basis of Windelband's taxonomy of the sciences—and his critique of psychology.
[31] .Ibid.

from two fundamental sources of the mind: the first is the capacity of receiving representations (receptivity for impressions), the second is the power of knowing an object through these representations (spontaneity in the production of concepts). Through the first an object is *given* to us, through the second the object is *thought* in relation to that given representation (which is a mere determination of the mind)."[32] Knowledge results, Kant explained, from the continuous interaction between the faculty of perception or sensibility and the faculty of reflection or thought. "Without sensibility no object would be given to us, without reflection no object would be thought. Concepts without percepts are empty, percepts without concepts are blind."[33] Kant's transcendental logic offered a critique not only of our empirical knowledge of objects given to the sensibility (Locke's theory of the tabula rasa) but of the a priori conditions necessary for such knowledge. As Windelband read Kant through the lens of late nineteenth-century science and philosophy, he understood that a genuine renewal of Kant's epistemology required a critique of the forms of thought and not merely the contents of perception.

Using Kant's schematic, Windelband divided the sciences not according to their object of research or their empirical content but according to their epistemological aims. In so doing he raised new questions about the conventional European tradition of the sciences based on substantive distinctions. Did the *Naturwissenschaften* share similar aims with the *Geisteswissenschaften*? Could there be any methodological basis for a comparison or any philosophical unity in their approach? Windelband answered these questions by describing *Naturwissenschaften* as "an inquiry into general laws" and *Geisteswissenschaften*, "an inquiry into specific historical facts": "In the language of formal logic, the objective of the first kind of science is the general apodictic judgement; the objective of the other kind of science is the singular assertoric proposition. Thus this distinction connects with the most important and crucial relationship in the human understanding, the relationship which Socrates recognized as the fundamental nexus of all scientific thought: the relationship of the general to the particular."[34] Modern natural science had stressed the general at the expense

[32] Immanuel Kant, *The Critique of Pure Reason*, trans. Norman Kemp Smith (London: Macmillan, 1929), 92.

[33] Ibid. The translation in the second sentence is a variant one based on the common English rendering of "percept" for *Anschauung* and "concept" for *Begriff*. Cf. Immanuel Kant, *Kritik der reinen Vernunft* (Hamburg: Meiner, 1956), 95.

[34] Windelband, "History and Natural Science," 175.

of the particular; as the technical mastery associated with natural science led to astonishing progress in various fields of research, many theorists attempted to apply these methods to the study of social and moral, rather than merely physical, phenomena. Within this tradition of reformist practice, Mill, in book 6 of his *System of Logic* ("On the Logic of the Moral Sciences"), had recommended that "the backward state of the moral sciences can only be remedied by applying to them the methods of physical science, duly extended and generalized."[35] His plan was to show how the same form of logic could apply to different sciences.

Historically, the entire development of logic had assumed the form of general apodictic propositions. All scientific research and verification aimed at the general, universally valid concept. In his *History of Philosophy*, Windelband demonstrated that as far back as the Greeks, the first principle of philosophy had been the universal study of nature, which resulted in much philosophical speculation on the development of the natural sciences. He noticed, however, a conspicuous lack of comparable reflection on the progress of the human sciences and the methodological problems of historical research. In the nineteenth century, with the work of Auguste Comte, Henry Thomas Buckle, and Mill, philosophers began to redress this imbalance by applying principles of natural science to the study of history, politics, aesthetics, and other humanistic disciplines. In the process of revising the traditional system of the sciences, however, these philosophers subsumed all the natural and human sciences under one form of philosophical logic. In their system of classification, positivism was established as the fundamental science of the sciences, a development that Windelband rejected.

By proceeding critically through the history of logic, Windelband attempted to dismantle the positivist claim for metalogical unity in the sciences, arguing instead that each realm of knowledge requires its own unique logical form. Windelband noted:

> In their quest for knowledge of reality, the empirical sciences either seek the general in the form of the law of nature or the particular in the form of the historically defined structure. On the one hand, they are concerned with the *form* which invariably remains constant. On the other hand, they are concerned with the unique, immanently defined *content* of the real event. The

[35] John Stuart Mill, *Collected Works*, vol. 8, *System of Logic* (Toronto: University of Toronto Press, 1974), 833; and ibid., 176–177.

former disciplines are nomological sciences. The latter disciplines are sciences of process or sciences of the event. The nomological sciences are concerned with what is invariably the case. If I may be permitted to introduce some new technical terms, scientific thought is *nomothetic* in the former case and *idiographic* in the latter case.[36]

The salient characteristics of these nomothetic and idiographic disciplines were as follows:

Nomothetic	Idiographic
1. General apodictic judgment	1. Singular assertoric judgment
2. Unchanging form of the real	2. Unique, self-determined content of the real
3. Universal	3. Particular
4. Idea (Platonic): in modern terms, natural law	4. Individual being, thing, or event
5. Epistemological aim: laws	5. Epistemological aim: structures
6. Abstraction	6. Perception
7. Sciences of law (*Gesetzeswissenschaften*)	7. Sciences of event (*Ereigniswissenschaften*)
8. *Naturwissenschaften*	8. *Geschichtswissenschaften*[37]

This analytical classification according to epistemological aims and pursuits was in no way intended to be an accurate description of the actual praxis of research. Windelband's criteria were conceived as "formal-logical" and not "content-real" principles. In particular, Windelband did not intend his logical categories to be in any way prescriptive; rather, his philosophical desideratum was methodological clarity. He was fully aware that the biologist in the laboratory and the historian in the archive would not attempt to rethink their professional tasks in terms of a logician's taxonomy. Scholarly research would proceed apace, unperturbed by the caviling of philosophers. Yet Windelband contended that the soundness of such research, as

[36] Windelband, "History and Natural Science," 175.
[37] This scheme helps clarify the basic differences between the nomothetic and idiographic sciences as expressed by Windelband in his rectoral address. The model I have used in the main text is based on the table in Herbert Schnädelbach, *Die Geschichtsphilosophie nach Hegel* (Freiburg: Alber, 1974), 140.

well as its truth-value, could not be left to intradisciplinary debates but must be decided philosophically. Philosophers might not be expected to assess the validity of meteorological investigations, but they were certainly capable of judging the logical coherence of such research. By means of this intense focus on the methodological problems of the sciences, Windelband hoped to secure a new status for philosophy in its post-Hegelian crisis-state. By redrawing the ambiguous lines between the disciplines, Windelband tried to show that philosophy's proper role was epistemological rather than empirical or practical.

On this basis Windelband persisted in demonstrating that the real contrast between nomothetic and idiographic research was really a question of ideal types. Accordingly, he maintained that no scientific datum is intrinsically nomothetic; rather, a datum might be categorized as nomothetic only by reference to the larger concerns of the researcher. Similarly, Windelband argued, there are no intrinsically "historical" facts or events. What lends historical significance to Napoléon's struggle at Waterloo (in contrast to yesterday's weather) is not its innate importance but "its relation to some high standard of value in life."[38] As he stressed again and again, the categories "nomothetic" and "idiographic" are referential distinctions, not absolute ones: "The difference between research in the natural sciences and history appears only when the issue concerns the cognitive—or theoretical use [*Verwertung*] of facts."[39] In other words, "facts" are not "given" ontologically but are the products of a cognitive synthesis in consciousness. Ever since Kant destroyed the illusions of dogmatic materialism by showing that truth is not based on the correspondence of an idea to an object *extra mentem*, object-focused epistemology was called into question.

Against the positivists and materialists, Windelband grasped truth not as an objective being (*Sein*) residing in the empirical world of our perceptions but as a transcendental idea, like Plato's forms or Kant's categorical imperative, which represents an absolute norm (*Sollen*). "Truth," Windelband wrote, "demands a validity in itself [*Geltung an sich*] without relation to a consciousness. . . . This philosophical idea of validity always points beyond the process of knowledge in empirical subjects. The validity of truth is independent of all behavior of

[38] Windelband, *Introduction to Philosophy*, 205.
[39] Windelband, "History and Natural Science," 178.

fallible and evolving subjects. A mathematical truth was valid long before anybody conceived it and it is valid even if an individual erroneously refuses his assent to it."[40] In methodological terms, the philosopher is thus required to distinguish between factual judgments (*Urteile*) that describe what is (*Sein*) and nonfactual judgments (*Beurteilungen*) that refer to what is valid (*Gelten*). Judgments of the first kind might determine that an object is "white," whereas judgments of the latter type might define it as "good."[41] For Windelband, these two realms of being and validity, which he sometimes called "the world of reality" (*Wirklichkeit*) and "the world of value" (*Wert*), could not be reconciled within a higher sphere. They represented the limits of each form of knowledge, limits marked by the aporia of philosophy itself as it tried to pose questions capable of resolving this breach.

The problem with most classificatory schemes of the sciences was that they either ignored this fundamental distinction between being and value and tried to unify the sciences under one method or they affirmed it merely on the basis of a materialistic ontology divided along the lines of nature/spirit, body/mind. In his lecture Windelband tried to establish a logical basis for this division which would categorize the various sciences according to differing cognitive values of research: nomothetic natural science and idiographic historical science. But he insisted that value, too, be understood logically rather than psychologically, because the science of psychology had conflated the object of research with the cognitive-theoretical interest of the researcher. Traditionally, psychology was labeled a *Geisteswissenschaft* because it had mind or psyche as its object of study. As it was practiced by Wundt, Fechner, and Helmholz, however, it had more to do with discovering universal laws than in revealing individual forms. Hence, in Windelband's program, psychology could now be classified as a *Naturwissenschaft*, for its methods conformed more appropriately to the nomothetic aims of the other natural sciences.

By redefining psychology as a natural science, Windelband hoped to offer some methodological clarity within the whole historicist tradition. Since the work of Vico, historicists had established the basis for separating the natural and human sciences in the hermeneutic understanding of the psychological subject. The Historical School had even argued that the aim of historical study was to recognize the unique,

---

[40] Windelband, *Introduction to Philosophy*, 183.
[41] Windelband, *Präludien*, 1:29.

individual, and unduplicable character of human consciousness so that one might better apprehend the total structure of all life relations in the world beyond the self. These historicists claimed that it was the historicity of human beings, their ontological dependence on the mutable, transient, and culture-bound, which enabled them to understand the various expressions of others—in the form of language, symbols, and signs. Vico had attempted to establish his "new science" of hermeneutic philology as a form of *rhetorica*, opposed to Cartesian *critica*, rooted in language and history rather than in mathematics. Following the Vichian tradition, Windelband's contemporary, Wilhelm Dilthey, looked to the science of psychology as the foundation on which to build his new hermeneutical *Grundwissenschaft*, for a time defining it as the most fundamental of all the *Geisteswissenschaften*. Windelband repudiated Dilthey's hermeneutical approach, however, because he believed it fostered a type of historical relativism and denied the possibility of any genuine scientific knowledge for the psychological-historical subject.

Psychologism and historicism represented the gravest dangers to philosophy, Windelband claimed, because both sought to reduce the principles of reason to mere temporal and psychical conditions independent of any transcendental source. In keeping with this emphasis on transcendental validity, Windelband rejected the historicity of understanding for ahistorical, transcultural principles of formal logic along Kantian lines. The Strassburg lecture set the terms for this more rigorously Kantian understanding of the crisis of nineteenth-century science as a conflict between two alternative visions of philosophy: the hermeneutical understanding of historicism and the atemporal validity of transcendental logic. For Windelband, these two alternative visions could never be resolved.

v. Windelband's Aporia: The Logical Problem of Method and the Metaphysical Problem of Freedom

Windelband's primary concern about the priority of the psychological or hermeneutical subject turned on the issue of cultural relativism. He feared that if one were to reduce the principles of validity to mere historical circumstance or to the subjective fancy of the psychological self, then the absolute character of all values would be forfeited. A Neo-Kantian science of universal values would combat these relativistic trends by focusing on a transcendental solution to the crisis of historicism. Within Windelband's axiology, the existence of historical truth would never depend on its discovery by a historian but would have a life of its own, like mathematically valid propositions that exist independently of mathematicians. Philosophy would then be left as the arbiter of values apart from history or any of the individual sciences. As Windelband declared: "It must be expressly stated that although historical validity provides a central problem for philosophy, in no way is this historical validity to be seen as the ground for philosophical validity. Were one to forget this, the result would be unholy relativism; this would truly mean the death of all philosophy."[42]

Thus, for Windelband, the generational debate in the human sciences about methods and historical values was transformed into a fundamental question concerning philosophy's own legitimacy. In a time of philosophical crisis, he believed that these methodological issues could not simply be reduced to terminological disputes or understood as the nagging complaints of quibbling logicians schooled in pettifoggery. As a Kantian, Windelband remained committed to the rigor of logic as the only legitimate way of settling the generational disputes about methodology. Yet in the end Windelband always redefined these logical disputes as issues of value; for him, the Kantian paradigm of rationality was not merely logical but also ethical. He always acknowledged the importance of Kant's second critique for the problems of the sciences. By drawing clear methodological lines between being and value, Windelband sought to preserve the ethical realm of human freedom which, he believed, could not be circumscribed within the realm of historicity. In a sense, his philosophical program on Neo-Kantian lines was conceived as an ethical response to the relativism that he perceived within the historicist tradition. Understood ethically, Windelband's theory of the sciences developed as a self-conscious response to two traditions. Against the historicists he appealed to standards of universal value; against the positivists he insisted that methodology could never be separated from axiology.

One year before his death, at the conclusion of his last work, *An Introduction to Philosophy* (1914), Windelband rephrased the methodological difference between *Natur-* and *Geisteswissenschaften* in terms of a metaphysical division between two realms:

[42] Wilhelm Windelband, *Die Philosophie im Beginn des 20. Jahrhunderts* (Heidelberg: Winter, 1907), 541.

This is the point at which the desire for a unified understanding of the world breaks down before an insoluble problem. The world of values and the world of reality, the provinces of "ought" and "must" are not foreign to each other. They are in mutual relation everywhere. But they are certainly not the same thing. There is a rent in the fabric of reality. . . . We cannot get over the contradiction. . . . The innermost meaning of temporality is the inalienable difference between what is and what ought to be, and because this difference, which reveals itself in our will, constitutes the fundamental condition of human life, our knowledge can never get beyond it to a comprehension of its origin.[43]

Ultimately, the careful divisions of logic and epistemology could not offer a metaphysical solution to the "rent in the fabric of reality." Windelband's taxonomy had set up an ideal logical state of two distinct forms of scientific inquiry—a natural-scientific logic that aimed at discovering general laws governing the process of a single phenomenon *and* a historical logic that affirmed the unique and unduplicable character of each phenomenon as an exception to all causal laws. Against the positivists he insisted on maintaining the recalcitrance of historical individualities to causal laws; against psychologism he maintained that laws of physiology and psychic process could never adequately grasp the measure of human values; and against the historicists he charged that cultural relativism could never have the last word in a scientific approach to reality. By rejecting all the attempts of scientism at discovering a universal method for *Natur* and *Geist*, Windelband determined a new *Fragestellung* for the Neo-Kantian theory of the sciences: one grounded in logic yet dependent on freedom. By drawing limits to the applicability and universality of scientific method, Windelband hoped to preserve the value of what lay beyond the limits—a newly configured Kantian realm of freedom. "In all the data of historical and individual experience," Windelband argued, "a residuum of incomprehensible brute fact remains, an inexpressible and indefinable phenomenon. Thus the ultimate and most profound nature of personality resists analysis in terms of general categories. From the perspective of our consciousness, this incomprehensible character of the personality emerges as the sense of indeterminacy of our nature—in other words, individual freedom."[44]

[43] Windelband, *Introduction to Philosophy*, 357–359. I have altered the translation in places for clarity. For the original German text, see Windelband, *Einleitung in die Philosophie* (Tübingen: Mohr, 1923), 433–434.
[44] Windelband, "History and Natural Science," 184.

Part of this indeterminacy that preserved the value of freedom was the radical split between *Natur* and *Geist*. Windelband recognized the aporia of his own historical logic—of a world sundered into being and value, ontology and axiology—but instead of seeing these limits as a contradiction within his own program, he seized on them as testimony to the ultimately insoluble, metaphysical quandary beyond which scientific reason could not go. At the very close of the rectoral address, Windelband confronted this problem within the frame of his own scientific values, abjuring the role of metaphysical prophet. Rational thought, he wrote, "can contribute nothing further to the resolution of these questions. Philosophy can identify the limits of knowledge in each of the individual disciplines. Beyond these limits, however, philosophy itself can no longer establish any substantive conclusions. The law and the event remain as the ultimate, incommensurable entities of our world view. Here is one of the boundary points where scientific inquiry can only define problems and only pose questions in the clear awareness that it will never be able to solve them."[45]

In strict Kantian fashion, Windelband set out to define the limits of scientific thought and to secure for reason the assurance and certainty of knowledge in contrast to mere metaphysical speculation. In an era dominated by anxiety concerning philosophy's status as rigorous *Wissenschaft* and not feuilletonistic *Weltanschauung*, Windelband tried to offer a rational alternative. By scrupulously attending to the logic of historical inquiry and offering an epistemological critique of historical practice, Windelband did succeed in making a clean break with the metaphysical tradition of speculative *Geschichtsphilosophie* common in the early nineteenth century. Yet for all his painstaking efforts at working out the taxonomy of scientific methods, Windelband never really produced a new logic of history worthy of its Kantian heritage. In no sense did he achieve the conceptual clarity that Kant, in his *Critique of Pure Reason*, had offered for the natural sciences. Windelband's programmatic taxonomy of the nomothetic and idiographic sciences provided only the skeletal outlines of a fully developed theory. Despite its shortcomings, however, the rectoral address provided the basic *Fragestellung* for the Neo-Kantian critique of historicism, a critique taken up with more epistemological rigor by Heinrich Rickert, Windelband's younger colleague at Freiburg.

[45] Ibid., 185.

CHAPTER THREE

Heinrich Rickert's Epistemology of Historical Science

We are not dealing with the history of philosophy as
something that has ceased to exist and has been left
behind, but with the actuality from which we of today
were long ago expelled, such that—afflicted with
blindness and vanity—we waste away with our own little
intrigues.
　　　　—Martin Heidegger, *Hegel's Phenomenology of Spirit*

i. Rickert's Response to the Contemporary Philosophy of Crisis

Windelband's efforts at taxonomy provided logical justification for the work of historicists such as Ranke, Humboldt, and Droysen. His analytic distinctions helped to establish a new epistemological program for defining the task of the various sciences. But at the time of Windelband's death in 1915, the controversies over historical values remained largely research-oriented and methodological. His work had helped to stabilize the role of philosophy as a science of knowledge, relegated to the logical task of determining the limits of other scientific disciplines. But the perception of crisis in the years following his death fundamentally altered the terms of his more traditional, value-focused *Fragestellung*. After the bitter lessons of the war, one can perceive a more urgent, apocalyptic tone in works on the philosophy of history, such as Spengler's *Decline of the West* (1918) and Lessing's *History as a Process of Conferring Meaning upon the Meaningless* (1919). The methodological controversies of the turn of the century assumed a new rhetorical form as polemics in the struggle for cultural identity.

This generational perception of crisis worked to intensify the merely academic debate about historical method and stimulated a wide-ranging discussion about the meaning and viability of historical values.

As both a student and colleague of Windelband, Heinrich Rickert was committed to a Neo-Kantian theory of values along transcendental lines. But where Windelband's relation of disciplinary research to problems of value was still tied to a primarily methodological debate, Rickert's defense of value-philosophy became a full-scale struggle against what he perceived as "the modish philosophical currents of our time": life-philosophy, historicism, biologism, Spenglerism, and the other expressions of crisis-thinking in the postwar era.[1] Rickert began his epistemological labors with technical works on the theory of definition and epistemology—*Die Lehre von der Definition* (1888) and *Der Gegenstand der Erkenntnis* (1892)—developing his craft as a careful logician in the process. In 1896 he published the first edition of his major work, *Die Grenzen der naturwissenschaftlichen Begriffsbildung*; in 1899, the shorter, more accessible *Kulturwissenschaft und Naturwissenschaft*; and in 1903, *Die Probleme der Geschichtsphilosophie*. After the war, however, he revised these works and published some newer, more polemical pieces such as *Kant als Philosoph der modernen Kultur* (1924) and *Die Philosophie des Lebens* (1920). In 1921 he also completed the first volume of his aborted three-volume systematic work on axiology, *System der Philosophie*.[2]

During the postwar era, Rickert acknowledged the threats to traditional science and philosophy emanating from the proponents of world-view philosophy, life-philosophy, and the fashionable Nietzsche cult. But he responded to the prophets of crisis by constructing a theory of value to counter the ethical relativism that he saw destroying the foundations of post-Kantian German thought. Rickert insisted that Windelband's theories on the differences between the sciences

[1] Heinrich Rickert, *Die Philosophie des Lebens: Darstellung und Kritik der philosophischen Modeströmungen unserer Zeit* (Tübingen: Mohr, 1922).
[2] Heinrich Rickert, *Kant als Philosoph der modernen Kultur* (Tübingen: Mohr, 1924); *Die Lehre von der Definition* (Freiburg: Mohr, 1888); *Die Probleme der Geschichtsphilosophie* (Heidelberg: Winter, 1924); *System der Philosophie* (Tübingen: Mohr, 1921); and *Der Gegenstand der Erkenntnis: Einführung in die Transzendentalphilosophie* (Tübingen: Mohr, 1928). *Die Grenzen der naturwissenschaftlichen Begriffsbildung: Eine logische Einleitung in die historischen Wissenschaften* (hereafter cited as *Die Grenzen*) (Tübingen: Mohr, 1929), and *Kulturwissenschaft und Naturwissenschaft* (hereafter cited as *KN*) (Tübingen: Mohr, 1926) both went through several editions and revisions. In general I will be using the pagination from the later editions because they reflect changes in Rickert's thinking after the war.

had fruitful consequences for scientific research. But he went beyond Windelband in attempting to establish a definitive *system* of values to overcome the perceived threat of value relativism. Rickert's universal philosophy of values was to provide an anchor for historical meaning, a transcendental solution to the anarchy of convictions, beliefs, and ideologies which, he determined, had brought on the crisis of historicism in the first place. In *Die Grenzen*, Rickert even went so far as to identify historicism with a form of nihilism, and yet despite this harsh judgment, he could also agree with his colleague Ernst Troeltsch that "the contemporary crisis of historicism is a deep inner crisis of our time; it is not merely a scientific issue but a practical problem of life."[3]

Within the context of the generational crisis of the sciences, Rickert decided that any revaluation of values in a Kantian sense had to engage the meaning of history. His polemical writings are filled with references to "historical objectivity," the "historical individual," "historical development," and the like, though he rejected speculative *Geschichtsphilosophie* in the manner of Hegel because, he argued, "a *metaphysics* of history in the old sense does not seem possible as a science."[4] Rickert was intent on offering a rigorously logical-epistemological critique of historical research as the only legitimate way of restoring its meaning as science, though he was careful to warn his contemporaries that "the philosopher can never be merely a historian; philosophy must never remain caught in its history. We should know the past well, for we can only practice philosophy as a science when we orient ourselves around it. But we want to study the past with a purpose: so that we might more readily overcome it."[5]

Like many of his contemporaries in the postwar era, Rickert still viewed history as something to be superseded or surmounted, as if history itself were a directional process that might be overcome. In effect he attempted a *supra*historical resolution of the crisis of historicism by turning away from historical experience to a transcendental theory of values. "Only from the standpoint of an absolute ideal that we take as the measure of empirical reality," he wrote, "can there be any meaning in interpreting historically determined cultural life in its

[3] Heinrich Rickert, *The Limits of Concept Formation in Natural Science: A Logical Introduction to the Historical Sciences* (hereafter cited as *Limits of Concept Formation*), trans. Guy Oakes (Cambridge: Cambridge University Press, 1986); *Die Grenzen*, 8; and Ernst Troeltsch, "Die Krisis des Historismus," *Die Neue Rundschau* 33 (June 1922): 586.

[4] Heinrich Rickert, *Science and History: A Critique of Positivist Epistemology*, translated by George Reisman (Princeton, N.J.: Van Nostrand, 1962), 154; *KN*, 140.

[5] Rickert, *Die Probleme der Geschichtsphilosophie*, 3–4.

uniqueness and individuality."[6] Hence, even as he engaged problems of historical value, he did so not "from a purely historical perspective" but rather measured "the values of the past against what *should be*."[7] This led him to a formidable paradox: he "overcame" the ethical dangers of historicism by turning to an epistemology of historical research which was itself grounded in logic and which knew no historical time. Ultimately, Rickert's work represented the culmination of the whole Neo-Kantian attempt to deny the reality of history and to resolve the crisis of the sciences in purely formal fashion.

During the 1920s Heidegger's phenomenological destruction of Neo-Kantian philosophy of history would help to reveal the contradictions in Rickert's work, refocusing the formal problem of historical epistemology by raising anew the question of historical being. Before we turn to Heidegger's critique, however, we must first understand the systematic side of Rickert's thought. In what follows I want to begin by offering a summary discussion of the basic themes in Rickert's work, leaving to the second part of the chapter a fuller treatment of his debate with Meinecke, Troeltsch, and the historicist tradition in general. What such a discussion shows, I think, is how clearly the Neo-Kantian mode of epistemological inquiry was at odds with the fundamental meaning of historicist thought, even as it attempted to "solve" its most pressing issues.

ii. Philosophy as *Wissenschaft* contra *Weltanschauung*

In the introduction to *Die Probleme der Geschichtsphilosophie*, Rickert remarked that "the philosophical sciences are today still characterized by the theme of restoration."[8] In his view, twentieth-century philosophy had been marked by the programmatic attempt to restore it to its former place as the science of sciences, a place it had lost with the decline of Hegel's metaphysical system. To secure the status of philosophy as this most fundamental of sciences, Rickert attempted to differentiate its subject matter from that of all other disciplines. In contrast to the empirical sciences of reality (physics, chemistry, biology, history, sociology, geology, and so forth), which had as their object the concrete experience of actual being-in-the-world, and against the

---

[6] Ibid., 142.
[7] Ibid., 131.
[8] Ibid., 1.

purely formal science of mathematics, philosophy was to have as its subject matter a theory of scientific knowledge. In Rickert's terms, it was to become the "*Wissenschaft der Wissenschaft*," or a scientific inquiry into the nature of scientific inquiry as such.[9] In this office of self-reflecting science, philosophy would reestablish itself on the firm ground of "logic, epistemology, and theoretical reason."[10] As Rickert emphasized in his lectures at the University of Heidelberg: "Theoretical philosophy is the doctrine of *Logos*; *Logos* is reason, *ratio*, *Vernunft*. *Logos* as logic, as epistemology, as theoretical philosophy is a doctrine of science [*Wissenschaftslehre*]. Whereas the other sciences have as their object something that lies outside of science itself, logic, or theoretical philosophy, has science itself as its object, and thus, it is the self-knowledge of science which is its aim."[11] Again, in this same series of unpublished lectures, Rickert stressed that "philosophy as science is possible only on a logical-epistemological basis."[12] Logic was to be "a philosophical *Grundwissenschaft*," or fundamental science, that would repudiate any pretenses to offering metaphysical insights about life, death, time, eternity, God, and the soul.[13] If, for Rickert, modish thinkers like Kierkegaard, Schopenhauer, Nietzsche, Bergson, and Haeckel had offered a much broader range for the work of philosophy by making it more meaningful for "life," they had also succeeded in rendering it dilettantish, unsystematic, and antiphilosophical. In his polemical *Die Philosophie des Lebens*, Rickert vehemently attacked the basic tenets of vitalism and tried to warn of its dangers. "If it achieves dominance," he wrote, "it is to be feared that the misological, modish philosophy of life will lead to the death of philosophy as a science. I believe, therefore, that I serve the life of philosophy when I attack this 'philosophy of life.'"[14] Throughout his career, Rickert continued to renew his attacks on vitalism, existentialism, pragmatism, biologism, and other *Weltanschauungen*, believing that only when one had separated oneself from personal interest and sociohistorical prejudice could one begin to see the world in its totality,

---

[9] Heinrich Rickert, *Heidelberg Ms. 59*, 4–4a. Throughout this chapter, I will refer to Rickert's unpublished writings, which are gathered in the university library at Heidelberg and include some 180 different entries. The above-cited manuscript is entitled "Einführung in die Erkenntnistheorie und Metaphysik." Hereafter, all Heidelberg manuscript citations will be noted as *Hd.Ms.*

[10] Ibid.

[11] Ibid.

[12] Ibid.

[13] Rickert, *Hd.Ms. 13*, 34.

[14] Rickert, *Die Philosophie des Lebens*, xiv.

apart from the cultural and psychological demands of the self.[15] *Lebensphilosophie* appeared to him as the most recent manifestation of the kind of *Weltanschauungsphilosophie* that had threatened the scientific character of German thinking.

In Rickert's interpretation, going back to the nineteenth century, there were two major *Weltanschauungen* that dominated German culture: naturalism and historicism.[16] Naturalism he defined as the attempt to ground the problematic of traditional philosophy in the scientific researches of the natural world. Rejecting the metaphysical speculation of the romantic nature-philosophers by limiting itself to an empirical investigation of reality, naturalists attempted to unify scientific inquiry with values and ideology. This scientific world view, or *wissenschaftliche Weltanschauung*, opened up a logical contradiction, according to Rickert, because it attempted to transform the world of history and culture by basing it on principles of nature. Against this kind of naturalist thinking, historicism sought to draw a fundamental distinction between nature and history which questioned the extension of naturalist principles beyond the domain of the physiochemical world. By emphasizing the unique, unduplicable character of historical phenomena, historicists turned to the self-understanding of spirit as the ground of human reality. For Rickert, however, "historicism [was] still more unphilosophical than naturalism, since history [was] not a systematic science."[17] If naturalism attempted to impose biological categories on the processes of history, historicism, in its turn, tried to historicize the biological, neglecting in the process the rigors of natural-scientific research. Each saw in their own special province the fundamentals for a new philosophy of life. "But although both are materially very different," Rickert noted, "their positions rest on the very same principle, namely, both wish to transform the concepts of a special discipline into a whole philosophy."[18]

Lebensphilosophie and the other *Weltanschauungen* shared the tendency to universalize the validity of their special science and to apply it uncritically to all other areas of life. But for Rickert, philosophy was not one among other sciences. It was the science of science itself and had as its special domain the study of the principles of knowledge.

[15] Heinrich Rickert, *Grundprobleme der Philosophie* (Tübingen: Mohr, 1934), 6–7.
[16] For a longer discussion of naturalism and historicism written by one of Rickert's contemporaries, see Ernst Troeltsch, *Der Historismus und seine Probleme* (Tübingen: Mohr, 1922), 102–110.
[17] Rickert, *Die Philosophie des Lebens*, 48.
[18] Ibid.

Following Fichte's principle of a foundational *Wissenschaftslehre* as the proper task of philosophy, Rickert endeavored to achieve a philosophical understanding of the natural and historical sciences by focusing on their logical and epistemological principles. If philosophy were to uphold its strict systematic character and not degenerate into mere "life-philosophy," Rickert believed it would have to focus on the *formal* principles of knowledge rather than on material content. To combat the metaphysical excesses of the life-philosophers, then, Rickert turned to the epistemological principles of Kant, which provided an anchor for his whole system. Kantian logic would prove a much-needed anodyne for the "disease" he called "historicism."[19]

iii. Rickert's Relationship to Kant's Transcendental Idealism

The popularity of life-philosophy in the nineteenth century was due in no small part to two important characteristics. First, it was easily appropriated by an intellectually sophisticated audience because, although philosophical in temperament, it broke with the style of technical philosophy. Life-philosophy was easily read, presented in the literary style of a Kierkegaard or the aphoristic style of a Nietzsche. It dispensed with the impenetrable argumentation of a Kant or a Fichte and prided itself on its new approach to the writing of philosophical discourse. Second, life-philosophy was not abstract or formal; it was concerned with problems of human existence and human values, focusing on issues of morality, aesthetics, social problems, and history. In his course "Die deutsche Philosophie von Kant bis Nietzsche," Rickert recognized its appeal for the general public, especially for the young university-trained intellectuals who were not academic philosophers. In these lectures Rickert acknowledged life-philosophy's powerful influence, yet he suggested that "what was new and essential in nineteenth-century German philosophy" could be traced back to its "preoccupation with the problem of values" and their relationship to human culture.[20] Here he saw Nietzsche as the apotheosis of a life-philosophy portraying itself as value-philosophy (*Wertphilosophie*). And although he had read Nietzsche with great in-

---

[19] Rickert, *Hd.Ms. 115*, 3, in which he insists there shall be "*kein Historismus!*" Similar pronouncements can be found in *Die Philosophie des Lebens*, 49, in *Hd.Ms. 13*, 27, and in *Die Grenzen*, 8.

[20] Rickert, *Hd.Ms. 31*, 4 and 10.

terest and enthusiasm, he came to the final decision that Nietzsche was nothing but an epigone of Kant.

In Rickert's survey, the period from 1781 (the publication of the *Critique of Pure Reason*) to 1888 (the date of *Ecce Homo*) represented a remarkable unity in German philosophy. It was during this period, he felt, that both Kant and Nietzsche had raised the problem of value to a central philosophical position. Yet where Nietzsche's genealogy of the Western tradition grounded value in the will, thus arriving at a new kind of voluntarist *Weltanschauung*, Kant had turned to reason as the source of value, thereby offering the solid foundation of *Wissenschaft*. Rickert believed that if one were intent on rehabilitating this axiological tradition, threatened on the one hand by the researches of the special sciences and on the other by the demand for existential meaning and universal value, one would have to focus on problems of philosophical method. Rickert hoped to resolve this crisis by re-uniting in one system what had been sundered by nineteenth-century life-philosophy. That is, he wished to harmonize a philosophy of values with a philosophy that was scientific and rooted in *Wissenschaft*. In developing a scientific form of value-philosophy, Rickert believed he would overcome the specious appeal of the life-philosophers and secure for the discipline of philosophy a special task that, though aimed at value and culture, rejected the prophet's mantle taken up by Nietzsche. In so doing, he would prove the worth of logic over clever aphorisms; as Rickert put it, "Every problem of a universal *Weltanschauung* and of life is transformed for us into a problem of logic and of epistemology."[21]

Before attempting to present Rickert's own value-philosophy, which he saw as crucial for understanding the debates concerning the *Natur-* and *Geisteswissenschaften*, I would like to explore his relation to Kant and show how his Kantian roots helped determine his approach to understanding both nature and culture. My intention here is not to offer a systematic view of Rickert's overall philosophy or to analyze the stages of its development; rather, my discussion will focus on the influence of Kantian thinking on Rickert's new form of historical logic. Both systematic philosophers and the adherents of *Lebensphilosophie* had concentrated their attention on the generational dispute over scientific method. As we saw in Chapter 2, Windelband had rejected the material division of scientific labor at the university and sought to clarify the relationship between the various scientific

[21] Rickert, *Die Grenzen*, 11.

disciplines along formal lines. Yet for him the ultimate problem was essentially one of classification. Rickert wished to go beyond the merely programmatic outline provided by Windelband and deal with the issue *philosophically*. By reformulating this taxonomical question about form and matter into a genuinely philosophical one, Rickert hoped to show the range and force of Neo-Kantian thinking.

To speak of the *formal* rather than the *material* differences between nature and history is already to betray a certain epistemological bias. In the argot of nineteenth-century German philosophy, such a distinction was a "critical" one. Kant's critical method, initiated by his Copernican turn, altered the naïve understanding of nature and consciousness. In the *Critique of Pure Reason* Kant focused all his energies on the resolution of the formal question in knowledge, the scholastic *quaestio juris*, rather than the empirical question, the *quaestio facti*.[22] In the preface, he referred to "the primary hypothesis of Copernicus," whose innovative astronomy inverted the relation of the earth to the solar system and helped Galileo and his followers found a modern form of physics.[23] Kant tried to achieve a similar revolution in philosophy, especially in relation to mathematics and the natural sciences. Unlike the British school of Locke and the empiricists, who put forth a mimetic theory of knowledge based on sensory impressions, Kant tried to demonstrate that it is not our concepts that conform to the natural object but, conversely, the natural object that conforms to our concepts.[24] By integrating this new Copernican insight, Kant believed that philosophy could dispense with the old methods of investigation and proceed with a new "critical" or "transcendental" method. To more fully understand the significance of this critical approach for Rickert, let us look a bit more closely at Kant's terminology.

"Transcendental" knowledge is, for Kant, "all knowledge which is occupied not so much with objects as with the mode of our knowledge of objects in so far as this mode of knowledge is to be possible a priori."[25] Accordingly, it is opposed to all empirical, physiological, psychological, metaphysical, or skeptical theories. Kant's aim is neither to deny that all our knowledge begins with experience nor to doubt the existence of given objects but rather to show how the existence of such objects can be conceived *scientifically*. To achieve this

---

[22] Immanuel Kant, *Critique of Pure Reason*, trans. Norman Kemp Smith (London, Macmillan, 1929), 120–122.
[23] Ibid., 22.
[24] Ibid.
[25] Ibid., 59.

scientific certitude requires that we admit that our knowledge begins with experience; yet Kant does not draw the conclusion that our knowledge is grounded in experience. For the scientific understanding of nature, we must, Kant insists, make a distinction between empirical, or a posteriori, and pure, or a priori, knowledge.[26] Our knowledge begins with experience, he contends, but has its origin in the a priori. This a priori element is, in fact, the condition on which all experience depends; it provides the "necessity and strict universality" for all our judgments about the world.[27] In this sense, transcendental knowledge is that form of knowledge which, though based on our experience, dispenses with the mere contents of experience, that is, the material component, and focuses on the forms of thought needed to organize such experience into a meaningful whole. This is the task of transcendental logic, which asks the question, "How are a priori synthetic judgments possible?"[28] Or, to pose this question in its modern form, "How is science [*Wissenschaft*] possible?"[29] For Kant, writing in 1781, science meant mathematics and physics; thus, the form of his transcendental critique concerning the possibility of a priori knowledge took the form of a critique of pure mathematics and pure natural science as the highest forms of pure reason. Writing over a century later, within a different scientific context, Rickert believed that the form of the Kantian inquiry must be extended beyond nature and mathematics to include a transcendental logic of history.

In the *Prolegomena to Any Future Metaphysics* (1783), Kant raised the question about the possibility of nature in its material and formal significance.[30] As ever, Kant's question focused not on the reality of nature itself as it existed apart from human beings but on nature as a possible object of human knowledge. Materially, Kant claimed, nature is the product of sensory experience; formally, it is the product of our rational understanding or consciousness. As he explained:

> Nature is the existence of things, so far as it is determined according to universal laws. Should nature signify the existence of things in themselves, we could never know it either a priori or a posteriori. Not a priori, for how

---

[26] Ibid., 42–43.
[27] Ibid., 44.
[28] Ibid., 55.
[29] This is the question raised in the two-volume study by Karl Vorländer, *Immanuel Kant* (Leipzig: Meiner, 1924), 1:270.
[30] Immanuel Kant, *Prolegomena to Any Future Metaphysics*, trans. Paul Carus (New York: Bobbs-Merrill, 1950), chap. 2.

can we know what belongs to things in themselves, since this never can be done by the dissection of concepts (in analytical propositions)? For I do not want to know what is contained in my concept of a thing (for that belongs to its logical essence), but what in the actuality [*Wirklichkeit*] of the thing is superadded to my concept [*Begriff*] and by which the thing itself is determined in its existence apart from the concept.[31]

In the transcendental aesthetic of his *Critique*, Kant demonstrated that nature, in its material form, is produced by our sensibility. In the transcendental logic, he argued that nature, in its formal aspect, is constructed through the work of concepts. Knowledge of nature thus becomes possible only when sensory intuitions are brought under the conceptual apparatus of consciousness. In this transcendental-logical sense, nature becomes an object constituted by consciousness or by the rules guiding our understanding. In this object-construction of the natural world lie the roots of Rickert's own transcendental philosophy.

Like Kant, Rickert made a categorical distinction between the reality of an object and our concept of the object, writing in *Science and History* that there is "a gulf between the content of concepts and that of reality which is as great as the gulf between the universal and the particular, and which cannot be bridged."[32] Whereas the life-philosophers sought to bridge this gulf by conceiving of a unity between human consciousness and the natural world, Rickert consistently emphasized the cleft between them. To achieve a truly scientific understanding of nature, Rickert claimed, one must distance oneself from experience and focus instead on the formation of concepts. As he explained in *Die Philosophie des Lebens*, "There is no science without conceptual thought, and that is precisely the meaning of each concept: that it distances itself from the immediate reality of life. The most vital of all objects ceases to live as something real as soon as it is conceived. *The dualism of reality and concept is never to be overcome.* To overcome it would be to overcome science itself. The essence of science rests on the tension between immediately experienced or real life and a theory of life or of reality."[33] With Kantian logic serving as the new organon for the European sciences, Rickert was determined to redraw the old lines of division between the *Natur-* and *Geistes-*

---

[31] Ibid., 42.
[32] Rickert, *Science and History*, 44; *KN*, 43.
[33] Rickert, *Die Philosophie des Lebens*, 110 (emphasis mine).

wissenschaften. But he first needed to rethink Windelband's old approach.

In his theory of the sciences, with its logical distinction between nomothetic and idiographic methods, Windelband had claimed that the same object could be the focus of both natural-scientific and historical research. What ultimately determined the meaning of the object was the subjective interest of the researcher. But Rickert felt that Windelband had not distinguished carefully enough between scholarly judgment and scientific concept-formation. "Facts" as objects of research were not simply given; they were first constituted by the work of scientific concepts that had to be taken into consideration before one arrived at a judgment. Seizing on the epistemological significance of his claim, Rickert went back to Kant's *Critique of Pure Reason* to reemphasize the logical priority of concept-formation to the activity of judgment (*Urteilstätigkeit*). This distinction made it necessary to view the difference between the *Natur-* and *Geisteswissenschaften* not as a problem of classification (as Windelband had) but as one of concept-formation.[34] Again in *Science and History* Rickert notes that "the formal character that determines the method of science must be implicit in the way it forms the concepts by which it grasps reality. Therefore, in order to understand the method of a science we have to know its principles of concept-formation."[35] Because this notion of concept-formation plays such a central role in Rickert's whole theory of the sciences, we will need to look at this term with some care.

Concept-formation, or *Begriffsbildung,* denotes for Rickert the process of structuring, ordering, and making rational the sensory material in the world of reality. As we have already seen, concept and reality are, for Rickert, two disparate elements in an understanding of an object. Reality as it exists apart from human beings is irrational; only through the process of conceptualizing it do we make it rational. All attempts to describe reality exactly "as it is"—that is, to achieve a conceptual representation faithful in all its details—are therefore doomed to failure.[36] Rickert emphasizes two reasons for his claim. First, the spatially extensive details of any process in nature are infinitely complex. Empirical reality, he argues, knows no sharp and absolute boundaries: "Nature makes no sudden leaps; everything is in

---

[34] Rickert, *Science and History,* 55–56; KN, 53–54.
[35] Rickert, *Science and History,* 38; KN, 37.
[36] Rickert, *Science and History,* 32; KN, 31 (cf. *Die Grenzen,* 36).

flux."[37] There is a continuous link between all parts of reality which make it impossible for the finite mind to grasp. This spatially *extensive* infinity Rickert calls "the theorem of the continuity of everything real."[38] Rickert then turns his attention to the *intensive* details of any one process in the empirical world and discovers that no one thing or event is completely identical with any other. At best, there is only similarity. Within each thing or each event, every part is distinct from every other part spatially and temporally, no matter how near or how far removed: "In other words, everything real exhibits a distinctive, peculiarly characteristic individual stamp. At least no one can say that he has ever encountered anything absolutely homogeneous in reality. Everything is different from everything else."[39] Rickert labels this "intensive infinity" of each part "the theorem of the heterogeneity of everything real."[40]

If we combine the theorem of continuity with the theorem of heterogeneity, Rickert indicates, wherever we look in the world we will find a "continuous differentiation."[41] By understanding reality as an irrational *heterogeneous continuum*, Rickert reaffirms the essential recalcitrance of the empirical world to all human attempts at description, reproduction, or representation. Rickert underscores this fact in *The Limits of Concept Formation in Natural Science*. "As a matter of principle," he writes, "it is an insoluble task for the finite mind to have knowledge of the world by individually representing in one's mind all the discrete phenomena as they concretely exist. . . . Whoever understands by 'knowledge of the world' an actual copy of it from the very outset has to renounce the idea of a science which would ever come near to representing knowledge of the world as a whole."[42] The heterogeneous continuum is reality as such before knowledge. If there is to be any knowledge at all, the infinite multiplicity of things has to be "eliminated or overcome," which can only be achieved through concepts.[43] Concepts simplify reality; they reduce to manageable pro-

[37] Rickert, *Science and History*, 33; KN, 31.
[38] Rickert, *Science and History*, 33; KN, 32.
[39] Rickert, *Science and History*, 33–34; KN, 32–33.
[40] Rickert, *Science and History*, 34; KN, 33.
[41] Rickert, *Science and History*, 34; KN, 33.
[42] This translation is taken from Thomas Burger, *Max Weber's Theory of Concept Formation* (Durham, N.C.: Duke University Press, 1976), 21, and is based on an earlier edition of Rickert, *Die Grenzen der naturwissenschaftlichen Begriffsbildung* (Tübingen: Mohr, 1902), 34. All other citations from *Die Grenzen* are from the 1929 edition cited above.
[43] Rickert, *Die Grenzen*, 42.

portions the mass of phenomena which the mind encounters, turning the real as such into something artificially rational. As Rickert made quite plain: "Without concepts . . . any knowledge of the smallest and simplest corporeal reality would be impossible. Concept-formation . . . is necessarily connected with any judgment about reality which can be expressed in words."[44]

Rickert's principle of concept-formation followed upon the whole modernist tradition of Cartesian-Kantian thought grounded in the epistemological distinction between subject and object. Appropriately, in the very first sentence of *Der Gegenstand der Erkenntnis* (*The Object of Knowledge*), Rickert stated unequivocally that "to the concept of knowledge there belongs, besides a subject that knows, an object that is known."[45] Against naïve realism and naturalism, however, Rickert argued that the object (*Gegenstand*) which stands opposite (*gegenübersteht*) can never be known in itself as part of reality but only in a reconstructed form as a concept. Knowledge of reality, then, can never be identified as, or coincide with, knowledge of being, because it is always the subject who first grounds the meaning of being. Spurred on by these Kantian motives, Rickert became persuaded that the whole enterprise of philosophy turns on the epistemological question concerning the ground of knowledge rather than on the ontological question concerning the ground of being—a distinction that was to have profound consequences for his methodology of the sciences.

iv. The Methods of Natural Science and History

a. *The Principles of Natural-Scientific and Historical Concept-Formation*

In Rickert's scheme of the sciences, reality itself is neither nature nor history; it exists apart from human consciousness as a heterogeneous continuum, infinitely varied and extensive, a kind of seamless fabric. Rickert himself often used the Heraclitean metaphor of a stream in constant flux.[46] Whenever we use our reason, he explained, we make little incisions into this seamless fabric; we artificially stop the river's flow. In deciding to analyze the river, we choose which

---

[44] Ibid.
[45] Rickert, *Der Gegenstand der Erkenntnis*, 1.
[46] Rickert, *Science and History*, 33; *KN*, 32; and *Die Grenzen*, 35.

part we will examine; similarly, when making incisions, we decide where to cut. Our choices are dictated by what we deem essential and inessential to our task. In terms of an overall theory of knowledge, to structure, transform, or conceptualize the empirical world of reality is to select out of it what is of value. To ensure that this act of choosing does not happen by whim or fancy, however, rules of choice must exist. These rules are themselves the very principles of science, Rickert argued, and it is philosophy's goal as the science of science to ensure their logical integrity. Such integrity can be achieved, however, only by recourse to the transcendental idea of an a priori. "If the construction of reality performed by the sciences is not to be arbitrary," Rickert wrote, "they require an 'a priori' or a prior judgment of which they can avail themselves in the delimitation of one part of reality from another . . . that is to say, they need a principle of selection with respect to which they can separate the essential from the inessential in the given material."[47]

The "a priori" principle of fact selection guarantees the scientific character of all reality construction. That is, it grounds the selection of facts not in the facts themselves but in the transcendental rules of logic by which the scientist must construct such facts. This guarantees against all arbitrary selection. Rickert designated the two logical methods of selecting the essential from the inessential as the natural-scientific method and the method of historical science. Understanding the essence of natural science or history, he argued, involves a close investigation of its principles of concept-formation rather than an analysis of any so-called material object categorized as either nature or history. It is precisely on this formal point of epistemology that the controversy between Rickert and the historicists turned.

b. Individualizing and Generalizing Sciences

In Rickert's scheme, the process of concept-formation depends on the goal that one seeks in selecting essential elements from the stream of reality. This goal in turn shapes the object that one selects. Rickert applied this insight to explain the difference between the two dominant methods of nineteenth-century research. In every interpretation of reality, he argued, there is a formal difference in the goal one seeks: either one focuses on the general characteristics that one particle of

---

[47] Rickert, *Science and History*, 36; *KN*, 35.

reality has in common with another, or one focuses on the differences between particles. In *The Limits of Concept-Formation, Science and History*, and in many articles, especially "Zwei Wege der Erkenntnistheorie," Rickert reemphasized that only two paths of knowledge exist. One can either transform the heterogeneous continuum of reality into a "homogeneous continuum," or one can make of it a "heterogeneous *discretum*."[48] That is, one can view all reality under the universal concept of similarity or the particular concept of dissimilarity. The one approach defines the procedure of natural science, and the other, the procedure of history.

According to Rickert, natural-scientific concepts reduce the infinite manifold of particular and discrete objects to a manageable number by concentrating on one central feature: what these things have in common. As he explained: "To use a felicitous metaphor of Bergson's, the natural sciences produce only ready-made clothes which fit Paul just as well as they do Peter because they are cut to the measure of neither. If they wanted to operate on a 'custom-made' basis, they would have to produce a *new* concept for every object they study."[49] But to produce an individual concept for every object would be logically contradictory because whenever the natural sciences do turn their attention to the individual exemplar, they look for a way to subsume it under a general principle. In so doing they simplify the complex elements of the individual thing itself. Thus, Rickert argued, "the particularity and individuality of the real world constitutes in every case the ultimate *limit of concept-formation in the natural sciences*."[50]

By using this logical method of concept-formation, Rickert hoped to prove that there was a necessary and absolute boundary that separates the *logical* essence of natural science from that of history. History's goal, as a form of science, is to extract the unique, particular, unrepeatable element from the continuous stream of reality and to present it with reference to its individual significance. As Rickert explained in *The Limits of Concept-Formation*,

> Every science, even history, has to transform its perceptual data and bring it under concepts. Thus, we wish to formulate the opposition of natural science and history in this way: Empirical reality . . . becomes nature when

[48] Rickert, *Die Grenzen*, 36–37; *Science and History*, 34–35; and *KN*, 33–34. This concept is also explained in Rickert's important essay "Zwei Wege der Erkenntnistheorie," in *Kant Studien* 14 (1909), 169–228.
[49] Rickert, *Science and History*, 45; *KN*, 44.
[50] Rickert, *Science and History*, 46; *KN*, 45; cf. *Die Grenzen*, 219.

we view it with respect to its universal characteristics; it becomes history when we view it as particular and individual. . . . The final difference of methods is to be found solely in that which the various concepts make out of reality and thus, the essential thing for logic is to see whether each seeks the universal or particular element in the real. The first task falls to natural science, the second to history.[51]

By dividing the sciences of nature and history according to their *logical* tasks, Rickert hoped, on the one hand, to overcome the old *Natur/Geist*, physical/psychological dualism of Mill and his German followers and, on the other, to avoid the positivist claim for adopting only one universal method. Comte and Buckle had identified the natural-scientific method with scientific method as such and attempted to transform history into a science by appropriating the principles of biology, chemistry, and physics. Rickert rejected the positivist program, however, and tried instead to construct his argument on the formal principles of logic developed by transcendental philosophy.[52] Following Kant, Rickert stressed that scientific method is not rooted in the material object but in the formal concept.

In the natural sciences, concept-formation is based on the generalizing method of the nomothetic approach, as Windelband had carefully argued. Natural-scientific inquiry seeks general laws by which to structure experience. Hence, Kant could define nature as "the existence of things, so far as it is determined according to universal laws."[53] Yet Rickert realized that nature itself is not law-abiding (in the sense that it follows Newtonian laws of physics); rather, we construct nature through our natural-scientific research according to scientific laws. This type of concept-formation selects the essential facts of reality from out of the lawless continuum of heterogeneous elements according to their conformity to laws. This is the generalizing method's sole aim: to impose lawfulness on the chaos of physical process.

In the *Geisteswissenschaften* such an approach was logically inconsistent. If history were to achieve the status of a science, it would have to follow its own logical approach based on the individualizing method of the idiographic disciplines. To borrow the same principles of concept-formation as the natural sciences and to apply their "laws" to the study of human history represented an error in logic. Buckle

---

[51] Rickert, *Die Grenzen*, 227.
[52] Rickert extends this argument in *Die Probleme der Geschichtsphilosophie*, 27–37.
[53] Kant, *Prolegomena*, 42.

and the other positivists who sought to discover "laws of historical inquiry" (thereby transforming history into a science) had, according to Rickert, confused the very issue of scientific "definition."[54] Science can either be generalizing, nomothetic, and law-seeking, or it can be individualizing, idiographic, and particular. It cannot be both at the same time. To clarify this logical confusion, Rickert focused on the problem of concept-formation as a way of defining the principle of selection in historical science. By turning to the philosophical problem of value as the basis of all principles of selection, he hoped to offer a way out of the cul-de-sac of traditional theory of science.

c. The Question of Value in Historical Method

In all areas of life, including science, Rickert observed, we are forced to choose between the valuable and the common. In *Die Grenzen*, he provided an example of this kind of choice by contrasting the value of a piece of ordinary coal with that of a diamond.[55] In so doing, he shed some light on the process of historical concept-formation. There are, he noted, many more pieces of coal in the empirical world than there are diamonds. The piece of coal is, however, like the diamond, a distinctive object different from all other worldly objects such as rocks, trees, birds, flowers, and so forth. Moreover, this one specific piece of coal is different from all other pieces by virtue of its singularity in time and space. What differentiates the coal from a diamond, however, is not merely the stamp of singularity. On closer scrutiny we find that what is really at issue in this separation is nothing other than the concept of value itself. Dividing the singular piece of coal into many parts does not lessen its value; the same cannot be said, however, of the diamond. As an *In-dividuum* the diamond's value rests precisely on its indivisibility. As Rickert explained: "The meaning that the diamond possesses rests on a *value* that in turn attaches to its irreplaceable singularity. The diamond *should* not be divided because it is valuable, a principle that holds for all other objects that are 'in-dividuals.'"[56] By applying this same axiological principle of individuality to the realms of history and culture, we will be better able to understand the role of historical concept-formation in Rickert's thinking.

[54] For an example of positivist historiography, see Henry Thomas Buckle, *History of Civilization in England*, vol. 1 (New York: Appleton, 1870), esp. 3–4.
[55] Rickert, *Die Grenzen*, 315–318.
[56] Ibid., 317.

For Rickert, value, or *Wert*, provides the central concept for understanding historical science. But one might legitimately ask, Where does this value come from? What is its source? How is it grounded? Following strictly Kantian principles, Rickert answered the question of ground (*der Satz vom Grund*) in purely transcendental terms. Values do not 'exist' ontologically, he argued; they neither possess material substance nor occupy space in the world of being but are based on formal principles. Their ground is logical or axiological rather than ontological—in Rickert's words, being "is," values are "valid" (*"Seiendes 'ist,' Werte 'gelten'"*).[57] In *System der Philosophie*, one of his most important works which was intended as the new organon for "value-philosophy," Rickert admitted, however, that "like all 'fundamental' concepts, the concept of value is indefinable."[58] One can think (*denken*) in terms of value, but the concept of value itself cannot be thought (*bedenken*).[59] To clarify this point, let us look more closely at Rickert's example of the piece of coal and the diamond.

As we saw earlier, the value of Rickert's diamond (in contrast to the commonness of the coal) does not reside in the material properties of the diamond itself. Instead, value attaches to the diamond through certain agreed-upon cultural concepts that shape the ontological singularity of this piece of rock and render it valuable. We can notice a similar logic at work when we consider the value of *historical* objects. In themselves, neither the life of Napoléon nor the French Revolution are essential to what we call "history." In and through them, however, we recognize certain values that become important to us. Only in relation to these values does the historical object become truly historical; apart from them it remains just another singular episode in the chaotic procession of human activity, equal in significance to the baking of bread or the brushing of one's teeth—topics which today have relevance for cultural historians but which for Rickert, with his tradi-

[57] For an excellent discussion of the fundamental tenets of *Wertphilosophie*, see Herbert Schnädelbach, *Philosophie in Deutschland, 1831–1933* (Frankfurt: Suhrkamp, 1983), 199–224; Johannes B. Lotz, "Sein und Wert," *Zeitschrift für katholische Theologie* 57 (1933): 557; August Messer, *Deutsche Wertphilosophie der Gegenwart* (Leipzig: Reinicke, 1926); and J. E. Heyde, *Wert: Eine philosophische Grundlegung* (Erfurt: Stenger, 1926). For a critique of this position, see Parvis Emad, "Heidegger's Value-Criticism and Its Bearing on a Phenomenology of Values," in John Sallis, ed., *Radical Phenomenology* (Atlantic Highlands, N.J.: Humanities Press, 1978).
[58] Heinrich Rickert, *System der Philosophie* (henceforth cited as *System*), (Tübingen: Mohr, 1921) 114.
[59] Johannes Berger, "Gegenstandskonstitution und geschichtliche Welt," Ph.D. dissertation, University of Munich 1967, 181, offers a critique of this position.

tional focus on political history and biography, held little interest. The cultural task of history is to bring a measure of self-consciousness to the enterprise of relating inessential episodes to essential values. As Rickert explained in his chapter "Die Logik der Geschichtswissen-schaft":

> The individual concrete meaning of [an object] . . . stands in the closest relation to universal concepts of value such that no historically meaningful object, to which we attach individuality, can attain historical meaning and significance without reference to a universal value. The concrete meaning is first 'constituted' historically through the universal value. The concrete meaning that is found in the real objects, as well as the historical principle of selection, lies not in the sphere of real *being* but in that of *value*, and it is from here that the connection between the individual value-related method and the meaningful material of history must be understood.[60]

If we go back to our initial inquiry concerning the ground of values and their relation to historical concept-formation, we find that for Rickert, values do not have their source in history; rather, history exists because of values. These values, which are transcendental and absolute, without existential or historical ground, cannot be known in themselves; they can be approached only through the objects that attach to them, objects that Rickert finds in the sphere of culture. Because of its singular role in historical concept-formation, Rickert singles out the concept of culture as an important starting point for reframing the question of value in the *Geisteswissenschaften*.

v. *Kulturwissenschaft* and *Naturwissenschaft*

Rickert's unfaltering emphasis on "culture" (*Kultur*) as the guiding principle for understanding the science of history must be explained within its own historical context. Writing in 1926, some forty years after Dilthey's *Introduction to the Human Sciences* (1883), Rickert wanted to reframe Dilthey's discussion about the epistemological distinctions between *Natur* and *Geist* by introducing a new terminological distinction between *Natur* and *Kultur*. Rickert praised Dilthey as a careful and erudite historian of ideas who possessed a "gift for 'reliving' and 'empathizing' with history [that] was extraordinary and per-

[60] Rickert, *Die Probleme der Geschichtsphilosophie*, 70.

haps unique in its time"; yet, he observed, "this estimable man was not gifted in the same measure with the capacity for rigorous conceptual reasoning."[61] Dilthey's identification of the natural sciences with the physical or corporeal and of the human sciences with the psychological or spiritual (*geistig*) was too focused on material and ontological elements. Such a distinction ignored the formal properties of value- and concept-formation. Thus, when Dilthey employed the Hegelian concept of *Geist* to anchor his system of scientific knowledge, Rickert dismissed it as inappropriate for historical study, labeling it "too narrow."[62] Rickert's response was to reformulate the traditional *Natur/Geist* division along more rigorously logical lines, offering instead an axiological split between nature and culture.

If Kant's definition of *nature* as "the existence of things so far as they are determined according to universal laws" adequately described the work of natural-scientific concept-formation, it did not provide an exhaustive model for all the sciences.[63] Rickert knew that he would have to rethink Kant's definition in light of the value-focused research of the cultural sciences, so that one would be able to define *culture* as "the existence of things so far as they are determined according to values."[64] In *Science and History* he provided a rationale for his definition by relating values to culture: "The idea of culture provides the historical sciences with a principle for the selection of the essential aspects of reality in the formation of their concepts, just as the idea of nature as reality considered from the point of view of universal laws and concepts does for the natural sciences. The concept of an historical individuality that can be represented as a real expression of complexes of meaning is first constituted by virtue of the *values* that attach to culture and through reference to them."[65] Natural science and cultural science are thus separated not according to the peculiarity of their objects but according to the logical difference in their methods, a division that was purely formal.[66]

Rickert acknowledged Windelband's claim that the method of natural science is generalizing, and the method of history, individualizing, but he believed that this distinction was too broadly drawn and inex-

[61] Rickert, *Hd.Ms. 31*, 203.
[62] Rickert, *Die Grenzen*, 526.
[63] Kant, *Prolegomena*, 42.
[64] Herbert Schnädelbach, *Die Geschichtsphilosophie nach Hegel* (Freiburg: Alber, 1974), 151.
[65] Rickert, *Science and History*, 83–84; *KN*, 81–82.
[66] Rickert, *Die Grenzen*, 523.

act. In his historical logic he tried to demonstrate that there are two kinds of individuality: mere singularity (the specifically given piece of coal) and essential singularity (the valuable diamond), two characteristics that could only be distinguished through a concept of value. Only on the basis of value distinctions that determined cultural concepts could the methodological problem of history be understood at all. In *Die Grenzen* he wrote, "The concepts of culture and of history are mutually conditioned and are connected to each in a double sense: cultural values alone make history as a science possible, and historical development alone brings forth real cultural objects to which cultural values attach themselves."[67]

vi. Values and Objectivity in Historical Science

Rickert's strategy in offering a new theory of cultural science was more radical than Windelband's taxonomical revision of the *Natur-* and *Geisteswissenschaften*. In a very practical way, Rickert sought to provide a logical theory that would ensure the scientific rigor of historical inquiry. If history's status as a science of culture were to be secured, it would have to withstand the many criticisms of the idealists, positivists, and practitioners of the old Historical School. Rickert was sensitive to these criticisms and, in fact, rewrote his major works, *The Limits of Concept Formation in Natural Science* and *Science and History*, many times to accommodate them; the former went through five different editions, and the latter, through seven.[68] Each time Rickert tried to answer the various criticisms of thinkers such as Becher, Frischeisen-Köhler, Troeltsch, Dilthey, Simmel, and Meinecke.[69] In what follows, I would like to focus on one aspect of this contemporary criticism—the problem of values and historical objectivity—in an effort to clarify the distinctiveness of Rickert's position.

As one studies the history of science from the time of Bacon, Kepler, Galileo, Newton, and Descartes, one notices how philosophers and scientists have sought to achieve a universal standard of objective and systematic investigation for scientific method. As these thinkers developed a radically new model of research, they gave precedence

[67] Ibid., 522–523.
[68] Ibid., vii–xxxi.
[69] For Rickert's comments on Becher, see *Die Grenzen*, 476 and 613; on Dilthey, 125, 181–183, and 488; on Simmel, 272 and 574; on Meinecke, xxvii and 335; and on Troeltsch, xxvii and 539.

to an ideal of objectivity as the most systematic way of advancing truth. Rickert's theory of value appeared to run counter to this long-standing and venerable tradition, for his principle of value seemed to be at odds with the demand for scientific objectivity. Yet Rickert attempted to overcome this apparent contradiction by providing a new kind of scientific logic which would achieve an epistemological balance between the competing claims of objectivity and subjectivity. As he explained in *System der Philosophie*:

> It appears inconsistent with the nature of science that values should play such a decisive role in its work, indeed, should even be the principles of its concept-formation. One rightly demands from the historian that he present things "objectively," and even if this goal is not wholly attainable, it nonetheless offers a logical ideal. How does this relate to the contention that the essence of historical method is in connecting objects with values? Does not each discipline that researches a part of the real world have to maintain its distance from all but the logical values if it is not to cease being a science of the real?[70]

Rickert tried to answer these questions by positing a logical distinction between the methods of natural- and cultural-scientific concept-formation. No one, Rickert argued, could seriously maintain that an absolute or value-free observation of reality is at all possible.[71] Each observation, each investigation of an object must, in some sense, "interest" the observer. With the admission of such an interest, one has also to admit the relevance of *value*. Logically, this value does not have to be one-sidedly subjective, however; it can also reflect an objective interest of the observer. The interest of natural scientists, for example, is guided by their focus on the general character held in common by each individual exemplar. Here, the value of commonality is decisive. For historians, however, the process of concept-formation proceeds differently, focusing instead on the precise singularity of the individual exemplar. As we have already seen in our example of the coal and the diamond, there are two distinct types of individuality for Rickert, both of which possess value: mere singularity and the unique individual or, in other words, the "inessential" and the "essential." But in *System der Philosophie*, Rickert claimed that such a distinction was not arbitrary: "The individual can only become

---

[70] Rickert, *System*, 219.
[71] Ibid., 218.

'essential' with reference to a value."[72] On the basis of this distinction, Rickert believed he could offer an epistemological solution to the problem of historical relativism.

Within Rickert's system of selection in natural science and history, value serves as a formal, a priori principle, transcendental in nature and valid (*geltend*) rather than real (*seiend*)—an absolute reference point by which all objects in the world of being can be judged. In concrete historical terms, this means that the values by which one judges real events are not themselves bound by the constraints of time. Rickert explained this paradox by referring these values to culture. Against the claims of historicists and life-philosophers, Rickert rejected the relevance of temporality and historicity and insisted that values are transhistorical and transcultural, as well as absolute and unchanging in their validity. They do not exist as such but find expression in cultural objects such as religion, art, the state, the community, economic organizations, ethical precepts, and others. With this separation of cultural values—whose ground is transcendental but whose expression is historical—Rickert was convinced that he had found a means to overcome the split between subjective, value-laden culture and objective, value-free cultural science.

In applying these insights to the specific problems of historical research, Rickert made a clear-cut distinction between "valuation," or *Wertung*, and what he called "value-reference," or *Wertbeziehung*. His argument proceeds as follows: For historians to engage in a particular area of research, such as the French Revolution, they must first have an interest in their topic. This interest need not undermine their objectivity, however, for one can have a practical interest in a subject and yet achieve theoretical objectivity. Practical valuation of the French Revolution need not be confused with theoretically referring it to values. Indeed, in many cases a historian's interest is really a cultural rather than a merely personal one, dependent on the consensus of the cultural community—its language, education, religion, art, economic structure, law, literature, science, and so forth. Thus, as a researcher, the historian might simply share in a common cultural value. For example, a French historian might not agree with certain political or social aspects of the French Revolution but could still be interested in their effects on the modern world. In appraising the Revolution, however, he or she would need to select out of an infinite number of

[72] Ibid.

historical facts those which seemed somehow relevant. In selecting these facts, the historian would be guided by a certain narrative tradition, deciding whether a political, cultural, economic, or intellectual critique would take precedence. Each different perspective would yield a different interpretation; nonetheless, each would be of value for a specific community of historical researchers. In Rickertian language, by selecting a fragment out of the heterogeneous continuum of French history and contextualizing it within a larger historical narrative, historians were referring to values but were not themselves evaluating.

Rickert consistently maintained that "practical valuation and theoretical reference to values are two logically *distinct* acts."[73] One could clearly identify a specific action (the execution of Louis XVI) as essential for the history of the French Revolution without acknowledging that such an act either promoted or impeded the achievement of a specific cultural value (political freedom). To clarify his position, Rickert explained:

> To treat an object as *important* for values and the realization of cultural goods does not at all mean that one values it, for valuation must always be either *positive* or *negative*. The positive or negative value attached to a segment of reality can be a matter of *dispute* even though its historical significance in virtue of its reference to some value is *beyond question*. Thus, for example, the historian as such is not in a position to decide whether the French Revolution was beneficial or harmful to France or Europe. Such a judgment would involve a valuation. . . . In short, valuations must always involve praise or blame. To *refer* to values is to do neither.[74]

In carefully distinguishing between the act of valuation and that of value-reference, Rickert hoped to provide a logical solution to the historicist problem of objectivity. Ranke, for example, had called for strict impartiality in his office as a scientific historian. Methodologically, he sought to achieve an "extinguishing of the ego" which would guarantee a re-creation of the historical epoch "as it actually happened."[75] Though Rickert was in sympathy with Ranke's desire for historical objectivity, he could not embrace the Rankean ideal uncritically. To be sure, one needed to overcome all arbitrary distortions of the historical

[73] Rickert, *Science and History*, 89; *KN*, 97.
[74] Rickert, *Science and History*, 90; *KN*, 88–89.
[75] For a fuller discussion of Ranke's position, see Leonard Krieger, *Ranke: The Meaning of History* (Chicago: University of Chicago Press, 1977).

facts; yet, he argued, "this does not mean that, as Ranke seems to have supposed, historical objectivity consists in a mere reproduction of the facts without any ordering principle of *selection*."[76] Rickert claimed that the historian, as a cultural scientist, always has to relate facts to values. If one had no criterion of selection, no special interest to guide one's research, then everything would be without meaning and would be reduced to mere value-free "nature."

Rickert did not dismiss this interest as being irrelevant or inappropriate; he admitted, rather, that in the practical world of historical scholarship, interests did determine value judgments. He was realistic enough to see that no historical work could ever be "entirely free from positive or negative valuations."[77] Yet he also maintained that historians were strictly accountable to render impartial judgments and preserve standards of scholarly objectivity. Historians might offer their own ideological interpretations of the French Revolution, but in so doing they were overstepping the proper bounds of scientific history. As cultural scientists, their task was to refer to values, not to evaluate. But Rickert's arguments were not as convincing for actual historians, many of whom believed that in focusing on the logic of research, he had missed the essential experience of historical reality.

vii. Causality and Values: Rickert's Transcendental Philosophy and Friedrich Meinecke's Historicism

Rickert's logical tour de force in *The Limits of Concept Formation in Natural Science* consisted of a sustained discussion involving the fine points of scientific labor. He intended his book to reformulate problems of historical values into epistemological questions concerned with the status of philosophy as the science of science itself. In this sense, Rickert's work marked a new phase in the development of historicism or, more precisely, in the philosophical response to the problems generated from out of the historicist tradition. For if the period from 1880 to 1930 represents the coming to self-consciousness of the philosophical problems of historicism, then the debates between the Neo-Kantians and Dilthey served to intensify this self-consciousness. What is remarkable here is how the conflict between Neo-Kantian logic and Dilthey's hermeneutics about questions of historical

[76] Rickert, *Science and History*, 85; KN, 83.
[77] Rickert, *Science and History*, 91; KN, 89.

objectivity, valuation, and prejudice helped to reinforce the basic philosophical presuppositions of the modernist era, bringing into focus the contradictions within subject/object metaphysics and its demand for scientific certitude. In Heidegger's *Destruktion* of Neo-Kantian logic, the bankruptcy of these metaphysical claims as a kind of hypostatization of historical experience was brought to light in a new way. And yet, for all its problems, Neo-Kantian thinking served a positive function. For it was only in this hypostatized form, Heidegger claimed, that the aporias of subject/object metaphysics could genuinely reveal themselves. Thus, for Heidegger, even though the Neo-Kantian "solution" to the crisis of historicism failed, in its failure it called attention to the inadequacy of the whole historicist *Fragestellung*. Heidegger understood Dilthey's work, on the other hand, as opening up the whole question of historicism in a new sense. In his view, Dilthey's inquiry into the question of historical being did not, as did Rickert's, reduce the problem of historical truth to a mere object of historical concept-formation but instead opened up the phenomenality and historicity of historical experience. In the next two chapters, I will discuss the implications of this shift more fully, but I will first explore what is at issue philosophically in Rickert's confrontation with historicism. I begin my discussion of Rickert's historical logic by looking at how his work was received by his contemporary Friedrich Meinecke.

Writing in 1928 in the *Historische Zeitschrift*, Meinecke tried to offer an alternative to Rickert's discussion of historical objectivity. In his essay "Causality and Values in History," he identified the fundamental polarity of cause and value with the Kantian antinomy of necessity and freedom, arguing that these categories were ultimately related to the philosophical logic that separated generalizing and individualizing methods within the sciences.[78] At the outset Meinecke identified three great traditions in German thought which attempted to resolve the causality-value problem: the positivist-naturalist school of empiricism, the vitalist (*Lebensphilosophie*) theory of *Verstehen* (understanding), and the Neo-Kantian tradition of historical logic.[79] The positivist tradition, Meinecke argued, attempted to eradicate subjective value

---

[78] Friedrich Meinecke, "Kausalitäten und Werte," in *Zur Theorie und Philosophie der Geschichte* (Stuttgart: Koehler, 1959), 61–89.

[79] For an extensive treatment of Meinecke's critique of these three traditions, see Walter Hofer, *Geschichtsschreibung und Weltanschauung*, pt. 1 (Munich: Oldenbourg, 1950), 39–318.

through objective science, whereas the vitalist stressed value at the cost of rigor; the Neo-Kantian, however, attempted to resolve the problem by applying the Kantian category of causality to the science of values. Meinecke had great sympathy for Rickert's epistemological labors and even supported his scientific aims; ultimately, though, he criticized Rickert for laying too much emphasis on questions of causality at the expense of the historian's life-interests and individual identity.

Against both the positivists and vitalists, Rickert tried to combine causality and values in a scientific manner, demonstrating that without the notion of cause, history as a form of science must peremptorily cease. He challenged the positivist assumption that historical causality could be explained in terms of the law-seeking, natural-scientific category of cause and effect. Historical causality, Rickert argued, was individual, not general, the result of a unique process of events causally ordered without being universally necessary.[80] The causes involved in Friedrich Wilhelm IV's rejection of the German crown, for example, were unique and unrepeatable. On the basis of this singular incident, one could not construct a universal theory of imperial succession. But historical research could still offer a scientific interpretation of events by relating the unique cause to a universal value, such as political power, thereby guaranteeing that what holds an interest for the historical scientist is never merely personal but is determined by the causal process of history itself. In this sense, history serves as the objectified expression of timeless universal values. In selecting pertinent material, the historian is not expressing a subjective opinion but is merely referring to values. Meinecke responded to Rickert's argument by claiming that this line of reasoning did not adequately reflect the realities of historical scholarship.

Meinecke agreed with Rickert that the historian selected out of an infinity of temporal events according to a certain principle of universally shared cultural values: "Behind the search for causalities there always lies, directly or indirectly, the search for values, the search for what is called culture."[81] Yet he did not accept Rickert's contention that historians, in their office as cultural scientists, had merely to refer to values rather than actually evaluate past events.[82] In answer to the

---

[80] Rickert, *Die Grenzen*, 376–377.
[81] Fritz Stern, ed., *Varieties of History* (New York: World, 1958), 273; and Meinecke, *Zur Theorie und Philosophie*, 68.
[82] Rickert, *Die Grenzen*, 335.

question of whether the historian could fulfill the condition of elim-inating all subjective tendencies, Meinecke simply replied, "It cannot be."[83] He maintained that: "Even the mere selection of value-related facts is impossible without an evaluation. It would only be possible if the values to which the facts related subsisted, as Rickert thinks, solely in general categories like religion, state, law, etc. But the histo-rian selects his material not only according to general categories like these but also according to his *living interest* in the concrete content of the material. He lays hold of it as something more or less of value, and in this he is evaluating it."[84]

For Meinecke, evaluation was "not merely a superfluous by-prod-uct of the historian's activity." He agreed with Rickert that "'the his-torian can abstain from value-judgment of his object'" but, he noted, "history written without such a valuation is either mere amassing of material and preparation for genuine historical writing or, in claiming to be genuine history, is insipid."[85] The historian must, Meinecke felt, take a stance on the valuation of historical material, and such a valua-tion had, necessarily, to be subjective. The subjectivity of one's posi-tion was part of one's method and defined one's activity as a scientist of cultural objects. In the fifth edition of *Die Grenzen* (revised espe-cially to answer Meinecke's objections), Rickert responded by arguing that any concession to subjectivity undermined the logical ideal of *Wissenschaft*.[86] To evaluate history subjectively was to move away from the objective demands of a science. At the heart of Rickert's dispute with Meinecke over questions of logic and objectivity, how-ever, was a fundamental disagreement over what constituted the proper sphere of philosophical "subjectivity." Whereas Rickert held to a Kantian notion of the transcendental subject, Meinecke (in following the historicist notion of *Verstehen*) defined subjectivity in vitalist terms as an ability "to enter into the very souls of those who acted [attempt-ing] through artistic intuition to give new life to life gone by—which cannot be done without a transfusion of one's own life blood."[87] On Meinecke's reading, subjectivity constituted in itself a singular value that secured for individuals their own raison d'être apart from any universal principle or law. Following Herder's neoclassical ideal of

[83] Stern, *Varieties of History*, 273; Meinecke, *Zur Theorie und Philosophie*, 68–69.
[84] Stern, *Varieties of History*, 273; Meinecke, *Zur Theorie und Philosophie*, 68–69.
[85] Stern, *Varieties of History*, 497; Meinecke, *Zur Theorie und Philosophie*, 68.
[86] Rickert, *Die Grenzen*, 335.
[87] Stern, *Varieties of History*, 283; Meinecke, *Zur Theorie und Philosophie*, 82.

Humanität, Meinecke believed that each individual entity is formed and shaped according to its own value, which in turn is always relative to its historical development. The optimistic tone of his liberal-humanist historicism notwithstanding, Meinecke understood that this doctrine of value relativity might still fall victim to the dangers of "relativism, anarchy, accident, and arbitrariness."[88] He remained adamant in his conviction that the only way to prevent the nihilistic consequences of relativism from overtaking German life would be a profound commitment to moral conscience and "faith."[89] Historical truth might be relative, but Meinecke remained convinced that there is an "unknown absolute" that serves as "the creative ground of all values." Even if "historicism and relativism belong together," Meinecke conceded, relativism need not be injurious.[90] The demands placed on the individual subject "could act as either life-enhancing or life-negating."[91] In any case, the consequences would be ethical and engage issues of life (*Leben*), not mere science (*Wissenschaft*). Ultimately, for Meinecke, questions of value and culture were religious and metaphysical and could never be resolved by logic or epistemology. The way out of the dangers of relativism, subjectivism, and historicism lay in the acceptance of "the primal irrational ground of the soul."[92]

viii. Rickert's Response to the Problems of Historicism

Meinecke's essay was animated by personal concerns about the vital character of historical scholarship, concerns that reflected his reading of Nietzsche's essay "On the Uses and Disadvantages of History for Life."[93] Like Nietzsche, Meinecke spoke of "the use of history for the creative life" and "the use of historical thought for the present,"

[88] Stern, *Varieties of History*, 283; Meinecke, *Zur Theorie und Philosophie*, 82.
[89] Stern, *Varieties of History*, 283; Meinecke, *Zur Theorie und Philosophie*, 82.
[90] Friedrich Meinecke, *Die Entstehung des Historismus* (Munich: Oldenbourg, 1965), 94 and 577; and *Zur Theorie und Philosophie*, 203.
[91] Meinecke, *Zur Theorie und Philosophie*, 204.
[92] Meinecke, *Die Entstehung des Historismus*, 95. See especially the excellent article by Jörn Rüsen, "Friedrich Meineckes *Entstehung des Historismus*," in Michael Erbe, ed., *Friedrich Meinecke Heute* (Berlin: Colloquium, 1981), 76–99.
[93] See the introduction to Friedrich Meinecke, *Historism*, trans. J. E. Anderson (London: Routledge, 1972), l–li. See also Friedrich Meinecke, *Vom geschichtlichen Sinn und vom Sinn der Geschichte* (Leipzig: Koehler and Amelang, 1939), 13; and Friedrich Nietzsche, *Untimely Meditations*, trans. R. J. Hollingdale (Cambridge: Cambridge University Press, 1983), 57–123.

invoking Goethe as his symbol for the creative historical sensibility.[94] Where Nietzsche saw the surfeit of historical culture as an expression of decadence, however, deeming it unhealthy and nihilistic, Meinecke embraced it as an affirmation of life's vital tendencies. He admitted that historicism might lead to relativism and nihilism, but he countered these apprehensions by pointing to the positive opportunities they opened up. He was convinced that facing the dangers of historical relativism would force one to confront an ethical choice in the present. In Meinecke's words, "That which makes us spiritually richer, which brings us into immediate 'life-contact' with the people and treasures of the past, which teaches us to *understand* the rhythm of eternal becoming and transformation in the fates of men and nations—all that can not only carry a destructive element but must also possess a creative power within itself."[95] Consequently, in his reflections on the crisis of historical relativism, Meinecke termed historicism a "life-problem in the highest sense."[96] To perceive historicism as a threat to culture was to misunderstand gravely its ethical value. In *Die Entstehung des Historismus*, Meinecke wrote: "We can discern in it [historicism] the highest stage so far reached in the understanding of human affairs and are confident that it will be able to develop sufficiently to tackle the problems of human history that still confront us. We believe that it has the power to heal the wounds it has caused by the relativizing of all values, provided that it can find the men to convert this '-ism' into the terms of authentic life."[97] For Rickert, the foundations of Meinecke's *Fragestellung*, the very terms in which he posed the question of historicism, were philosophically inadmissible.

Meinecke's emphasis on life as the starting point of historical inquiry seemed fanciful and destructive to Rickert. In his polemical *Die Philosophie des Lebens* (1922), Rickert rejected Meinecke's vitalist presuppositions, insisting that "in philosophizing about life, a philosophy of *mere* life is not enough."[98] Philosophy required the rigor of logic and *Wissenschaft*. Life experience, hypostatized as an epistemological principle, undermined both. In identifying the source of value as life and the ethical demands made on life by conscience and faith, Meinecke had succumbed to the relativizing of all value. His

[94] Meinecke, *Vom geschichtlichen Sinn*, 13 and 97.
[95] Ibid. In "Values and Causality in History" Meinecke writes, "Without a strong desire for values, causal inquiry becomes a lifeless task." Stern, *Varieties of History*, 276.
[96] Meinecke, *Zur Theorie und Philosophie*, 341.
[97] Meinecke, *Historism*, lvii.
[98] Rickert, *Die Philosophie des Lebens*, vii.

emphasis on vitalist, romantic, and Nietzschean readings of value had only succeeded in reproducing the clichés of historicism, making it a surrogate form of *Weltanschauung.*

Rickert countered Meinecke's vitalist historicism with a transcendental critique of historical method. Rejecting the hermeneutic theory of *Verstehen*, Rickert argued that to have knowledge of an object was not to experience it intuitively or through sympathetic identification but to construct it formally according to principles of concept-formation. Understanding, for Rickert, was a logical rather than psychological process that overcomes the subjectivity of historical experience by appealing to a nonhistorical subject: Kant's transcendental ego. In the *System der Philosophie*, Rickert tried to establish the logical ground of value by reference to a "third realm"—the "pro-physical"—a realm of formal validity independent of the two realms of mind and body, *Geist* and *Natur*, on which the old classification of the sciences rested. In this formal realm of values—a logician's Elysian fields—Rickert believed he could offer a remedy for the poisons of Meinecke's historicism.

For Rickert, the pro-physical world differs from the world of traditional metaphysics not by being "above" or "beyond" (*meta*) the experiential physical world but by being "prior to" or "before" (*pro*) it. Priority, in Rickert's terms, is not to be understood in a temporal sense, however, as coming before the physical world chronologically. Rather, pro-physical means that this realm precedes the physical world conceptually. That is, unlike the world of experience which is bound to objects and to the necessary conditions that govern their existence, the pro-physical world is pre-objective and without necessary condition. For example, Rickert maintained that all our perceptions of objective reality (trees, rocks, flowers), as well as our understanding of nonobjective complexes of meaning (*Sinngebilde*, e.g., the semantics of a sentence, the meaning of a Beethoven adagio, mathematical functions), despite their many differences, all share one common function: each stands apart from us as things (*Gegenstände*) rather than as subjects. These *Gegenstände* are bound by laws of causal necessity within a specific space-time continuum. As empirical subjects with both physical and psychological properties, we, too, Rickert argued, stand under the same causal laws. But what enables us to bridge the chasm between the empirical subject and the empirical object is a nonempirical, transcendental realm which is *conceptually* prior to experience and which grounds all our knowledge in a priori validity. Within Rickert's philosophy, value is grounded in a pro-physical, transcendental realm that has only axiological validity and not ontological existence. All our experience in the temporal world is at first made possible by this transcendental ground, which, in contrast to the causal laws guiding nature, allows for a dimension of freedom. As Rickert explained in his *System*, "The freedom of the act lies prior to or before the reality of causally conditioned objects. It makes this reality at all 'possible.'. . . Causality reigns over the real world of objects and the world of the psychological subject; however, this world would be without any basis if there were not a realm of freedom, through which we had to pass in order to attain it."[99] All causality, all objectivity, Rickert goes on to say, would be impossible without freedom. It is only the free act of the subject which first grounds the world of the object and which allows us to conceive of such a world, thus making knowledge at all possible. In his appeals to this third pro-physical realm of freedom, Rickert believed he could overcome the vitalist and hermeneutic tendencies in Meinecke's understanding of history and prepare the way for a thoroughgoing critique of historicist principles. Historicist *Verstehen* had merely elevated subjective inferences to the status of a methodological precept, raising practical evaluation over theoretical value-reference. Such an approach, Rickert charged, was "monstrous."[100]

In *Die Probleme der Geschichtsphilosophie*, Rickert spoke out clearly against historicism, seeing it as part of the whole crisis mode of Weimar culture:

> Indeed, this historicism, which appears as something so positive, proves itself (as soon as it is carried to its logical conclusion) as a form of relativism which can only lead to nihilism. . . . This kind of historicism, if it were truly logical, would have to admit every temporal object as worthy of being historical and, therefore, could attach itself to no thing precisely because it would have to attach itself to all things. Historicism thus makes a principle out of thinking without principles and raises that to a *Weltanschauung*. As such, it is to be decisively combated by both the philosophy of history and philosophy in general.[101]

In his unpublished lectures he continued his assaults, calling historicism "unsystematic," "relativistic," and "antiphilosophical."[102] In *The*

---

[99] Rickert, *System*, 305.
[100] Rickert, *Die Probleme der Geschichtsphilosophie*, 129.
[101] Ibid., 129–130.
[102] Rickert, *Hd.Ms. 115*, draft no.1, 3; *Hd.Ms. 115*, draft no.2, 4; *Hd.Ms. 13*, 27; and *Hd.Ms. 31*, 760. These phrases recur frequently throughout the various manuscripts.

Limits of Concept Formation in Natural Science, he made it clear that he "decisively rejected all forms of historicism" as "dangerous and one-sided"; historicism "was either relativistic and nihilistic or it covered its negativity and emptiness by choosing this or that form of historical life in order to find the contents of its *Weltanschauung*."[103] In the *System der Philosophie*, he echoed similar sentiments.[104] The problem with Meinecke, Troeltsch, and the other historicists was that they refused to go beyond the "merely historical."[105] As Rickert always maintained, "History was in no position to solve philosophical problems for itself."[106] The answers must come from philosophy. Any solution to the crisis concerning historical knowledge must itself be free of historical relativism. Hence, as Rickert saw it, if philosophy were truly to "overcome" the crisis of historicism, it would first have to redefine the basic *Fragestellung* of historical inquiry. In an effort to do so, Rickert turned to the Kantian principle of ethics.

If the values of Meinecke and other historicists represented a personal decision of conscience and conviction, Rickert's timeless, absolute values constituted an ethical imperative (*Sollen*) of universal humanity. These values were in themselves ahistorical and without content, just as the historical world was in itself valueless and ethically neutral. Rickert's task was to show how these ahistorical values could serve as the ground for a transcendental subject who stood opposed to the empirical-psychological subject of the historical world. In actual practice, Rickert admitted, the historical subject attempts to concretize ethical demands by bringing to fruition certain projects, goals, aims, and so forth, which we call culture. In culture one seeks to reconcile the gap between the "is" and the "ought" (*Sein* and *Sollen*), between meaningless being and meaning-laden history. Such a reconciliation can never be completed, however, because there is always some imperfect distance between the reality of history and the ideality of value. And yet the meaning of historical life is grounded in the attempt to overcome this distance and achieve a universal value— a task that is "insoluble," according to Rickert. Consequently, the philosophy of history is never able to offer a final truth. The values that it attempts to systematize serve as a kind of "Kantian *Idee* whose realization becomes the goal for all cultures that must, nonetheless, labor

[103] Rickert, *Die Grenzen*, 8 and 736.
[104] Rickert, *System*, 19 and 321.
[105] Rickert, *Die Grenzen*, 697.
[106] Ibid.

under the knowledge that theirs is a never-ending task."[107] These transcendental values serve a dual function in that they guide the scientist's search for objectivity as well as providing cultural meaning for the historical process itself. In this sense, they offer a practical solution to problems of historical knowledge and meaning by demonstrating that the subject, too, stands under the imperative to attain an ethical goal. As Rickert wrote in *Grundprobleme der Philosophie*: "Without the tension between two forms of being—i.e., without the duality of what is [*Sein*] real and what is not yet real but which should become real [*Sollen*]—there is absolutely no meaning to life. Without this tension the striving to realize unique values in cultural objects would not come to pass."[108] It is precisely this ethical imperative that guides the work of both the natural scientist and the historian, Rickert insisted, for scientific activity is nothing but the attempt to bridge the chasm between what is and what ought to be. Truth itself, as the highest value of science, demands that science be grounded in freedom and not necessity. Only this freedom to move from *Sein* to *Sollen* can bring about the realization of truth as the expression of value. Thus, Rickert concluded: "We must see all the theories that believe they can reject the idea of freedom as being theoretically invalid. The crucial reason for this is that science itself needs freedom even when investigating causal connections. Only a theoretical (transcendental) subject who is not dependent on causality can take a position on the value of truth. Only when we grant the possibility of such a subject can we recognize something as being true and meaningful."[109]

In recognizing the primacy of freedom as an ethical imperative within science itself, Rickert believed he had transformed Windelband's methodological inquiries into genuine questions of value. Epistemological considerations aside, Rickert could agree with his adversary Nietzsche that "the question of value is more fundamental than the question of certainty: the latter becomes serious only by presupposing that the value question has already been answered."[110] Within the realm of freedom, Rickert believed he had overcome charges of formalism, because freedom implied autonomy, and autonomy, activity. Ultimately, the fundamental goal of his philosophy of

---

[107] Rickert, *Die Probleme der Geschichtsphilosophie*, 119.
[108] Rickert, *Grundprobleme der Philosophie*, 228–229.
[109] Ibid., 231–232.
[110] Friedrich Nietzsche, *The Will to Power*, trans. Walter Kaufmann and R. J. Hollingdale (New York: Random House, 1968), 322.

history was not theoretical or formal method but practical, vital truth. Rickert's final answer to the crisis of historicism was to affirm the primacy of Fichte's transcendental subject, a subject that grounded itself through its own freedom and through its practical demand for self-realization (*Bildung*), thereby providing ethical meaning (*Sinn/Sollen*) in the meaningless world of historical being (*Sein*).

ix. Rickert's Philosophy of History

Despite Rickert's attempts to overcome charges of formalism in his work, many felt his approach to problems of historical life remained insular and overly theoretical. Ernst Troeltsch, for example, criticized Rickert for being too formal in both his system of values and his understanding of concrete historical experience. He argued that Rickert's transcendental logic explained all psychological facts as part of the spatial-physical "heterogeneous continuum" without acknowledging the role of the irrational.[111] The effect of such an approach was to undermine the very bond that allowed the historian to understand the past; as Troeltsch put it, "As soon as one starts from ideas and standards, one falls into an unhistorical rationalism and loses contact with empirical history and its practice."[112] Friedrich Meinecke, in an essay written a few years after Troeltsch's death, expressed similar sentiments. Although praising Rickert for his noteworthy methodological contributions, Meinecke nonetheless tried to show that philosophy could only go so far in explaining historical reality: "Determination of the essence of values is the chief concern of modern philosophy. The historian may seek to learn from this discussion, but he need not and cannot refrain from forming an idea of the essence of values based on his own *experience*. From the standpoint of the philosopher, this idea will appear to be too sketchy, ambiguous, and therefore insufficient. But because it is drawn from the practice of historical inquiry, it will possess more instinctive certainty, perhaps, than the one which arises from more logical-abstract procedures."[113] Meinecke's critique was echoed by many of his contemporaries.

[111] On his critique of Rickert, see especially Ernst Troeltsch, "Die Geisteswissenschaften und der Streit um Rickert," *Schmoellers Jahrbuch* 46 (1922): 35–64.

[112] Troeltsch, *Der Historismus und seine Probleme*, 162. For another approach to Rickert's transcendental theory of value, see Alfred Stern, *Philosophy of History and the Problem of Values* (Berkeley: University of California Press, 1962), 134.

[113] Friedrich Meinecke, "Values and Causality in History," in Stern, *Varieties of History*, 277–278; and Meinecke, *Zur Theorie und Philosophie*, 74.

In writing his own logic of historical inquiry, *The Problems of the Philosophy of History*, Georg Simmel warned of the dangers of being too abstract when dealing with the actual experience involved in historical research. To do so created a state of "artificial isolation in which epistemology transposes or displaces methods that are inextricably linked in the actual praxis of research . . . in consequence, the epistemological analysis of these sciences does not seem to be germane to their real structure at all. By reflecting on the process of research, it seems to create its own structure of the sciences, a structure which it projects into their real form."[114] Simmel, Meinecke, and Troeltsch were only a few of those who criticized Rickert for what they felt to be his neglect of the actual circumstances of historical praxis. These life-philosophers and historicists wished to inquire into the vital and historical ground of knowledge, an area that Rickert, with his transcendental system of value, had sorely neglected. The most prescient critique, however, came from Dilthey, who agreed with Rickert that value was the key to historical science. In his *Nachlass* Dilthey wrote that "without the determination of values in the historical material and the historical process, neither historical reality nor historical study are conceivable." Only when "such values are not transcendental values, but life-values," Dilthey explained, could they have any meaning for history.[115] Rickert had erred when he wished to interpret historical life-values as the expression of "a priori objective-teleological values" akin to Kant's categories.[116] Historical values, Dilthey insisted, derived their validity not from their ideal status as the transcendental ground of activity but in their real effect on historical beings.[117]

In his "Critique of Historical Reason," Dilthey attempted to overcome Rickert's "transcendental formalism" by rooting the method of the *Geisteswissenschaften* in the historical development of *Geist* itself. Like Rickert, he was interested in developing a new theory of historical knowledge which would secure the status of genuine science for historical inquiry while simultaneously granting its independence from all natural-scientific method. But where Rickert had undertaken a transcendental approach modeled on Kant's critique of natural

[114] Georg Simmel, *Problems of the Philosophy of History* (New York: Free Press, 1977), 147.
[115] This quotation from Dilthey is part of the unpublished *Nachlass* but has been cited by Michael Ermarth, *William Dilthey: The Critique of Historical Reason* (Chicago: University of Chicago Press, 1976), 194.
[116] Ibid.
[117] Ibid, 193–197.

science and mathematics, Dilthey pressed for a radically human-centered, hermeneutic form of logic. In Dilthey's reading, differences between nature and history could not be traced back merely to contrasting forms of concept-formation. Rather, he argued, there was something in our experience itself which made us capable of understanding history that could not be circumscribed by natural-scientific method. He concurred with Rickert that the proper approach to history must be scientific, but his aim was to establish a science whose ground was history itself. Human beings "belonged to history," Dilthey contended, and their knowledge of the historical world was grounded in this "belonging." Hence, for Dilthey, history was never merely an object, never a *Gegen-stand* that stood over and apart from a subject. A theory of the sciences which insisted on the *Gegenständlichkeit* (objectivity) of history could never hope to capture this uniquely human bond to the past.[118]

Neo-Kantian epistemology was rooted in the Kantian question, How is objective (*gegenständliche*) experience possible? By following the basic tenets of Kant's theory of natural-scientific knowledge, Rickert believed he could offer an epistemologically secured theory of historical truth. But in carrying over the Kantian critique of nature to a transcendental critique of history, Dilthey claimed, Rickert left out the essential character of the historical experience itself, namely, its historicity. For Rickert, the historical object, much like the object that we term "natural," was simply "there" for the historical observer, its reality having already been determined by a transcendental concept-formation generated out of the categories of mind. Following this Kantian outline, Rickert argued that a science of history must interrogate the historical object in terms of its logical structure, an approach that defined the very method of Neo-Kantian thinking. Historicist thinkers such as Meinecke and Troeltsch, however, had serious misgivings about this Neo-Kantian strategy. Though they acknowledged that by stressing ideas of value and individuality Rickert had captured the essence of historical thinking, they nonetheless believed that in so doing he had also denied the possibility of genuine historical development.[119] In their view, Rickert's tendency to overemphasize the

---

[118] To define history as a *"Gegenstand"* was to see it as only an inert "fact," not as a vital, living, and organic bond to the present—namely, as something experienced. This, in fact, is the key difference between Dilthey's understanding of history in hermeneutic terms and Rickert's view of a logic of historical knowledge.

[119] Troeltsch, *Der Historismus und seine Probleme*, 236.

Kantian category of causality succeeded only in eliminating the dynamic and vital process of historical becoming. That history was essentially *past* history and not something that was simply "there" in
the present for the historian waiting to be "known" was completely
overlooked by Rickert. In effect, the fact of temporal distance did not
constitute a logical problem in Rickert's theory of historical concept-
formation.[120] He was far more interested in the forms of scientific presentation and in the logical synthesis of historical material. He hardly
noticed that the historical individual was not a given "fact of knowledge" (like Hermann Cohen's mathematical-logical *Faktum der Erkenntnis*) but was itself subject to the myriad changes and interpretive possibilities of temporal being.[121] As Troeltsch noted, "He knows or
recognizes only the Kantian mathematical concept of time and not the
concept of historical time or concrete duration."[122] Ultimately, Rickert's
Kantian causality, when applied to history, resulted in a world of
static historical objects without any development. In this world of discrete objects without temporal change, there was only factuality, no
historicity.

Rickert's critics were also concerned about his blind disregard for
the historicity of the human being. They maintained that his notion of
the transcendental subject missed the essential attributes of historical
consciousness, because a subject grounded in logic rather than historical reality could hardly be expected to understand the concrete dynamic of cultural change. Against Rickert's timeless, transcendental
subject, Troeltsch and Meinecke argued for a temporal subject who
understands that history offers a "horizon" for the human understanding of the past. In affirming the positive sense of this boundary
line beyond which human thought could not go, Troeltsch and
Meinecke were following Nietzsche, who, in the second of his "Untimely Meditations," spoke of "the historical horizon" of human consciousness as a life-enhancing possibility.[123] All knowledge takes the

[120] This basic criticism is a Heideggerian one and has been put forth in an excellent
dissertation by Berger, "Gegenstandskonstitution," who treats Rickert's epistemology
from a hermeneutic perspective.
[121] For a fuller discussion of Hermann Cohen, see Klaus Christian Köhnke, *Entstehung
und Aufstieg des Neukantianismus: Die deutsche Universitätsphilosophie zwischen Idealismus
und Positivismus* (Frankfurt: Suhrkamp, 1986).
[122] Troeltsch, *Der Historismus und seine Probleme*, 236.
[123] Nietzsche mentions this idea in his second "untimely meditation" of history, but
the concept is rich in meaning within the German tradition at large. For a more modern
view, see Hans-Georg Gadamer, *Kleine Schriften*, vol. 1 (Tübingen: Mohr, 1970), 7. Ludwig Landgrebe, *Major Problems in Contemporary European Philosophy*, trans. Kurt Rein-

form of interpretation, Nietzsche argued. We can only approach truth from a limited perspective that is bound temporally by a historical horizon and bound spatially by cultural tradition. We are embedded in a historical moment, Nietzsche wrote, so that the more actively we seek to step out of this congeries of prejudice and circumstance to deny the limitations of the moment, the further we move away from any knowledge that has claim to human value. But Rickert was not moved by Nietzsche's critique or the historicist writings of Troeltsch and Meinecke. In an effort to "overcome" the limitations of the "horizon," Rickert sought to ground history in a timeless system of absolute validity. In turning away from the perspectivism of the moment, he offered a transcendental theory of history which did not really resolve the underlying crisis in historicist thinking.

The most powerful critique of Rickert's work came from one of his students at the University of Freiburg, Martin Heidegger, who pointed toward the untenability of his transcendental *Fragestellung*.[124] Heidegger, following Dilthey, stressed that the ground of historical science was not logic but the temporal categories of human existence. Heidegger went on to affirm that an object "becomes" historical not as a result of logical concept-formation but from its rootedness in temporal being. The historical object must not be seen as a mere "fact" that is "there" for historical science but should be understood as a form of being that has taken on the character of temporal distance. To reduce history to a mere object is to lose the fundamental connection to the past. As Heidegger explained in *Being and Time*:

> Even if the problem of 'history' is treated in accordance with a theory of science, not only aiming at the 'epistemological' clarification of the historical way of grasping things (Simmel)—or—at the logic of concept-formation in an historical presentation (Rickert), but doing so with an orientation towards 'the side of the object,' then, as long as the question is formulated this way, history becomes accessible only as the *object* of a science. Thus the basic phenomenon of history (which is prior to any possible thematizing by historical science) has been irretrievably put aside. How history can become a possible *object* for historical science is something that may be gathered

hardt (New York: Unger, 1966), 17, defines "horizon" as "the situational locus in which man finds himself embedded at any given time."

[124] Heidegger wrote his habilitation under Rickert in 1916; within months, Rickert moved to Heidelberg to replace Windelband, and Heidegger began to work more closely with Husserl. For more on Heidegger's critique of Rickert, see Chap. 5.

only from the kind of being which belongs to that which is historical—from its historicity and from the way it is rooted in temporality.[125]

By 1927, when Heidegger's *Being and Time* was published, Neo-Kantianism was on the wane. Rickert was nearing the end of his career, and his influence was diminishing. The charges of "formalism" and of "transcendental abstraction" were still leveled by the historicists and life-philosophers, but now a whole new critique of Rickert's historical logic began to emerge. With Heidegger's new emphasis on the historicity of being, the fundamental question of the Neo-Kantians had been altered. As Ludwig Landgrebe noted, Heidegger's true contribution to the debate concerning the crisis of historicism was to show that "a philosophical foundation of the Geisteswissenschaften could not be attained without a new ontology"—the task of *Being and Time*.[126] There, as in his Marburg lectures, *The History of the Concept of Time* (1925), Heidegger attacked both Windelband and Rickert for what he called their "empty methodology."[127] In stressing the transcendental conditions of our knowledge, he claimed: "No longer do they inquire into the structure of these realities themselves. Their theme is merely the question concerning the logical structure of scientific presentation. This goes so far that in Rickert's theory of the sciences, the sciences that he treats are no longer recognizable. He merely lays down schemes of sciences. This disfiguring and trivialization of Dilthey's *Fragestellung* had the dubious result of hiding its genuine meaning and of hindering until now its positive consequence."[128]

It was Dilthey's positive accomplishment, according to Heidegger, to move away from the Neo-Kantian concern with "empty method" and redirect philosophy's attention to reality itself. Against the pure formalism of the Baden school, in his work Dilthey turned to the temporal-historical dimension of life as the basis for the study of the *Geisteswissenschaften*. And yet in the "trivialization" of Dilthey's *Fragestellung* by Rickert and Windelband, Heidegger identified an impasse, or aporia, in the work of academic philosophy which helped spur a crisis in history, philosophy, and the other sciences. From the

---

[125] Martin Heidegger, *Being and Time*, trans. John Macquarrie and Edward Robinson (New York: Harper and Row, 1962), 427; *Sein und Zeit* (Tübingen: Niemeyer, 1976), 375.

[126] Landgrebe, *Major Problems in Contemporary European Philosophy*, 119.

[127] Martin Heidegger, *Prolegomena zur Geschichte des Zeitbegriffes*, *Gesamtausgabe* 20 (Frankfurt: Klostermann, 1979), 20.

[128] Ibid.

period of Heidegger's *Being and Time*, one can speak of an "ontological turn" in German philosophy which was to have profound consequences for the traditional approach to the human sciences. With this new emphasis on the meaning of historicity in the work of Dilthey and Heidegger, the very form of the question concerning historical truth shifts from Rickert's epistemological inquiry to an ontological concern with historical being, an issue that will command our attention in the next two chapters.

In focusing on this ontological reading, I want to show that an understanding of the crisis of historicism requires a broader *Fragestellung* than the one offered in the standard interpretations of scholars such as Iggers, Rüsen, and others. Their outstanding work has helped to clarify the disciplinary matrix and professional aims of historicist thinkers. By laying bare the ideological presuppositions and political loyalties in historicist thought, these historians have succeeded in opening up the whole controversy over methods in the late nineteenth and early twentieth centuries. But this disciplinary focus on the historical profession has obscured the real contribution of philosophers to the historicist tradition. The emphasis on problems of research, methodology, and objectivity by both the Neo-Kantians and Dilthey should not conceal the underlying meaning of their generational debate, which is, I believe, ultimately philosophical rather than historiographical. What interested these philosophers were the epistemological, axiological, and ontological consequences of the historicist position, especially as they related to the question of scientific truth. Historicism comes to prominence within the frame and structure of a science and challenges the traditional understanding of natural-scientific logic as a universal standard of truth. The "crisis" of historicism in this sense is really nothing other than the coming to self-consciousness of the temporal, historical, cultural, and institutional character of scientific inquiry itself—a topic that we now conveniently label "postmodern." But in opening up the metaphysical contradictions at work in the scientific demand for objective truth, historicism simultaneously reveals the contradictions at the heart of the modernist vision. Writing at the time of this emergent modernist tradition, Heidegger and Dilthey were both aware of what was at stake in the whole discussion about "crisis."

Heidegger's *Destruktion* of subject/object thinking develops as a response to the kind of scientific-historical questions posed by Rickert and Dilthey. As he tries to show in his critique of Spengler, historical thinking can never be understood merely in terms of history or historiography but is always tied to a metaphysical interpretation of human being within the horizon(s) of time. In this temporal sense, history (*Geschichte*) is first and foremost a "happening" (*Geschehen*), a phenomenon of historical enactment rather than a cultural object or scientific source. Dilthey's work helped to make this processual character of historical existence clear. But, again, the real focus of his critique was not historical research as such but the meaning of historicity for human existence. Hence any attempt to connect the work of Heidegger or Dilthey to the tradition of *Historik* (disciplinary reflection on the research practices of history) remains problematic at best. What remains central to their work is an awareness that the crisis of historicism—or, more properly, what is at issue in this crisis—represents the tensions within the project of modernity itself: of a subject/object tradition of scientific inquiry which goes back to the Cartesian demand for a reliable method of philosophical inquiry. These contradictions can be clearly seen in Dilthey's work, which offers a model for the kind of crisis-thinking which marks German philosophy in the first quarter of the twentieth century.

CHAPTER FOUR

Wilhelm Dilthey's Critique of Historical Reason

The knife of historical relativism . . . which has cut to pieces all metaphysics and religion must also bring about healing. Only we need to be thorough. We have to make philosophy itself an object of philosophical concern.
—Wilhelm Dilthey, *Zur Weltanschaungslehre*

i. Dilthey's Project

Writing in the *Preussische Jahrbücher* of 1871 to pay tribute to a colleague, the recently deceased historian of philosophy Friedrich Überweg, Dilthey offered some thoughts on the contemporary situation within nineteenth-century German philosophy. After praising Überweg for his splendid multivolume *History of Philosophy* and his *System of Logic*, Dilthey went on to offer a note of criticism. Despite his impressive erudition and careful scholarship, Überweg, Dilthey explained, had failed to address "the fundamental and one of the most important tasks in philosophy today: the establishment of a valid theory of scientific knowledge."[1] Like his contemporaries Rickert and Windel-

[1] Wilhelm Dilthey, *Gesammelte Schriften*, vol. 15 (Göttingen: Vandenhoeck & Ruprecht, 1970), 156. The collected works of Dilthey, which extend to twenty volumes, were first published in 1914 and interrupted for some two decades by various problems. The first twelve volumes were reprinted after 1956, and only then were later ones added. Volume 19 was published in 1982, and volume 20, in 1990. Two volumes of a projected six-volume edition of Dilthey's *Selected Works*, edited by Rudolf Makkreel and Frithjof Rodi, have already been published by Princeton University Press. For a fuller bibliographic history of the Dilthey project, see Ulrich Herrmann, *Bibliographie Wilhelm*

band, Dilthey was convinced that establishing just such "a valid theory of scientific knowledge" stood as the great task confronting German philosophy.

With the publication of his *Introduction to the Human Sciences* (1883), Dilthey presented his first conception of such a theory. For the next three decades, he set to work on providing a fully developed epistemology of the human sciences in a range of studies on psychology, anthropology, logic, hermeneutics, literature, social thought, and history. Although the subject matter of these writings was diverse, ranging from the poetry of Hölderlin and the metaphysics of Descartes to the psychology of Brentano and the hermeneutics of Chladenius, the essential form of the question about the "ground" of knowledge in the human sciences remained the same.[2] How can we, Dilthey asked,

---

Dilthey: Quellen und Literatur (Basel: Beltz, 1969). For a more recent discussion of the Dilthey literature, see the yearly reviews in the *Dilthey-Jahrbuch*, vols. 1–8. A helpful summary of the recent trend in Dilthey interpretation can also be found in the first chapter of Hans-Ulrich Lessing, *Die Idee einer Kritik der historischen Vernunft* (Freiburg: Alber, 1984), in the introduction to Hans-Ulrich Lessing and Frithjof Rodi, *Materialien zur Philosophie Wilhelm Diltheys* (Frankfurt: Suhrkamp, 1984), and in the two excellent collections of essays edited by Ernst Wolfgang Orth, *Dilthey und die Philosophie der Gegenwart* (Freiburg: Alber, 1985) and *Dilthey und der Wandel des Philosophiebegriffs seit dem 19. Jahrhundert* (Freiburg: Alber, 1984), both from the Dilthey Conference of 1983, which celebrated the centennial publication of Dilthey's *Einleitung in die Geisteswissenschaften*. Also helpful are Hans-Ulrich Lessing's introduction to *Wilhelm Dilthey: Texte zur Kritik der historischen Vernunft* (Göttingen: Vandenhoeck & Ruprecht, 1983), 9–24; Otto Pöggeler's introduction to Wilhelm Dilthey, *Das Wesen der Philosophie* (Hamburg: Meiner, 1984), vii–xlvi; and Rudolf Makkreel and Frithjof Rodi's introduction to Wilhelm Dilthey, *Introduction to the Human Sciences* (Princeton, N.J.: Princeton University Press, 1989), 3–42. In the notes that follow, all references to the *Gesammelte Schriften*, 20 vols. (Göttingen: Vandenhoeck & Ruprecht, 1957–1990) will be noted as *GS* with the corresponding volume and page number; when I use the notation *GS* after an English translation (separated by a semi-colon) this refers to the corresponding German source.
[2] The term *Geisteswissenschaft(en)* is a crucial one for Dilthey and needs to be understood within the context of late-nineteenth-century German thought in general. Translated variously as "human sciences," "human studies," or "humanities," the term goes back to the 1849 Schiel translation into German of John Stuart Mill's *System of Logic*. Ironically, the German word first appeared as a rough equivalent of Mill's term "moral sciences," but this concept is far too narrow and specific to capture the full meaning of the word. Hegel used the phrase *Wissenschaft des Geistes*, and it is the Hegelian notion of *Geist* (bound up with all the historical, cultural, and metaphysical implications of a "philosophy of mind" or "philosophy of spirit") which influenced Dilthey. Erich Rothacker has written a systematic account of the German tradition of the *Geisteswissenschaften* in *Die Logik und Systematik der Geisteswissenschaften* (Munich: Oldenbourg, 1926). Extremely helpful are Erich Becher, *Geisteswissenschaften und Naturwissenschaften* (Munich: Duncker & Humblot, 1921); Otto Bollnow, *Die Methode der Geisteswissenschaften* (Mainz: Gutenberg, 1950); and Hans-Georg Gadamer, "Wahrheit in den Geisteswissenschaften," in *Kleine Schriften*, vol. 1 (Tübingen: Mohr, 1967), 39–46. The term signified for Dilthey that group of studies dealing with the cultural spirit of humanity: history, psychology, economics, sociology, philology, anthropology, politics, religion, literature, and others. It is to be carefully differentiated from the term *Naturwissenschaft*,

---

secure scientific knowledge of the human world which is as truly "scientific," or *wissenschaftlich*, as the knowledge of nature obtained by the natural sciences? And even if we should succeed in fulfilling this imperative toward scientific knowledge, can we still preserve the truth of the human spirit? Can we do so in a way that its vitality and immediacy are not compromised by lifeless theorizing? Dilthey re-phrased, reconstructed, and transformed these questions throughout his life, approaching them from a variety of perspectives in philosophical, aesthetic, pedagogical, and psychological studies. If we are to understand Dilthey's relationship to historicism properly, we need to keep in mind the place of historical knowledge within this larger *Fragestellung*.

At first glance, Dilthey's work appears to be a fragmentary collection of sketches, notes, drafts, or uncompleted manuscripts. Although his collected writings now number twenty volumes, only a few of them were published in finished form during his lifetime; most of the remaining volumes were part of Dilthey's extensive *Nachlass*, a collection of writings whose unity has been hard to determine.[3] In a way, Dilthey's work resembles Nietzsche's in that it also needs to be reinterpreted in light of unpublished manuscripts that were never given final form.[4] Despite this complex textual history, however, I want to

---

which includes all the fields in the natural sciences. The differences between these two branches of study are not merely terminological but, more fundamental, also methodological. Nature is "explained," as Dilthey puts it, but spirit, or *Geist*, is "understood." This difference between explanation (*Erklären*) and understanding (*Verstehen*) points to the centrality of hermeneutics for a theory of the human sciences.

[3] There were many critics who felt that Dilthey's work was fragmentary not only in a textual sense but in a philosophical sense as well. Dilthey wrote on such a variety of topics that his contributions seem to lack a theoretical unity. Yet, as I will argue throughout this chapter, all his scholarly endeavors were part of a systematic effort to unify the praxis *and* theory of research in the *Geisteswissenschaften*. For one particularly caustic review of Dilthey's work from a contemporary source, see Jonas Cohn in *Logos* 12 (1923–24):297. See also the insightful study by Michael Ermarth, *Wilhelm Dilthey: The Critique of Historical Reason* (Chicago: University of Chicago Press, 1978), 5–6, and Lessing, *Die Idee einer Kritik der historischen Vernunft*, 14–15. Dilthey's *Nachlass* contains some of the most important fragments of the whole Dilthey project. Volume 19, for example, contains the extensive drafts of his projected multivolume work *Die Einleitung in die Geisteswissenschaften*, of which only the first part was published. The first draft of circa 1880–1890, called the "Breslau Draft," and the second from 1893, the "Berlin Plan," are crucial to an understanding of Dilthey's overall critique of historical reason. Volume 20 of the collected writings contains important lecture notes on the subjects of logic and epistemology and an overall theory of the projected *Einleitung* (cf. GS 19: xl–xli). The status of the "Nachlass" is also discussed in Ermarth, *Wilhelm Dilthey*, 6–10; Lessing, *Die Idee einer Kritik der historischen Vernunft*, 14–31; and Frithjof Rodi, "Zum gegenwärtigen Stand der Dilthey-Forschung," in *Dilthey-Jahrbuch*, 1 (1983): 260–67.

[4] Werner Stegmaier, *Philosophie der Fluktuanz: Dilthey und Nietzsche* (Göttingen: Van-

argue for the underlying unity within Dilthey's project. In his first major work, *The Introduction to the Human Sciences*, Dilthey articulated the need for a unified critique of historical reason whose purpose would be "to develop an epistemological foundation for the human sciences . . . [which would determine] the capacity of the human being to know itself and the society and history which it has produced."[5] This new critique, while following the critical imperative of Kant, would seek to ground the truth of the individual human sciences in the actual terms of social and historical reality.

Throughout the many phases of Dilthey's long and productive life, this single project was to offer a reference point by which to evaluate and consider any new influences. Thus, although Dilthey did experience many crucial shifts in his thought from his early university days in 1852 until his death in 1911, they were shifts in emphasis rather than fundamental changes in direction. As Anna Tumarkin, one of his students, put it, despite the apparent gaps and contradictions in his studies, Dilthey's work "resembled an organic development with its concentric circles: ever in a more profound and original manner the same question would be pursued from new sides."[6] Following Tumarkin's conception, many Dilthey scholars have distinguished three "phases" in Dilthey's thought: (1) the early phase, from about 1852 to 1876, characterized by the influence of positivism and the natural sciences and culminating in the essay "Über das Studium der Geschichte der Wissenschaften vom Menschen, der Gesellschaft, und dem Staat" (1875); (2) the middle phase, from about 1877 to 1900, marked by a concern with the methodology of the human sciences and psychology, resulting in the publication of *Introduction to the Human Sciences* (1883) and *Ideas concerning a Descriptive and Analytic Psychology* (1894); and (3) the late phase, from 1900 to 1911, the last years of Dilthey's career, during which he was concerned with the problem of hermeneutics, a doctrine of *Weltanschauung*, and the growing influence of Edmund Husserl's *Logical Investigations* (1900) on the theory of the human sciences.[7] The question of "phases" and "shifts" in intel-

denhoeck & Ruprecht, 1992), provides an interpretation of Dilthey and Nietzsche within the context of nineteenth-century German philosophy.

[5] Dilthey, *GS* 1:116 and *GS* 8:264.

[6] Anna Tumarkin, "Wilhelm Dilthey," *Archiv für Geschichte der Philosophie* 25 (1912): 151.

[7] The question of "phases" in Dilthey's intellectual development has proven to be a matter of great debate among scholars. For a history of this controversy, the following articles are helpful: Hans Ineichen, "Von der ontologischen Diltheyinterpretation zur

lectual history is oftentimes problematic, serving more to segregate the important influences in a philosopher's work than to affirm their unity and continuity. Ironically, Dilthey confronted this same problem in his own work—both in his intellectual biography of Schleiermacher and in his study of the early Hegel.[8] Until recently, most Dilthey scholarship had been dominated by this phase approach, finding a so-called hermeneutic turn in Dilthey's thinking (signaled by the 1900 essay "The Rise of Hermeneutics") which constituted an important break with the earlier work.[9] Bernhard Groethuysen argues, for example, that after Julius Ebbinghaus's savage attacks on the psychological studies of 1894–1896, Dilthey reformulated his ideas and abandoned his earlier "psychological" attempts to ground the human studies in favor of a new "hermeneutical" grounding. On his reading, hermeneutics becomes for the later Dilthey the new "fundamental science," serving as the foundation for all studies of history, society, literature, and the other sciences of spirit.

In itself, this "phase-oriented" approach to Dilthey might seem a minor point of internal criticism, of concern only to those schooled in the particulars of Dilthey philology. But when viewed against the background of nineteenth-century German philosophy (and the crisis of historicism), this argument about phases becomes important because it interprets Dilthey's hermeneutics as a turn away from the earlier epistemologically grounded tradition of psychology. In more-recent criticism, Hans-Ulrich Lessing and Frithjof Rodi have broken with this line of interpretation, arguing instead for the unity of the epistemological-psychological-hermeneutic strains within Dilthey's thought.[10] These philosophers see Dilthey's project of a critique of historical reason as a philosophical attempt to unify the various shifts or

---

Wissenschaftstheorie in praktischer Absicht: Neue Dilthey-Literatur," *Philosophische Rundschau* 22 (1976): 493–509; and Bernard Eric Jensen, "The Recent Trend in the Interpretation of Dilthey," *Philosophy of the Social Sciences* 8 (1978): 419–438; Peter Hünermann, *Der Durchbruch geschichtlichen Denkens im 19. Jahrhundert: Johann Gustav Droysen, Wilhelm Dilthey, Graf Paul Yorck von Wartenburg* (Freiburg: Alber, 1967), deals extensively with the question of phases in Dilthey's work and, in fact, sees five of them. This question is also raised by Lessing, *Die Idee einer Kritik der historischen Vernunft*, 27–31; Ermarth, *Wilhelm Dilthey*, 3–12; Theodore Plantinga, *Historical Understanding in the Thought of Wilhelm Dilthey* (Toronto: University of Toronto Press, 1980) 3–23; and Ilse Bulhof, *Wilhelm Dilthey: A Hermeneutic Approach to the Study of History and Culture* (The Hague: Martinus Nijhoff, 1980), 1–9.

[8] Dilthey, *GS* 4, *GS* 13, and *GS* 14.
[9] Dilthey, *GS* 5: 317–331. For example, see the introduction by Dilthey's student Bernard Groethuysen in Dilthey, *GS* 7:v–x.
[10] Lessing and Rodi, eds., *Materialien zur Philosophie Wilhelm Diltheys*.

turns within his thinking, an argument that I find persuasive. If after 1900 Dilthey thematizes hermeneutics in a more self-conscious fashion, then perhaps we should see this not as a break with his earlier work but as a modification of emphasis. Dating back to his Schleiermacher biography, Dilthey wrote extensively about the specific problems of understanding, interpretation, and psychology.[11] Later, in his essay "The Development of Hermeneutics" (1900), he stressed that "within the context of the epistemology, logic, and methodology of the human sciences, the theory of interpretation becomes a vital link between philosophy and the historical sciences, an essential part of the foundation of the human sciences."[12] In both cases, one can clearly see the influence of hermeneutical thinking at work.

What remained crucial for Dilthey's overall project, however, was his unfaltering commitment to an epistemological *Fragestellung*, a commitment that he shared with his Neo-Kantian contemporaries Windelband and Rickert. What he wrote in 1883 in the preface to his *Introduction to the Human Sciences* could as easily have been written in 1911, the year of his death: "Only in inner experience, in the facts of consciousness, have I found a firm anchor for my thinking. . . . All science is experiential; but all experience must be related back to and derives its validity from the conditions and context of consciousness in which it arises, i.e. the totality of our nature. We designate as 'epistemological' this standpoint which consistently recognizes the impossibility of going behind these conditions. . . . Modern science can acknowledge no other than this epistemological standpoint."[13] In approaching Dilthey's work, I will emphasize the unity and continuity

---

[11] Dilthey, *GS* 15: 395–787.

[12] Dilthey, *GS* 5: 330. As Ernst Wolfgang Orth has argued in "Historical and Critical Remarks on the Relation between Description and Hermeneutics in Phenomenology," *Research in Phenomenology* 15 (1984): 1–18: "It would be a complete misunderstanding of the professionally historical and professionally philological argumentation in Dilthey's late essay on hermeneutics to attempt to interpret it as a hermeneutic turn in his philosophy. In Dilthey, understanding is a way of apprehending which still connects descriptive, psychological, and hermeneutical motifs. He makes use of them ingenuously and in a superior manner. To think that a traditional special discipline could simply become the instrument of a first philosophy is rather unusual with regard to Dilthey's way of thinking. Admittedly, he did not coin any term to name his foundational discipline, his philosophy of deliberation (*Besinnung*). It is Dilthey's merit here of having avoided mistakes by his terminological reservations (except for the equivocal term *Geisteswissenschaften*). As little as a complete system of psychology can be taken as a presupposition of an epistemology, as little can a complete system of hermeneutics be presupposed to reformulate this epistemology in order to build a fundamental ontology" (11).

[13] Dilthey, *Introduction to the Human Sciences*, 50; *GS* 1: xviii.

of this epistemological standpoint as I explore his writings on descriptive psychology, the method of *Verstehen*, problems of historical relativism, and his concept of *Erlebnis* (lived experience).

ii. The Unity of the *Introduction to the Human Sciences* (1883)

In the preface to *Introduction to the Human Sciences*, Dilthey explained his reasons for undertaking his philosophical-methodological study of historical knowledge. Such a project was, he noted, the direct outgrowth of his own efforts to complete a two-volume biography on Schleiermacher's life and thought. In 1870 Dilthey published the first volume, which covered the period from 1768 to 1802. The second volume, which was to have included lengthy discussions of Schleiermacher's dialectics, ethics, aesthetics, psychology, and hermeneutics (contrasted with the thought of Hegel, Kant, Fichte, Schelling, and Schlegel) remained in notes and draft and was never finished. Dilthey believed that to complete such an extensive study on the intellectual history of the "Age of Goethe," he would need the proper philosophical tools. First and foremost, he would require a clear conception of the various branches of the human sciences, a kind of unifying theory of their individual contributions. Only then would he be able to make sense of the complex of ideas which formed the matrix of Schleiermacher's intellectual universe. As he readily acknowledged, the genesis of his methodological inquiry into the form and structure of the *Geisteswissenschaften* had practical roots in the biography, for "the presentation and critique of Schleiermacher's system everywhere presupposed an investigation into the ultimate questions of philosophy."[14]

Dilthey's study of Schleiermacher made it apparent to him that the practical problems of historical research are always tied to the theoretical problems of philosophical critique; both are mutually determinative. Consequently, at the very outset of his project concerning a critique of historical reason, Dilthey explained that he did not favor an orthodox Kantian approach to knowledge. Knowledge requires no theoretical architectonic, Dilthey claimed, but is rooted in the actual experience of life itself. With specific regard to the human sciences, knowledge can never be purely abstract or theoretical but must itself

[14] Dilthey, *GS* 1: xx.

reflect the actual development of these sciences throughout history. Hence, any proposed logic of the human sciences must begin with a study of their history. As Dilthey himself emphasized, "Insight into the historical development of the human sciences is the empirical foundation for a true understanding of their logical constitution."[15] In the preface to the *Introduction*, he again declared that "the historical description [of the human sciences] prepares the ground for their epistemological foundation."[16]

Here, one can clearly see how Dilthey's starting point was very different from that of his Neo-Kantian contemporaries. Unlike Rickert, for example, he did not attempt to find an a priori ground for our knowledge of human culture; rather, he thought of knowledge as bound up with the culture it attempts to know. Because all knowledge is ultimately self-reflexive, philosophy cannot begin from an absolute ground. "There is no absolute starting point," Dilthey insisted. "Every beginning is arbitrary."[17] And yet as he turned his attention to the history of metaphysics, Dilthey discovered that Western philosophy had proceeded as if there were some fixed point of departure for establishing a metaphysical foundation for science. Seeking to avoid the pitfalls of an Archimedean metaphysics, Dilthey realized that philosophy had to be supplemented with history; history had to be fortified with philosophy. Among his predecessors, only Hegel had attempted to think through this relationship of history to philosophy in a fundamental way. By emphasizing the historical aspects of philosophy as the ground for an *epistemological* account of the human sciences, Dilthey succeeded in overcoming the purely formal and insular character of Neo-Kantian epistemology.

The Dilthey project outlined in the *Introduction to the Human Sciences* was originally conceived as a multivolume undertaking made up of six sections, of which only the first two were published in Dilthey's lifetime.[18] The first book attempted to describe the state of the *Geisteswissenschaften* in Dilthey's own time while demonstrating the

[15] Cited from the unpublished *Nachlass* in Ermarth, *Wilhelm Dilthey*, 94.
[16] Dilthey, *GS* 1: xv.
[17] Dilthey, *GS* 5: cx and *GS* 1: 419.
[18] For the complete details of the six-book project, see the "Vorbericht" to *GS* 19 by F. Rodi and Helmut Johach, esp. pp. xl–xli. For Dilthey's own extensive analysis of his intentions, the "Althoff Brief" of 1882 is crucial; see *GS* 19: 389–392. The basic premise of the *Einleitung* was, as Dilthey put it, "to see how—from the experience of mental life—one could achieve a science of man, society, and history" (390).

need for a new epistemological foundation. This book was merely introductory, and in it Dilthey wished to outline the differences between the natural sciences and the human sciences according to their method and object of study. As he wrote to a contemporary: "The first book of the first volume seeks, in contrast to the presently popular approach of the Comte and Mill school, to grasp the truly inner structure of the human sciences as they have developed historically. From this I hope to show the necessity of a general grounding [of the human sciences]."[19] The second book, entitled "Metaphysics as Foundation of the Human Sciences: Its Dominance and Decline," attempted a historical analysis of the idea of *Wissenschaft* in Western philosophy from the ancient Greeks until the Middle Ages. "The second book demonstrates," as Dilthey explained, "that metaphysics is no longer capable of providing a universally acceptable grounding of the individual sciences. . . . I attempt, by means of a historical description of metaphysics, to prove the fruitlessness of every such undertaking."[20] In short, for Dilthey, the age of a metaphysical grounding of the human sciences had come to an end. Book 3, which was to continue the general theme of Book 2 from the Renaissance until Dilthey's own day, was never completed.[21] Books 4, 5, and 6, published as part of the *Nachlass*, were conceived by Dilthey as his "own attempt to provide an epistemological foundation for the human sciences."[22] Here Dilthey was to provide the philosophical justification for the historical critique worked out in Books 2 and 3. Throughout this chapter I want to focus attention on this project, begun in the *Introduction* and developed in the "Breslau Draft" of the early 1880s and what has been called the "Berlin Plan" of a decade later.[23] In no sense, however, should we see these later manuscripts as having a different aim than the earlier studies dealing with the history of metaphysics. In the

[19] Cited from Dilthey's unpublished letter, the so-called Schoene Brief of 1882, in Lessing, *Die Idee einer Kritik der historischen Vernunft*, 111.

[20] Ibid.

[21] Volume 2 of the *Gesammelte Schriften, Weltanschauung und Analyse des Menschen seit Renaissance und Reformation*, covers only the period up through the seventeenth century. Dilthey never formally completed his study of the nineteenth-century hermeneutic tradition.

[22] Dilthey, *Introduction to the Human Sciences*, 51–52; *GS* 1: xix.

[23] I would argue that the *Aufbau der geschichtlichen Welt in den Geisteswissenschaften* (1910) and the *Ideen über eine beschreibende und zergliedernde Psychologie* (1894) (perhaps Dilthey's two most famous works besides the *Introduction*) are a continuation of the project begun in 1883 rather than a new "psychological" or "hermeneutic" phase of Dilthey's thought.

preface to the *Introduction*, Dilthey explained that in his work, "historical reflection is as valuable as epistemological self-reflection."[24] Dilthey believed that any new theory of the *Geisteswissenschaften* had first to overcome the actual historical theory that had been left to it, the detritus of the metaphysical approach, before it could offer any helpful solution to the crisis of scientific philosophy.

iii. Dilthey's Relationship to Positivism, Idealism, and the Historical School

Dilthey's antimetaphysical stance was, of course, consonant with the mood of post-Hegelian German philosophy in general. The Historical School of Ranke, Droysen, and Savigny had protested against the speculative side of Hegel's philosophy of spirit. Their critiques were intensified by the empirical approach of positivism and the natural-scientific research of university-trained scholars. As we have already seen, both within the natural sciences and the sciences of history, Hegel's philosophy came under severe attack after mid-century. Dilthey's ideas were formed in this positivist, anti-Hegelian climate, but his attitude was in no sense typically antimetaphysical, like the historicists. Dilthey held Hegel in high regard and believed that metaphysics could not be dismissed offhand as an unscientific aberration of the human spirit but rather had to be grasped *historically* as an attempt to establish a valid starting point for scientific inquiry.

Dilthey understood metaphysics in the Aristotelian sense as first philosophy: the *Wissenschaft der Wissenschaft*—scientia scientiarum.[25] According to Dilthey, the guiding principle of metaphysics was the "principle of sufficient reason" (*Satz vom Grund*), which, as the principle of all principles, grounds all worldly phenomena.[26] Dilthey tried to show that belief in this science of first principles had determined the actual practice of those engaged in researches of the physical and historical world. He even claimed that the actual division of the sciences according to nature and spirit (*Natur-* and *Geisteswissenschaft*)

---

[24] Dilthey, *Introduction to the Human Sciences*, 52; GS 1: xix.

[25] Dilthey, *Introduction to the Human Sciences*, 178; GS 1: 129.

[26] Dilthey, *Introduction to the Human Sciences*, 221–223; GS 1: 388–390. There is also a long discussion of the *Satz vom Grund* in Dilthey GS 19: 43–44, and 71–81. Also helpful in this context are the comments by Manfred Riedel, "Diltheys Kritik der begründenden Vernunft," in Orth, ed., *Dilthey und die Philosophie der Gegenwart*, 185–210, and the introduction to volume 7, *Geschichte der Philosophie, 19. Jahrhundert: Positivismus, Historismus, Hermeneutik*, ed. Manfred Riedel, 7–28 (Stuttgart: Reclam, 1981).

was based on these metaphysical principles of first philosophy. Beginning with Aristotle and culminating in the thought of Hegel, Dilthey
identified a powerful trend within metaphysics to orient all science
(and, more fundamentally, all aspects of being) to a logical ideal: that
of *logos*, or *Vernunft* (reason). Accordingly, Dilthey referred to metaphysics as a *Vernunftwissenschaft*, or a "science of reason."[27] But because the actual praxis of the natural and human sciences had weak-
ened belief in the logical character of nature and history in the
nineteenth century, Dilthey began to speak of "the euthanasia of
metaphysics."[28] In this period at "the end of metaphysics" (to borrow
Heidegger's phrase), Dilthey turned to the empirical work of the positivists and the Historical School to inaugurate his critique. As Ranke
had already shown in his reading of Hegel, rational metaphysics had
undermined the very nature of historical experience by abstracting
from the empirical datum and denying the reality of historical praxis.
Hence, as Dilthey understood it, metaphysics, which originally
sought to provide a logical ground for all types of *Wissenschaft*, ironically came to undermine the very praxis of *Wissenschaft* itself. In this
sense, Dilthey came to speak of a conflict between metaphysics and
Wissenschaft, which he hoped to resolve by offering his own critique
of historical reason as an alternative to Hegel's metaphysical science
of reason.

Dilthey's antimetaphysical stance was, in some respects, related to
the positivist critique of Hegel, but it would be unfair and misleading
to overestimate the influence of thinkers such as Auguste Comte or
John Stuart Mill on his work.[29] Dilthey shared with the positivists a
desire to restructure the system of the sciences according to a new
methodological ideal: the commitment to empirical research in place
of abstract systematizing. In the end, however, he wholly repudiated
any attachment to Comte's positive sociology or Mill's logic of the
moral sciences. Yet his reasons for rejecting positivism were not the
result of a simple leaning toward romanticism—as some have argued

[27] Dilthey, *Introduction to the Human Sciences*, 228; GS 1: 395.
[28] Dilthey, *Introduction to the Human Sciences*, 238; GS 1: 405.
[29] Hans Sommerfeld wrote the dissertation "Wilhelm Dilthey und der Positivismus,"
University of Berlin, 1925; more recently, Jürgen Habermas, *Knowledge and Human Interests* (Boston: Beacon, 1971), has treated the problem in depth, and Hans-Helmuth Gander, *Positivismus als Metaphysik: Voraussetzungen und Grundstrukturen von Diltheys
Grundlegung der Geisteswissenschaften* (Freiburg: Alber, 1988), follows on the problem of
Dilthey and positivism. The influence of positivism on Dilthey's thought is also mentioned in previously cited works by Ermarth, Bulhof, Plantinga, and Lessing, among
others. Dilthey discusses his early relationship to positivism in the 1870s in GS 5: 3–6.

—but grew out of his rigorous devotion to an ideal of *Wissenschaft*, free of both speculative excess as well as "the orgies of empiricism."[30] Even in his early career, Dilthey had plans for an essay entitled "An Introduction to Scientific Studies from the Standpoint of Reality and Experience in Contrast to Empiricism and Speculation," which contained a critique of both Hegel and the positivists.[31] In this early work, Dilthey sought an approach to reality which would stress the experiential element in human knowledge, "a philosophy of experience" led by the call for "empiria, but not empiricism."[32] By "empiria," Dilthey meant the actual experiences of life in their undiluted, nonscientific form; to these he contrasted the metaphysical approach of "empiricism."

The empiricist philosophy of science (rooted in the English tradition of Locke, Hume, and associationist psychology) claimed to derive its methods from rigorous external observation, attempting to analyze the given world in contrast to the abstract world of consciousness. Comte, for example, held that to understand human mental functions, one needed to pursue physiology and sociology because the only data of significance were external rather than within consciousness itself. The putative "science" of psychology he declared to be logically contradictory, because introspection itself is an impossible task; the only genuinely scientific study of human life, Comte argued, requires the kind of exact observation found in the natural sciences. Thus, in his attempts to found a new science of human life—sociology—Comte denied the value of psychology as a science and subordinated all historical and social inquiry to the methodological principles of the natural sciences. In the final analysis, Dilthey concluded that Comte's attempts at empiricism followed the path of a "crude

[30] Dilthey, *GS* 1: 135 and *GS* 4: 434. In his Ph.D. dissertation, "Historicity and Hermeneutic" (Vanderbilt University, 1969), David Linge argues that Dilthey rejected positivism not, as some have argued, out of a romantic disillusionment with the "system" of Comte and Mill but due to his conviction that positivism was a veiled form of metaphysics—unempirical in bent and dogmatic in method. Jeffrey Barnouw also argues for Dilthey's commitment to "empiricism" rather than a knee-jerk form of positivism in *Review of Metaphysics* 32, no. 4 (June 1979): 746–750. See also Elisabeth Paczkowska-Lagowska, "Dilthey's Reform of Psychology," *Reports on Philosophy* 7 (1983): 13–16.
[31] Dilthey, *GS* 5: 434.
[32] The motto *"Empirie und nicht Empirismus"* is found in a draft of the *Introduction to the Human Sciences* from *GS* 5: 434, where Dilthey uses it as a chapter heading for a future manuscript. This phrase is also found in an early letter of Count Paul Yorck von Wartenburg to Dilthey in November 1877, published in *Briefwechsel zwischen Wilhelm Dilthey und dem Grafen Paul Yorck von Wartenburg, 1877–1897*, ed. Sigrid von der Schulenburg (Halle: Niemeyer, 1923), 2. In *GS* 1: 81, Dilthey also speaks of *die unbefangene Empirie* (an impartial empirical approach).

naturalistic metaphysics" that "approached the facts of the historical process in a much less satisfactory manner than did Hegel or Schleiermacher."[33]

If Comte's error lay in his unempirical attempts at empiricism, the same could be said, from Dilthey's standpoint, of Mill. Mill did not view psychology as scientifically inadmissible; in fact, he attempted to use it as the keystone for his "logic of the moral sciences," a project that Dilthey shared. Nonetheless, despite Mill's antimetaphysical pursuit of the logical foundations of experience, Dilthey rejected his approach as "unfruitful" because it subordinated the autonomy of the *Geisteswissenschaften* to the methodological ideal of the natural sciences.[34] Mill's efforts to establish the "moral sciences" by appealing to the sciences of nature were, according to Dilthey, another attempt at undermining the "empiria" of human experience. The human sciences required a method all their own, Dilthey claimed, a method that reflected the actual research of its practitioners. What the empiricists had overlooked was "the full, untruncated experience" of historical life; abstracting from the genuine phenomena of social and cultural existence, they erected a gossamer edifice of theory and intellection. Dilthey's critique was unremitting: "Empiricism has been just as abstract as speculative thought. The human being that influential empiricist schools have constructed from sensations and representations, as though from atoms, contradicts the inner experience from whose elements the idea of the human being is, after all, derived."[35] In the marginalia to his copy of Mill's *Logic*, Dilthey wrote: "Mill is dogmatic due to his lack of historical education. Only from Germany can there come a truly empirical method to replace the prejudicial method of dogmatic empiricism."[36] By following the path of a different empirical tradition practiced by the German Historical School, Dilthey believed he had found a way to overcome the one-sided empiricism of the positivists and ultimately to ground scientific truth in historical reality.

As we begin to approach his own philosophy, we need to recognize that Dilthey never appropriated the work of the German historicists as an appendage to his philosophical labors. For him, history was less a field of study or disciplinary paradigm than a way of understand-

[33] Dilthey, *Introduction to the Human Sciences*, 154–157; *GS* 1: 105–107.
[34] Dilthey, *Introduction to the Human Sciences*, 158; *GS* 1: 108.
[35] Dilthey, *Introduction to the Human Sciences*, 173; *GS* 1: 123–124.
[36] Cited by Georg Misch in his preface to Dilthey, *GS* 5: lxxiv.

ing and revealing human perceptions of the world. He had studied at the University of Berlin and had attended the lectures of Ranke, Jakob Grimm, August Boeckh, Theodor Mommsen, and Franz Bopp.[37] And from his early days as a student of theology, while he was working on the analysis of Schleiermacher's ethics, he had always valued the "historical" approach as highly as the "systematic," being convinced that there could be no system without history.[38] It was in this sense that Dilthey spoke of his own work as "historical research with a philosophical aim."[39] Unlike Kuno Fischer or Friedrich Überweg, however, Dilthey was never committed to solving philosophical problems through historical analysis. History was always linked in Dilthey's work to the project of critique. As he explained in a speech given to commemorate his seventieth birthday, he not only "attempted to write a history of literary and philosophical movements" but also "undertook to examine the nature and condition of historical consciousness—a critique of historical reason," generated by his reading of the Historical School.[40]

According to Dilthey, it was the Historical School that "had recognized the historicity of humans and of all the social order" by defining the individual as an "essentially historical being," a discovery that he termed "the emancipation of historical consciousness."[41] This new insight into the historicity of the human condition had led, in Dilthey's interpretation, to a radical break with the eighteenth-century notions of natural law, natural religion, abstract political theory, and abstract political economy. Politically, it represented a triumph over the spirit of the French Revolution and the Napoleonic codes by reclaiming the thousand-year tradition of German history which had been undermined by French philosophers and their ideas of social systems.[42] In scientific terms, the achievements of the Historical

[37] For a personal sketch of Dilthey's reminiscences of the Historical School and his early days at the University of Berlin, see GS 5: 7–9.
[38] Dilthey, Introduction to the Human Sciences, 47; GS 1: xv.
[39] This is an often-repeated motto in Dilthey's work. Cf. Dilthey, GS 5: xliii, 35 and GS 3: 42–44, 222.
[40] Dilthey, GS 5: 9.
[41] Ibid., 11. Clara Misch, ed., Der junge Dilthey (Göttingen: Vandenhoeck & Ruprecht, 1960), 124; and Dilthey, GS 1: xv. In his study of Friedrich Christoph Schlosser, Dilthey also wrote, "It is the essence of the human being that he is historical" (GS 11: 140).
[42] Dilthey's interpretation of "historicism" is, in many ways, close to that of Friedrich Meinecke in his book Die Enstehung des Historismus (Munich: Oldenbourg, 1965). Dilthey, as Meinecke did later, spoke of "the emancipation of historical consciousness" as a positive turn in Western thought (GS 1: xv–xvi). In many other ways, Meinecke follows Dilthey, especially in his view of Leibniz as one of the great originators of

School liberated German science from the metaphysical systems of universal reason. Its work represented, in Dilthey's words, "a purely empirical mode of observation . . . aiming to determine the value of a particular state of affairs solely from the context of its development."[43] The significance of this new historical approach was that it offered the historicophilological sciences a methodological ideal different from the sciences of nature by affirming the autonomy of their subject areas and styles of presentation. Yet despite its powerful sense for the concrete details of historical life, Dilthey found the approach of the Historical School philosophically naïve. As he explained in his preface to the *Introduction*: "Even today the Historical School has not yet succeeded in breaking through the inner limits which have necessarily inhibited its theoretical development and its influence on life. Its study and evaluation of historical phenomena remain unconnected with the analysis of the facts of consciousness; consequently, it has no grounding in the only knowledge which is ultimately secure; it has, in short, no philosophical foundation. Lacking a healthy relationship to epistemology and psychology, this school has not attained an explanatory method."[44] Hence, although Dilthey still respected the Historical School for helping to break down metaphysical notions of *Wissenschaft*, ultimately he believed that the "historical turn" of nineteenth-century German scholarship lacked a genuinely scientific foundation.

As an example of a philosophically naïve attitude toward historical consciousness, Dilthey cited the great master of historicism, Leopold von Ranke.[45] The Rankean ideal of "self-extinguishment" (*Selbstauslöschung*) represented for Dilthey an "impossible" contradiction.[46] The contemplative bearing of a Rankean researcher fostered a kind of aesthetic ocularism—a vision of the past which defined history as a spectacle or an assemblage of museum pieces. Yet by pressing to an extreme the detached ideal of objective contemplation, Dilthey believed

German historical consciousness. For Dilthey's view, see *GS* 11: xv ("Leibniz is the first thinker in whose work one can notice the development of historical consciousness").

[43] Dilthey, *Introduction to the Human Sciences*, 48; *GS* 1: xvi.

[44] Dilthey, *Introduction to the Human Sciences*, 48; *GS* 1: xvi.

[45] For a more detailed analysis of Ranke's methodology, see Herbert Schnädelbach, *Die Geschichtsphilosophie nach Hegel* (Freiburg: Alber, 1974). For Dilthey's praise of Ranke, see *GS* 7: 101–103. In *GS* 1: 94, Dilthey criticizes the Rankean ideal of *Selbstauslöschung* (self-extinguishment) and offers a psychological interpretation instead. The whole problem of Dilthey's relationship to the Historical School and its adherents' ideal of interpretation is provided by Elisabeth Paczkowska-Lagowska in "The Humanities in Search of Philosophy: Wilhelm Dilthey and the Historical School," *Reports on Philosophy* 6 (1982): 1–16.

[46] Dilthey, *GS* 5: 281.

that the Rankean approach undermined the vital force of human historicity. In the *Introduction to the Human Sciences*, Dilthey sought to overcome the limits of Ranke's method by offering a "philosophical foundation for the principle of the Historical School" which would link its notion of historicity to an epistemological critique of consciousness.[47] As he explained in the preface: "All science and scholarship is empirical, but all experience is originally connected, and given validity, by our *consciousness* (within which it occurs) indeed, by our whole nature. We call this point of view—which consistently recognizes the impossibility of going behind consciousness (to see, as it were, without eyes or to direct a cognitive gaze behind the eye itself) —the *epistemological* point of view. Modern science can acknowledge no other."[48]

If we are to make sense of the influence of positivism and the Historical School on Dilthey's thinking, we will need to take him seriously when he maintains that he "found a firm anchor for [his] thought only in inner experience, in the facts of consciousness." By focusing on experience as the primary datum of knowledge, Dilthey hoped to overcome the crisis within German philosophy which led to "the growing separation between life and scientific knowledge."[49] Through a historical critique of Kant's own model of experience, ordered and filtered through the prism of consciousness, Dilthey sought to bring a new kind of philosophical certitude to the naïve empiricism of Mill and Ranke. But to do so, he first had to work through the implications of Kant's critical thinking for his critique of history.

iv. The Kantian *Fragestellung* and Dilthey's "Critique of Historical Reason"

Dilthey's critique has obvious connections to Kant's critical project, and yet, as with his relations to the positivists and the Historical School, we should not assume that thematic affinity translates into philosophical agreement. In many ways it is Dilthey's divergence from Kant which proves decisive in understanding his work. This is not to suggest that in some fundamental sense Dilthey and Kant are

[47] Dilthey, *Introduction to Human Sciences*, 49; *GS* 1: xvii.
[48] Wilhelm Dilthey, *Selected Writings*, ed. H. P. Rickman (Cambridge: Cambridge University Press, 1976), (hereafter cited as *SW*), 161; *GS* 1: xvii.
[49] Dilthey, *SW*, 161; *GS* 1: xvii.

at odds epistemologically, for despite their differences, Dilthey remains tied to the Cartesian-Kantian "early modern philosophy of consciousness."[50] But Dilthey subjects Kant to a new kind of criticism different from that of Neo-Kantians such as Cohen, Natorp, Lange, Windelband, or Rickert—a criticism that is not formal, aprioristic, physiological, axiological, or natural-scientific. Dilthey's accomplishment, rather, is to take seriously the achievements of the Historical School and to use them as a starting point to criticize Kantian ideas. That is, Dilthey attempts a historical, anthropological, psychological, and hermeneutic critique of the Kantian tradition. He historicizes

[50] For a similar analysis, see Lessing, *Die Idee einer Kritik der historischen Vernunft*, 138–139, and Hans Ineichen, "Diltheys Kant Kritik," *Dilthey-Jahrbuch* 2 (1984): 59–64. By the phrase "early modern philosophy of consciousness," I mean to translate the German concept *neuzeitliche Bewußtseinsphilosophie*, which is currently used in German philosophy to designate a certain epistemological tradition from Descartes through Leibniz to Kant. Heidegger, Gadamer, and others define this tradition by its tendency to ground truth not in divine revelation but in the perceptions, reflections, opinions, and ratiocinative activities of the human being. The self—or the consciousness known by the self as self—becomes the ground of scientific certitude. This involves a new relationship between self and world, one based on the understanding of world as an object "there" for a subject. This subject-object dichotomy places the human being at the center of all being (both epistemologically and ontologically). Simply put, *die Bewußtseinsphilosophie der Neuzeit* finds the ground of truth *within* human consciousness, defined as the Cartesian cogito. As Dilthey put it in his "Breslau Draft": "Whatever is there for us—because and insofar as it is there for us—is subject to the *condition* of being given in consciousness," *Introduction to the Human Sciences*, 246–247; and *GS* 19: 60. Dilthey is not alone in seeing *Bewußtsein*, or "consciousness," as the key to epistemology or to philosophy as a whole. For the *Neuzeit* (early modern period) the cogito becomes, as it were, an Archimedean point on which to found all certainty and knowledge. See Jürgen Mittelstrass, *Neuzeit und Aufklärung* (Berlin: de Gruyter, 1970), 156–166. As a result of this central focus on the cogito and its rigorous demand for critical and self-critical knowledge rooted in scientific method (a method that demands *universal* knowledge rather than the merely subjective knowledge of the individual), there arises a *new* relationship between human beings and the world. "Mind," or *Geist*, is defined as *res cogitans*, while "Nature," or *Natur*, is defined as *res extensa* (cf. Heidegger's comments in *Nietzsche*, vol. 4, trans. Frank Capuzzi [New York: Harper and Row, 1982], 116; the distinction is also discussed in *Being and Time*). This epistemological distinction between *Geist* and *Natur* has, as we have seen, a profound influence on the methodological and practical developments within the sciences. After Galileo, Descartes, Copernicus, Kepler, and Bacon, *Naturwissenschaft* comes to replace the medieval and Renaissance "humanities" as *the* standard of truth. Truth is no longer rooted in authority (the church), in doctrine, in Aristotle, or in the past (history) but is now grounded in the cogito. For the classification of philosophy into *Antike*, *Mittelalter*, and *Neuzeit*, see Mittelstrasse, *Neuzeit und Aufklärung*, 166; Friedrich Überweg, *Grundriß der Geschichte der Philosophie der Neuzeit* (Berlin: Mittler, 1897); August Messer, *Die Geschichte der Philosophie von Beginn der Neuzeit* (Leipzig: Quelle & Meyer, 1918); Johann Fischl, *Die Geschichte der Philosophie* (Graz: Pustet, 1950); Hans-Georg Gadamer, ed., *Philosophisches Lesebuch* (Frankfurt: Fischer, 1967); Rüdiger Bubner, ed., *Geschichte der Philosophie* (Stuttgart: Reclam, 1984); and many others. For a critical discussion, see Wilhelm Kamlah, "'Zeitalter' überhaupt, 'Neuzeit,' und 'Fruhzeit,'" *Saeculum* 8 (1957): 313–332.

"reason" yet remains tied to the Kantian idea of an epistemological subject. To clarify the implications of this position more fully, I will begin by outlining a few important themes in Dilthey's corpus.

In his inaugural address at the University of Basel in 1867, Dilthey began by declaring that "the fundamental problem of philosophy seems to me to have been determined for all time by Kant. It is the highest and most universal task of all human researches, namely: in what form is the world (which is there only in our perceptions and representations) given to us?"[51] In another set of lectures, "Logic and the System of the Philosophical Sciences," Dilthey claimed that "the fundamental problem of philosophy" was formulated by Kant: "Through which means and within what bounds is knowledge of the phenomenal world (given in inner and outer perception) possible?"[52] For Dilthey, this question remained basic to his overall project. In 1890 he published an essay entitled "Contributions to the Solution of the Question concerning the Origin of Our Belief in the Reality of the External World and Its Justification."[53] Four years later he turned his attention to a project he called "Ideas concerning a Descriptive and Analytic Psychology."[54] In 1896 he also published "On Comparative Psychology," and in the *Nachlass* he left behind the chapters "Perception of the External World," "Inner Perception," and "The Psychological Context of Perceptions."[55] Throughout his career Dilthey continued to rethink the question of phenomenal knowledge in terms of the actual research done by his academic colleagues in philosophy, psychology, and the other sciences, altering its character and substance, yet retaining the Kantian focus. Hence, despite Dilthey's unequivocal disagreements with Rickert, Windelband, Cohen, and other Neo-Kantians (on questions of terminology, method, subject matter, and so on), he nonetheless shared with them the basic *Fragestellung* of Kantian epistemology. Like Rickert, Dilthey always maintained that the ground of knowledge lay in human consciousness. He might argue the question of how one defined human consciousness and under what conditions one chose to study it, yet in spite of these differences (and there were many), Dilthey remained squarely committed to the Cartesian-Kantian approach. As explained in one of his lectures from

---

[51] Dilthey, *GS* 5: 12.
[52] Wilhelm Dilthey, *Grundriß der Logik und des Systems der philosophischen Wissenschaften* (Berlin: Mittler, 1865), 3.
[53] Dilthey, *GS* 5: 90–138.
[54] Ibid., 139–240.
[55] Ibid., 241–316; and Dilthey, *GS* 19: 75, 174, 195.

"The System of Philosophy": "Kant's point of departure, like that of all early modern philosophy since Descartes, lies in the principle that every form of knowledge and perception is given to us in *consciousness*. Consciousness is the point where perception and knowledge begin. . . . Whatever exists beyond consciousness cannot be expressed."[56]

Dilthey believed that Kant had succeeded in dismantling the speculative excesses of metaphysics—"these shimmering castles in the air of the scientific imagination"—by systematically demonstrating that all human knowledge begins within consciousness and hence within our experience.[57] In Dilthey's view, Kant had rehabilitated metaphysics by limiting its sphere of concern and focusing on the possibility and ground of scientific knowledge against the vaporous ruminations of the school-philosophers. And yet even if Dilthey could maintain that Kant's "question concerning the conditions of rigorous knowledge as the question concerning the condition for science" had succeeded in transforming philosophy into a rigorous science of experience, he still believed that the Kantian program was not critical enough.[58]

Kant had lived in an age dominated by a paradigm of science which was defined largely in terms of mathematics and physics. As such, he determined that scientific knowledge, if it were to be worthy of its name, must be necessary and universal. But Dilthey believed that in an age marked by the historicophilological labors of the German academy, this view of science had to be critically amended. He began by challenging the spurious Kantian distinction between "pure" and "empirical" knowledge, attempting to rephrase Kant's question concerning the conditions of human knowledge by redefining the meaning of consciousness itself.[59] In Dilthey's interpretation, consciousness is never "pure" or absolute but exists only within the context of human life, which is temporally and culturally determined. Thus consciousness is always a specific consciousness, *my* consciousness, part of the totality of my own biography within a specific historical milieu. "It is Kant's error," Dilthey claimed, "that he did not pos-

[56] This quotation is taken from the *Nachlass* and is reprinted in Dietrich Bischoff, "Diltheys Kant-Darstellung in seiner letzten Vorlesung über das System der Philosophie," in *Wilhelm Diltheys geschichtliche Lebensphilosophie* (Leipzig: Teubner, 1935), 46–63, esp. 54–55.

[57] Dilthey, *SW*: 192; *GS* 1: 359.

[58] Dilthey, *GS* 13: 98.

[59] Immanuel Kant, *The Critique of Pure Reason*, trans. Norman Kemp Smith (London: Macmillan, 1929), 41–43.

sess this historical breadth of observation."[60] In the *Critique of Pure Reason* Kant attempted to resolve the problems of epistemology by reference to a priori conditions that he believed opened up the possibility for knowledge of the external world. But Dilthey countered the Kantian view by stressing that historical experience is the only genuine a priori condition of life as it is lived in the world. As Dilthey wrote in the *Nachlass*:

> Kant's a priori is rigid and dead; the real conditions of consciousness and their presuppositions are, as I conceive them, part of a living, historical process, a development; they have a history, and the process of this history is their conformity to an ever more exact, inductively known manifold of sensory contents. The life of history encompasses as well the apparently rigid and dead conditions under which we think. These historical conditions of consciousness can never be destroyed, because it is through them that we are able to think. They are themselves, rather, being developed.[61]

The actual conditions of human life are, Dilthey emphasized, the necessary starting point for any inquiry into the world of nature or history. Neither a doctrine of "pure" reason nor one of absolute a priori knowledge can serve the needs of a developing science of life-in-the-world. Because life is always changing, *Wissenschaft* (which is part of life) can never be removed from the process of change which is its very ground. If reason were able to provide a theory of knowledge for human history, it would first have to abandon its timeless, changeless, fixed, and hypostatized point of departure. Dilthey insisted that this precondition must exist for any new critique of reason which wished to stress the empirical, rather than the pure, character of human knowledge. Kant's understanding of human reason proved unworkable for Dilthey because it measured human consciousness against the lifeless archetypes of logic and mathematics, spurning the actual experience of historical being. Moreover, Kant's table of twelve categories served only to constrain the vital impulses of human desire against a fixed scheme of cognition. In a well-known passage from the *Introduction to the Human Sciences*, Dilthey explained:

> No real blood flows in the veins of the knowing subject constructed by Locke, Hume, and Kant; it is only the diluted juice of reason, a mere pro-

[60] Bischoff, *Diltheys geschichtliche Lebensphilosophie*, 55.
[61] Dilthey, *Introduction to the Human Sciences*, 500–501; *GS* 19: 44 (translation mine).

cess of thought. Cognition seems to develop concepts such as the external world, time, substance, and cause from perception, imagination, and thought. However, my historical and psychological studies of man as a whole led me to explain cognition and its concepts in terms of the powers of man as a willing, feeling, and imagining being. So I have used the following method: I have related every constituent of present-day, abstract scientific thought to the whole of human nature (as experience and the study of language and history reveal it) and sought to connect them. As a result, the most important constituents of my picture and knowledge of reality—personal individuality, external world, other persons, their temporal life, and interaction—can be explained in terms of the whole of human nature in which willing, feeling, and thinking are only different aspects of the real process of life. The questions which we ask of philosophy cannot be answered by rigid *a priori* conditions of knowledge but only by a history which starts from the totality of our nature and sketches its development.[62]

Dilthey's attitude was determined in large part by his rejection of the rigid and scholastic elements in Kant's thinking. He challenged, for example, the abstractness and formality of Kant's theory of time, claiming that any attempt at reducing time to an ideal form for intuiting phenomena misses its reality as immediate experience.[63] Since Kant's analysis had been derived from a mathematico-physical model of time as constant observation and enduring presence, Dilthey argued, it could not adequately grasp the temporality and historicity of lived experience. Nonetheless, Dilthey sought to reclaim what was meaningful within Kant's thought by raising the question of whether "an epistemology of history, which he himself did not provide, is possible within the framework of his concepts."[64] Thus, while seeking on the one hand to revitalize Kant's demand for scientific rigor, Dilthey also understood the pressing need for dismantling the Kantian *Fragestellung* and returning to the vitality of historical experience. By historicizing reason and reclaiming "the full, total, and unmaimed experience of life . . . against the contemporary dominance of the Kant cult," Dilthey hoped he could heal the rift between life (*Leben*) itself and the lifeless grounding of the sciences (*Wissenschaften*).[65] The success of his project was undermined, however, by contradictions in his

[62] Dilthey, *SW*, 162; *GS* 1: xviii.
[63] Dilthey, *SW*, 209–211; *GS* 7: 192–193.
[64] Dilthey, *SW*, 208; *GS* 7: 192.
[65] Dilthey, *GS* 8: 171.

appropriation of Kant, which persisted throughout his work and helped to shape his attitude toward the Neo-Kantians and their theory of historical knowledge.

v. Dilthey and the Philosophy of Crisis

Dilthey's position between Kant and the Historical School developed out of his own imaginative reading of European intellectual history, a reading sensitive to the tensions within late-nineteenth-century German culture. As early as 1873, Dilthey wrote: "The great crisis of the sciences and European culture, which we are now living through has so deeply and totally taken possession of my spirit that the desire to be of some help in it has extinguished every extraneous and personal ambition."[66] In his short essay "The Dream," Dilthey repeated the same theme, pointing to "the frightful anarchy of thought" that afflicted modern culture, and even confessed that "a strange anxiety overcame me caused by seeing philosophy seemingly divided and torn in three or more directions—the unity of my own being appeared to be rent apart."[67] Again from the *Nachlass*, in a passage titled "Contemporary Culture and Philosophy," Dilthey identified "the deep contradiction running through the present age" which mocked the rapid progress of the sciences.[68] In almost all Dilthey's work, one finds these themes of crisis, anarchy, contradiction, and anxiety defining the path of inquiry and the mode of interrogation.[69] His extraordinary sensitivity to these currents helped him to recast the problems of contemporary academic philosophy by abandoning its strictly methodological focus for what he believed was the only genuine concern of modern thought: the understanding and interpretation of historical existence.

Contemporary academics, especially those who followed the Neo-Kantian school of Rickert and Windelband, had presumed to define philosophy's essential task as the classification and legitimation of knowledge in the *Natur-* and *Geisteswissenschaften*. As part of their program, Windelband and Rickert separated nature from history and

[66] Misch, *Der junge Dilthey*, vii; and Ermarth, *Wilhelm Dilthey*, 15.
[67] Dilthey, *GS* 8: 223–224.
[68] Ibid., 197.
[69] For similar pronouncements, see Dilthey, *GS* 5: xlii; *GS* 19: 48; *GS* 10: 14; *GS* 6: 246. See also *Briefwechsel*, 156 and 228.

culture on the basis of a transcendental theory of knowledge rooted in a "supra-empirical subject."[70] Dilthey rejected this approach, however, arguing that "the transcendental method means the death of history for it precludes any penetration of given realities by fruitful historical concepts."[71] Against the Neo-Kantians, Dilthey claimed that it is not the transcendental, transhistorical, and transcultural "self" that experiences historical life but the vital, living, pulsating human being conditioned in its historical place and time. Dilthey responded to Rickert's approach by emphasizing that "we must move out of the pure, fine air of the Kantian critique of reason in order to do justice to the wholly different nature of historical objects."[72] Any science of history, culture, or *Geist* must ground its theory in the actual experience of historical life. The Kantian theory of the sciences had separated *Wissenschaft* and *Leben*. In fact, Rickert had proclaimed all *Lebensphilosophie* as the death of true *Wissenschaft*. But Dilthey wished to reverse the antihistorical, antilife attitude within Neo-Kantianism by focusing on the bundle of instincts and the labyrinth of psychological and social relations that constitute human being. By stressing the primacy of *Erlebnis*, or lived experience, he hoped, on the one hand, to secure the connectedness of science to life and, on the other, to establish the unique epistemological validity of the *Geisteswissenschaften* and their methods. "If the mind sets itself over its own creations as something merely objectively empirical and analyzes them according to the external method of natural science," Dilthey argued, "then there occurs a self-alienation of mind in regard to its own creations."[73] Whereas the positivists had tried to apply the methods of natural science to the study of human history and culture, Dilthey reminded his contemporaries that history, unlike nature, is "not merely an appearance given in external sensation as a mere phenomenal reflex" but rather "an inner reality directly experienced from within."[74] As inner experience, history requires an approach and a method based not on the causal continuity of natural processes but on a structural, inner unity peculiar to *Geist* itself: the method of *Verstehen*.

We can understand history, culture, and society because, as human

[70] Dilthey, *GS* 7: 285.
[71] Ibid.
[72] Ibid., 278.
[73] Dilthey, *GS* 6: 126.
[74] Dilthey, *SW*, 247; *GS* 5: 317–318 (translation mine).

beings, we, too, are bound up in traditions, customs, practices, and institutions that have been historically conditioned. This kind of knowledge differs from the knowledge of the natural world, for it is grounded in the lived experience of historical humanity—a fundamental fact of human consciousness which allows us to "understand" history rather than merely "explain" it. Explanation, or *Erklären*, as the epistemological approach of empiricism, is based on external observation; conversely, understanding, or *Verstehen*—the approach of hermeneutics—is based on lived experience. We, as humans, understand history, Dilthey argued, because we are part of it: "The first condition for the possibility of historical science lies in the fact that I myself am a historical being, that he who inquires into history is the same as he who makes it."[75]

Historical knowledge is radically different from the knowledge of nature, then, not only in a methodological or even epistemological sense. For although Dilthey acknowledged the validity of a Kantian approach for a theory of the sciences, his real aim was a hermeneutic understanding of life itself. The roots of this mode of questioning go back to Vico and his famous dictum *"verum et factum convertuntur."* If for Vico only what the human being created (the *factum*) was true (*verum*), for Dilthey, "only that which the mind has made can it fully understand."[76] But Dilthey's theory of the *Geisteswissenschaften*, dependent as it is on the work of both Vico and Kant, cannot be explained solely against this background. Dilthey did not want to understand the critique of historical reason as merely an epistemological inquiry into the grounds of historical science. For Dilthey, *historical* reason also involved an anthropological study of human life as it is lived in the world. In concrete terms Dilthey concentrated his philosophical attention on the living human subject, which is itself histori-

[75] Dilthey, *GS* 7: 278.

[76] *The New Science of Giambattista Vico: Unabridged Translation of the Third Edition (1744) with the addition of "Practic of the New Science,"* trans. Thomas Goddard Bergin and Max Harold Fisch (Ithaca, N.Y.: Cornell University Press, 1984), 96; and Dilthey, *GS* 7: 148. Dilthey held Vico in high regard. In fact, in his Schleiermacher biography he referred to *The New Science* as "one of the greatest triumphs of modern thought" (*GS* 14, pt. 2, 698). For articles dealing specifically with Vico and Dilthey, see Howard Tuttle, "The Epistemological Status of the Cultural World in Vico and Dilthey," in Giorgio Tagliacozzo and D. P. Verene, eds., *Giambattista Vico's Science of Humanity* (Baltimore: Johns Hopkins University Press, 1976), 241–250; and H. A. Hodges, "Vico and Dilthey," and H. P. Rickman, "Vico and Dilthey's Methodology of the Human Studies," both in Giorgio Tagliacozzo, ed., *Giambattista Vico: An International Symposium* (Baltimore: Johns Hopkins University Press, 1969), 439–456.

cal and whose being is determined by an awareness of its own historicity, rather than on the prosaic narrative of historical events. By focusing on the ontological consequences of historicity, Dilthey offered a new approach to the crisis of the sciences in the late nineteenth century. His hermeneutical manner of questioning helped transform the problem of historicism from a taxonomical dispute about method and logic to a philosophical reflection on the meaning of historical existence. He believed that in doing so he could present contemporary philosophy with a way out of the epistemological cul-de-sac of Neo-Kantianism which marked the crisis mentality of German thought. In his essay "The Problem of History in Recent German Philosophy" (1943), Hans-Georg Gadamer offered an insightful assessment of this aspect in Dilthey's work, seeing it as the first indication of a phenomenological critique of nineteenth-century science: "Dilthey appears to share with the Neo-Kantians the epistemological point of view . . . that merely inquires into the possibility of historical science and neglects the question of 'being' in history. In truth, however, he does not limit himself to reflect only on historical knowledge as it is present in the science of history; rather, he reflects on the being of the human being which is conditioned by a knowledge of its own history."[77]

Dilthey's radical indictment of the Neo-Kantian project was animated by a fundamental awareness of metaphysical residues in its approach to history. For example, Rickert's attempt to solve the crisis of relativism by appealing to a suprahistorical concept of value seemed to Dilthey to deny the value of historicity. By rejecting the historicity of science, Rickert had also denied the possibility of any kind of human understanding, because Dilthey argued, science itself (especially the human sciences) could be understood only in a historical context. "I am, to the impenetrable depths within myself, a historical being," Dilthey wrote; only on the basis of this lived historical being can one hope to understand history.[78] Both within the intellectual history of the West and within the historical experience of living human beings, history is essentially a form of past life. Consequently, before we turn to a more explicit discussion of Dilthey's understanding of historicity, we will first explore his notion of life (*Leben*) and lived experience (*Erlebnis*).

[77] Hans-Georg Gadamer, "Das Problem der Geschichte in der neueren deutschen Philosophie," *Kleine Schriften*, vol. 1 (Tübingen: Mohr, 1967), 4.
[78] Dilthey, *GS* 7: 278.

vi. Dilthey's Concept of *Erlebnis* and Its Relation to the Human Sciences

In an essay written in 1895 on comparative psychology, Dilthey stated that the aim of the human sciences is to take the products and expressions of the sociohistorical world given to us in life and "to transpose them back into the vital, living, spiritual reality from which they derive."[79] As it presents itself to us within our experience, Dilthey argued, life is not a haphazard collection of sensory impressions or curiosities but the unity of fragments within a psychically organized whole. Against the fiction of a monadic, autonomous, and self-determined subject propagated by eighteenth-century social contract theory, Dilthey defined the self by its embeddedness in life and by its participation in language, custom, and tradition. As Dilthey wrote in a fragment from the *Nachlass*:

> The human being knows itself only in history, never through introspection; indeed, we all seek it in history. Or, to put it more generally, we seek what is human in it, such as religion, and so on. We want to know what it is. If there were a science of human beings it would be anthropology that aims at understanding the totality of experience through the structural context. The individual always realizes only one of the possibilities in its development, which could always have taken a different turning whenever it had to make an important decision. The human being is only given to us at all in terms of its realized possibilities.[80]

For Dilthey, self-knowledge does not derive from an interiorized monologue or through rigorous introspection but through an awareness of the "interwoven texture of world and self," where there is no separation of the processes of consciousness from the "external" object being perceived.[81] Within this *Lebenszusammenhang*, or life-nexus —accessible only through the immediacy of lived experience—Dilthey finds the structural unity of historical interpretation.

To analyze fully the significance of *Erlebnis* for Dilthey's theory, I will proceed in two directions. First, I will inquire into the relationship between Dilthey's theory of consciousness and his "philosophy

---

[79] Dilthey, *GS* 5: 265.
[80] Wilhelm Dilthey, *Pattern and Meaning in History: Thoughts on History and Society*, ed. H. P. Rickman (New York: Harper and Row, 1962), 138 (translation altered); Dilthey, *GS* 7: 279.
[81] Dilthey, *GS* 19: 167.

of life." Second, I will try to explain how Dilthey's interpretation of *Erlebnis* (in contrast to that of the romantic tradition) can be used as the starting point for a new theory of the human sciences.

In the "Breslau Draft," Dilthey attempted to relate the problem of the life-nexus to a theory of human consciousness. He began by examining what he called the "first principle" of philosophy, the "principle of phenomenality," which he traced to the early modern philosophy of consciousness in Descartes and Leibniz.[82] According to the principle of phenomenality, all objects and persons to which I stand in relation are "there for me" only as facts of my consciousness. As Dilthey explained: "I only *appear* to live among things that are independent of my consciousness; in reality, my self distinguishes itself from facts of my own consciousness, formations whose locus is in me. My consciousness is the locus which encompasses this seemingly immeasurable external world; it is the stuff from which the objects which press on one another in that world are woven. . . . The object is simply this representation, this fact of consciousness which, through a process which needs to be investigated, I place over against myself."[83] In "Contributions to the Solution of the Question concerning the Origin of Our Belief in the Reality of the External World," Dilthey went even further, suggesting that "the highest principle of philosophy is the 'principle of phenomenality' according to which everything that is 'there for me' stands under the general condition of being a fact of my consciousness. Even every external thing is given to me only as a connection of facts or processes of consciousness. An object or thing is only 'there' for and in consciousness."[84]

Following this early modern philosophy of consciousness, Dilthey rejected the naïve belief in a world of objects separate from consciousness which impinge on it from without. Rather, as Dilthey saw it, objects exist for us only through the condition of their being known. Yet, at the same time, these "facts of consciousness" are not merely the representations of a purely logical subject riven from the world. Were this the case, Dilthey's epistemological first principle would lead to a radical phenomenalism, presenting only pure images on the screen of subjectivity. Instead, Dilthey defined these facts of consciousness as *Erlebnisse*, or life experiences, that cannot be known through pure cognition but only in the mediated context of a world.

[82] Dilthey, *Introduction to the Human Sciences*, 245; GS 19: 58.
[83] Dilthey, *Introduction to the Human Sciences*, 245–246; GS 19: 58–59.
[84] Dilthey, GS 5: 90.

Hence, to overcome the solipsistic implications of pure phenomenality, Dilthey added a second philosophical principle, that of the totality of experience. This second principle (intimately bound up with the first) holds that all the so-called facts of consciousness can only be grasped as part of the totality of our life-nexus.[85] Accordingly, as Dilthey explained, "The nexus that encompasses the facts of consciousness—including perceptions, memories, objects and representations of them, and finally concepts—is psychological, i.e., it is contained in the totality of our psychic life."[86] All the facts of our consciousness, from the simplest memory of childhood to the most complex scientific theory of matter, are parts of a unified tapestry of life experience and may never be abstracted from it and reduced to "pure" data. Any theory of the human world which seeks to objectify these life experiences as historical facts of research or as the phenomenal representations of an abstract subject can never approach the genuine sense of the life-nexus as a unity. In its totality, life is performative, interactive, and reflexive; an epistemology that denies this movement and seeks to isolate consciousness in the abstract frame of the cogito only alienates philosophical reason from its own life source. In an effort to get back to this fundamental and immediate vital ground, Dilthey seized on the notion of *Erlebnis* as a way of overcoming the bloodless theorizing of the philosophical sciences.

Erlebnis, in Dilthey's sense, can never be wholly understood in a

[85] Dilthey called this principle the *Satz von der Totalität des Erlebens* (see GS 19: 75 ff.). For an analysis of this and the other "fundamental" principle of Dilthey's philosophy, *Satz von Phänomenalität*, refer to the excellent introduction by Otto Pöggeler in Wilhelm Dilthey, *Das Wesen der Philosophie* (Hamburg: Meiner, 1984), viii–xlvi, esp. xvii–xix. Also helpful on Dilthey and hermeneutics is Pöggeler, *Heidegger und die hermeneutische Philosophie* (Freiburg: Alber, 1984), chap. 4, 256–263. See also two articles in collected essays: Erwin Hufnagel, "Hermeneutik als Grundlegung der Geisteswissenschaften," in Ulrich Nassen, ed., *Klassiker der Hermeneutik* (Paderborn: Schöningh, 1982); and Heinrich Anz, "Hermeneutik der Individualität: Wilhelm Diltheys hermeneutische Position und ihre Aporien," in Hendrik Birus, ed., *Hermeneutische Positionen* (Göttingen: Vandenhoeck & Ruprecht, 1982). Among other studies on Dilthey and hermeneutics which are helpful are the following: Paul Ricoeur, "The Task of Hermeneutics," in Michael Murray, ed., *Heidegger and Modern Philosophy* (New Haven, Conn.: Yale University Press, 1978), 141–160; Michael Ermarth, "The Transformation of Hermeneutics," *Monist* 64, no. 2 (April 1981): 175–194; Hans-Georg Gadamer, "The Problem of Historical Consciousness," *Graduate Faculty Philosophy Journal* 5 (1975): 3–52; Richard Palmer, *Hermeneutics* (Evanston, Ill.: Northwestern University Press, 1969); and Manfred Riedel's two outstanding contributions: "Einleitung," in Wilhelm Dilthey, *Der Aufbau der geschichtlichen Welt in den Geisteswissenschaften* (Frankfurt: Suhrkamp, 1970), 9–80, and his essays on Dilthey in *Verstehen oder Erklären? Zur Theorie und Geschichte der hermeneutischen Wissenschaften* (Stuttgart: Klett-Cotta, 1978). I should also mention the first-rate contributions to Dilthey scholarship by Stefan Otto, *Rekonstruktion der Geschichte: Zur Kritik der historischen Vernunft* (Munich: Fink, 1982).

[86] Dilthey, *Introduction to the Human Sciences*, 264; GS 19: 75.

theoretical way but must be viewed in its fully concrete manifestations as the product of a thinking, willing, feeling, and living human creature. As early as 1883, in the *Introduction*, Dilthey spoke of experience (*Erfahrung*) as having its "originary nexus" in "the conditions of consciousness."[87] In the *Erlebnis*—"the basic unit of life"—reality is revealed to us; it is the medium through which we come to know the world.[88] According to Dilthey: "The consciousness of an experience and its constitution are the same: there is no separation between what is there-for-me and what in experience is there-for-me. In other words, the experience does not stand like an object over against the one who experiences it, but rather its existence is undifferentiated from what is there present for me in it."[89] The implications of Dilthey's insights within the context of late-nineteenth-century German philosophy are profound. Against the claims of positivism and naturalism, Dilthey argued that nature remains something external and recalcitrant to us because it is something we have not ourselves made; history, on the other hand, opens itself up to us in a way that we understand because we are already involved in it. Its structure is hermeneutical; that is, it is open to us through the process of interpretation. To comprehend fully the effect of our primal life relation to history—which Dilthey used as the cornerstone for his theory of the human sciences—we must first understand what Dilthey meant by his technical use of the term *life*, or *Leben*. We can then proceed to explore the hermeneutic significance of life and relate it to Dilthey's theory of historical consciousness.

In the "Breslau Draft," Dilthey defined *life* in these terms:

> The term "life" expresses what is to everyone the most familiar and intimate, but at the same time the darkest and even most inscrutable. What life is, is an insoluble enigma. All reflection, inquiry, and thought arise from this most inscrutable of things. All knowledge is rooted in this never wholly knowable thing. One can describe it. One can accentuate its singular, characteristic traits. One can, as it were, pursue its tone, rhythm, and stirring melody. But one cannot dissect life into its constituent parts; it cannot be reduced to analysis. What it is cannot be expressed in a simple formula or explanation. . . . Thought cannot fully go behind life, for it is the expression of life.[90]

[87] Dilthey, *GS* 1: xvii.
[88] Dilthey, *GS* 7: 161.
[89] Ibid., 139.
[90] Dilthey, *GS* 19: 346–347. Both Ermarth (*Wilhelm Dilthey*, 197–209) and Palmer (*Hermeneutics*, 108) argue that Dilthey's theory of *Erlebnis* was a move in the direction of

Because life itself was so difficult to reduce to any workable philosophical expression, Dilthey tried in a variety of ways and contexts to communicate what he meant by it. "Life," he wrote, "is the primary thing—in it are woven all our impressions, thoughts, and perceptions."[91] "Life is its own proof"—one cannot ground it in anything other than itself.[92] "Always and everywhere life remains for thought *unergründlich*, or incapable of being grounded."[93]

Despite the mystical and romantic overtones implicit in these various descriptions, however, Dilthey never intended his notion of life to be metaphysical, irrational, or speculative. For Dilthey, life always meant life as it is lived by human beings in the world, that is, "*das von den Menschen gelebte Leben.*"[94] As he explained in one of his drafts for "The Categories of Life," "I use the technical term 'life' in my work on the human sciences specifically in regard to life in the human world."[95] In contrast to the biological, cosmic, and aesthetic implications of nineteenth-century French and German life-philosophy, Dilthey set as his goal "the foundation of a descriptive and analytic psychology which would proceed from the structure of our psychic life itself and would seek, within the realm of methodical *Wissenschaft*, a more modest, restricted, and less arbitrary solution to the task that contemporary life-philosophers have set before themselves."[96] Because *Erlebnis* alone does not give us a sense of the full dimensions of life but only of life's structural units as experienced within a specific

---

twentieth-century phenomenology. The contributions in Orth, *Dilthey und die Philosophie der Gegenwart*, esp. pt. 1, "Beziehungen zur Phänomenologie," 29–182; Rudolf Makkreel, "Husserl, Dilthey, and the Relation of the Life-World to History" *Research in Phenomenology* 12 (1982): 39–58; and the early study by Ludwig Landgrebe, "Wilhelm Diltheys Theorie der Geisteswissenschaften," *Jahrbuch für Philosophie und phänomenologische Forschung* 9 (1928): 238–266, all show distinct connections between the late thought of Dilthey and the contributions of the young Edmund Husserl. Dilthey's theory of *Leben*, *Erlebnis*, and *Lebenszusammenhang* were far more than the romantic musings of a late nineteenth-century irrationalist. Dilthey's theory of consciousness was rigorously *wissenschaftlich*, and his penchant for "empirical" researches and *objektive Gültigkeit* (objective validity) shows a clear connection to the kind of philosophy practiced by Husserl in the early years of the twentieth century. If there is any doubt concerning Dilthey's status as a "romantic," one should carefully read his letters to Husserl reprinted in "Der Briefwechsel Dilthey-Husserl," *Man and World* 1 (1968): 423–446, with an introduction by Heidegger's student Walter Biemel.

[91] Dilthey, *GS* 19: 345.
[92] Dilthey, *GS* 5: 131.
[93] Dilthey, *GS* 19: 347.
[94] Dilthey, *GS* 8: 78 and 121.
[95] Dilthey, *GS* 7: 228.
[96] Dilthey, *GS* 5: 371 and also *GS* 19: 37–43 for similar sentiments.

temporal context, Dilthey proposed that philosophers engage in the work of what he called "descriptive psychology."

Descriptive psychology was to be a new discipline in both aim and function. In Dilthey's view, it was to supplant the natural-scientific psychology of the German university, which rooted its study of mind in laboratory experiments and human physiology, by focusing on the "living unity" of consciousness. As Dilthey wrote in his *Ideas concerning a Descriptive and Analytic Psychology* (1894):

> The self finds itself in a variety of states which are recognized as unified through the consciousness of the identity of the person. At the same time, each self finds itself conditioned by an external world and reacting to it. The self then grasps this world in its consciousness and determinately knows it by acts of sensory perception. Since this living unity finds itself thus conditioned by the milieu in which it lives and to which it in turn reacts, there emerges an articulated organization of its inner states. This I call the structure of psychic life. By grasping this structure, descriptive psychology discovers the principle of coherence which connects the psychic series into a whole. This whole is life.[97]

Whereas the older, natural-scientific study of psychology had "in dead abstraction attempted to approach the problem of the original constitution of the individual severed from the historical trunk of society and its interactions," Dilthey's psychology sought to ground all our *Erlebnisse* in the sociohistorical context from which they originated.[98] In this sense his descriptive psychology was intended as a study of the objectifications of human consciousness within time, within the process of historical life. In the *Ideas*, Dilthey explained:

> We find in language, myth and religious ritual, customs, law and in the external organization of society, the products of the collective spirit in which, in Hegel's terms, human consciousness is objectivated and thus can withstand analysis. Man does not apprehend what he is by musing over himself, nor by doing psychological experiments, but rather by history. This analysis of the products of human spirit—destined to open for us a glance at the genesis of the psychic nexus, of its forms and its action—must, in addition to the analysis of historical products, observe and collect everything which it can seize of the *historical processes* wherein such a nexus

[97] Wilhelm Dilthey, *Descriptive Psychology and Historical Understanding* trans. Kenneth Heiges and Richard Zaner (The Hague: Martinus Nijhoff, 1977), 81–82; and Dilthey, *GS* 5: 200.

[98] Dilthey, *GS* 5: 63.

becomes constituted. It is precisely on the combination of these two methods that every historical study of the genesis, forms, and action of the psychic nexus in man depends.[99]

Natural-scientific psychology had conceived of the human being in atomistic fashion as a psychological ego set against history and society. It sought to isolate the universal element in psychic life and, through the study of physics and mechanics, to arrive at a theory of human perception. But Dilthey insisted that perception, like all mental functions, can never be isolated from the thing perceived. Everything is of a piece, a structural unity whose center is the matrix of experience. Dilthey's task was to arrive at a theory of structural unity whereby the complexes of these *Erlebnisse* could provide a universal framework for the particular life experience. In individual life, this unity is provided by one's own life history. From the matrix of a single experience, one can proceed to understand, reflexively, its part within an overall structure. One understands the tolling of bells, for example, within the nexus of other experiences; it conjures memories of Sunday morning service, perhaps, or the funeral of a public figure. Yet, no matter what the memory, each experience extends beyond the boundaries of the individual self. One's own life history is necessarily a part of a larger cultural life-nexus, and only within such a broader structure can the individual find meaning. Even language, the very instrument of self-reflection, is itself the product of this broader cultural structure. Hence, Dilthey began to see individual life—or autobiography—as an important model for an understanding of the human world that made history possible. But in no sense was this focus egological or psychologistic, for Dilthey always viewed the individual experience of life within a structural nexus of part-to-whole relations. By emphasizing the centrality of this part-to-whole relationship, Dilthey was able to move from a descriptive psychology focused on "structure" to a hermeneutical theory of history which understands life as a "phenomenon."

Rickert and Windelband had posited a theory of consciousness which defined the transcendental subject as a hermetic and lifeless entity, a Cartesian fiction measured against the categories of Kant. Dilthey sought to break with this insular tradition of academic *Kathederphilosophie* and its rostrum-style pronouncements. Against Rick-

---

[99] Dilthey, *Descriptive Psychology*, 62–63; *GS* 5: 180.

ert's theory of concept-formation, Dilthey turned to a hermeneutical method for understanding nature and history not simply as objects "there" for consciousness but also as modes of experience within the unity of a life history. Dilthey was careful, however, to avoid the illusion of an immediate consciousness of things or of the direct accessibility of consciousness to itself posited in the Cartesian cogito. To overcome this extreme subjectivism, Dilthey attempted to think of consciousness both within its own life history and within its cultural and historical context. Because life itself is part of a larger whole (the history of human life), Dilthey maintained that to understand it, one had to consider more than the data of biography, memory, or self-reflection; one also needed to understand the historical objectifications of life as they are studied in the human sciences. In Dilthey's words: "Life is the fullness, variety, and interaction—within something continuous—experienced by individuals. Its subject matter is identical with history. At every point of history there is life, and history consists of life of every kind in the most varied circumstances. History is merely life viewed in terms of the continuity of mankind as a whole."[100] By contextualizing history both within individual lives and within the life of the species, Dilthey had hoped to lay the foundation for a new philosophical anthropology focused on the historical essence or historicity of the human being. In a well-known passage from "The Dream," Dilthey claimed, "What the human being is can be told only from its history."[101] Similarly, in "Introduction to the Philosophy of Life," he explained that "what the human being is and what it desires, it experiences only in the development of its nature through the centuries; it is never to be found in universal concepts but only in living experience itself, which springs from the depths of its whole being."[102] But Dilthey's emphasis on the historicity of the individual raised a problem when considered from the standpoint of a scientific study of human life. For, if one remained committed to a rigorous epistemology, then how—from the limited historical perspective of finite human experience—could one attain a larger, scientific truth applicable beyond the life experience of one individual?

[100] Dilthey, *Pattern and Meaning*, 163; *GS* 7: 256.
[101] Dilthey, *GS* 8: 226.
[102] Dilthey, *GS* 6: 57. For similar pronouncements by Dilthey in a variety of contexts, cf. *GS* 1: 98 and 271, *GS* 2: 170, *GS* 3: 210, *GS* 4: 528, *GS* 5: 425, *GS* 8: 4 and 166, and *GS* 9: 173. This notion of the historically bound nature of humanity, namely, human historicity, is a recurrent theme for Dilthey and will be treated in more detail later in this chapter.

What scientific criteria, what form of inquiry, what particular method could one employ to offer some modicum of certitude for the claims of the human sciences? Dilthey himself realized the broad implications of this problem, posing the decisive question, "How are we to overcome the difficulty that everywhere weighs upon the *Geisteswissenschaften* of deriving universally valid propositions from inner experiences that are so personally limited, so indeterminate, so compacted and resistant to analysis?"[103] The question itself was not new. The problem of how to establish a historical method that would guarantee a measure of objectivity against the dangers of subjective relativism had also preoccupied the early historicist tradition. Dilthey tried to go beyond the merely historiographical focus of early historicism, however, by reconciling "the most profound fact of the human sciences—the historicity of mental life which expresses itself in each cultural system that humanity produces" with the methodological demands of hermeneutics. By avoiding both the ahistorical tendencies of Neo-Kantianism and the philosophical impoverishment of historicism, Dilthey hoped to overcome the fundamental split between scientific knowledge and historical life which had marked the crisis of the sciences. As he reconsidered these relations, Dilthey turned to a philosophical rehabilitation of hermeneutics.

vii. Historicity and Hermeneutics

Dilthey's work marks an important shift in philosophical reflection on historicism, appearing as it does during the era of Neo-Kantian dominance at the German university. If the methodological contributions of Rickert and Windelband solidified the scientific status of historical research, they also contributed to the profound alienation of historical spirit from its roots in actual historical existence. Against this kind of abstract theorizing, Dilthey's persistent tendency was to acknowledge the significance of human historicity, viewing it as a hermeneutical indication for understanding life, not as a transcendental condition for the possibility of knowledge. In his continuing dialogue and correspondence with his close friend Graf Paul Yorck von Wartenburg, Dilthey moved further away from the methodological focus of Neo-Kantian theory of science toward a hermeneutic of historical understanding. Understanding, in Dilthey's interpretation, sig-

---

[103] Dilthey, *GS* 6: 107.

nified not only the specific procedure of the human sciences but the fundamental movement of human historical life as well, a movement whose beginning is impossible to isolate epistemologically. Neo-Kantianism had erred in its attempt to secure a logical starting point for historical inquiry and understanding. But Dilthey emphasized that knowledge begins in the middle. Within the sphere of individual life, one moves from the context of familiarity (an understanding of oneself) to the larger nexus of all life-relations (an understanding of others) in a circular fashion; as Dilthey phrased it, "Understanding is a rediscovery of the I in the Thou."[104]

We come to understand the emotions, acts, impulses, desires, thoughts, and expressions of other persons, Dilthey argued, by virtue of a shared psychic structure. In the forms of everyday human expression—gestures, facial movements, speech, intonation, and so on —the world of human psychology opens itself to us to be interpreted. The process of understanding such signs, expressions, and other objectifications of life Dilthey referred to as *Verstehen*.[105] *Verstehen* in this special sense means not only the understanding of an individual person or mind (*Geist*) but also the social and cultural products of mind,

---

[104] Dilthey, *GS* 7: 191.

[105] Dilthey defines *Verstehen* as follows: "Understanding and interpretation is the method used throughout the human studies. It unites all their functions and contains all their truths. Understanding opens up the world. Understanding of other people and their expressions is developed on the basis of experience and self-understanding and the constant interaction between them. Here, too, it is not a matter of logical construction or psychological dissection but of an epistemological analysis. We must now establish what understanding can contribute to historical knowledge" (translated by H. P. Rickman in *SW*, 219; Dilthey, *GS* 7: 205). He also writes: "The course of every person's life is a process of continuous determination in which the possibilities inherent in him are narrowed down. The crystallization of his nature always determines his further development. . . . But understanding lays open for him a wide range of possibilities that are not present in the determination of his actual life. For me as for most people today, the possibility of experiencing religious states of mind in my personal existence is sharply circumscribed. However, when I go through the letters and writings of Luther, the accounts of his contemporaries, the records of the religious conferences and councils, and the reports of his official contracts, I encounter a religious phenomenon of such eruptive power, of such energy, in which the issue is one of life or death, that it lies beyond the experiential possibilities of a person of our time. But I can re-live [*nacherleben*] all of this. . . . And thereby this process opens up for us a religious world in Luther and in his contemporaries in the early Reformation that enlarges our horizon by including possibilities that are available to us only in this way. Thus man, who is determined from within, can experience many other existences in imagination. Although he is limited by his circumstances, foreign beauties of the world and regions of life that he could never reach himself are laid open to him. To put it in general terms, man, bound and determined by the reality of life, is made free not only by art—which has often been pointed out—but also by the understanding of things historical" (translated by Theodore Plantinga in *Historical Understanding in the Thought of Wilhelm Dilthey*, 23; Dilthey, *GS*, 7: 215–216).

which are objectified in such things as art, poetry, literature, music, laws, science, and philosophy. These expressions Dilthey referred to as *objective mind* (*objektiver Geist*), a term he borrowed from Hegel.[106] In a draft for his "Critique of Historical Reason," which merits extended quotation, Dilthey defined objective mind and its relation to his theory of *Verstehen* as a central fact of the human sciences:

I have shown how significant the objective mind is for the possibility of knowledge in the human studies. By this I mean the manifold forms in which what individuals hold in common have objectified themselves in the world of the senses. In this objective mind the past is a permanently enduring present for us. Its realm extends from the style of life and the forms of social intercourse, to the system of purposes which society has created for itself, to custom, law, state, religion, art, science, and philosophy. For even the work of genius represents ideas, feelings, and ideals commonly held in an age and environment. From this world of objective mind the self receives sustenance from earliest childhood. It is the medium in which the understanding of other people and their expressions take place. For everything in which the mind has objectified itself contains something held in common by the I and the Thou. Every square planted with trees, every room in which seats are arranged, is intelligible to us from our infancy because human planning, arranging, and valuing—common to us all— have assigned its place to every square and every object in the room. The child grows up within the order and customs of the family which it shares with the other members and its mother's orders are accepted in this context. Before it learns to talk it is already wholly immersed in that common medium. It learns to understand the gestures and facial expressions, movements and exclamations, words and sentences, only because it encounters them always in the same form and in the same relation to what they mean and express. Thus the individual orientates himself in the world of objective mind.

[106] For Dilthey's discussion of *objektiver Geist*, see *GS* 7: 208–210. Dilthey's notion of objective mind differs from Hegel's in that it is rooted principally in lived experience rather than in a metaphysical process of historical development. Although Dilthey *did* borrow from Hegel in viewing all human reality in terms of objective mind, he conceived of this in a hermeneutical rather than a metaphysical fashion. All our understanding is grounded in the cultural artifacts that compose our lives: religion, society, language, custom, and others, yet understanding—given within a specific temporal-spatial context—first allows us to make sense of the unity of objective mind and our own subjective life experience. Life experience implies objective mind; objective mind implies life experience. The structure of our understanding is circular, or hermeneutic. But there is also a crucial link here to the notion of the *Geisteswissenschaften* in that they study human life—not just my life but "human" life reconstituted as the interwoven texture of *all* human lives in objective mind. As Dilthey put it in the "Nachlass," "The human sciences have as their comprehensive reality—objective mind" (translated by Ermarth in *Wilhelm Dilthey*, 277).

From this there follows a consequence important for the process of understanding. The expression of life which the individual grasps is, as a rule, not simply an isolated expression but filled with a knowledge of what is held in common and of a relation to the mental content.[107]

Whereas the understanding of everyday life occurs within a context of changing impressions and familiar points of reference, the understanding of objective mind demands a more rigorous approach. Its expressions are "fixed" in a given form: in poetic meter, in musical cadence, in architectural buttresses, in literary prose. Understanding and interpreting these "fixed life expressions" (as Dilthey called them) requires a method with specific rules and procedures, attentive to the concept of cultural development and change: the method of hermeneutics. Through a hermeneutic approach to *Verstehen*, Dilthey hoped to provide a scientifically verifiable procedure capable of explicating the expressions of objective mind. This hermeneutic approach would, if successful, grant "the possibility of universally valid interpretation" and resolve the problems of relativism which were plaguing the human sciences.[108] In "The Rise of Hermeneutics" (1900), Dilthey argued that "in the context of the epistemology, logic, and methodology of the human studies, the theory of interpretation [that is, hermeneutics] becomes an important link between philosophy and the historical sciences, an essential part of the foundation of the human studies."[109]

Traditional hermeneutics—in the manner of Ast, Wolf, Ernesti, Michaelis, and Semler—had focused on exegetical criticism of classical texts and the Bible.[110] For them, hermeneutics was primarily a *technique* with philological applications and ambitions. With the romantic hermeneutics of Schleiermacher, however, the grammatical, syntactical, and stylistic emphasis of these earlier critics was amended, thus placing new significance on *psychological* analysis within a historical context. Dilthey, who had spent much of his early career researching the intellectual background of Schleiermacher, conceded the importance of psychological interpretation for understanding historical

[107] Dilthey, *Pattern and Meaning*, 120–121; GS 7: 208.
[108] Dilthey, GS 5: 329.
[109] Ibid., 331.
[110] For a fuller treatment of the hermeneutic tradition, see Jean Grondin, *Einführung in die philosophische Hermeneutik* (Darmstadt: Wissenschaftliche Buchgesellschaft, 1991), and the classic work by Hans-Georg Gadamer, *Truth and Method* (New York: Crossroad, 1989), pt. 2. Dilthey's own reflections on the hermeneutic tradition are included in his multivolume biography of Schleiermacher; GS 13, and especially GS 14: 595–787; and in his essay "The Rise of Hermeneutics," in GS 5: 317–331.

texts. But he went even further. Whereas for Schleiermacher hermeneutics was primarily textual—in the sense that it was used to interpret literary works, codes of law, historical documents, business contracts, letters, and so forth—for Dilthey it became a means of interpreting life itself. "Life"—in the technical sense Dilthey gave it—is a text whose parts are the *Erlebnisse* of the psychological subject. Every part of life, every *Erlebnis*, has significance for the whole. And, in turn, the whole determines the significance of each part. Life expresses itself to us within a context of meaning whose unity is based on this part-to-whole relationship, following a hermeneutical structure.[111] Because "life" is not only individual life but also the product of historical forces and circumstance, it cannot be interpreted solely within the life-nexus of a single human being. To interpret life properly, one must understand all its various expressions "in the world," within language, culture, and history—something that, Dilthey believed, could be done only through an analysis of objective mind. In seeing the human world in this way as a "text" that required interpretation, Dilthey radically altered the meaning of hermeneutics within German philosophy. Whereas hermeneutics had been, for Savigny, Ranke, and Boeckh, a methodological tool used to guarantee the scientific rigor of philological and historical understanding, for Dilthey it became an "essential part of the foundations of the human sciences."[112]

Dilthey's appropriation of hermeneutic principles for an understanding of historicism helped to shift the focus of its *Fragestellung* away from the problem of method to an emphasis on historical experience itself. As an exegete of *Geist*, Dilthey attempted to see all methodological access to history as something grounded in the part-to-whole interplay of self and world, a context of shared meaning which opens itself up to us in various linguistic, cultural, and psychological forms. This common hermeneutical structure of experience, Dilthey argued, enables the scholar to achieve a certain measure of historical understanding. In one of his important drafts for a "Critique of Historical Reason," Dilthey explained that "the principles of historical science find no equivalents in abstract theories. . . . The totality of our being lies in experience alone. This is what we reconstruct through

[111] Dilthey, *GS* 7: 130–138.
[112] Dilthey, *GS* 2: 115 and *GS* 5: 331. Dilthey often makes this connection between hermeneutics and his critique of historical reason, see *GS* 1: 116, *GS* 7: 191–294, and *GS* 8: 264–266.

understanding, and it is here that the principle of the commonality of individuals is given."[113]

In Dilthey's interpretation, "historical consciousness"—or the consciousness of one's own historicity—constitutes a break with both historicist fact-collecting and the early modern philosophy of consciousness, Ranke's *Selbstauslöschung* and Descartes's cogito. Unlike Nietzsche, who in "The Uses and Disadvantages of History for Life" pilloried historical consciousness for its diseased and life-wearying antiquarianism, Dilthey insisted that "historical consciousness has, finally, no 'use'; it is rather a way of viewing things which is applicable to every phenomenon."[114] Even as Dilthey raised historical consciousness to the highest form of reflexive awareness, however, he still remained committed to the Cartesian project of securing certitude for scientific knowledge. If historical consciousness represented to him the highest form of self-knowledge—the only genuine means of grasping lived experience—it also signified a limit beyond which scientific consciousness could not proceed. Dilthey's work is marked by this persistent tension between the claims of scientific knowledge for universal validity and the finitude of temporal, historical being. To reconcile these competing claims, Dilthey turned to the problem of philosophical "categories" derived from the work of both Aristotle and Kant.

Categories, Dilthey observed, are "concepts that express or establish a context, relation, or nexus" and can be classified as either "formal" or "real."[115] Formal categories are grounded in reason itself as an abstract, timeless form of consciousness, for example, identity, difference, causality, substance, and so forth. Real categories, on the other hand, are "not grounded in reason but in the life-nexus itself" and hence serve as "life-categories" rather than as calcified formal relations of pure reason.[116] Dilthey stressed that the essential difference between formal categories and life-categories has to do with their relation to time. Whereas the Kantian categories are "rigid and dead," the categories of life express a dynamic, interactive process between

[113] Dilthey, *GS* 7: 278.
[114] Dilthey, *GS* 11: xix.
[115] Dilthey, *GS* 19: 360. Dilthey's *Kategorien des Lebens* are a revision of the Kantian categories, which, according to Dilthey, are fixed and rigid (see *GS* 19: 44 and *GS* 7: 228). These new "life-categories" aim at historicizing Kant and focusing on the actual living, breathing, and feeling human person in history. They are not "formal" or "abstract" but "real." For a scholarly assessment of this project, see Lessing, *Die Idee einer Kritik der historischen Vernunft*, 249–257.
[116] Dilthey, *GS* 19: 361.

the knowing subject and the world, a hermeneutic relation grounded in temporal context. In Dilthey's work, "Life stands in close relation to the filling of time. Its whole character, its relation to corruptibility and ephemerality, the fact that it forms a nexus that has a unity (namely, the self), is determined by time."[117] This meant, first, that all our experience, "everything which is there for us, is there only as a given in the present. Even when an experience is past, it is there for us only as a given present experience."[118] The priority of the present as a way of organizing, synthesizing, and giving meaning to the temporal flow of experiential reality provided Dilthey with the conceptual means of understanding the unity and totality of life as "temporality." Temporality, he maintained, is "the categorical determination of life" which provides the foundation for all the other categories; it not only provides a unifying focus for bringing together all the various fragments of our own experience but also allows for the understanding of others as members of cultural and historical communities.[119] But human temporality can never be reduced to the present understanding of any context. Understanding is always bound up with the history of our own lives and other lives in the past: "Knowledge of the human world lies in the relation of common human vitality to individuation and in the relation of individuation to the concept of historicity."[120] Historicity, which for Dilthey constituted "the fundamental fact of the human sciences," helps to define the temporal structure of an individual life in relation to the whole of history, a relation that stresses the limits of our knowledge and our rootedness in time.[121] This meant, as Dilthey put it, that "there are always walls enclosing us; we are always attempting tumultuously to free ourselves from them . . . [yet we must realize] the impossibility of such an attempt, for here, as everywhere, one encounters the fundamental characteristic of all human consciousness: its historicity."[122]

[117] Dilthey, *GS* 7: 229.
[118] Ibid., 230.
[119] Ibid., 192.
[120] Dilthey, *GS* 5: 266.
[121] Dilthey, *GS* 6: 108.
[122] Dilthey, *GS* 8: 38. *Historicity*, or *Geschichtlichkeit*, plays an important role in Dilthey's thinking. Although according to Hegel biographers Karl Rosenkranz and Rudolf Haym the term and concept appear in Hegel, *Sämtliche Werke*, 20 vols., ed. Hermann Glockner (Stuttgart: Frommann, 1961), esp. vol. 17, 189 and vol. 19, 137, the first significant usage occurs in the correspondence between Dilthey and Graf Yorck from 1877 to 1897. In January of 1888 Yorck writes to Dilthey: "The germinal point of historicity is

Dilthey's insight into the historicity of consciousness transformed Kant's formal categories through a hermeneutic refashioning of the basic problem of human knowledge. All knowledge, for Dilthey, proceeds from the limited perspective of the self (part) to the universal perspective of all human history (whole) in a circular, reflexive manner. A human being can never stand outside of time and view the world from an absolute perspective or assume that the viewpoint of a single individual could provide a foundation for human-scientific inquiry. The individual does not invent language, custom, or tradition but finds them "there" within the world, pressing their claims and demands everywhere, leaving one caught in a *circulus vitiosis*, or "vicious circle." We move from self to world and back to self in a circular fashion as we attempt to integrate our own aims, ambitions, and goals into the larger world about us.[123] The Kantian concept of abso-

---

not that the whole psycho-physical datum *is* but rather lives," *Briefwechsel*, 71. Both Dilthey and Yorck agreed that "historicity" and "temporality" are categories of life and not merely of abstract metaphysics (see *Briefwechsel*, 91, and *GS* 6: 314).

By *historicity* Dilthey meant not only that all things are historically determined but also that human beings themselves are historically determined in their position as human beings. This meant that both the object of historical study (*Historie*) and the actual subject of lived temporal experience (*Geschichte*), that is, humanity, are likewise historical in essence. As Gadamer put it, this notion of historicity meant that not only *historische Erkenntnis* but also *die geschichtliche Seinsweise des Menschen* is a fundamental structure of human life. Or as Dilthey said, "Man's nature is his history!" (*GS* 8: 224). It is this *ontological* condition of human historicity rather than only the epistemological condition of historically determined knowledge that is crucial for an understanding of the *Geisteswissenschaften*. David Linge wrote: "Since man is radically historical, there is no possibility of founding our knowledge of life on a prior, metahistorical basis. Because of his own historicity, knowledge of man is knowledge of him *in and through his history*" ("Historicity and Hermeneutic," 116). The relationship between human beings and their history is, then, circular, reflexive, or hermeneutical, an insight that was to have a profound effect on Martin Heidegger in *Being and Time*, especially in his long section on Dilthey and Graf Yorck.

For the meaning of *Geschichtlichkeit*, see Hans-Georg Gadamer, "Geschichtlichkeit, in *Religion in Geschichte und Gegenwart*, vol. 2, 1496–1498; Leonhard Renthe-Fink, "Geschichtlichkeit" in *Historisches Wörterbuch der Philosophie*, vol. 3 (Basel: Schwabe, 1974), 404–408, and also Renthe-Fink, *Geschichtlichkeit: Ihr terminologischer und begrifflicher Ursprung bei Hegel, Haym, Dilthey, und Yorck* (Göttingen: Vandenhoeck & Ruprecht, 1964), and Renthe-Fink, "Zur Herkunft des Wortes 'Geschichtlichkeit,'" *Archiv für Begriffsgeschichte* 15 (1971): 306–312; Gerhard Bauer, *Geschichtlichkeit* (Berlin: de Gruyter, 1963); Linge, "Historicity and Hermeneutic"; Heribert Boeder, "Dilthey 'und' Heidegger: Zur Geschichtlichkeit des Menschen," in Orth, ed., *Dilthey und der Wandel des Philosophiebegriffs seit dem 19. Jahrhundert* (Freiburg: Alber, 1984), 161–177; David Hoy, "History, Historicity, and Historiography," in M. Murray, *Heidegger and Modern Philosophy*; and Otto Pöggeler, "Historicity in Heidegger's Late Work," *Southwestern Journal of Philosophy* 4 (1973): 53–73.

[123] Dilthey spoke of the circular or hermeneutical relation of man to world and life to history as a *structural* one based on the part-to-whole relationship in a variety of con-

lute time which dominated the method of the natural sciences could never adequately grasp this circular movement of an understanding structured by temporal relationships. Kantian epistemology posited the object of scientific inquiry as something static and present at hand, "there" for analysis; but Dilthey patiently stressed that the temporality and historicity of life undermine the fixity of any object of knowledge.

Through an ontology of historical experience, grounded in the awareness that "the essence of the human being is historical," Dilthey tried to show the bankruptcy of traditional subject/object metaphysics. Traditional hermeneutics had opened the path for this type of criticism by demonstrating that all knowledge is given to us in the form of a part-to-whole relationship. Yet the older approach of the romantic school had focused on the structure of the *object* given to consciousness, viewing it within its own historically determined context. Ranke had even argued for the "extinguishing" of the subject, seeking thereby to eliminate all personal prejudice. But although Ranke was exemplary in understanding the historicity of the object, his approach to the subject was less successful; the effect of his historical theory was to isolate the subject in a state of hypostatized, ahistorical meditation. Against this approach, Dilthey's hermeneutics sought to fuse the historicity of both object and subject by focusing on the dynamic interplay of consciousness and world as the basis for all historical interpretation. In Dilthey's thought, consciousness itself is marked by the same temporality and historicity as the historical world. Dilthey never succeeded in finally synthesizing the categories of temporality and historicity into a coherent *Grundwissenschaft* that would unify the insights of descriptive psychology, hermeneutics, historical science, and epistemology; he nonetheless continued to insist on the need for a more originary mode of questioning to dissolve and overcome the subject/object presuppositions of traditional philosophical thinking. His hermeneutic approach pointed to the vital ground of all scientific inquiry; yet even as he celebrated the life-nexus as the

texts, but most especially in his "Entwürfe zur Kritik der historischen Vernunft" (see *GS* 7: 262–264 and 277–280). This close relationship between hermeneutics and the historical character of life, namely, "historicity," is pursued by Helmut Diwald in *Wilhelm Dilthey: Erkenntnistheorie und Philosophie der Geschichte* (Göttingen: Musterschmidt, 1963), 198–203; Linge, "Historicity and Hermeneutic," pt. 1; John Maraldo, *Der hermeneutische Zirkel: Untersuchungen zu Schleiermacher, Dilthey, und Heidegger* (Freiburg: Alber, 1974), 65–88; and Peter Hünermann, *Der Durchbruch geschichtlichen Denkens im 19. Jahrhundert: Johann Gustav Droysen, Wilhelm Dilthey, Graf Paul Yorck von Wartenburg* (Freiburg: Herder, 1967) 156.

germinal focus of the *Geisteswissenschaften*, he was plagued by the immanent historicity of knowledge which undermined its value as truth. To evaluate Dilthey's work, we will need to consider this problem of historicity more fully in terms of the crisis of relativism which gripped the historicist tradition in the early twentieth century.

viii. The Crisis of Historical Relativism

In his "Critique of Historical Reason," Dilthey struggled to avoid the contradictions that he saw emerging between two distinct epistemological traditions: the Kantian ideal of scientific rationality and the Rankean practice of historical consciousness. In many ways his history of the human sciences is an attempt to reconcile these traditions through a hermeneutic refashioning of scientific knowledge itself. Dilthey instinctively recognized that the sources for the "crisis" of historicism lay in the conflicting demands for a scientific methodology that would reflect the hermeneutic insight into the historicity of truth. He rejected the Neo-Kantian efforts to forge a transcendental-logical theory of values which would overcome the relativism of merely "historical" judgments. By defining *history* as an aggregation of facts constituted under the category of value and *nature* as an assemblage of data constituted under the category of laws, Rickert and Windelband had evaded the actual sources of human experience and historical life.[124] Abstract epistemology, riven from its historical context and measured against a lifeless, logico-mathematical model of time, offered little hope, in Dilthey's estimation, of solving the crisis of historical values. As he noted in the *Nachlass*: "Rickert wants to arrive at reality as a transcendental object solely through inference on the basis of mere logical relations of an epistemological subject—and he finds that this will not work. This is the error of his method. The real method must proceed from the empirical consciousness. This method recognizes that it is futile to undertake constructions on the basis of abstract concepts. It also recognizes that reality cannot be constructed or be fully demonstrated logically, but only made plausible."[125]

If for Rickert history, or the historical datum, appeared as an object

[124] See the penetrating critique by Manfred Riedel, *Geschichte der Philosophie* 7, 331–332.
[125] From the unpublished "Nachlass," translated in Ermarth, *Wilhelm Dilthey*, 197.

constructed by an epistemological subject, for Dilthey history was something more spiritual (*geistig*), a process of vital life relations rather than an individual, discrete entity. We know the past, Dilthey claimed, not as a detached "datum" but as a meaningful part of our own existence, temporally removed but psychologically immediate. In hermeneutical terms, Dilthey understood historical reflection not as a process of scholarly judgment but as a human deliberation about the possibilities and limits of an individual's existence within a specific historical-cultural milieu. Hence he stressed the importance of autobiography and philosophical anthropology as disciplines that would situate human experience within both the individual life and the life of the species. Human reflection, Dilthey insisted, is conditioned by specific historical circumstances; at no point can human beings remove themselves from the historical process and achieve a form of absolute knowledge. Our knowledge *of* history, which appears to us as an exclusively epistemological concern, is always bound up with our being *in* history, which requires an awareness of our ontological condition. For Dilthey this ontological dimension of human history—its embeddedness in being and its reflexive relation to time—constitutes the genuine meaning of "historicity": human beings interpret life not in terms of categories derived from logic but from a reflexive awareness (*Innewerden*) of their own hermeneutic situation.

Against the Neo-Kantian tendency to define history through logic, methodology, and transcendental or "pure" reason, Dilthey committed his philosophical effort to a critique of historical reason, in which reason is interpreted by way of its historicity. But if human consciousness is reflexively thrown back on its own historical ground, then how can one account for historical truth? Can one ever withdraw from the hermeneutic circle of self-reflection and overcome the circularity of all truth claims? Can there be some way to achieve epistemological certitude without abandoning the ontological insights of Dilthey's hermeneutics? For Rickert, Dilthey's attempts to historicize reason led to an unsystematic affirmation of everything relative and fragmentary that could never achieve the genuine goal of all philosophy: systematic knowledge of the absolute. On his side, Dilthey rejected Rickert's stratagems for grounding truth in a priori values, transcendental subjectivity, "normative consciousness," and the "prophysical" realm of *Sollen*. As Dilthey continually reminded his contemporaries in ever new ways and within different contexts, "The problem of how scientific history is possible arises once we replace Hegel's universal reason by life in its totality"; against the metaphysical totality of the absolute, Dilthey stressed "the totality of life," "the connectedness of the facts of consciousness," "the unity of consciousness," "the totality of human nature."[126] "There is no absolute point," Dilthey proclaimed, and yet he was sensitive to the need for connecting discrete, particular, individual life expressions with the totality of historical life. How from the particularity of human consciousness, Dilthey asked, can one achieve the universal validity of knowledge? If he never succeeded in finally answering this question, Dilthey did nonetheless direct his efforts at overcoming the mere relativity of historical truth.

And yet despite their many differences and points of contention, Dilthey and Rickert shared a fundamental aim: to resolve the crisis of historical knowledge by providing a scientific methodology capable of overcoming the relativity of cultural values. Though Dilthey could admit that "everything historical is relative," which on the surface "seems to work towards dissolution, skepticism and impotent subjectivity," at the same time he also insisted that "what is relative must be brought into a more profound and deeper relation to what is universally valid."[127] The task of epistemology (or a logic and methodology

[126] These phrases recur both in the published writings and in the "Nachlass"; cf. Dilthey, GS 1: xvii; GS 8: 180; and GS 19: 75 and 140.
[127] Translated by H. P. Rickman in Dilthey, SW, 121; GS 8: 204. This point—of attempting to unify "the relative" and "the universally valid"—seems to be lost on many Dilthey commentators. Gerhard Masur argues, for example, that "Dilthey was an avowed relativist," in Prophets of Yesterday (New York: Macmillan, 1961), 167; H. Stuart Hughes contends that "Dilthey struggled—without success—for an escape from the skeptical and relativist implications of his own thought" (Consciousness and Society [New York: Knopf, 1958], 199). This charge of relativism and skepticism is also levied by a number of Marxist critics, such as Guntolf Herzberg, "Wilhelm Dilthey und das Problem des Historismus," diss., Humboldt University of Berlin, 1976, who, for all his labors, misconstrues Dilthey as a relativist committed to irrational Lebensphilosophie. Historicism is, for Herzberg, a form of bourgeois imperialist thought unable to escape the relativist contradictions of its own position. For a similar approach, one can also read Robert Steigerwald, Bürgerliche Philosophie (Frankfurt: Verlag Marxistische Blätter, 1979); I. S. Kon, Die Geschichtsphilosophie des 20. Jahrhunderts (Berlin: Akademie, 1964); and the work of Georg Lukács, The Destruction of Reason (London: Merlin, 1980), who has a chapter on Dilthey and Lebensphilosophie.
There is a close connection between the categorization of Dilthey as an "irrational" proponent of Lebensphilosophie and the charge that he is a thoroughgoing relativist. Part of this problem stems from the early Dilthey-Rezeption in Germany of the 1920s–1950s. Historians of philosophy such as Willy Moog, Die Deutsche Philosophie der Gegenwart (Stuttgart: Enke, 1922); Ernst von Aster, Philosophie der Gegenwart (Leiden: Sijthoff, 1935); Hans Meyer, Geschichte der abendländischen Weltanschauungen, vol. 5 (Paderborn: Schöningh, 1947); Gerhard Lehmann, Die deutsche Philosophie der Gegenwart (Stuttgart: Kröner, 1943), and Lehmann, Die Geschichte der Philosophie, vol. 10 (Berlin: Göschen,

of the human sciences) was to determine whether or not valid, objective knowledge of the human world is possible, because, in Dilthey's words, "every science implies a claim to validity."[128] In his *Essence of Philosophy* (1907), Dilthey observed: "It is not the relativity of each world view that is the last word of the human mind that has traversed them all but the sovereignty of mind in regard to each one of them—and at the same time the positive consciousness of how, in the different ways that the mind, the one reality of the world, exists for us. In contrast to [a philosophy of] relativism . . . it is the task of the philosophy of world views to relate the human mind to the riddle of the world and of life."[129]

Dilthey has been misinterpreted by some scholars who have maintained that he was a thoroughgoing historical relativist.[130] Certainly he

---

1957); and even Georg Misch—Dilthey's son-in-law, who, in his *Lebensphilosophie und Phänomenologie* (Leipzig: Teubner, 1931), tried to unify the vitalist and phenomenological sides of the Dilthey tradition—all helped to categorize Dilthey and to put him into a convenient tradition, namely, late-nineteenth-century irrationalism. Even one of Dilthey's most perceptive early commentators, Otto F. Bollnow, in *Die Lebensphilosophie* (Berlin: Springer, 1958) and *Dilthey: Eine Einführung* (Stuttgart: Kohlhammer, 1955), tended to see Dilthey in these traditional terms. Of course, as we have already seen, Heinrich Rickert, in *Die Philosophie des Lebens* (Tübingen: Mohr, 1922), had earlier criticized Dilthey for his irrational tendencies. Yet, as I have consistently argued, although there are relativist, historicist, vitalist, and even irrational elements in Dilthey's thought, the unifying element is his "Critique of Historical Reason," whose goal is *always* to establish *"allgemeingültige Erkenntnis"* ("universally valid knowledge") (*GS* 8: 179) or *"eine erkenntnistheoretische Grundlegung der Geisteswissenschaften"* ("an epistemological grounding of the human sciences") (*GS* 1: xix). The task is not "irrational"; it is based on an *"Erkenntnistheorie, Logik, und Methodenlehre"* (*GS* 8: 179). For a sophisticated discussion of the *tension* between this epistemological ideal and the "relativist implications of Dilthey's thought," see Franco Bianco, "Dilthey und das Problem des Relativismus," in Orth, ed., *Dilthey und die Philosophie der Gegenwart*, 211–230. For a good selection of Dilthey's own views on his project, see his *Texte zur Kritik der historischen Vernunft*, and for a thoroughgoing refutation of charges concerning Dilthey's "avowed relativism," see Dilthey, *GS* 8: 13.

[128] Translated by H. P. Rickman in Dilthey, *SW*, 183; and Dilthey, *GS* 7: 137. Dilthey wrote in a letter to Count Yorck on December 31, 1884: "My real goal is a methodology of the human sciences" (*Briefwechsel*, 48). This was the motivating force behind all Dilthey's various *wissenschaftliche* efforts.

[129] Dilthey, *GS* 5: 406.

[130] For those who argue that Dilthey was a relativist, see Wolfgang Müller-Lauter, "Die Konsequenzen des Historismus in der Philosophie der Gegenwart," *Zeitschrift für Theologie und Kirche* 59 (1962): 226–255; and Maurice Mandelbaum, *The Problem of Historical Knowledge: An Answer to Relativism* (New York: Liveright, 1967), lxvii and 418. For treatments of Dilthey as "historicist," see Calvin Rand, "Two Meanings of Historicism in the Work of Dilthey, Troeltsch, and Meinecke," *Journal of the History of Ideas* 25 (1964): 503–518; Schnädelbach, *Geschichtsphilosophie nach Hegel*, esp. 115; Jörn Rüsen, "Theorien im Historismus," in Jörn Rüsen and Hans Süssmuth, eds., *Theorien in der Geschichtswissenschaft* (Düsseldorf: Schwann, 1980). See also Masur, *Prophets of Yesterday;* Hughes, *Consciousness and Society;* and Georg Iggers, *The German Conception of History* (Middletown, Conn.: Wesleyan University Press, 1968). My own views are more in line

did acknowledge that "every world view is historically conditioned and hence, limited and relative."[131] And throughout this chapter we have seen how Dilthey's work was informed by the influence of historicist ideas. Yet in a letter to Edmund Husserl in 1911, Dilthey explicitly denied all charges that he was a "historicist" or someone committed to historical relativism. "I am not," he wrote, "a philosopher of intuition, nor a historicist, nor a skeptic."[132] In fact, in a second letter to Husserl, who in his *Logos* article hinted at Dilthey's affiliation with a "relativism that has a close affinity to psychologism," Dilthey reaffirmed his "orientation toward a universally valid foundation for the human sciences and toward a presentation of the objectivity of historical knowledge."[133] Like Husserl, Dilthey rejected the purely subject-focused, self-contained consciousness of introspection for a self-reflexive, intentional, and phenomenologically engaged awareness of life as it is lived in the world, directed neither inward nor outward but involving an awareness that "life is structure, and structure is lived coherence."[134]

Dilthey responded to Husserl's charges of relativism by referring to his essay "The Essence of Philosophy," in which he addressed the problem of world views. "It is the task of the theory of world views," Dilthey explained, "to describe methodically on the basis of an analysis of the historical development of religion, poetry, and metaphysics —but in contrast to relativism—the relationship of the human mind to the enigma of the world and of life."[135] In developing a theory of world views, which he described as philosophical, theological, and poetic conceptions of the world-nexus (*Weltzusammenhang*), Dilthey

with those of Bernard Eric Jensen, who, in an article titled "The Role of Intellectual History in Dilthey's *Kritik der historischen Vernunft*," *Dilthey-Jahrbuch* 2 (1984): 65–91, argues that although the historicist tradition is important to Dilthey, he never uncritically accepts fundamental tenets. As I see it, Dilthey never succeeded in resolving the problems of his "Critique of Historical Reason" *within* the *Fragestellung* of historicism, but he did adopt certain philosophical positions that were in line with historicist views, namely, the fundamental *"Geschichtlichkeit des menschlichen Daseins"* ("historicity of human being"). As I will argue, Dilthey's stress on historicity was not only an epistemological concern, i.e., related to problems of scope and method of historical science, but was *ontological* in nature and involved a full recognition of humanity's historical being.

[131] Dilthey, *GS* 8: 224.
[132] From "Der Briefwechsel Dilthey und Husserl," ed. Walter Biemel, *Man and World* 1 (1968): 428–446.
[133] Ibid. Edmund Husserl argues for such an ideal in his essay "Philosophie als eine strenge Wissenschaft," *Logos* 1 (1911): 289–341.
[134] Dilthey, *GS* 19: 355.
[135] Dilthey, *SW*, 123; *GS* 5: 406.

believed he could break down the superficial contrast between *Welt-anschauung* and *Wissenschaft* which dominated the work of Husserl, Rickert, and his contemporaries. In *The Types of World View and Their Development in the Metaphysical Systems* (1911), Dilthey strove to overcome the mere "relativity" of individual, historically limited world views by reconciling the variety of philosophical systems with their own history. Instead of deciding either "for" or "against" Heraclitus and Parmenides, for example, in an artificially posed "struggle of world views," Dilthey's task was "to examine what is true in each and to unify these truths."[136] Rather than giving himself over to the multiplicity, anarchy, and chaos of differing world views and accepting a philosophy of relativism, Dilthey affirmed the possibility of scientific truth. Every world view is one-sided, Dilthey acknowledged, but at the same time "all world views, if they seek a complete solution to life's enigmas, invariably contain the same structure."[137] By focusing on the structural similarities within these individual, historical world views and relating them to one another in a system of historical world views (*Weltanschauungslehre*), Dilthey believed he could provide a unifying "philosophy of philosophy" that would reconcile the historicist ideal of individuality with the Kantian demand for universally valid scientific knowledge.[138]

Those who attacked Dilthey for his commitment to historicist relativity often missed the subtlety of his position. For even as he affirmed the relativity of historical world views, he was careful to distinguish it from relativity within the sphere of scientific claims.[139] Dilthey always understood that there is a difference between our vital commitments to world views which are determined by our values *and* a scientific-philosophical reflection about world views which is informed by the value of universal truth. As individuals we choose among different value systems based on our disposition, background, and sensibility; as scientists and scholars, however, we have the responsibility to understand our particular values within the system of historicoscientific development. And yet, confronted by the anarchy of world views and the variability of historical values, Dilthey admitted in a sketch from the *Nachlass*, "Modern Man and the Conflict

[136] Dilthey, *GS* 8: 148.
[137] Ibid., 82.
[138] Ibid., 206–211.
[139] See the excellent study by Michael Ermarth, "Objectivity and Relativity in Dilthey's Theory of Understanding," in Rudolf Makkreel and John Scanlon, eds., *Dilthey and Phenomenology* (Washington, D.C.: University Press of America, 1987), 84–88.

of World Views," that "I can only live in the total objectivity of thought. In my most trying hours I have been attracted to the force of personality in Rousseau or Carlyle. Yet I have always felt within myself the strongest thirst for objective truth."[140] If there were historicist tendencies at work in Dilthey's doctrine of world views, then they must be understood against his expressed commitment to "the total objectivity of thought."

The blind affirmation of nineteenth-century historicism—brilliantly parodied by Robert Musil in *The Man without Qualities*—would have resulted in the construction of an "imaginary museum" of ideas, each valid and binding in its own historical context yet sterile in their effect on human consciousness.[141] Indifferent to the meaning of belief and commitment, this version of historicism would be a mere cataloging of philosophically relative truths. But Dilthey emphasized the reflexive awareness of historical consciousness which preserved the life-related meaning of historical truth. To see each world view as an individual, disparate, and relative frame of reference without also acknowledging its life-meaning was to embrace ethical and epistemological skepticism. But Dilthey wanted to affirm the life-related meaning of history and to combine it with a philosopher's commitment to universality which was neither sterile nor abstract. In his famous "Seventieth Birthday Address" of 1903, Dilthey explained:

> I undertook an investigation of the nature and conditions of historical consciousness—a critique of historical reason. This task led me to the most general problems: a seemingly insoluble contradiction arises if we pursue historical consciousness to its last consequences. The finitude of every his-

[140] Dilthey, *GS* 8: 233.

[141] Karl-Otto Apel makes a fascinating connection between the thought of Dilthey and the "nihilistic" historicism of Robert Musil in "Scientistics, Hermeneutics, Critique of Ideology: An Outline of a Theory of Science from an Epistemological-Anthropological Point of View," in *The Hermeneutics Reader: Texts of the German Tradition from the Enlightenment to the Present* (New York: Continuum, 1984), 320–345. Apel writes: "If the practical (existential) consequences of this conception are taken seriously, it leads to the problem of nihilistic 'historicism,' which Dilthey himself had clearly recognized and which the writer Robert Musil, in reference to the thought of Nietzsche, later brought under the heading *The Man without Qualities*. Indeed, a man who had scientifically objectified all binding truths and norms and had gathered them all together into the simultaneity of an 'imaginary museum' of merely passively understood meaning would be like a being who was capable of gaining any qualities, a pure 'man of possibilities,' as Musil also says, a man who would be able to actualize his life. He would have lost all ties to tradition and it would have been the historical-hermeneutical sciences themselves which would have reduced him to just this ahistorical state. They themselves—i.e., their neutralizing objectivation of binding norms and truths—would have taken the place of effective tradition and, thus, of history itself" (333).

torical phenomenon, whether it be a religion, an ideal, or a philosophic system, hence the relativity of every sort of human conception about the connectedness of things, is the last word of the historical world view. All flows in process; nothing remains stable. On the other hand, there arises the need of thought and the striving of philosophy for universally valid cognition. The historical way of looking at things (*die geschichtliche Weltanschauung*) has liberated the human spirit from the last chains which natural science and philosophy have not yet torn asunder. But where are the means for overcoming the anarchy of convictions which threatens to break in on us?

I have worked all my life on problems which link themselves as a long chain to this problem. I see the goal. If I fall by the wayside, I hope that my younger companions and students will go on to the end of the road.[142]

ix. The Antinomy of "Historical" Reason: The Historicity of Truth and the Demand for a Scientific Method

Dilthey never really resolved the tension between the finitude of historical consciousness and the scientific demand for universality. He could admit that "the development of historical consciousness destroys faith in the universal validity of any philosophy" at the same time as he charged historical reflection with the task of finding validity within the realm of the relative.[143] But the tensions within Dilthey's

---

[142] Translated by Georg Iggers in *German Conception of History*, 143–144; and Dilthey, *GS* 5: 9.

[143] In remarks presented to the "Dilthey-Tagung" in April 1983, Hans-Georg Gadamer summarized Dilthey's achievement in general terms. In his essay "Dilthey nach 150 Jahren: Zwischen Romantik und Positivismus," in Orth, *Dilthey und die Philosophie der Gegenwart*, 157–182, Gadamer praised Dilthey for his universal breadth, his erudite learning, his masterful contributions to German *Geistesgeschichte*, his "*wahrhaft episches Temperament.*" But despite this, he noted, Dilthey lacked a distinctive "conceptual power" ("*Mangel an begrifflicher Kraft*"), a lack that overshadowed his work and its influence. Unlike Heidegger, Dilthey never achieved (Gadamer added) a philosophical precision that might have helped scholars bent on a new *Dilthey-Rezeption*. I think that this general remark sheds some light on the reasons for so much debate and confusion among Dilthey scholars. Was Dilthey a historicist? A relativist? A *Lebensphilosoph*? A positivist or a romantic? A phenomenologist? A committed follower of psychologism, of existentialism, or of hermeneutics? Was he a Kantian? A Hegelian? This line of inquiry is sometimes confusing because Dilthey himself was writing in an age of great upheaval and transition. His career spanned from the Hegelianism of the 1850s to the phenomenology of Husserl, crisscrossing the major developments in late-nineteenth-century European thought. As I have argued throughout this study, Dilthey's basic mode of questioning brought together strands of historicism, psychologism, *Lebensphilosophie*, positivism, and hermeneutics. But it was always within the parameters of the "Critique of Historical Reason," which would establish an epistemological foundation of the *Geisteswissenschaften* on the basis of the ontological insight into human his-

thought are not unique; they reflect contradictions within German philosophy itself. The concurrent demands for a historical and a scientific approach to the human world in the late nineteenth century were part of both the historicist and the Kantian traditions. By looking at Dilthey's project against the background of what I will call the antinomy of "historical" reason, I want to reveal the impasse in philosophical thinking which helped shape the crisis of historicism.

Antinomy meant for Kant a contradiction within reason itself. All events or, to be more strict, all human experience of such events could, in Kant's view, be circumscribed rationally and hence grounded in a principle of reason (*Satz vom Grund*). There were, however, some rare cases in which the laws of reason came into conflict. As Kant himself described it in a letter to his friend Christian Garve: "Not the investigation of the existence of God, of immortality, etc., but the antinomy of pure reason was the point from which I began: 'The world has a beginning—it has no beginning, etc., to the fourth: There is freedom in human beings—against: there is no freedom, rather everything is natural necessity'; it was this that first woke me from my dogmatic slumber and drove me to the critique of reason itself to dissolve the scandal of the contradiction of reason with itself."[144]

This "contradiction of reason," or "antinomy," posed an important problem for Kant in *The Critique of Pure Reason* as he tried to account for the problem of "pseudo-rational doctrines" and wondered "whether and in what way, despite this contradiction, there still remains open to reason a path to certainty."[145] But Dilthey also recognized the formidable problem of antinomy in his own critique of his-

---

toricity. Dilthey's *terms* were not always clear, he did lack *"begriffliche Kraft,"* yet his *Fragestellung* was consistent. This is what provides unity in Dilthey's thought, not the security of any specific "-ism." For a review of the various approaches in more-recent Dilthey literature, see those works mentioned in this chapter, nn. 1 and 7; see also the review by Michael Ermarth, "Historical Understanding in the Thought of Wilhelm Dilthey," *History and Theory* 20, no. 3 (1981): 323–334.

[144] Immanuel Kant to Christian Garve, September 21, 1798, in Immanuel Kant, *Gesammelte Schriften* (Berlin: Walter de Gruyter, 1983), 12: 257–258. For the importance of the concept of "antinomy" to Kant, see his *Gesammelte Schriften*, 4:338 and 341 n, 10: 252, and 18: 60–62; and Norbert Hinske, "Kants Begriff der Antinomie und die Etappen seiner Ausarbeitung," *Kant Studien* 56 (1965): 485–496. Also on the idea of "antinomy" in Kant, see Michael Gillespie, *Hegel, Heidegger, and the Ground of History* (Chicago: University of Chicago Press, 1984), 24–55 and 183. For Dilthey's use of the term *antinomy*, see GS 8: 3–9, and for Gadamer's critique, see *Truth and Method*, 192–214, and "The Problem of Historical Consciousness," 21–37. For criticisms of Gadamer's *Dilthey-interpretation*, see Frithjof Rodi, "Dilthey, Gadamer, and Traditional Hermeneutics," *Reports on Philosophy* 7 (1983): 3–14, and Stefan Otto, "Dilthey und der Begriff des empirischen Apriori," *Philosophisches Jahrbuch* 91, no. 2 (1984): 376–382.

[145] Kant, *Critique of Pure Reason*, 394.

torical reason. In a chapter entitled "The Antinomy between the Claim of Every Life- and World-View to Universal Validity and the Claim of Historical Consciousness" from a late work, Dilthey described the anarchic situation of German philosophy at the turn of the century and pointed to a "contradiction" between scientific and historical consciousness.[146] Philosophy itself, torn between the competing claims of *Weltanschauung* and *Wissenschaft*, provided the site for this generational conflict.

On one side, the historicist tradition was preoccupied with establishing a harmonious balance between the claims of historical truth and the demands of a scientific and empirical method. Ranke's *Weltgeschichte*, Droysen's *Historik*, the hermeneutical-critical approach of the Historical School—all were concerned with the tension between historical knowledge and its value for human life. The Neo-Kantians, on their side, grappled with the problem of how science could serve as an antidote to the poisons of historical relativism. They understood value as a scientific question whose ground was neither life nor history but transcendental consciousness. Dilthey's own program was an attempt to mediate between the life-related concerns of the historicists and the scientific concerns of the Neo-Kantians. Following Kant, he intended to write his own critique of the limits of reason aimed at establishing universally valid knowledge. But in the manner of the Historical School, he understood his task hermeneutically. Because reason is neither absolute nor pure but historical and tradition-bound, it, too, is subject to the claims of historicity. Yet by historicizing reason and affirming the life-sources of historical consciousness, did Dilthey simultaneously undermine his goal of legitimating historical knowledge as an "objective science"? Did he ever resolve the contradiction between the historicity of reason and the rationality of history—the antinomy of historical reason—providing a viable solution to the "crisis of historicism"?

Hans-Georg Gadamer, in "The Problem of Historical Consciousness," acknowledges that Dilthey was troubled by "the question of how to assume objectivity in the midst of relativity," but he observes that "nevertheless, we ask Dilthey in vain for an effective answer to the problem of relativism."[147] Gadamer finds contradiction and "inner disunity" at the heart of Dilthey's thought and argues that Dilthey's

[146] Dilthey, *GS* 8: 3–9.
[147] Gadamer, "The Problem of Historical Consciousness," 30.

effort to ground the human sciences in history and lived experience is never really reconciled with the natural-scientific model of objectivity he derived from Kant: "Emphasize as he might the contemplative tendencies of life itself, the attractions of something 'solid' that life involves, his concept of 'objectivity' (as he reduced it to the objectivity of 'results') remains attached to an origin very different from lived experience. This is why he was unable to resolve the problem he had chosen."[148] Dilthey affirmed that "life is an insoluble riddle . . . incapable of analysis," drawing the conclusion that "because life always remains for us a riddle, so, too, must the universe."[149] In the Berlin *Nachlass*, Dilthey likewise spoke of "the unfathomability [*Unergründlichkeit*] of life."[150] Yet, conversely, Dilthey also expressed his commitment to "the principle of sufficient reason" (*Satz vom zureichenden Grunde*), which asserts that every phenomenon can be explained rationally in terms of a ground or cause.[151] Following this claim to fundamental rationality, the task of philosophy becomes "the establishment of a valid theory of scientific knowledge."[152] Or, as Dilthey put it in another context: "The coherence of all knowledge from which all efforts at foundation must proceed stretches beyond the thought of separate persons and contains the inner necessity of a scientific conclusion. . . . How this coherence arises—this coherence of the totality of knowledge—that is what we must search for; it offers the basic foundations for a true theory of knowledge. . . . There is no perspective without an objective order. This is the fact which is finally the guarantee for the objective and real validity for our knowledge."[153]

But are historicity and the hermeneutical understanding of truth compatible with Dilthey's demand for the "objective and real validity of our knowledge"? Can the subjective and temporal conditionality of historical experience yield the apodictic certainty of rigorous science? Dilthey never finally succeeded in resolving the antinomy of historical reason which figures so prominently in his work. Despite his repeated efforts in drafts and manuscripts, he never felt he could publish his work in definitive form under the title "Critique of Historical

[148] Ibid., 37.
[149] Dilthey, *GS* 19: 346–347.
[150] Ibid. See also Dilthey, *GS* 8: 70, 145, 225, and 226, where Dilthey refers to *Leben* as a "riddle," as "unfathomable," "unanalyzable," "insoluble," and so forth.
[151] Dilthey, *GS* 1: 44.
[152] Dilthey, *GS* 15: 156. Refer back to the first page of this chapter for Dilthey's analysis of Überweg.
[153] Translated by Ermarth, from Dilthey's unpublished Berlin "Nachlass," in *Wilhelm Dilthey*, 239.

Reason." And yet this failure to resolve the so-called crisis of historicism lay not in any conceptual inadequacy on Dilthey's part. As with my critique of Rickert, I will now look at the questions asked rather than at the answers proffered for understanding the limitations of Dilthey's position.

Dilthey grounded the truth of the human sciences in the inner experience of the historical subject. All truth, he claimed, is rooted in life, in lived experience, in the self-reflection of historical consciousness. And yet, starting from this position of subjective experience, he wished to guarantee that experience itself would be approached objectively. The Neo-Kantians perceived the contradiction between historical subjectivity and epistemological objectivity and sought to construct a transcendental subject whose consciousness was grounded not in time (as was Dilthey's) but outside of time, in the a priori—an approach that was formal and ahistorical. Dilthey rejected their solution out of hand. Yet he agreed with them that the truth of historical experience must have the same methodological validity as those investigations of the natural sciences. Following Kant's critical philosophy, but sensitive to the hermeneutic demands of historical interpretation, Dilthey rejected Kant's transcendental method for an empirical method grounded in life and human historicity. Despite the real differences between the Kantian program and Dilthey's hermeneutics, each nonetheless shared a common philosophical heritage, one derived from Descartes and committed to a notion of epistemological objectivity. These Cartesian traces in Dilthey's thinking marked his entire project; if we follow their logical path, they can help to explain the inner contradictions between historicity and universal validity which led to the antinomy in his critique of historical reason.

In his hermeneutic critique of Neo-Kantian epistemology, Dilthey achieved a new understanding of the human being which affirmed the radical historicity of lived experience. The earlier adherents of the Historical School had stressed the historicity of the object—its unique, unduplicable essence within the development of time and culture. But Dilthey now emphasized the historicity of the subject as well; he recognized that no objective methodology could adequately explain what it means to "be" historical or to understand ourselves as historical beings. Dilthey understood that the effects of historicity go beyond epistemological questions about historical relativism to affect the ontological status of human being itself. In the words of H. Richard Niebuhr, "Historical relativism affirms the historicity of the subject even more than that of the object; man . . . is not only in time, but time is in man."[154] With this new emphasis on the historicity of the human being, Dilthey called into question the nonhistorical anthropology of his predecessors but he remained committed, in some fundamental sense, to their nonhistorical ideal of interpretation, that is, to apodictic certitude and universal validity. Thus even as he succeeded in overcoming the certitude of Enlightenment and romantic metaphysics, he still remained tied to the old epistemological *Fragestellung* of Descartes, Kant, and the early modern philosophy of nature. Consequently, one can always notice a certain ambivalence in Dilthey's work between two contrasting positions: the sense of liberation engendered by the destruction of the dogmatic certitude of metaphysics and the feelings of uncertainty and anxiety produced by the awareness of historical relativity. It was Heidegger who recognized these contradictions in Dilthey's work between epistemological certitude and ontological historicity and tried to reframe Dilthey's basic question about historicism and the methodology of the human sciences.

Dilthey's theory of the human sciences, Heidegger argued, was still conceived as a theory of "method" aimed at "scientific objectivity," like that of most early modern philosophy of the sciences. For Heidegger, "The way to knowledge is known in the sciences by the title of method." But, he explained, " 'Method' here is not to be understood 'methodologically' as a manner of investigation or research, but metaphysically as a way to a definition of the essence of *truth*, a definition that can be grounded only through man's efforts."[155] In contrast to the medieval view, in which certitude is found only on the path to salvation and the transmission of truth is achieved through *doctrina*, early modern philosophy, Heidegger claimed, conceived of truth only in terms of method. This revolution in philosophy was heralded by Descartes's *Discourse on Method* (1637), a work that expresses the essence of the modern world view. In a chapter from his lectures on *Nietzsche*, "The Dominance of the Subject in the Modern Age," Heidegger emphasized that it is in Descartes's cogito that a new form of subjectivity is introduced into Western thought; for the first time in Western philosophy, truth is grounded in the certitude of the self-

[154] H. Richard Niebuhr, *The Meaning of Revelation* (New York: Macmillan, 1941), 13.
[155] Martin Heidegger, *Nietzsche*, 4: 89; German edition, *Nietzsche*, II, 135.

knowing subject. Henceforward, that kind of truth which character-izes this self-knowing subject, namely, "certitude," becomes the stan-dard by which to measure all other truth claims: "Because truth now means the assuredness of presentation-to, or *certitude*, and because being means representedness in the sense of such certitude, man, in accordance with his role in foundational representation, therefore be-comes the subject in a distinctive sense."[156] This new form of truth is not to be conceived, however, as simply "subjective." That is, it is not based on individual feelings, desires, opinions, and beliefs but is grounded in the essential *form* of self-consciousness, which Heidegger referred to as "subjectivistic" rather than "subjective."[157]

By understanding human self-consciousness in its "subjectivist" and Cartesian sense, Heidegger attempted to show the relationship between the demand for truth and the reliance on method. Heidegger wrote of Descartes's metaphysics:

> Man is the distinctive ground underlying every representing of beings and their truth, on which every representing and its represented is based and must be based if it is to have status and stability. Man is *subjectum* in the distinctive sense. The name and concept "subject" in its new significance now passes over to become the proper name and essential word for man. This means that every nonhuman being becomes an *object* for this sub-ject. . . . "Method" now takes on a metaphysical import that is, as it were, affixed to the essence of subjectivity. "Method" is no longer simply a se-quence arranged somehow into various stages of observation, proof, expo-sition, and summary of knowledge and teachings, in the manner of a scho-lastic *Summa*, which has its own regular and repetitive structure. "Method" is now the name for the securing, conquering, proceeding against beings, in order to capture them as objects for the subject.[158]

In quest of that certitude which it knows within its own self-reflec-tions, the Cartesian cogito now views the external world as an "ob-ject" there to be known in all its certainty by a "subject." Within this subject-object relationship, knowledge of the world proceeds apace through the use of rigorous Cartesian method. Heidegger insisted, however, that this fundamental shift in thinking was not peculiar to Descartes but was at the root of all early modern philosophy, espe-cially that of Kant. According to Heidegger, in Kant's thinking the

---

[156] Heidegger, *Nietzsche*, 4: 117; *Nietzsche*, II: 166.
[157] Heidegger, *Nietzsche*, 4: 96; *Nietzsche*, II: 141.
[158] Heidegger, *Nietzsche*, 4: 119–120; *Nietzsche*, II: 168–170.

being of objects consists in their objectivity, determined a priori by our consciousness, which provides the precondition and ground for the possibility of experiencing them as objects at all.[159] If for Kant and Descartes all scientifically valid claims to objectivity must be certain or must be grounded in the certainty of the self-knowing subject, then for later philosophers themes such as subjectivity and objectivity, as well as truth and certitude, would always be joined together.[160]

Clearly, Dilthey's philosophical enterprise was grounded in the Cartesian certitude of the self-reflecting subject. His "principle of phenomenality," following in the tradition of the early modern philosophy of consciousness, affirmed that "everything is 'there-for-me' only as a fact of my consciousness."[161] Dilthey underscored that "even every external thing is given to me only as a nexus of facts or process of consciousness."[162] In strictly Cartesian fashion, Dilthey always conceived the problem of historical knowledge within the early modern framework of subjectivity-objectivity, an epistemological bias that he never abandoned. Even as he recognized the necessity of Cartesian certitude and objectivity, he also acknowledged the limits of human certainty and the positive meaning of relativity and historicity for an understanding of historical consciousness. Subjective prejudice could never be reconciled with the demands of science, however. Hence the early modern philosophy of consciousness, derived from Descartes and committed to a scientific ideal of methodological objectivity, proved to be an unworkable *Fragestellung* within which to resolve the problem of historicism. Dilthey still conceived of method in the human sciences according to the same epistemological biases as in the

[159] See especially Martin Heidegger, *Einführung in die Metaphysik* (Tübingen: Niemeyer, 1953), 14. See also *Sein und Zeit* (Tübingen: Niemeyer, 1976). For an analysis of Kant and Heidegger, see Frank Schalow, *The Renewal of the Kant-Heidegger Dialogue* (Albany: State University of New York Press, 1992).

[160] Heinrich Rickert, in a series of unpublished lectures entitled "Einführung in die Erkenntnistheorie und Metaphysik" (Heidelberg Universitätsbibliothek, ms. 59), sees Descartes as a crucial figure in the history of philosophy. It is with Descartes, he contends, that consciousness is seen as the ground of objective reality. (For the connections with Dilthey, cf. n. 50 above, where the Cartesian philosophy of consciousness is discussed as a crucial element of *die neuzeitliche Bewußtseinsphilosophie*.) Rickert asks the question: "Gibt es eine (vom Bewußtsein unabhängige) Welt, die wir im Bewußtsein aufnehmen und dadurch erkennen? Oder: ist alles was sich wissen läßt notwendig im Bewußtsein beschlossen?" (Is there a world independent of consciousness which we take up and know through consciousness? Or: is everything that is knowable necessarily contained in consciousness?") Like Dilthey's assertion in *der Satz von Phänomenalität*, Rickert maintains that everything is "there-for-me" *only* within consciousness.

[161] Dilthey, *Introduction to the Human Sciences*, 245; *GS* 19: 58.

[162] Dilthey, *GS* 5: 90.

natural sciences. But, by the terms of his own argument, Dilthey's understanding of historical knowledge was rooted in lived experience, not scientific method. As he himself knew, any attempt to purge the historical subject of its temporal-cultural horizons, limits, and prejudices would undermine the very historicity that is the productive ground for understanding. By positing a model of interpretation informed by the subject-object dichotomies of Cartesian metaphysics, Dilthey reinforced the aporia of the historicist tradition—its simultaneous affirmation of the objective goals of *Wissenschaft* and the subjective values of *Weltanschauung*. Given the basic framework of historicist thinking and its unacknowledged reliance on natural-scientific ideals of "proof," "certitude," "rigor," "impartiality," and "validity," the fundamental aporia within historicism could never be resolved. In this sense, Dilthey's work serves as a model of the genuine achievement of historicist thinking in the crisis mode. But Dilthey was never able to resolve the crisis or come to an original understanding of the antinomy of historical reason. And yet, ironically, it was Dilthey's failure to "overcome" the crisis of historicism which helped to bring the idea of crisis itself a new meaning in the work of Heidegger.

Heidegger's ontological reading of historicism was an attempt to break free of Descartes's and even Dilthey's distinctions between subject and object which have traditionally dominated Western metaphysical thinking. By recasting the historicist's epistemological question about the objectivity of historical knowledge as an ontological question about the meaning of historical being, Heidegger began to deconstruct or dismantle the crisis in Weimar academics. Focusing on the aporetic moment of Dilthey's thinking which he defined by its problematic relation to subjectivity, Heidegger tried to account for the impasse in historicism in terms of an overall theory of crisis. Crisis now came to signify not only the methodological aporia in historicism but also the aporia within Western metaphysics itself in the era of modernity. For Heidegger, "crisis" and "modernity" were thought together as mutually determinative characteristics and possibilities of thinking, cultural symbols of a fundamental turning in Western philosophy which were both warning signs of the older tradition's collapse ("the end of philosophy") and intimations of an "other beginning" that would initiate a new kind of thinking. This effort to think through the ontological implications of the Cartesian tradition would, Heidegger hoped, heal the wounds inflicted by "the knife of historical relativism," to use Dilthey's metaphor.[163] But Dilthey's knife proved double-edged. As Heidegger dismantled the metaphysics of crisis-thinking, he initiated a new kind of crisis, political in scope and committed to a revolutionary overturning of contemplative academic research and theory. In the wake of Dilthey's aporia, Heidegger turned to history, and the history of metaphysics, to rehabilitate the positive sense of crisis that he believed defined the project of modernity. By examining his work from 1919 to 1927, I hope to show how Heidegger helped to transform the narrowly academic crisis of historicism into a crisis about crisis itself and about the meaning of modernity as an epoch of crisis-thinking.

[163] Dilthey, *GS* 8: 234. This is a well-known phrase coined by Dilthey and later used by Friedrich Meinecke to speak of the "crisis of historicism." On Meinecke's use of the metaphor "healing the wounds of historicism," see *Die Entstehung des Historismus* (Munich: Oldenbourg, 1965), 4 and 496, and "Geschichte und Gegenwart," in *Zur Theorie und Philosophie der Geschichte* (Stuttgart: Koehler, 1959), 94. Meinecke writes, "We believe that it [historicism] has the power to heal the wounds that it has inflicted through the relativization of all values—provided that it can find human beings who will convert this '-ism' into the terms of authentic life" (*Die Entstehung des Historismus*, lvii), and again, "Historicism must itself attempt to heal the wounds it has inflicted" (418). And, finally, "This is the great question: Does historicism (and the relativism that it has produced) possess the power to heal the wounds that it has inflicted upon itself?" (*Zur Theorie und Philosophie der Geschichte*, 94). The full sentence from Dilthey reads: "The knife of historical relativism which, at the same time, has wounded all metaphysics and religion, must also bring with it a healing touch."

CHAPTER FIVE

"The Time Is Out of Joint": The Young Heidegger's *Destruktion* of Historicism

Every vital kind of philosophizing must grow out of the present situation.

—Martin Heidegger,
"Phänomenologie der Anschauung und des Ausdrucks"

i. The Revolutionary Language of Theology: Karl Barth's "Epistle to the Romans"

The collapse of historicism, both as a world view and as a viable model for academic research, was not marked by any sudden ceremony heralding its demise. On the contrary, despite Dilthey's warnings about the "Janus face" of philosophy, with its irreconcilable tension between "universally valid knowledge" and a wisdom concerning "the enigma of life," historicism dominated German thinking, even in its decline.[1] As the theologian Friedrich Gogarten wrote in a 1924 essay: "The historicizing of all our thinking has been carried out today to the extent that it has become impossible for any of our ideas to escape it. . . . Our question then is not whether the historicizing of all thinking has actually occurred . . . but whether the historicizing which actually did take place is valid."[2] After Germany's experience in the First World War, the

---

[1] Wilhelm Dilthey, "The Dream," in Hans Meyerhoff, ed., *The Philosophy of History in Our Time* (Garden City, N.Y.: Doubleday, 1959), 41; and *Gesammelte Schriften*, vol. 8 (Göttingen: Vandenhoeck and Ruprecht, 1962), 224.

[2] Friedrich Gogarten, "Historicism," in James M. Robinson, ed., *The Beginnings of Dialectical Theology* (Richmond, Va.: John Knox Press, 1968), 343–354.

terms of the historicist question had changed radically. Sixteen million casualties later, the intricacies of Rickert's logic no longer offered the same assurance about the "meaning" (*Sinn*) of history. Troeltsch's learned polemics notwithstanding, the new voices of Oswald Spengler and Karl Barth spoke to a generation that had witnessed revolutionary upheavals that transformed German life. The unthinkable had happened: there was no Kaiser, and Germany had lost a war. The violent destruction of political and social life left little promise for the reinstatement of civic order and historical continuity. Hastily, workers and soldiers councils were being formed as many older imperial structures collapsed. In the midst of all the turmoil, there emerged a revolutionary imperative to tear down the old and begin anew.

If historicism had any relevance within this new configuration, it was more as an index to the "crisis" of culture than as a viable movement in its own right. What I find curious about the fate of historicism in this postwar era is how its inner logic and metaphysical character revealed themselves much more clearly in decline than they had in the dominant period of historicist thinking during the nineteenth century. The historicist faith in the meaning and coherence of human history had been shattered. Most concretely, on the barricades in Berlin and at the battlements of Verdun, the bourgeois narrative of order and optimism received a terrible blow. The faith of the liberal epoch in progress, culture, and *Bildung* was at an end. As the soldiers returned from the front, the mood at home became bleak and ominous. Two popular books published in Munich in 1918 captured this mood perfectly: Paul Ernst's *Collapse of German Idealism* and Oswald Spengler's *Decline of the West*.[3] Their very titles represented an assault on the reassuring platitudes of prewar Europe. Spengler's book in particular, despite (or rather owing to) its popularity, came under a barrage of criticism—and rightly so. His jargon-laden "mathematics" of culture, with its allusions to "Apollonian number" and "the symbolizing of extension," was crude and pretentious, and his colleagues in geometry and the natural sciences let him know as much.[4] Yet despite these sweeping and sometimes virulent attacks, the book's real point was

[3] Paul Ernst, *Der Zusammenbruch des deutschen Idealismus* (Munich: G. Muller, 1918); and Oswald Spengler, *The Decline of the West*, trans. C. F. Atkinson (New York: Knopf, 1926).
[4] The 1921 issue of *Logos: Eine Internationale Zeitschrift für Philosophie der Kultur* was devoted to a critique of Spengler.

often missed. What characterized Spengler's work was not its theory of numbers, its morphology of history, or its Faustian grasp of space and time but its cultural pessimism. Spengler's book was a clear sign of the collapse and destruction of the old, worn values of the prewar world. Spengler, or rather "the Spengler phenomenon," revealed that German culture was experiencing a "crisis" concerning its own fundamental history and identity, a crisis that threatened the meaning and continuity of the historicist tradition.

Historicism was, from its very beginnings, committed to a fundamental faith in history, a faith that, in thinkers such as Ranke, Droysen, and Troeltsch, revealed a theological dimension as well. Liberal theologians such as Adolf von Harnack inherited this faith and sought, by means of critical scholarship, to unite religion and culture in an ideal of ethical-historical progress. Harnack's *Kulturprotestantismus* blended the economic and political optimism of middle-class German Protestants with the self-congratulatory stance of cultural liberalism. In his lectures on "the essence of Christianity" at the University of Berlin (Winter Semester 1899/1900), Harnack assured his listeners: "We have received from the very foundation of our religion a lofty and noble ideal, an ideal that should be kept in view as our historical development proceeds, as its goal and lodestar. Who can tell whether man will ever achieve it? But we can and ought to draw nearer to it, and today—as opposed to two or three hundred years ago—we are already aware of a moral obligation to proceed in this direction, and those among us whose experience is more subtle and therefore prophetic no longer look upon the kingdom of love and peace as a mere Utopia."[5] In the aftermath of Versailles, Harnack's exultant meliorism held little appeal for the new generation of German intellectuals weaned on the realities of the war experience. In this atmosphere of skepticism and political disaffection, Karl Barth suddenly effected a theological volte-face in 1919 with his *Epistle to the Romans*.

Although Barth's message was very different from Spengler's, he shared with him two fundamental traits: the radical rejection of the historicist faith in the meaning of history and the awareness of a fundamental "crisis" in the foundations of German *Bildung* and *Wissenschaft*. Barth's *Romans* was a "revolutionary eruption" that challenged

---

[5] Adolf von Harnack, *What Is Christianity?* (New York: Harper, 1957), 113–114.

the very premises of liberal theology (and, by extension, German liberal culture at large) by questioning its understanding of language.[6] With writerly intensity, Barth made Paul's epistles speak again in a genuine idiom, in concert with the understanding of postwar experience. For Barth, the scriptures of the New Testament were not merely historical documents but also living testimony to the vitality and power of the true word of God. Through close textual readings of Paul's letters to the Romans, the language of faith was opened up in all its radicality. The Word that spoke in Barth's text was not merely the historical and cultural legacy of the early Christian Church but the reality of living experience. In a radical break with the spirit and aim of Harnack and his nineteenth-century predecessors, Barth's *Romans* reconceived the basic project of liberal and historical theology. Rejecting the historicist task of reconstructing the historical position from which Paul wrote, Barth wanted to stand before his theological situation as if he were Paul's contemporary. For Barth, "If we rightly understand ourselves, our problems are the problems of Paul."[7] If we could patiently attend to the message of the word, Barth believed that the Pauline epistles would speak to us or, rather, make a claim and judgment on us in their contemporaneity.[8] It was precisely this judgment of the word, salvaged from the pious obscurantism of historical erudition and revitalized by the eschatological force of Paul's language, which helped to precipitate a genuine "crisis" in theology.

Throughout Barth's commentary one could detect the influence of Kierkegaard, Dostoyevsky, Nietzsche, and Nietzsche's friend Franz Overbeck—voices that served to indict the cultural platitudes of German science and religion.[9] Theologically, a new beginning was announced: a *Stundenull* (zero hour) that Barth, cribbing from Nietzsche, called a "revaluation of all values." The old concepts, categories, and structures of thinking were declared bankrupt and unfit for a true revelation of God's word.[10] Like the young Luther in his *Lectures on Romans*, Barth initiated a radical reform of the Christian message in

[6] See, for example, the judgment of Hans-Georg Gadamer in *Truth and Method*, trans. Joel Weinsheimer and Donald G. Marshall (New York: Crossroad, 1989), 509; *Wahrheit und Methode* (Tübingen: Mohr, 1975), 481.
[7] Karl Barth, *Epistle to the Romans* (Oxford: Oxford University Press, 1989), 451.
[8] In Greek, *krisis* indicates both a "judgment" and a "turning." Henry George Liddell and Robert Scott, *Greek-English Lexicon* (Oxford: Oxford University Press, 1990), 997.
[9] For the influence of Kierkegaard, see also *Dostoyevsky* (Richmond, Va.: John Knox Press, 1964) by Barth's friend Eduard Thurneysen.
[10] In the first edition of Barth's *Epistle to the Romans* (1919), chap. 2, secs. 14–19 are titled "Revaluation of All Values."

light of the new situation within which the word spoke—and was interpreted.[11] In a way, Barth's writings served as a kind of "hermeneutical manifesto" that called for an end to traditional research practices so that the living word could speak in the contemporary situation. Barth's "crisis theology," as it was called, began with the judgment (*krisis* in Greek) of God (Rom. 2:1–6), which was beyond the scope of all knowledge or *Wissenschaft*. In its original Greek sense, *krisis* (from *krinein*) meant a kind of sifting or separating that was, at the same time, a selecting or judging that culminated in a de-cision.[12] In German, the same linguistic play with *Scheidung* (separation, scission) and *Entscheidung* (decision) is preserved; crisis is, literally, a decisive judgment understood as a critical (also derived from *krinein*) turning point.[13] For Barth, crisis signified the realization that "genuine faith is a void" and that human beings must confront a kind of "either/or" between the flesh, "which occurs *in* time," and the spirit, which is the "moment beyond all time."[14] Out of this void the word erupts and lays claim to the truth of spirit; for Paul as well as for Barth, the void itself reveals and bears witness to the crisis that is "the present time."

The genuine meaning of "crisis theology" was not, however, narrowly theological but lay in its radical indictment of the conceptual foundations that had sustained most of nineteenth-century German thought and culture. In *Romans* Barth proclaimed an end to the liberal era by focusing his attention on the sterility and spiritual exhaustion that had claimed the German world. Yet his task was neither to erect a new theological model nor to destroy the old one for its own sake. He sought, rather, to radicalize faith through an encounter in "the present time" with the eschatological message of Paul: "And this do, knowing the time, that now it is high time to awake out of sleep: for now is our salvation nearer than when we believed. The night is far spent, the day is at hand: let us therefore cast off the works of darkness, and let us put on the armour of light" (Rom. 13:11–13).

In the same spirit as Barth, Friedrich Gogarten tried to understand Paul's message as a genuine call for renewal in an age of crisis. For

---

[11] Martin Luther, *Lectures on Romans*, vol. 25 of *Luther's Works*, ed. Hilton C. Oswald (St. Louis: Concordia, 1972).

[12] Joseph Shipley, *The Origins of English Words* (Baltimore: Johns Hopkins University Press, 1984), 177 and 350; see also Eric Partridge, *Origins: A Short Etymological Dictionary of Modern English* (New York: Macmillan, 1958), 130.

[13] Wolfgang Pfeifer, ed., *Etymologisches Wörterbuch des Deutschen*, vol. 2 (Berlin: Akademie, 1989), 934.

[14] Barth, *Epistle to the Romans*, 33, 283, 304.

Gogarten, Barth's book (like Spengler's) signaled the end of a historical epoch and an awareness of a new crisis-consciousness. Reacting to the collapse of liberal values in history, Gogarten wrote:

> It is the destiny of our generation to stand between the times. We never belonged to the period presently coming to an end; it is doubtful whether we shall ever belong to the period which is to come. . . . So we stand in the middle—in an empty space. We belong neither to the one nor to the other. . . . Therefore, we were jubilant over Spengler's book. It proved, whether or not it is true in detail, that the hour has come in which this refined intelligent culture, through its own intelligence, discovers the worm in itself, the hour in which trust in progress and culture receives the death blow. And Spengler's book is not the only sign. Whoever reads can find it in nearly every book and essay.[15]

In this void "between the times" the work of Spengler and Barth came to signify the very crisis of German culture which had been spawned by the war. Neither *The Decline of the West* nor *Epistle to the Romans* offered a new beginning for *Wissenschaft* or for faith; each concentrated on the work of demolition and subversion. Barth, in particular, felt it presumptuous to offer new foundations while rubble lay everywhere in view. Yet the experience of waste and devastation, if entered into and endured, might, Barth considered, prove more valuable in the end than all attempts at hurried reformation. The only meaningful possibility left for theology lay in the effort to dismantle its inherent structures and return to the primordiality of authentic religious experience expressed in the living language of the word. Writing to a friend "from the front" in early November 1918, the young Heidegger echoed some of Barth's concerns. Disdaining the "nibbling dilettantism" of academic life, Heidegger insisted that "theoretical discussions yield little fruit; only personal experience can bring clarity." In his letter Heidegger went on to offer some admonitions about scholarship (*Wissenschaft*) and warned his friend about the dangers of an overly academic approach to the living word: "What you are seeking you will find in yourself; the path leads from originary religious experience to theology but it *must* not lead from theology to the vitality of religious consciousness."[16]

---

[15] Friedrich Gogarten, "Between the Times," in Robinson, *Beginnings of Dialectical Theology*, 277–280.

[16] Martin Heidegger and Elisabeth Blochmann, *Briefwechsel, 1918–1969*, ed. Joachim W. Storck (Marbach: Deutsche Schillergesellschaft, 1989), 9–10.

ii. The Crisis of Faith

Heidegger was twenty-nine when he returned home from the war suffering from an intense personal crisis. Ever since his early school days, he had remained a strict and devout Catholic. The son of a Messkirch sacristan, Heidegger himself originally trained for the priesthood at a Jesuit novitiate in Feldkirch before health problems forced him to withdraw.[17] He left the seminary in 1911 to attend the University of Freiburg, where he studied Catholic theology for four semesters and began to take up the study of philosophy. In 1915 he completed his *Habilitationsschrift* (inaugural dissertation) on the scholastic theologian Duns Scotus and soon thereafter started "delivering philosophical courses for theologians" with his Catholic colleague Professor Engelbert Krebs.[18] For seven years, from 1909 to 1916, Heidegger's academic and religious pursuits converged, leading in 1916 to a nomination for the chair in Catholic philosophy in Freiburg.[19] Drafted in 1917, intermittent military obligations forced him to interrupt his teaching for almost two years. During this time his life changed dramatically. In March 1917, Heidegger married a young Lutheran, Elfriede Petri, and began to read from the works of the great Protestant theologians, especially Luther and Schleiermacher.[20] In August he gave a lecture to a private group on Schleiermacher's second speech from *On Religion*. Months later he was called up to the front as a weatherman and helped "prepare poison gas attacks on American soldiers during their final push from Verdun to Sedan in early October."[21]

By the time Heidegger resumed his teaching duties at Freiburg during the war emergency semester of 1919 (January 25–April 16), his

[17] For a copy of Heidegger's early curriculum vitae and an in-depth discussion of his early education and career up to July 1915, see Thomas Sheehan, "Heidegger's *Lehrjahre*," in John Sallis, Giuseppe Moneta, and Jacques Taminiaux, eds., *The Collegium Phaenomenologicum: The First Ten Years* (Dordrecht: Kluwer, 1988), 77–137.

[18] Heidegger's *Habilitationsschrift* has been translated by Harold Robbins as his doctoral dissertation for DePaul University, 1978, under the title *"Duns Scotus' Theory of the Categories and of Meaning* by Martin Heidegger"; Martin Heidegger, *Frühe Schriften*, *Gesamtausgabe* 1 (Frankfurt: Klosterman, 1978). Initially, each separate volume of the *Gesamtausgabe* will be cited in full and thereafter as *GA* with volume number and page reference. For a study of Heidegger's early religious training at Freiburg, see Bernhard Casper, "Martin Heidegger und die Theologische Fakultät Freiburg, 1909–1923," in *Kirche am Oberrhein* (Freiburg: Herder, 1980), 534 ff.

[19] Cited after Husserl's letter to Paul Natorp, by Thomas Sheehan, "Heidegger's Early Years: Fragments for a Philosophical Biography," in Sheehan, ed., *Heidegger: The Man and the Thinker* (Chicago: Precedent, 1981), 7.

[20] Thomas Sheehan, "Reading a Life: Heidegger and Hard Times," in Charles Guignon, ed., *The Cambridge Companion to Heidegger* (Cambridge: Cambridge University Press, 1993) 70–96.

[21] Ibid.

solidly Catholic world view had come under assault.[22] In a letter to his friend Father Krebs, Heidegger wrote on January 9, 1919, that "epistemological insights, extending to the theory of historical knowledge, have made the *system* of Catholicism problematic and unacceptable to me—but not Christianity and metaphysics (although these in a new sense)."[23] From this same period there are two other documentary sources that confirm Heidegger's crisis of faith after 1917. His mentor, Edmund Husserl, in a letter of 1919 to the theologian Rudolf Otto spoke of the "radical changes in [Heidegger's] basic religious convictions," changes occasioned by "difficult inner struggles."[24] And Krebs's diary gives an account of Frau Heidegger's visit of late December 1918, where she came to explain why she and her husband could not baptize their son-to-be in the Catholic faith: "My husband has lost his church faith and I have not found mine. . . . Together we have read, spoken, thought and prayed much, and the result is that we both think only as Protestants. That is, without any strong dogmatic ties, we believe in a personal God and pray to Him in the spirit of Christ without, however, Protestant or Catholic orthodoxy."[25] Heidegger explained to Krebs that "for the past two years I have struggled for a fundamental clarification of my philosophical position"; finally, he had decided to break with the whole "system" of Catholicism to follow his own "inner calling" (*inneren Beruf*).[26]

Heidegger's "difficult inner struggles" notwithstanding, his experience of a "religious crisis" could hardly be thought of as unique. In the turbulent period after the war, crisis itself became a cliché, and religious crisis was no exception. (Husserl's letter to Otto also spoke of Heidegger's friend Heinrich Ochsner, who experienced a religious conversion at about the same time.) Husserl went on to say that his own "philosophical effect has something remarkably revolutionary about it: Protestants become Catholic. . . . Catholics become Protestant."[27] In this context of religious crisis, Heidegger's religious shift

---

[22] Martin Heidegger, *Zur Bestimmung der Philosophie, Gesamtausgabe* 56/57 (Frankfurt: Klostermann, 1987), 215. See also Hugo Ott, *Martin Heidegger: Unterwegs zu seiner Biographie* (Frankfurt: Campus, 1988), 106–119.

[23] Ott, *Martin Heidegger*, 106.

[24] Quoted by Thomas Sheehan in "Heidegger's 'Introduction to the Phenomenology of Religion,' 1920–21" (hereafter cited as "Heidegger's 'Introduction'"), in Joseph Kockelmans, ed., *A Companion to Martin Heidegger's "Being and Time"* (Washington, D.C.: University Press of America, 1986), 43.

[25] Quoted by Ott in *Martin Heidegger*, 108.

[26] Ibid., 108–109.

[27] Quoted in Sheehan, *Heidegger*, 23 ff.

was closely tied to the concrete situation in German theology in 1919, symbolized especially by the work of Barth. What makes this so important in the larger context of a study of historicism is how this religious crisis itself becomes philosophically revolutionary—and how Heidegger's religious questions come to affect the very notion of historical consciousness so prevalent in German historicist thinking.

Barth and Gogarten both believed that genuine Christianity involves a contradiction between faith and knowledge. Religion, for them, was not primarily a cultural inheritance or the manifestation of a historical world view. Rather, it evoked a living encounter with the word of God whereby "the conversation between the original record and the reader moves round the subject-matter, until a distinction between yesterday and today becomes impossible."[28] In Barth's words, the eschatological message of Paul's epistles revealed the genuine meaning of religion as "the permanent *Krisis* of the relation between time and eternity."[29] Despite their many differences, Heidegger shared with Barth and Gogarten a common concern for early Christian thinking as well as a hermeneutical approach to its understanding and interpretation. In his newly begun reading of Luther, Schleiermacher, and Overbeck, Heidegger discovered a Christianity at odds with the medieval scholasticism of his own faith. These radical thinkers taught him a new skepticism concerning the Christian faith as it was practiced in the churches and interpreted by the theologians. By radically dismantling and destroying the scholastic-academic dogmas of inherited Christian tradition, these theologians, or rather antitheologians, discovered the "fundamental character of originary Christianity in its world-denying expectation of the End."[30] Heidegger transformed these eschatological traces into an "indication" (*Anzeige*) of a "genuine beginning" for philosophy. Concretely, that meant a transformation of the old scholastic categories that, in their Neo-Kantian form, Heidegger had employed in his book on Duns Scotus.[31] In its conclusion Heidegger spoke about problems of a "metaphysical origin" concerning "time and eternity" which were reflected upon "in a scientific

[28] Barth, *Epistle to the Romans*, 7.
[29] Ibid., 10–11.
[30] Martin Heidegger, *The Piety of Thinking*, trans. James G. Hart and John C. Maraldo (Bloomington: Indiana University Press, 1976), 4; *Phänomenologie und Theologie* (Frankfurt: Klostermann, 1970), 8.
[31] I would like to thank John van Buren for allowing me to read a draft of his unfinished manuscript, *The Young Heidegger* (Bloomington: Indiana University Press, 1994), in which he discusses Heidegger's early work in detail and offers a penetrating reading of the *Habilitationsschrift*.

and theoretical way by history and philosophy." These disciplines defined the problems in terms of both "the formation of values" and "the validity of values," themes that the young Heidegger, in a footnote, associated with "a consideration of Catholic theology from a scientific standpoint."[32] He also noticed that connections between Neo-Kantian value-philosophy and scholastic logic had been important in the scientific understanding of theology, but he realized that neither of these influences had helped him genuinely to understand the originary power of religious faith.

As he began to move away from "scientific" Catholic theology through his readings of Luther, Schleiermacher, and Overbeck, Heidegger's philosophical position changed. Despite his persistent claims that "philosophy itself is, as such, atheistic if it understands itself radically," Heidegger's early philosophy was always marked by the presence of religious thinking.[33] In his new lecture courses "Introduction to a Phenomenology of Religion" (Winter Semester 1920/21) and "Augustine and Neo-Platonism" (Winter Semester 1921/22), Heidegger provided a hermeneutic reading of Christian faith derived from Husserl's phenomenological insight that the "essence" of entities is neither their substance (whatness) nor value but the way they disclose themselves within the structure of intentionality.[34] Husserl's work offered an alternative to both the Neo-Kantianism of his earlier work and the scientific theology of the Freiburg faculty; but the lines of influence went both ways. If phenomenology helped Heidegger to break with his theological past, his new interest in Protestant theology helped him to move away from Husserl. From the concrete understanding of factical life as a "situation" in Paul's epistles, Heidegger rethought Husserl's notion of anonymous intentionality, which he now saw as overly theoretical because it did not engage the factical world of decision making. And yet, in one sense, phenomenology and radical-skeptical theology had the same aim: to win genuine access (*Zugang*) to the originary structures of experience. Traditional forms of philosophical and theological research had focused too much attention on historical-cultural development and an analysis of world views. But phenomenology and radical theology sought to break through these calcified research practices by destroying the very structures of scientific tradition which made them possible.

[32] Heidegger, *GA* 1: 410.
[33] Martin Heidegger, *Phänomenologische Interpretationen zu Aristoteles: Einführung in die phänomenologische Forschung*, Gesamtausgabe 61 (Frankfurt: Klostermann, 1985), 199.
[34] Sheehan, "Heidegger's 'Introduction.'"

196 Heidegger, Dilthey, and the Crisis of Historicism

Heidegger's radicality consisted in a curious appropriation/transformation of theological and phenomenological sources from within his own historical situation, a practice that, in the summer semester of 1920, he termed *Destruktion*.[35] This key term in Heidegger's early writings served as a kind of shorthand definition for his own understanding of phenomenology, especially as a way of reinterpreting the history of philosophy. Although the term has roots in his reading of the young Luther, especially the "Heidelberg Disputation" (1518) and *Lectures on Romans* (1515/16), Heidegger's usage is unique.[36] Luther employed the Latin term *destruere* ("to destroy") in an effort to "destroy" the scholastic theology of glory derived from the philosophy of Aristotle. "He who has not been broken and brought low by the Cross," Luther argued, can never know God.[37] The puffed-up and distended "wisdom" of the learned theologian could hardly penetrate the inward core of genuine faith, which was possible only through experiencing for oneself the pain and suffering of the theology of the cross. Heidegger followed Luther's destruction of scholastic philosophy with a *Destruktion* of Neo-Kantian *Kathederphilosophie*. As a modern

[35] *Destruktion* in Heidegger's sense connotes something other than mere "destruction"; it also has the positive sense of removing obstacles by de-structuring them and opening up a space wherein what is de-structured can reveal itself. As Heidegger writes in *Sein und Zeit* (Tübingen: Niemeyer, 1976), 22 (English translation, *Being and Time*, by John Macquarrie and Edward Robinson [New York: Harper and Row, 1962], 44): "If the question of being is to have its own history made transparent, then this hardened tradition must be loosened up, and the concealments which it has brought about must be dissolved. We understand this task as one in which by taking the question of being as our clue, we are to de-structure the traditional content of ancient ontology until we arrive at those primordial experiences in which we achieved our first ways of determining the nature of being—the ways which have guided us ever since. . . . We must, on the contrary, stake out the positive possibilities of that tradition, and this always means keeping it within limits. . . . To bury the past in nullity is not the purpose of this de-structuring; its aim is positive; its negative function remains unexpressed and indirect" (translation modified). The French translator of *Sein und Zeit*, François Vezin, translates *Destruktion* as *désobstruction*, which carries the sense of removing obstructions, or de-obstructing. See *Entre et Temps* (Paris: Gallimard, 1986), 45. "De-obstruction" is the authentic meaning of *Seinsforschung*; this requires a hermeneutic removal of the obstructions posed by metaphysics and its "oblivion of Being." In Summer Semester 1923 Heidegger declared: "Hermeneutics is de-structuring!" Only in "concrete historical investigations" can "this hermeneutic–de-structuring research be demonstrated" (*Ontologie: Hermeneutik der Faktizität, Gesamtausgabe* 63 [Frankfurt: Klostermann, 1988], 105). Even for the later Heidegger, "*Destruktion* must be strictly understood as de-structuring (*de-struere*), dismantling [*Ab-bauen*], and not as devastation [*Verwüsten*]" (*Seminare, Gesamtausgabe* 15 [Frankfurt: Klostermann, 1986], 337).
[36] Luther used the term in the "Heidelberg Disputation" when he spoke of God's "destroying" the wisdom of the wise. *Werke*, vol. 50 (Weimar: Böhlau, 1883–), 362; in English, vol. 31 of *Luther's Works*, ed. Harold I. Grimm (Philadelphia: Muhlenberg, 1957), 53. See also *Werke*, vol. 56, pp. 371–372, and *Works*, 25:361. For a fuller discussion, see van Buren, *Young Heidegger*.
[37] Luther, *Werke*, 50:362–363.

counterpart to medieval scholasticism, *Kathederphilosophie* (which derives literally from the ponderous "rostrum"-style philosophizing at German universities) was, for Heidegger, a philosophy of dispassionate and detached ocularism. In its overreliance on theory and self-congratulatory scholarship, it had forgotten philosophy's roots in factical-historical life. In the war emergency semester, Heidegger spoke out against the reified "primacy of the theoretical" that dominated academic language, subjecting it to a new kind of destruction by emphasizing prefixes and introducing hyphens in words such as *Ent-lebnis* ("de-living"), *ent-geschichtlicht* ("de-historicized"), and *ent-deutet* ("de-signified"), terms that captured the wizened, desiccated spirit of *Kathederphilosophie*.[38]

A year later, in his lectures titled "Phenomenology of Intuition and Expression (Theory of Philosophical Concept-Formation)," Heidegger tried to explain the difference between the negations of *Kathederphilosophie* and his own practice of *Destruktion*:

> Philosophy is neither science nor a theory of world views. Its task is not an a priori grammar of reason, nor can it offer an epistemological description of consciousness, because by doing so it merely deteriorates. The result is a series of negations. One can easily include this philosophy of negation within German *Kathederphilosophie*: each happily slaying the other. However, *Destruktion* is pursued with none of this negative and deprecating flavor; it is an expression of philosophizing: of rendering uncertain one's own existence [*Dasein*]. Here, the real aim is clear: to grasp radically the idea of phenomenology. In phenomenology the originary motives of philosophizing become vital again in their purity.[39]

The new practice of *Destruktion* was Heidegger's call to the "vitality of genuine research" and to a new language that would transform philosophy from the "obscurities, comforts, unverified traditions, and matters of taste" plaguing Neo-Kantian scholasticism and the modish world-view philosophies.[40] Husserl's phenomenology had shown him that the return to origins must be the primary task of philosophy, but Husserl had bracketed the factical-historical world of experience.[41] It

---

[38] Heidegger, *GA* 56/57: 89.
[39] This quotation is taken from F. J. Brecht's *Nachschrift* of Heidegger's lecture course from Summer Semester 1920, "Phänomenologie der Anschauung und des Ausdrucks: Theorie der philosophischen Begriffsbildung" (hereafter cited as "PAA"), July 26, 1920.
[40] Heidegger, *GA* 56/57: 5, and *GA* 61: 39.
[41] In his lectures from Summer Semester 1923, Heidegger spoke of "the ahistoricality

was the language of Paul, Luther, Augustine, and the Protestant theologians which offered Heidegger a hermeneutic understanding of Christian experience apart from the deadening influence of the rostrum and the pulpit. The "struggles" of philosophy (a constant theme in his early work) were not about incessant conferencing and armchair pyrotechnics but concerned the "one thing that mattered."[42] Augustine's battle with Neo-Platonism and Luther's "struggle" with Aristotelianism, far from being historical curiosities, were alive and raging in the present situation.[43] From within this situation, Heidegger retrieved the sources of philosophy and theology, salvaging them from the realm of "objective truth," as he wrote to Karl Löwith in 1921, by "being there with them" in one's "own facticity."[44]

Heidegger's affinity for these theological sources is itself a model of his new "hermeneutic breakthrough" after 1917. In his *Destruktion* of liberal-theological hermeneutics, Heidegger came to grasp hermeneutics in a radically new sense: as an "indication" for the understanding of factical-historical life.[45] Scientific theology, in the form of historical and cultural erudition, could not break free from the abstract language of conceptuality which had dominated scholastic metaphysics. In fact, Heidegger believed that academic religious learning had become pharisaical as it denied the experiential roots of factical life.

Heidegger's sources for this critique were rich and varied: Braig, Dostoyevsky, Deissmann, Kierkegaard, Luther, Pascal, Aristotle, Eck-

---

of phenomenology" and took Husserl to task for his lack of historical consciousness. See *GA* 63: 75. Compare Husserl's remarks on relativism in his *Logische Untersuchungen*, vol. 1 (Tübingen: Niemeyer, 1968), 117; translated by J. N. Findlay as *Logical Investigations*, vol. 1 (London: Routledge, 1970), 140.

[42] A rich source for Heidegger's early thought comes from his student Karl Löwith, who provides his own reading in his tendentious autobiography, *Mein Leben in Deutschland vor und nach 1933: Ein Bericht* (Stuttgart: Metzler, 1986). On p. 29 Löwith cites the catchword of Heidegger's early thinking—"*das Eine was Not tut*" ("the one thing that matters")—which he links to Heidegger's readings, especially of Van Gogh, Rilke, Pascal, Barth, Dostoyevsky, and Kierkegaard. Löwith discusses these same themes in his article "The Political Implications of Heidegger's Existentialism," trans. Richard Wolin, *New German Critique* 45 (Fall 1988): 117–134.

[43] See Otto Pöggeler, "Neue Wege mit Heidegger," *Philosophische Rundschau* 29 (1982): 57.

[44] Some of the important letters that Heidegger wrote to Löwith have finally been published. Among these is one long letter from 1921 which provides some textual evidence for Heidegger's notion of "facticity": see "Drei Briefe Martin Heideggers an Karl Löwith," in Dietrich Papenfuss and Otto Pöggeler, eds., *Zur Philosophischen Aktualität Heideggers*, vol. 2, *Im Gespräch der Zeit* (Frankfurt: Klostermann, 1990), 30.

[45] For a fuller discussion of Heidegger's term *formal indication* (*formale Anzeige*), see Theodore Kisiel, *The Genesis of Heidegger's "Being and Time"* (Berkeley: University of California Press, 1993), and van Buren, *Young Heidegger*. Kisiel also discusses Heidegger's relations to Schleiermacher.

hart, Jaspers, and Lask.[46] An untiring reader, Heidegger was well informed about the various academic controversies in the early years of the Weimar era. Like any good mandarin, he read Barth and Spengler and was sensitive to the watchwords *Krisis* and *Untergang* (decline). But Heidegger's *destruktive*-hermeneutic relation to his sources transformed them from the shibboleths of cultural history and bad sociology to a "formal indication" (*formale Anzeige*) of a "new beginning" for philosophy and theology.[47] He did not merely borrow ideas from theology; he forged them into a new language that he hoped would work against the abstract conceptuality of metaphysics and call attention to the "crisis" of Western culture and history. Four hundred years after Luther's defense at Wittenberg, this other Catholic apostate reframed the language of the school-philosophies into the living word of his own experience. We need to take the late Heidegger very seriously when he says that "without this theological provenance I would never have come onto the path of thinking."[48] A letter from Heidegger to Löwith in August 1921 echoes this sentiment: "I work concretely and factically out of my 'I am,' out of my intellectual and wholly factic origin, milieu, life-contexts, and whatever is available to me from these as a vital experience in which I live. . . . To this facticity of mine belongs what I would in brief call the fact that I am a 'Christian theo*logian*.' This involves a particular radical personal concern, a particular radical scientificity, a strict objectivity *in* the *facticity*; in it is to be found the historical consciousness, the consciousness of 'intellectual and cultural history.' And I am all this in the life-context of the university."[49]

---

[46] Heidegger was a voracious reader and in his early years read widely, especially in theology but also in other areas. In his 1925 Kassel lectures, "Wilhelm Diltheys Forschungsarbeit und der Kampf um eine historische Weltanschauung" (hereafter cited as "KV," with pagination based on the original manuscript copy from Walter Bröcker at the Dilthey-Forschungsstelle, Ruhr University, Bochum), Heidegger even refers to mathematicians and physicists whom he read during the early twenties. The Kassel lectures are forthcoming in Frithjof Rodi, ed., *Dilthey-Jahrbuch für Philosophie und Geschichte der Geisteswissenschaften.* I am indebted to Professor Rodi for generously providing me with a copy before publication. For Heidegger's reading of Eckhart, Schleiermacher, Overbeck, Deissmann, and others, the best accounts are provided by Theodore Kisiel in his various articles and in his book, *The Genesis of Heidegger's "Being and Time."*
[47] See Heidegger, *GA* 61: 19, 32–34, 141–42, and 183 for examples of Heidegger's usage.
[48] Heidegger, *On the Way to Language*, trans. Peter D. Hertz (New York: Harper and Row, 1971), 10; *Unterwegs zur Sprache, Gesamtausgabe* 12 (Frankfurt: Klostermann, 1985), 91.
[49] Papenfuss and Pöggeler, *Zur Philosophischen Aktualität Heideggers*, 2:29; trans. Theodore Kisiel in "Heidegger's Apology: Biography as Philosophy and Ideology," *Graduate Faculty Philosophy Journal* 14, no. 2–15, no. 1 (1991): 376.

As a "Christian theo*logian*," Heidegger set out to interpret the word (*logos*) of God (*theos*); his response to the crisis within theology was to turn to this word (*Wort*) as an anti-word (*Ant-wort*) or counter-*logos* to the language of liberal theology.[50] As a radically factical practice, hermeneutics sought to destroy, de-structure (*Destruktion*), dismantle, and un-build (*Abbau*) the research-oriented mode of traditional hermeneutics and burrow beneath its critical-exegetical method of inquiry to get at the factical "I am" of vital experience. No longer primarily a text-oriented strategy, in Heidegger's situation of crisis, "hermeneutics is the annunciation or becoming manifest in language of the being of that which is in its being to—(me)."[51] In Heidegger's hands, the "crisis of theology" proves not to be theological at all but a crisis concerning the very nature of language, meaning, and being. Or rather, theology (like philosophy or history) becomes meaningful only in and as "crisis." More than even those heralds of crisis Spengler and Barth, Heidegger's work of the 1920s is incomprehensible without an understanding of the factical-historical conditions of Weimar in an era of cultural upheaval. Inauthentic existence, idle chatter, the predominance of curiosity, "masking oneself" (*Larvanz*), "everydayness" (*Alltäglichkeit*), "falling" (*Abfall*), and the imminence of death—all these prominent themes attest to Heidegger's constant return to the sources of practical existence.

Yet, if these categories seem to reflect an inordinate concern on Heidegger's part for sociological anomie or cultural disenchantment, their genuine meaning lies elsewhere. Heidegger's preoccupation with the language of crisis is transformed through his hermeneutic break with the tradition and itself becomes a way of rethinking "crisis" in its phenomenological or originary meaning. Early in his youth, as a subscriber to the avant-garde Catholic literary journal *Der Brenner*, Heidegger read the first installments of Kierkegaard's *Two Ages*, translated by Theodore Haecker with the German title *Kritik der Gegenwart* (*Critique of the Present Age*).[52] Kierkegaard's acerbic, ironic assessment of the contemporary situation (which he claimed was

---

[50] See Otto Pöggeler, "Heidegger und die hermeneutische Theologie," in Eberhard Jüngel, ed., *Verifikationen: Festschrift für Gerhard Ebeling* (Tübingen: Mohr, 1982), 475–498.
[51] Heidegger, *GA* 63: 10.
[52] See Allan Janik, "Haecker, Kierkegaard, and the Early Brenner: A Contribution to the History of the Reception of *Two Ages* in the German-Speaking World," in Robert Perkins, ed., *International Kierkegaard Commentary: Two Ages* (Macon, Ga.: Mercer University Press, 1984), 189–222.

marked by a "fossilized formalism" and a "narrow-hearted custom and practice") focused attention back on the individual, who was then forced to decide about the ethical possibility of authentic existence.[53] The very lack of certainty which Kierkegaard discerned in the present age became, through philosophical critique, a condition for the possibility of an ethical turn or movement. In the hermeneutic situation "between the times," Heidegger committed himself to the Kierkegaardian task of offering a genuine "critique of the present age" which would address the prevailing crisis in German thinking.[54] In a phenomenological sense, "crisis" came to mean not merely the Spenglerian diagnosis of cultural decline or the social and political changes brought on by the war. The crisis of the 1920s signified, rather, an indication of the nihilistic character of the history of Western thought.[55] Spengler's thesis of "decline" proved to be only a vulgar adaption of Nietzsche's genealogical narrative of nihilism. Still, Heidegger believed that Spengler's epochal understanding of Western destiny did provide some structural hints for understanding the history of being as a decision or turning point (a fundamental *Krisis*) within being itself.[56] All the various manifestations of the contemporary cultural crisis (in theology, mathematics, physics, and history) were, for Heidegger, only the marks of this decisive epochal turning.

Heidegger's much-discussed *Kehre* (often translated misleadingly as "reversal") must be interpreted in this light. Heidegger's *Kehre* was a "turning" that had more than idiosyncratic or biographical consequences. What was at stake for Heidegger in the rhetorical figure of a "turning" was not a shift within his own thinking (whether one dates

[53] Søren Kierkegaard, *Two Ages*, trans. Howard Hong and Edna Hong (Princeton, N.J.: Princeton University Press, 1978), 72, 78. See also Perkins, *Kierkegaard Commentary*, 234–248.

[54] In 1920 Friedrich Gogarten published an essay entitled "Zwischen den Zeiten" in *Die Christliche Welt*, the chief organ of liberal theology. Gogarten explicitly referred to Kierkegaard and his "critique of the present age," arguing that religion always addresses the crisis of culture. Two years later, Gogarten, Barth, Thurneysen, and Georg Merz founded a new journal, *Zwischen den Zeiten*, which took its name from Gogarten's essay. The journal became the leading voice of "crisis theology" in Germany.

[55] For various etymological treatments of *Krisis*, see Paul Grebe, ed., *Duden: Etymologie* (Mannheim: Bibliographisches Institut, 1963), 371; Hjalmar Frisk, *Griechisches Etymologisches Wörterbuch*, vol. 2 (Heidelberg: Carl Winter, 1970), 20; Wilhelm Pape, *Griechisch-Deutsches Handwörterbuch* (Braunschweig: Vieweg, 1880), 1510–1511; and Adolf Kaegi, ed., *Benselers Griechisch-Deutsches Schulwörterbuch* (Leipzig: Teubner, 1904), 515–516.

[56] In his lectures of Summer Semester 1920 ("PAA," May 11, 1920), Heidegger stated that Spengler's "principal foundations are essential"; again, in Winter Semester 1921–1922 (*GA* 61: 74), he criticized Spengler, although he thought Spengler had expressed one of the "decisive tendencies" of the time.

the *Kehre* after *Being and Time* or, as some more-recent scholarship suggests, after 1917) but a turning of/within the history of being, understood epochally.[57] *Kehre*, in this sense, is Heidegger's name for a turning toward a new beginning within the history of Western thought, as well as a turning from the oblivion-bringing metaphysics of science and technology. But part of the dynamic of this turning depends on a re-turn (*Rückkehr*) to the origins of Western thinking in the Greeks. Heidegger's *Kehre* was thus intended not only as a historical return but also as a *destruktive* retrieval of that hidden part of the tradition leveled by the normalizing practices of intellectual and cultural history. After his turn away from scholastic metaphysics and toward the Protestant theological reading of Paul, Heidegger found phenomenological indications for a new beginning of thinking in the eschatological consciousness of the early Christians. In the early Christian experience of time, Heidegger saw a model of factical-historical life free from the historicist notion of developmental time and recalcitrant to any scientific-scholarly "analysis." The early Christians, in Heidegger's reading, faced a critical situation similar to the contemporary crisis of Weimar culture; in their decision to be ever watchful to "the signs of the times" (Matt. 16:3), they offered alternative possibilities to the abstract conceptuality of Greek metaphysics. Precisely in this phenomenon of "watchfulness" or "vigilance," Heidegger found a way to come to grips with the crisis of the sciences within the German university.

iii. The Situation of University Philosophy

Heidegger's religious crisis of 1917–1919 marked a significant change in his early thinking. In his letter to Krebs, he alluded to "epistemological insights extending to the theory of historical knowledge" which made "the system of Catholicism problematic and unacceptable to [him]."[58] Ultimately, his doubts about historical epistemol-

---

[57] For an excellent discussion of *die Kehre* in Heidegger's works, see Jean Grondin, *Le tournant dans la pensée de Martin Heidegger* (Paris: Presses universitaire de France, 1987), and Theodore Kisiel, "Das Kriegsnotsemester 1919: Heideggers Durchbruch zur hermeneutischen Phänomenologie," *Philosophisches Jahrbuch* 99 (1992): 105–123. See also Martin Heidegger, "Die Kehre," in *Die Technik und die Kehre* (Pfullingen: Neske, 1962); translated by William Lovitt as "The Turning," in *The Question concerning Technology* (New York: Harper and Row, 1977).
[58] For the text of the letter, see Ott, *Martin Heidegger*, 106; translated in Sheehan, "Reading a Life," 71–72.

ogy resulted in a turn toward the historicity of life, a theme that Heidegger kept coming back to and rethinking in various forms as "factical life experience," "the temporally particular hermeneutic situation," "the hermeneutics of facticity," and "the existential analytic of *Dasein*" right up through *Being and Time*.[59] This turn toward historicity and hermeneutics must not, however, be understood as a turning away from theology or from theological questioning. Heidegger's break with the system of Catholicism, like his move away from scholastic philosophy, was a radicalization of his original mode of questioning rather than a rejection of it. His turn toward Paul, Luther, Overbeck, and Schleiermacher paralleled his phenomenological investigations by focusing on the *historical* context of self-disclosure and intentionality. If philosophy were to offer some measure of help in the contemporary crisis, it would first have to examine its own factical-historical situation in the present. And, for Heidegger, that meant above all a consideration of its role within the modern university system.

Since the founding of the Humboldt University of Berlin in 1809, philosophy as a discipline had been separated into two different, sometimes hostile approaches in Germany: the "systematic" and the "historical."[60] In general terms, the systematic approach proceeded on a scientific basis, without regard to questions of historical development. The historical approach, conversely, focused on problems dealing with the history of concepts (*Begriffsgeschichte*) and the importance of tradition and continuity in philosophical education. In the context of Heidegger's early thinking, the polemical essay written by his mentor Edmund Husserl, "Philosophy as a Rigorous Science" (1911), and the work of the elder Dilthey on historical world views represented these two basic approaches. As early as his *Habilitationsschrift* on medieval logic, however, Heidegger tried to collapse this distinc-

---

[59] Heidegger uses the term *hermeneutics of facticity* (1923) in *GA* 63:5–14; *factical life experience* (1919) in "Anmerkungen zu Karl Jaspers 'Psychologie der Weltanschauung,'" *Wegmarken, Gesamtausgabe* 9 (Frankfurt: Klostermann, 1976), 91; and *the temporally particular hermeneutic situation* (1922) in "Phänomenologische Interpretationen zu Aristoteles," *Dilthey-Jahrbuch für Philosophie und Geschichte der Geisteswissenschaften* 6 (1989): 237.

[60] See, for example, the terminological distinction used in the popular reference work by Johannes Hoffmeister, *Wörterbuch der philosophischen Begriffe* (Leipzig: Meiner, 1944), 678. This distinction between "historical" and "systematic" philosophy was dominant in German faculties at the beginning of the century and might roughly be compared with the "continental"/"analytic" distinction that dominates American universities today. In the conclusion to his *Habilitationsschrift* (*GA* 1), Heidegger tried to overcome the superficial distinction between "historical" and "systematic."

tion by insisting that "a theoretical-systematic evaluation of scholasticism is not possible without a certain measure of historical interest."[61] A philosophy caught between the demands of *Wissenschaft* and *Weltanschauung* would hardly be able to grasp the meaning of "crisis" in an originary fashion.

In his lectures on Aristotle (Winter Semester 1921/22), Heidegger tried to dispense with this traditional separation of *Wissenschaft* and *Weltanschauung* and de-structure the methods of philosophy by going back to their roots in factical-historical life: "Philosophizing, as a fundamental knowing, is nothing other than the radical enactment of the historical facticity of life such that the historical and the systematic are equally foreign to it and all the more superfluous, as is their separation."[62] Later, in *Being and Time*, Heidegger would return to this same theme by citing Count Yorck's observation that "the separation between systematic philosophy and historical presentation is essentially incorrect."[63] The real question for philosophy was neither the systematic, system-building methods of the school-philosophers nor the merely cultural dilettantism of the world-view advocates. Genuine philosophical questioning would make a demand on one's life and radicalize it by returning it to the questionability of life itself. But the institutional pressures brought to bear on philosophical and scientific work in a modern research university tended to cover over and obscure the factical roots of life. The details of appointments, promotions, and committee meetings and the pressure to conform to contemporary standards of research all tended to trivialize the meaning of philosophical labor—a trend that Heidegger, naturally, opposed. In a letter to his student Karl Löwith Heidegger wrote: "I work concretely and factically out of my 'I am.' . . . I do not separate . . . the life of scientific, theoretical, conceptual research and my own life."[64] As he returned from the war in 1919, the young Heidegger was intent on engaging the reality of factical-historical life against the theoretical tendencies within university *Kathederphilosophie*.

On the very first day of the new war emergency semester, Heidegger turned to the topic of university reform. In a curious and new language that spoke of "genuine" reform, "the originary authentic"

[61] Heidegger, *GA* 1: 195.
[62] Heidegger, *GA* 61: 111.
[63] Heidegger, *Being and Time*, 454; *Sein und Zeit*, 404.
[64] Papenfuss and Pöggeler, *Zur Philosophischen Aktualität Heideggers*, 29.

problematic, "the original radical" meaning, "the genuine origin" of spirit, and twice more of "the genuine" problem, Heidegger declared: "Today we are not yet ready for the *genuine* reform of the university. Becoming mature enough for this is the topic [*Sache*] of a *whole generation*. The renewal of the university means a rebirth of genuine scientific consciousness and the context of life. Life relations renew themselves, however, only in the return to the genuine origins of spirit. . . . Only life constitutes an 'epoch,' not the tumult of overhasty cultural programs."[65] The new "topic" was life: life as the origin of scientific consciousness, of university research, of philosophical theory. "The scientific scholar only has an effect," Heidegger emphasized, "through the vitality of genuine research."[66] If philosophy were to have any meaning in the new postwar situation of the university, where for the first time imperial educational policy had been replaced by "modernizing" forces, then it would have to return to the genuine facticity of life and the life-context of research. The so-called university reform program of mandarin pedagogues such as Eduard Spranger merely revealed, in Heidegger's words, "a total misunderstanding of all genuine revolutionizing of the spirit."[67] With Kierkegaardian fervor, Heidegger worked for a reform of the German university in and through the radicalizing of philosophy itself; that is, he abandoned the notion of philosophy as either rigorous science or as a world view for a "pre-theoretical or supra-theoretical (in any case a non-theoretical) science, a genuinely primordial science [*Ur-wissenschaft*] from which the theoretical itself takes its origin. This primordial science is so constituted that it not only *needs* to make no presuppositions but it *can never* do so because it is not a theory. It lies then *before* or above the spheres where discourse about presupposition has any meaning at all. *This* meaning first originates [*ent-springt*] from the origin [*Ursprung*]."[68]

Traditional philosophy, argued Heidegger, is dominated by the "primacy of the theoretical," which leads to the objectification, hypostatization, and calcification of all lived experience. It continues to grasp the originary experience of life in an epistemologically reified fashion according to traditional Cartesian-Kantian notions of the sub-

[65] Heidegger, *GA* 56/57: 4–5.
[66] Ibid., 5.
[67] Ibid., 4. For a comparison to other pedagogical claims during Weimar, see Fritz Ringer, *The Decline of the German Mandarins* (Cambridge: Harvard University Press, 1969).
[68] Heidegger, *GA* 56/57: 96–97.

ject and its object. But as traditional philosophy (in its various forms as critical realism, psychologism, Neo-Kantian idealism) attempts to understand this experience, it refuses to give up its epistemological categories and presuppositions. Hence, it always speaks of the world as an already "given."[69] Introducing a new language of experience into philosophy—exemplified in his expression "*es weltet*" (literally, "it worlds")—Heidegger challenged the theoretical comportment of his academic colleagues and their attitude of "de-living" (*Ent-lebung*).[70] Life lives itself, said Heidegger; it is not primarily the psychological subject that lives; rather, living occurs in and as the phenomenon of lived experience. In his lectures Heidegger tried to communicate what he meant by "lived experience" (*Erlebnis*) through a simple comparison drawn from modern physics and ancient tragedy. He went on to contrast the behavior of astronomers bent on investigating the phenomenon of a sunrise to the Theban chorus in Sophocles' *Antigone* which, on the morning after a victorious battle, views the ascent of the sun with joyous thanks. The difference between these two modes of seeing, Heidegger told his students, lies in the problem of *how* one experiences. In genuine experience, "Experience (*Er-leben*) doesn't pass before me as a thing that I set there as an object; rather, I myself appropriate it (*er-eigne es*) to me, and it properly happens or 'properizes' (*es er-eignet*) according to its essence."[71] In this event of appropriation, understood as *Ereignis*—which *gives* being, yet itself *is* not (*es gibt*)—Heidegger returned to the basic theme of the lecture course: the relation of science to life.

For the remainder of his so-called phenomenological decade, Heidegger kept returning to this problem in various forms, but the theme or matter (*Sache*) remained the same. Behind the theoretical structures of analysis and description, there is a pretheoretical, factical-historical world, which "worlds." Two years later, near the beginning of his lectures on Aristotle, Heidegger repeated the theme. "Philosophy can not be defined," he insisted, "only experienced."[72] If in the process of definition things are sundered, the concrete, factical world of experience reveals that "in temporalizing enactment, things are originarily 'one.'"[73] From his reading of Schleiermacher, Heideg-

---

[69] Ibid., 88.
[70] Ibid., 73, 88–89.
[71] Ibid., 75. For references to "*es gibt*" ("it's giving, there is"), see p. 62.
[72] Heidegger, *GA* 61: 14.
[73] Ibid., 62.

ger had found an "indication" of this originary understanding of factical life before its sundering into theory. In the second of his speeches from *On Religion*, Schleiermacher described the life-unity of experience that analysis can never know:

> One can break down the fluids of an organic body into its constituent parts; but now take these separated elements, mix them in every proportion, treat them in every way. Will you be able to make life's blood out of them again? Will what was once dead be able to move again in a living body and become one with it? . . . The first mysterious moment that occurs in every sense perception, before intuition and feeling have separated, where meaning and its objects have, as it were, flowed into one another and become one before both turn back to their original position—I know how indescribable it is and how quickly it passes away.[74]

Heidegger found in Schleiermacher's "moment . . . where meaning and its objects . . . become one" another way of reading the experience of intentionality, that most difficult of Husserlian problems. For the early Heidegger, intentionality was not the activity of a subjective consciousness toward the world or a kind of psychophysical coordination of mind and environment. It was a movement of meaning, a "worlding" of the world in and as an enactment (*Vollzug*) out of a specific factical-historical *situation* (a new term he employed after reading Jaspers). In his Aristotle lectures of Winter Semester 1921/22, Heidegger continued to argue that theory alone could never find its way inside this situation as situation; it always remained on the outside. Because the very questions and difficulties of philosophy were tied to its position as a form of learning within the German university, any genuine access to its problems had to begin there: "The difficulties of access do not occur sometime or somewhere nor are they enacted by someone. We live within them here and now—at this place, in this lecture hall. You before me, I before you. We designate this fixed situation of a shared, environing world . . . with the title: *University*."[75]

By beginning in the factical situation of university life in the twenties, Heidegger hoped to return philosophy to the very sources from which it had become alienated. As he explained, traditional university

---

[74] Friedrich Schleiermacher, *Über die Religion* (Hamburg: Meiner, 1958), 41 and 43; *On Religion*, trans. Richard Crouter (Cambridge: Cambridge University Press, 1988), 112 and 114.
[75] Heidegger, *GA* 61: 63.

philosophy had extinguished factical life by fostering an attitude of presuppositionless theorizing as the basis of academic research. But theory alone covers over and disguises the genuine origins of scientific practice in their institutional and existential roots. The real question of/for philosophy is the questionability of life itself. Going back to the discussion of virtue in the *Nicomachean Ethics* (1106b), Heidegger repeated Aristotle's original insight about the difficulty of life. On the one hand, factical life reveals the tendency of human beings to seek the easy way out and to fall back into the carefree oblivion of all that is familiar.[76] With a precipitous haste to achieve certainty and security, factical life covers over its origins and attempts to disguise the incertitude that lies at the heart of existence. And yet, on the other hand, there is within factical life a countermovement to this dissimulation, a genuine searching after the origins of that which is.

For Heidegger, philosophy is this countermovement within factical life; it literally provokes a *Kampf*, or "battle," against the routinized practices of everyday indifference. And yet, in pushing philosophy back to its roots in factical life, Heidegger saw that within the university, philosophy itself had become part of the tendency toward ease and comfort. The effect of theory and "scientific rigor" had been to cover over the difficulties of life, thus making philosophy artificial, cerebral, and impotent. Heidegger's early lectures reveal a different kind of philosophy, however, a philosophy at odds with its own history and institutional identity. Again, the sources for his critique came from theology, especially Paul and Luther. For example, in his letter to the Colossians, Paul admonished his listeners to "see to it that no one makes a prey of you by philosophy and empty deceit" (Col. 2:8), and the young Luther, in his *Lectures on the Romans*, cautioned:

> But alas, how deeply and painfully we are ensnared in categories and questions of what a thing is; in how many metaphysical questions we involve ourselves! When will we become wise and see how much precious time we waste on vain questions, while we neglect the greater ones? . . . Indeed I for my part believe that I owe to the Lord this duty of speaking out against philosophy. . . . Therefore I warn you all as earnestly as I can that you finish these studies quickly and let it be your only concern not to establish and defend them but treat them as we do when we learn worthless skills to destroy [*destruere*] them and study errors to refute them.[77]

[76] Ibid., 108–109.
[77] Luther, *Lectures on Romans*, 361. See also Edmund Schlink, "Weisheit und Torheit,"

In his lectures from the summer semester of 1923, "Ontology: Her-meneutics of Facticity," Heidegger spoke of "phenomenology taking on its battle position" against contemporary forms of philosophy. Cit-ing Luther, he claimed that philosophy "has become the pimp to the public whore of spirit, *fornicatio spiritus*, the fornication of the spirit (Luther)."[78] He followed Luther's destruction of the quietist and con-templative forms of scholastic philosophy with his own *Destruktion* of Neo-Kantian epistemology and popular world-view philosophies. If Luther and Paul both attacked philosophy for its systematic detach-ment from the world of faith and suffering, Heidegger repeated their battle (*Kampf*) by pointing to the "aestheticizing obfuscation," "care-freeness," and "security" fetish of modern university philosophy.[79] In its comfortable university setting, philosophy had adopted a jargon of technical expertise and exclusion. Only by returning to the spirit of Luther's basic insight about suffering and the theology of the cross could philosophy retrieve the fundamental movement of human life in all its factical care and worry. "The phenomenon of *care* [*Sorge*]," Heidegger insisted, "must be seen as a *fundamental problem of Dasein*. It cannot be pieced together out of theoretical, practical, and emo-tional parts. It must first be made clear how, in *Dasein*, care itself (grasped in its originary state before any analysis), the care of mere seeing and mere questioning, is grounded in the being of human exis-tence."[80]

Heidegger discovered in the phenomenon of care a way of ques-tioning the fundamental meaning of human existence. Caring—as a basic experience of facticity—presented another way of thinking about experience in contrast to the torpid musings of university phi-losophy. But if phenomenology were to succeed in rethinking the con-temporary situation, it would first have to work through the history of the philosophical tradition.

Kerygma und Dogma 1 (1955): 6 and 16–22. Schlink argues that "Luther's paradoxes carried out an attack on the basic ontological structure of Aristotelian thought, and it permeated the core of the Aristotelian-scholastic form of thought with historical-exis-tential thinking. Therefore, it is not accidental that the early Heidegger was so strongly influenced by Luther's lecture on Romans in his work before *Being and Time*. To be sure, Heidegger's existential analytic of human *Dasein* is a radical secularization of Luther's anthropology" (translation by van Buren in *Young Heidegger*, notes to chap. 5, sec. 3).

[78] Heidegger, *GA* 63: 46.
[79] Heidegger, *GA* 61: 109–111.
[80] Heidegger, *GA* 63: 103–104.

iv. Heidegger's Practice of *Destruktion*

Heidegger found in Luther's attack on scholastic theology a strategy for coming to terms with the lifeless theory of *Kathederphilosophie*. In the new crisis situation of 1920s Weimar, Heidegger interpreted Luther's contest between *either* the theology of glory *or* the theology of the cross as a battle against contemporary scholastics.[81] But now Luther's "either/or" (appropriated through Kierkegaard's critique of the present age) was made more radical. It would have been all too easy for Heidegger to pose this either/or in terms of the traditional split in university philosophy between *Weltanschauung* and *Wissenschaft*. But Heidegger sought to challenge this superficial dichotomy by repeating Luther's destruction of theology with a *Destruktion* of contemporary philosophy. To "repeat" (*wiederholen*) the past was not, however, to slavishly reenact it just as it had been.[82] By *Wiederholung* Heidegger also meant a "retrieval" of the past within the horizons of the present and the future. In his readings of Luther, Paul, Augustine, Kierkegaard and others, Heidegger discovered that the past exists not *as* a past but as a futural possibility. In terms of a *destruktive* history of philosophy, this recognition signified a new way of conceiving the tradition freed from the metaphysical notions of "objectivity," "scientific rigor," "historical erudition," and "history of concepts" (*Begriffsgeschichte*) spawned by *Wissenschaft/Weltanschauung* philosophy.

Heidegger's retrieval of Luther's either/or was now transformed into a radical decision between *either* history of philosophy as mere cultural and intellectual history (*Geistesgeschichte*) *or* the enactment (*Vollzug*) of philosophy within the facticity of contemporary life. "The *Destruktion* of the intellectual-historical tradition," Heidegger insisted, "is tantamount to the explication of those motive-giving originary situations from which fundamental philosophical experiences spring."[83]

---

[81] Luther, "Heidelberg Disputation," 31:35–70. In the essay by Otto Pöggeler, "Heidegger und die hermeneutische Theologie," 492, and in his full-length study *Martin Heidegger's Path of Thinking*, trans. Daniel Magurshak and Sigmund Barber (Atlantic Highlands, N.J.: Humanities Press, 1987), 28, he refers to Heidegger's unpublished lecture course of Summer Semester 1921, "Augustinus und der Neuplatonismus," which explicitly thematized the work of the early Luther, especially the 1518 "Heidelberg Disputation."

[82] See John Caputo, *Radical Hermeneutics* (Bloomington: Indiana University Press, 1987), 60–61, for a discussion of Heidegger and Kierkegaard on "repetition" and "retrieval" (*Wiederholung*).

[83] Heidegger, *GA* 9: 73.

That is, the *Destruktion* of the history of philosophy was not a mere "destruction" of what was "given" in the tradition, but a "de-structuring," "unbuilding," "building back," or "dismantling" (*Abbau*) of all "givenness" to its roots in factical life. *Destruktion*, then, was merely another form of retrieval, for in de-structuring the past, one reclaimed it for the present and the future. For Heidegger, philosophical research (*Forschung*) would no longer be conceived from within the scientific strictures of the academy but would "make the productivity of the past vital again—and bring it into a future."[84]

In the early Christian experience of "being wakeful" (*wachsam sein*) for the second coming of the Lord (1 Thess. 5:4–8), Heidegger found another source for a critique of all fixed, present-at-hand, or given philosophical meaning.[85] The ever watchful and vigilant mode of early Christian anticipation offered him a model of factical life experience, for in the Christian's openness to the future, a new experience of time—as temporality—emerges. *Destruktion* as a practice remains sensitive to the situational character of all thinking, both religious and philosophical. If, for the early Christians, the meaning of the *parousia* is understood as a second coming, then the time of the coming is not a futural "when." Instead, the primary question concerns one's proper attitude toward the coming itself, a question of "how" one waits.[86] So too, in philosophy, Heidegger interpreted "being wakeful" as a model experience of *Dasein* in its facticity, which he saw as the basis of a hermeneutics of facticity. Being wakeful means understanding one's own *Dasein* where "understanding is . . . not a kind of self-comportment (intentionality) but a *how of Dasein* itself; terminologically, it is from the outset established as *Dasein's being wakeful* for itself."[87]

The Christian experience of wakefulness revealed to Heidegger two fundamental themes that determined his path of thinking right through *Being and Time*: a new understanding of temporality and a radically *destruktive* understanding of hermeneutics. Rejecting the calendrical time (*chronos*) of worldly reckoning for the "moment" (*kairos*) of insight and revelation, the early Christians came to experience time

[84] Martin Heidegger, *Logik: Die Frage nach der Wahrheit*, Gesamtausgabe 21 (Frankfurt: Klostermann, 1976), 14.
[85] See Heidegger, *GA* 63: 15, 18–20, and 30 for various examples of *Wachsein* and *wach werden*.
[86] Sheehan, "Heidegger's 'Introduction,'" 57–58.
[87] Heidegger, *GA* 63: 15.

within their particular "historically enacted situation."[88] That is, they understood time not as chronology or history but as "historicity." Moreover, by thematizing the mode of expectation as a "how" rather than in terms of a "when," the early Christians gained insight into the fundamentally interpretative, or hermeneutical, character of all experience. As Heidegger approached philosophy's "historically enacted situation" within the university of his own day, he transformed these two fundamental Christian insights into a *destruktive* reading of the history of philosophy. By "situation" Heidegger meant "a certain unity in natural life experience. Situations permeate one another; their times of duration do not exclude one another (for example, a year at the front, a semester: these are not objective concepts of time). In each situation there is present a unifying tendency. They contain no static moments, rather they are 'appropriate happenings' ['*Ereignisse*']."[89]

The "appropriate happening" within a situation involves the full participation of what he called "the situations-ego" or "the 'historical' ego." Because every event has a certain unity within a historical situation, one cannot circumvent the participation of the historical subject by focusing solely on the "theoretical" ego. The grave failing within most university philosophy, Heidegger maintained, was the tendency toward exactly this kind of overtheorizing and "de-historicization." The natural scientist, for example, observed nature apart from any "situations-ego" and described it, lifelessly according to Heidegger, in terms of physical-mathematical theory.[90] But the university philosophers were hardly better. The Neo-Kantians began their scientific inquiry with "the fact of science" (*das Faktum der Wissenschaft*) while the world-view philosophers investigated the history of philosophy as if it were a museum full of conceptual artifacts. And instead of pursuing their work in an original way, they accepted the conventional division of the sciences according to nature and spirit, organized as natural sciences and human sciences. In 1923 Heidegger even criticized Husserl for his overly theoretical attitude that betrayed the "ahistoricality of phenomenology."[91] "From their beginning," Heidegger claimed, "traditional philosophy and philosophical research oriented themselves toward a certain kind of knowing, namely, the truth

[88] Sheehan, "Heidegger's 'Introduction,'" 57–58.
[89] Heidegger, *GA* 56/57: 205.
[90] Ibid., 207.
[91] Heidegger, *GA* 63: 75.

of theoretical knowing."[92] But the Pauline experience of wakefulness indicated to Heidegger another kind of knowledge, grounded in the factical experience of life and "historical" in character.

This early Christian sense of history was not, however, an objective experience of the past (*objektgeschichtlich*) but rather an enacted, living, and factical awareness of the meaning of history from within the present situation, what Heidegger (in his analysis of Paul) termed "*die vollzugsgeschichtliche Situation.*"[93] From within the situation of wakefulness, Paul admonishes the Thessalonians to be watchful "concerning the times [*chronon*] and seasons [*kairon*] . . . let us not sleep, as others do but let us watch and be sober. For those who sleep, sleep at night, and those who get drunk are drunk at night. But let us who are of the day be sober, putting on the breastplate of faith and love and as a helmet the hope of salvation" (1 Thess. 5:1–8). Paul's letter makes a claim on his readers and moves attention away from the objective time (*chronos*) of history to the experiential time (*kairos*) of enactment. But it also understands this *kairos* as a "decisive turning point" or "time of crisis" within the Christian situation: either one succumbs to the soporific allures of sleep and drink or one decides to remain wakeful for the second coming.[94] No theoretical detachment is possible; only through a decision (understood as *Krisis*) can one grasp Paul's authentic message. Heidegger's historically enacted situation demanded the same commitment to either/or decision making, for like Paul he rejected the sleep-inducing narcotic of theory for the decisive resoluteness of lived experience.

The historical situation of the sciences in the 1920s appeared to Heidegger, from within this originary experience of Christian *kairos*, as a "crisis" in a new sense. All the earnest pronouncements about the crisis of the sciences which filled the scholarly journals and academic conferences, however, struck him as endless prattle. In one of

[92] Heidegger, *GA* 21: 8.
[93] Heidegger, *GA* 9: 93.
[94] In his lectures of Winter Semester 1921/22 (*GA* 61: 164), Heidegger, echoing Paul, warned that "one should be on one's guard against using the idea of absolute truth as a soporific opiate." Christian *kairos* functioned as a mode of temporality which stressed the wakeful vigilance of the early Christian church. For some theological evidence of *kairos* as a "decisive turning point," see Gerhard Kittel, ed., *Theological Dictionary of the New Testament*, vol. 3 (Grand Rapids, Mich.: Eerdmann's, 1965), 455–456. In William F. Arndt and F. Wilbur Gingrich, *A Greek-English Lexicon of the New Testament* (Chicago: University of Chicago Press, 1957), 396, *kairos* is defined as "the time of crisis." My point here is to show how early Christian eschatology and Weimar sociology converge in a peculiar fashion in the young Heidegger's work, linking "crisis" to both a theory of history and temporality.

his letters to Löwith, for example, he greeted the publication of the new academic journals *Ethos* and *Kairos* (and the already outmoded *Logos*) with bitter sarcasm: "What will next week's joke be? I believe that a madhouse has a clearer and more rational inner aspect than does this epoch."[95] But despite his sensitivity to the clichés and pretensions of the moment, the appearance of a "crisis consciousness" seemed to Heidegger an indication of a genuine turning point between epochs, a time of fateful decision for a history of the West. Spengler's sermonizing about the decline of Western culture, despite its self-aggrandizing bombast, appeared to him as the contemporary sign of a profoundly Nietzschean nihilism. The crisis of the twenties entailed more than a decline of values, the threat of unbridled relativism, or the uncertainty brought on by new methods of research. For Heidegger, *crisis* itself was a term that pointed to the primordial state of all genuine science and history as it resisted the prevailing tendencies of theory for the radical decision of a new either/or. In this decisive moment of crisis, there emerged a new wakefulness for the genuine question of all science and philosophy, "the question of being."

"At the birth of every science," Heidegger wrote in *Being and Time*, "there falls a principal decision, and science lives on the basis of this."[96] Through the accumulated weight of history and tradition, however, this original decision had long been forgotten. What persisted in its place was the calcified practice of an academic industry, comfortably ensconced in a university structure where the original decision (or what Heidegger, in another context, referred to as "an original interpretation") had become formalized.[97]

v. Heidegger's Crisis and the Crisis of Western Thought

The situation of crisis in the twenties opened up for Heidegger a space in which he believed genuine thinking could take place. By questioning the given structures of scientific inquiry, he hoped to turn

---

[95] Quoted in Karl Löwith, *Mein Leben*, 28. This same critical attitude toward contemporary academic philosophy can be seen in Heidegger's letters to Karl Jaspers in Walter Biemel and Hans Saner, eds., *Martin Heidegger/Karl Jaspers Briefwechsel, 1920–1963* (Frankfurt: Klostermann, 1990), in which Heidegger derided "the gurgling of contemporary philosophy" in a letter from June 27, 1922 (29).

[96] Heidegger, *GA* 61: 29.

[97] Martin Heidegger, *Prolegomena zur Geschichte des Zeitbegriffs, Gesamtausgabe* 20 (Frankfurt: Klostermann, 1988), 4; translated by Theodore Kisiel as *History of the Concept of Time* (Bloomington: Indiana University Press, 1985), 3.

the occasion of crisis into a "new beginning" for thought. Obviously, the subsequent history of Heidegger's involvement with National Socialism makes the optimistic tone of this new beginning no small matter for reflection and critique, a critique that we will consider at the end of this chapter.[98] Yet in the historical context of early Weimar, Heidegger's thematization of crisis offered a productive way of rethinking the very foundations of the sciences as they had been defined in the Western tradition since Plato and Aristotle. In a new *destruktive* history of tradition, Heidegger transformed "crisis" from the modish watchword of feuilletonistic apocalypse to one of his fundamental categories for understanding an epochal turning in the history of the West. For Heidegger, "crisis" retained its original Greek connotations of separation and judgment and came to describe a decision concerning the meaning of Western history itself, especially in the epoch of modernity. Crisis theology, the crisis in mathematics, the crisis in physics, the crisis of historicism—all offered concrete and factical indications of a crisis-phenomenon that went beyond the mere institutional anomie of a post-Versailles realignment of the sciences and challenged the traditional Cartesian and Kantian notion of scientific truth.

The crisis of the sciences, in Heidegger's reading, opened up a crisis in the foundations of "classical science" as a whole. For over three centuries Galilean science had presented a world sundered into subject and object, defined by a fundamental faith in the certitude of scientific method as a way to secure truth. This schema of a subject/object bifurcation had become, for Heidegger, inseparable from the idea of crisis itself. Nihilistic notions about a crisis of values, a crisis of relativism, a crisis of historicism, and so on were merely the other side of the abiding faith in classical science which characterized the modern era as a whole. In his lectures "Ontology: Hermeneutics of Facticity," Heidegger addressed the roots of this crisis in traditional subject/object metaphysics, exhorting his students:

Steer clear of *the schema: there are subjects and objects,* consciousness and being; being is an object of knowledge; authentic being is the being of na-

[98] For more-recent work on Heidegger's affiliation with National Socialism, see Richard Wolin, *The Politics of Being: The Political Thought of Martin Heidegger* (New York: Columbia University Press, 1990); the series of articles and primary sources gathered in the New School for Social Research's *Graduate Faculty Philosophy Journal* 14, no. 2–15, no. 1 (1991); Thomas Sheehan, "'Everyone Has to Tell the Truth': Heidegger and the Jews," *Continuum* 1, no. 1 (Autumn 1990): 30–44; and Tom Rockmore, *On Heidegger's Nazism and Philosophy* (Berkeley: University of California Press, 1992). These provide only a sampling of more-recent titles on this topic.

ture; consciousness is "I think," hence "I-like," "I-pole," center of acts, person; over against egos (persons) there are: beings, objects, natural things, things of value, goods. The relation between subject and object is to be determined and is a question of epistemology. . . . This almost ineradicable fore-having [*Vorhabe*] constructed through the obstinacy of a calcified tradition, fundamentally obstructs [*verbaut*] access forever to that which is indicated as factical life [*Dasein*]. . . . The dominance of this epistemological problem (which has its equivalent in other disciplines) is often characteristic of a type kept alive especially in science and philosophy.[99]

For Heidegger, issues concerning certitude, proof, methodological rigor, and indubitability were not recent problems emanating from the crisis-debates in science during the early twenties. They were bound up with the same subject/object thinking that had lain at the heart of modernist science and metaphysics since Descartes. Heidegger's answer to these problems was not to offer a "new" philosophical foundation for modernity but to approach them in a way that would obviate the need for foundations. In Heidegger's terms, the very notion of crisis was bound up with the demand for proof and indubitability which plagued the definition of truth in the natural and human sciences. Heidegger detected a "scandal" at the heart of these Cartesian-Kantian demands for "proof," writing in *Being and Time*: "The 'scandal of philosophy' is not that this proof has yet to be given, but that *such proofs are expected and attempted again and again*. Such expectations, aims, and demands arise from an ontologically inadequate way of starting. . . . If Dasein is understood correctly, it defies such proofs, because in its being, it already *is* what subsequent proofs deem necessary to demonstrate for it."[100]

In a radically original destruction of the history of ontology, Heidegger saw the problems between natural versus historical science, *Wissenschaft* versus *Weltanschauung*, and object versus subject as "inappropriate formulations of the question" of foundations. Unlike most of his vitalist and Neo-Kantian contemporaries, Heidegger rejected the prevailing idea that the appropriate scientific method is derived either from the object of research (that is, from the fact of nature or history) or from the concept of value employed by the researcher (nomothetic/generalizing or idiographic/individualizing). What was at stake for Heidegger, rather, was what he variously called "an original relationship to the matters themselves [*zu den Sachen selbst*]," "an

[99] Heidegger, *GA* 63: 81.
[100] Heidegger, *Being and Time*, 249–251 (translation modified); *Sein und Zeit*, 205–207.

original interpretation," or "a more original understanding" of the fundamental concepts of science.[101] In a crucial passage from his introduction to the *History of the Concept of Time*, Heidegger wrote:

> If the sciences are not to be regarded as a spurious enterprise, founding their justification merely by invoking the prevailing currents of the tradition, but instead are to receive the possibility of their being from their meaning in human *Dasein*, then the decisive question and the place where an answer to the crisis is to be found, is in bringing the subject matters under investigation to an original experience, before their concealment by a particular scientific inquiry. Here we restrict ourselves to the domains of history and nature, which are to be exhibited in their original mode of being.[102]

Scientific research, Heidegger argued, takes place within structures that have already been worked out before any genuine encounter with the phenomena being observed. Yet the meaning of this encounter for human *Dasein* can never be fixed within the logical structures of the prevailing natural and human sciences. These structures merely cover over and conceal the "original experience" of *Dasein*, which alone can provide genuine meaning. Heidegger likewise rejected the traditional concepts of understanding (*Verstehen*) and explanation (*Erklären*) as ways to organize our experience, because they merely reinforce the same subject/object dichotomies of university philosophy. Heidegger sought instead to get behind all epistemological distinctions to the lived, factical roots of human experience "before their concealment by a particular scientific inquiry." But how is this possible? Because the sciences already determine the space within which such inquiries can be conducted, how can one circumvent the research imperatives within the sciences themselves? Would not all such circumvention result in merely accepting the relativistic implications of the world-view philosophers?

By investigating the "situation" of philosophy at the turn of the century, Heidegger came to understand that the basic terms of these questions were not inherent to the sciences themselves but were products of two fundamental developments. First, in the wake of the collapse of idealism and the growing prestige of the natural sciences, philosophy felt increasing pressure to abandon its speculative meta-

---

[101] Heidegger, *History of the Concept of Time*, 4, 3; *GA* 20: 6, 4, 3.
[102] Heidegger, *History of the Concept of Time*, 4–5; *GA* 20: 6.

physical excesses and concentrate on providing a theory and logic of the sciences. Second, this movement toward a theory of science did not take place "in an original return to the matters at issue but by going back to a historically established philosophy, that of Kant."[103] In the Neo-Kantian philosophy of consciousness, Heidegger maintained, "the structure of knowledge itself, the structure of research, of the access to the realities in question, are no longer investigated, much less the structure of these realities. The sole theme is the question of the logical structure of scientific representation."[104] The effect of a Neo-Kantian theory of the sciences was to reinforce the Cartesian split between the subject and object, thereby valorizing the epistemological standpoint as the most fundamental. But the great irony was that in attempting to establish "new" foundations for a science of consciousness, these academic epigones were merely rehabilitating a "historically established philosophy." To reclaim its primary meaning, Heidegger wished to bring an original experience of history to bear on this historical rehabilitation.

For Heidegger, the genuine meaning (*Sinn*) of history lay neither in the established framework of a "science of history" nor in the return to a system of thinking "in" history (for example, Neo-Kantianism, Neo-Thomism, Neo-Aristotelianism, Neo-Fichteanism, all of which flourished at the early part of the century). Only through the "preliminary research" of phenomenology (that is, through "an understanding beforehand of the area of subject-matter underlying all the objects a science takes as its theme") could the originary meaning of historical experience reveal itself.[105] This required that philosophy dismantle the traditional scientific ideas of "logic," "method," and "concept-formation." As Heidegger indicated in the introduction to *Being and Time*: "What is philosophically primary is neither a theory of the concept-formation of historical science nor the theory of historical knowledge nor even the theory of historical experience as the object of historical science. Rather, what is primary is the interpretation of authentic historical being in its historicity."[106] The originary Christian experience of time in Paul's epistles revealed to Heidegger a very different understanding of historical meaning than that which dominated the prevailing sciences of history and humanity. It called into

[103] Heidegger, *History of the Concept of Time*, 13; GA 20: 13.
[104] Heidegger, *History of the Concept of Time*, 17; GA 20: 20.
[105] Heidegger, *Being and Time*, 30; *Sein und Zeit*, 14.
[106] Heidegger, *Being and Time*, 17; *Sein und Zeit*, 20.

question the primacy of a detached, theoretical consciousness associated with the scientific philosophy of Neo-Kantianism. As he retrieved the authentic meaning of Christian *kairos* through a new understanding of time as historicity, Heidegger found a way of breaking with the traditional framework of the sciences within university philosophy—a break that was to have a profound effect on his reading of historicism.

By grasping the fundamental happening of history (*Geschichte*) not as historical science (*Historie*) but as historicity (*Geschichtlichkeit*), Heidegger transformed the meaning of history from a question of logical method and scientific research to an ontological exploration of the roots of human being in the world. In a very basic sense Heidegger understood that the sciences of history and nature were not pregiven structures or entities but grew out of historically specific life situations. Because science itself was a form of life, it was grounded in the same temporal structures of experience as other forms of life, such as wakefulness, care, anxiety, and "fallenness." The objective model of time used in physics and biology, for example, could never reveal the interior structure of situational awareness. Nor could the science of history, based on the developmental model of objective natural time, reveal the genuine experience of what it meant "to be" historical. The prevailing historical sciences saw the past as a collection of already given, pre-formed artifacts "there-for-me," waiting to be empathically re-lived and understood. Ranke, for one, aimed at reconstructing the factually given state of affairs in the past. But Heidegger rejected Rankean factuality for a new form of hermeneutic facticity; what mattered was not the theoretical or empirical givenness of an object but its "situation character" in concrete factical and historical terms. The genuine experience of history for Heidegger was not about reconstructing facts but about retrieving the meaning of the past within the situation of the present as a possibility for one's own future.

Because historical science was organized around the theme of narrative, developmental time, it tended to conceal the genuine meaning of temporality as a unity of what Heidegger termed three temporal *ecstases*: "the phenomenon of the future as a 'coming-toward' [*Zukunft*], the past as a 'having been' [*Gewesenheit*] and the present as a 'waiting-toward' [*Gegenwart*]."[107] In their haste to complete their nar-

---

[107] Heidegger, *Being and Time*, 377 (translation modified); *Sein und Zeit*, 329.

ratives, historians had forgotten that the unity of these three temporal ecstases lay not in "time" itself as a fixed and objective entity but in the primordial temporality of human being. Heidegger's aim was to destroy the traditional understanding of time in the historical and natural sciences so that he might reclaim it in a radically hermeneutic fashion. He was convinced that the basic theory and logic of the sciences was constructed on a metaphysics of time which undergirded the very notions of truth in contemporary epistemology. Debates about objectivism and relativism, which seemed to concern issues of value judgments and research methods, appeared to him as misconceived interpretations of human temporality. In a crucial passage from "The Concept of Time," his 1924 lecture, Heidegger explained:

> The present generation thinks that it has found history and is even overburdened by it. It moans about historicism—*lucus a non lucendo*. It gives the name "history" to something that is not history at all. . . . The common interpretation of *Dasein* is threatened by the danger of relativism; but the anxiety concerning relativism is anxiety in the face of *Dasein*. The past as authentic history is retrievable in "how" one exists. *The possibility of access to history is grounded in the possibility (according to which it understands the present as temporally particular) to be futural. This is the first principle of all hermeneutics.* It says something about the being of *Dasein*, which is historicity itself. Philosophy will never be able to grasp what history is as long as it analyzes it as the object of contemplation for a method. The enigma of history lies in what it means *to be* historical.[108]

From within the theory and logic of the sciences, the meaning of any "possibility of access to history" is extinguished by the demand for neutrality, self-extinguishment, and objectivity. But Heidegger reclaimed the past by insisting that its authentic meaning does not lie within the past itself (as an object there for researching) but in the way the past is appropriated. Husserl had attempted to overcome this traditional research model by focusing on the implicit fore-structure that makes experience possible, the basic intentionality of consciousness. Suspending all metaphysical hypotheses and bracketing out the purely contingent, situational character of human intentionality, Husserl undertook an austere description of the phenomenality of experience without any ontological presuppositions. In principle, this rigorously phenomenological attending to the things themselves sought

---

[108] Martin Heidegger, *Der Begriff der Zeit* (Tübingen: Niemeyer, 1989), 25.

to obviate the need for a Neo-Kantian methodology of the sciences and to reject the competing claims of psychologism and historicism.[109]

Heidegger had learned from Husserl to take the issue of fore-structure very seriously. He quarreled with his mentor, however, about the metaphysical implications of any attempt to allege "pure" intentionality. Hermeneutically insisting on the interpretational situatedness of all human understanding, Heidegger set out to unmask all claims of ontological neutrality, whether in the form of Husserl's "transcendental ego" or the Neo-Kantian "pro-physical subject." These programmatic attempts at solving the problem of neutrality, Heidegger argued, gained access to the prescientific structures of consciousness only to lose the positive meaning of historical experience. By returning to the sources of hermeneutic experience, Heidegger hoped he could reframe the terms of Husserl's phenomenology and Neo-Kantian philosophy of consciousness.

Although most contemporary observers continued to define the crisis of the sciences in terms that had changed little since the time of Herder and Humboldt, Heidegger set about destroying or dismantling the basic meaning of crisis itself. Ironically, his attempt was misread as yet another contribution to the philosophy of crisis.[110] From Herder to Dilthey, the rise of historical consciousness had been conceived as a great liberation from the slumbering dogmatism of metaphysics and an alternative to overarching schemes of historical theory. But Heidegger challenged this interpretation, revealing historical consciousness as something essentially metaphysical, caught up in the objectivist vision of the early modern sciences of nature. Traditionally, historicism was understood, by the defenders of scientism, as a form of unbridled relativism, because it aimed at grasping historical phenomena within their own specific cultural and historical milieux. But Heidegger reframed this discussion by focusing on the objectivist motives latent within historicism, which appeared to him as a kind of

[109] See Edmund Husserl, *Logische Untersuchungen*, vol. 2, pt. 2, 1–127 (the Sixth Investigation) (Tübingen: Niemeyer, 1968); *Logical Investigations*, 2: 667–770, (London: Routledge, 1970). For a close reading of the young Heidegger's notion of intentionality and its relation to Husserl, see Theodore Kisiel, "Heidegger (1907–1927): The Transformation of the Categorial," in H. J. Silverman, John Sallis, and T. M. Seebohm, eds., *Continental Philosophy in America* (Pittsburgh: Duquesne University Press, 1983). Kisiel argues that "intentionality is another name for the phenomenon par excellence of phenomenology" (177).
[110] See Georg Misch, *Lebensphilosophie und Phänomenologie: Eine Auseinandersetzung der Diltheyschen Richtung mit Husserl und Heidegger* (Stuttgart: Teubner, 1967), originally published in 1930.

covert scientism. Later, in his 1946 essay on Anaximander, Heidegger identified historicism as merely another form of technological thinking and compared its reframing of historical objects to the technical organization of radio and press.[111] In *Being and Time* he wrote, "The emergence of a problem of 'historicism' is the clearest symptom that historical science attempts to alienate *Dasein* from its authentic historicity."[112]

Heidegger shared with Dilthey, Rickert, and Windelband the aim of combating the relativistic implications of historicism. But *Being and Time*, understood within its own problematic, is hardly a considered response to the historicist debate. If the Neo-Kantians and Dilthey sought to overcome the crisis of historicism by a more original grounding of science, Heidegger's task was to invert the idea of "grounding" itself, laying bare the skeletal structure of all epistemological claims to objectivity. In the sections that follow, I would like to explore Heidegger's response to the Neo-Kantians and Dilthey, because it is through his critical and *destruktive* reading of these thinkers that his own project becomes clearer. Heidegger rejected the idea of presuppositionless and autochthonic philosophizing, insisting instead on the retrieval of hints or traces (*Spuren*) from within the tradition. Throughout the period from 1919 to 1927, he offered lectures and seminars on Plato, Aristotle, Leibniz, Descartes, Luther, Dilthey, Scheler, Husserl, Rickert, and others.[113] But his interest was not "historical" in the sense of Windelband's or Überweg's magisterial histories of philosophy. In section 77 of *Being and Time*, Heidegger approvingly cited a comment from Graf Yorck to the effect that "there is no longer any actual philosophizing which would not be historical."[114] But his understanding of "historical" here is a radical departure from the tradition of Ranke, Droysen, and Meinecke.

Although it may be enlightening to focus on the historical aspects of Heidegger's thought, especially his *Destruktion* of the history of philosophy, we must not forget that history as such was never his foremost concern. Ultimately, Heidegger attempted neither to over-

[111] Martin Heidegger, *Holzwege* (Frankfurt: Klostermann, 1972), 301. Translated by David F. Krell in *Early Greek Thinking* (New York: Harper and Row, 1984), 17.

[112] Heidegger, *Being and Time*, 448; *Sein und Zeit*, 396.

[113] For a list of Heidegger's courses and lectures, see the *Prospektus*, which was published for the *Gesamtausgabe* in November 1991 by Klostermann and which updates the list in William Richardson, *Heidegger: Through Phenomenology to Thought* (The Hague: Martinus Nijhoff, 1963).

[114] Heidegger, *Being and Time*, 454; *Sein und Zeit*, 402.

come the aporia of historicism nor to provide a new theoretical founding of the human sciences but to "raise anew the question of the meaning of being."[115]

vi. Heidegger's Quarrel with Neo-Kantianism

In any discussion of the early Heidegger, some mention of his Neo-Kantian roots seems almost inevitable. These facts are fairly clear. He wrote his doctoral dissertation in 1912 and later, under Rickert's guidance at Freiburg, his *Habilitationsschrift* in 1915. His *Habilitationsvortrag*, "The Concept of Time in the Science of History," reflected the traditional Neo-Kantian division of the sciences along the lines of Windelband's nomothetic and idiographic schema. In this essay Heidegger repeated the Neo-Kantian truism that the research methods of the various sciences should be understood in terms of their "logical structure" rather than merely according to conventional distinctions between nature and spirit.[116] But after his return home from the front in 1918, Heidegger's earlier veiled criticisms of Neo-Kantian logic became explicit. In the lectures of Summer Semester 1919, "Phenomenology and Transcendental Value Philosophy," Heidegger offered an extended critique of the Neo-Kantian *Fragestellung*. In his lecture courses over the next eight years, there are many references to Rickert (fewer to Windelband), almost all critical, as well as many discussions of contemporary philosophical positions in which the Neo-Kantians remain silent dialogue partners.

Rather than going through a point-by-point discussion of Heidegger's painstaking analysis of Neo-Kantian *Kulturphilosophie* in 1919, I want to focus on Heidegger's reasons for rejecting the basic approach and foundations of the Neo-Kantian program. My aim is to offer a concrete example of Heideggerian *Destruktion*, especially in regard to the generational debate concerning historicism and relativism. Ironically, as I tried to show earlier, the roots of Heidegger's *Destruktion* of Neo-Kantianism are more theological than philosophical. The Pauline insight into the kairological character of time opened up for Heidegger the possibility of an "other" beginning for philosophy whereby

[115] Heidegger, *Being and Time*, 19; *Sein und Zeit* 1.
[116] Heidegger, *GA* 1: 358; translated by Harry S. Taylor and Hans Uffelmann as "The Concept of Time in the Science of History," *Journal of the British Society for Phenomenology* 9 (1978): 3–10.

the timeless validity of transcendental values is de-structured through the insight into the temporality of being. Yet had Heidegger insisted on "replacing" the atemporal structures of logic with the temporality of being, he would only have repeated the same Neo-Kantian indifference to factical experience. Paul's emphasis on the radical facticity of life was not an epistemological judgment but an ethical call that demanded a decision: whether to respond to the crisis of faith brought on by the *parousia* or to fall back into the familiar structures of everyday, anonymous existence. If the crisis of historicism were to have any authentic meaning in the modern world, Heidegger believed, it would have to be understood in the genuine Pauline sense of "crisis" as a call toward a decision. Epistemological neutrality was hardly the proper response. Heidegger's basic critique of Neo-Kantianism grew out of this theological turn toward radical, factical experience understood as temporality. But, before discussing the problem of temporality and the three ecstases of time, we must first return to the fundamental questions of Neo-Kantianism.

According to Rickert and Windelband, the fundamental characteristic of science is the arrangement of reality through the concept (*Begriff*); reality itself is an incalculable, irrational manifold and can be understood only through conceptual simplification that, on the basis of determined interests or values, recasts and transforms the real. Because human knowledge can never reproduce this infinite, multiform reality, we are forced to select what we deem essential based on specific cognitive interests. The question for philosophy thus becomes, How are concepts to be formed so that our cognitive interests are realized in our methods of scientific inquiry? Because reality as such, as it "is," can never be the aim of science, Rickert believed that philosophy would be better served by abandoning the quest for ontological foundations and focusing instead on the limits of what we can know, on epistemology, an ultimately Kantian project. This Kantian approach led Rickert to abandon the material and substantive distinctions of nature and spirit for a formal-logical taxonomy of the sciences based on theoretical goals and cognitive interests.

In his theory of the natural and "cultural" sciences, Rickert followed Windelband's famous distinction between the nomothetic or law-seeking sciences and the idiographic, individualizing sciences. The concept of culture makes possible, in Rickert's view, individualizing concept-formation, for it "offers a principle of selecting the historically essential from the historically inessential. 'It is through the

values that attach to culture that the concept of a historically represented individuality is first constituted.'"[117] By following this path of
questioning, Rickert discerned an inner unity to history and culture
(because it is the individualizing method of history which attaches to
recognized cultural values). Rickert defined nature, on the other
hand, as that realm independent of values. The importance of this
insight for a theory of the sciences is considerable: it offers a way to
extend the basic Kantian question—How is natural science possible?
—to the realm of history. Rickert could now ask, How is history as
science possible? and respond by arguing that (in Heidegger's words)
"that which makes history as science at all possible is the *concept of
culture.*"[118]

Like natural science, history cannot reproduce the infinite manifold
or "heterogeneous continuum" of reality. Again, it depends on a principle of selection based on values. But Rickert argued that scientific
inquiry need not—indeed, must not—be evaluative; instead of offering a value judgment (*Werturteil*), the cultural scientist can offer a
purely theoretical relation (*Wertbeziehung*) of cultural objects to values.
This insight allowed Rickert to propose a transcendental solution to
the crisis of historical relativism because he no longer needed to consider any historical justification for the existence of specific values.
Values, in his scheme, do not "exist" at all; they are, rather, "valid."
Values are a kind of transcendental repository of logical meaning—
formally valid but never real. In Rickert's theory of the sciences, then,
values are neither subjective nor objective but constitute "an autonomous sphere that lies beyond subject and object."[119]

Early in his career, Heidegger followed Rickert (and Windelband)
in accepting the logical separation of the natural and human sciences.
In his speech on "The Concept of Time in the Science of History," he
based his remarks on Rickert's idea that "the selection of the historical
from the abundance of what is given is based on a value-relation."[120]
He went on to say that "the goal of historical science is, accordingly,
to present the effective and developmental context of the objectifications of human life in their individuality and uniqueness, which one
can understand through their relation to cultural values." At the end

[117] Heidegger, *GA* 56/57: 174.
[118] Ibid., 173.
[119] Heinrich Rickert, "Vom Begriff der Philosophie," *Logos* 1 (1910–11): 12. See also
Rickert, *Gegenstand der Philosophie* (Tübingen: Mohr, 1928).
[120] Heidegger, "Concept of Time in the Science of History," 8; *GA* 1: 427.

of the speech, as if wishing to leave no doubt where his allegiances lay, Heidegger repeated the Rickertian claim that "the principle of historical concept-formation manifests itself as the relation to values."[121] Yet even in this early work Heidegger provided a hint of how he would later approach the Neo-Kantian theory of the sciences. While still clinging to the timeless validity of values as the ground for historical meaning, Heidegger tried, nonetheless, to propose a principle for distinguishing natural and historical science based on their different concepts of time: if, in physics, time is measured quantitatively by mathematically determined units, in history, time is qualitatively grasped in terms of its significance by relating it to values.

Clearly, Heidegger's notion of time played an important role in helping him break away from the Neo-Kantian model of philosophy. But Husserl's phenomenological approach also offered him an alternative to Rickert's theory of logic by focusing his attention on the problems of *intentionality* ("*Intentio* literally means *directing-itself-toward*. Every lived experience . . . directs itself toward something") and *categorial intuition* ("Simply apprehending the bodily given as it shows itself," conceptually grasped as a category).[122] By the war emergency semester of 1919, his project of a Neo-Kantian phenomenology lay in ruins. Even though the next semester's lectures (in the summer of 1919) explicitly dealt with a phenomenological critique of Rickert's and Windelband's value-philosophy, already in the current semester Heidegger had begun to approach problems of value from a hermeneutic perspective: as he put it, "'worlding' ['*es weltet*'] does not coincide with 'valuing' ['*es wertet*']."[123] Now Heidegger explicitly thematized experiences from the environing world (*Umwelt*) which, in their character as events ("*Er-eignisse*"), do not lend themselves to theoretical or transcendental-logical solutions. The Neo-Kantian bent toward theorization merely de-worlds, de-lives (*Ent-lebnis*), de-historicizes (*ent-geschichtlich*), and de-signifies (*ent-deutet*) our original experience in/of the world.[124] Heidegger went so far as to say that the primacy of theory leads to a "destruction of the experience of the environing world."[125] Philosophy is pretheoretical, Heidegger argued, but not in the sense of a temporal a priori. Rather, Heidegger saw the

---

[121] Heidegger, "Concept of Time in the Science of History," 10 (translation modified); GA 1: 433.

[122] Heidegger, *History of the Concept of Time*, 29, 47; GA 20: 37, 64.

[123] Heidegger, GA 56/57: 73.

[124] Ibid., 89.

[125] Ibid., 85.

fundamental task of philosophy as the phenomenological description of experience *before* its definition (deformation) and constitution (concealment) by the natural or human sciences, whether in the form of value theory or fact-seeking positivism.

Windelband and Rickert had artificially separated the problems of theory and experience into the realms of value and being; in so doing, they failed to grasp the primordial character of truth. Rickert's philosophy was marked by its uncompromising insistence on the subject/object distinction (as Rickert put it, "to the concept of knowledge belongs, besides a subject who knows, an object that is known") and its immanentist view that "the being of every reality must be seen as a being in consciousness."[126] As far as Heidegger was concerned, neither of these principles offered an original or radical interpretation of the event-character of truth. Moreover, Rickert's twofold claim that being has a meaning only as part of a judgment and that judgments are made exclusively in terms of a transcendental "ought" were rejected by Heidegger as eristic and empty. Heidegger ended his lecture of Summer Semester 1919 by challenging Rickert's thesis that meaning is nothing other than a value. He went on to suggest that by putting aside phenomenal events and failing to gain insight into the "research of experience" (*Erlebnisforschung*), Rickert had missed the genuine meaning of meaning as it relates to beings and existentialia. Truth is not subordinate to value, Heidegger claimed; it is a primordial "worlding" or "eventing" (*es er-eignet*) whose grammatical structure follows neither the subject nor the predicate but takes the form of the "middle voice."[127]

Where Rickert insisted that the truth attaching to judgments is neither psychologically nor historically grounded, Heidegger agreed. In fact, Heidegger shared with Rickert a number of problems, besides the question of meaning. Right up through *Being and Time*, Heidegger's thought was marked by a concern for a transcendental solution to the crisis of the sciences and to the problem of historical relativism. Like Rickert, he, too, insisted on the primacy of philosophy as a form

[126] Quoted by Heidegger in *GA* 56/57: 182; on pp. 49 and 75 he refers to *Wahrsein* as *aletheia*. Charles Guignon, in his perceptive book *Heidegger and the Problem of Knowledge* (Indianapolis: Hackett, 1983), 143–145, speaks of a comparison between the "depth grammar" found in Wittgenstein's *Philosophical Investigations* and Heidegger's idea of language in *Being and Time*.

[127] For a more complete discussion of the significance of the middle voice in Heidegger, see Charles Scott, *The Language of Difference* (Atlantic Highlands, N.J.: Humanities Press, 1987), 67–87, and John Llewelyn, *The Middle Voice of Ecological Conscience* (New York: St. Martin's, 1991).

of *Wissenschaft* against all world-view philosophy. And yet even as early as 1919, Heidegger had already established the groundwork for his critique of Neo-Kantian value-theory. Rickert nowhere explained what meaning "is," Heidegger wrote; he maintained that "a meaning lies . . . before all beings and cannot be grasped by ontology."[128] It is simply "valid." There is, in his view, always a gap between validity and being or value and existence, for validity is neither "in" beings or "in" being but in the formal realm of transcendental logic. In this sense Rickert's "meaning" is a logical rather than an ontological condition. Hence, Rickert claimed that only an epistemological approach to the questions of formal meaning, one that directs its gaze to the pure norms of a transcendental consciousness, could offer a legitimate *Fragestellung* for the crisis of meaning in the human or cultural sciences.

Heidegger saw at work here the same worldless, ahistorical theorizing that Kierkegaard had detected in Hegel's "philosophy of reflection": in his earnest effort to solve the problems of the sciences, Rickert had reflected on only his reflections of things, not on the things and problems themselves. In his 1925 lectures on the "history of the concept of time," Heidegger complained that Rickert had been phenomenologically naïve, merely assuming a kinship between judgment and representation without even raising the issue of the intentionality of representation; thus, he claimed, "Rickert arrived at this theory not from a study of the matters themselves but by an unfounded deduction fraught with dogmatic judgments."[129] And, in "Phenomenology of Intuition and Expression (Theory of Philosophical Concept-Formation)," Heidegger said of Rickert: "It is easier, on the basis of a finished system, to offer finished answers than it is to keep oneself constantly open to the problematic of life."[130]

Heidegger continually maintained, even in his later thinking, that genuine philosophy never offers a system or a proof but is always preparatory, always "underway" (*unterwegs*).[131] The task of philosophy is not to resolve questions but to abide in the questionability of the question itself, to question the very logic of question and answer. In Heidegger's well-known discussion of the "scandal of philosophy" in *Being and Time*, he spoke to the whole Cartesian-Kantian tradition

---

[128] Heidegger, *GA* 56/57: 199.
[129] Heidegger, *History of the Concept of Time*, 33; *GA* 20: 43.
[130] Unpublished lecture by Heidegger, "PAA," July 26, 1920.
[131] See, for example, his essays collected in *Unterwegs zur Sprache, GA* 12.

and concluded that the very demand for proof and certitude in epistemological questioning is an "ontologically inadequate way of starting." What is needed, Heidegger claimed, "is the basic insight that while the different epistemological directions which have been pursued have not gone so very far off epistemologically, their neglect of any existential analytic of Dasein has kept them from obtaining any basis for a well secured phenomenal problematic. Nor is such a *basis* to be obtained by subsequently making phenomenological corrections on the concepts of subject and consciousness. Such a procedure would give no guarantee that the inappropriate *formulation of the question* would not continue to stand."[132] Insofar as Neo-Kantian idealism emphasized the fact that being and reality are only "in consciousness" and hence cannot be explained through an analysis of beings, it moved away from simple realism and positivism. But when the idealist refuses to inquire into the ontological consequences of this position (namely, what it means to *be* "in"), the interpretation becomes meaningless. The consequences of this question for Heidegger's own *destruktive* retrieval of Neo-Kantianism were profound, for Heidegger's debate with Rickert rested on a quarrel over the meaning of being for the transcendental project.

Rickert insisted that the proper sense of transcendental is always tied to a transhistorical, timeless, and logical subject, not Dilthey's historical subject. Accordingly, Rickert consistently interpreted Kant's first *Critique* as a transcendental analysis of the conditions of the subject's knowledge of objects, or *Gegenstände*. Heidegger, while rejecting the implicit subjectivity of Rickert's position, nonetheless managed to retrieve from the transcendental project another, nonsubjective understanding of "transcendental." What he tried to communicate with his new term *Dasein* was something nonsubjective, something that destructures the anthropological sense of a person or the humanist understanding of an individuated ego. *Da-sein*, literally, is a place, a *topos*, a "there" *in* being, an event marked by temporality rather than a thing weighted down with substance. In this place, being and beings come into play, take on meaning, and open themselves up in the space of a question; *Dasein* is, in its questioning, the place for the condition of the being of mortal beings, of the possibility to be at all. Heidegger understood this possibility in a transcendental sense, namely, as "the condition for the possibility of." But whereas Rickert

---

[132] Heidegger, *Being and Time*, 250–51 (translation modified); *Sein und Zeit*, 207.

focused his attention on the strict possibility of *knowledge*, thereby cal-
cifying the dynamic ontological meaning of the transcendental, Heidegger found in the very notion of transcendental possibility a crucial
insight into the aletheic unfolding of being in the "there" of *Da-sein*.[133]

Rickert was hardly alone in offering this subject-grounded definition of "transcendental"; it marked the whole Kantian tradition of
epistemic thinking. And yet Heidegger felt that within the problematic of "idealism" there lay the possibility of a *destruktive* retrieval:

> If what the term "idealism" says, amounts to the understanding that being
> can never be explained by beings but is already that which is "transcenden-
> tal" for all beings, then idealism affords the only correct possibility for a
> philosophical problematic. If so, Aristotle was no less an idealist than Kant.
> But if "idealism" signifies tracing back all beings to a subject or conscious-
> ness whose sole distinguishing features are that it remains *indefinite* in its
> being and is best characterized negatively as "un-Thing-like," then this ideal-
> ism is no less naïve in its method than the most grossly militant realism. . . .
>
> Our discussion of the unexpressed presuppositions of attempts to solve
> the problem of Reality in ways which are just "epistemological," shows that
> this problem must be taken back, as an ontological one, into the existential
> analytic of *Dasein*.[134]

By focusing his attention away from the subject/object dichotomies
of Neo-Kantian logic, Heidegger hoped to reclaim the ontological
condition of beings in the "existential analytic of *Dasein*." In Husserl's
notion of intentionality—*intentio* as a "directing-itself-towards"—Heidegger found a way of overcoming the formal-logical approach to
meaning that characterized Rickert's thought. "Every lived experience," Heidegger argued, "directs itself toward something"; that is, it
is not an *intra mentem* coordination of the physical and the psychical
but a kinetic, dynamic center, a movement of meaning (*Sinn*) which
breaks with the Cartesian, objectless subject who first must proceed
outward toward the object. Husserl had already shown in the sixth of
his *Logical Investigations* that consciousness can never be a self-en-
closed receptacle of meaning but that meaning is a pre-conceptual
and pre-predicative dimension of being.[135] Heidegger transformed this

---

[133] Heidegger, *Being and Time*, 26–27; *Sein und Zeit*, 7, for example.

[134] Heidegger, *Being and Time*, 251–252 (translation modified); *Sein und Zeit*, 208.

[135] On intentionality, see Heidegger, *History of the Concept of Time*, 27–47; *GA* 20: 34–63.
See also Husserl, *Logische Untersuchungen*, vol. 2, pt. 2, 1–127.; *Logical Investigations*,
667–770.

doctrine of intentionality into a critique of the Kantian tradition. By retrieving Husserl's notion of "being-meaning" (*Seinssinn*) into three intentional moments of "content-meaning" (*Gehaltssinn*), "relational meaning" (*Bezugssinn*), and "enactment-meaning" (*Vollzugssinn*) or "temporalizing-meaning" (*Zeitigungssinn*), Heidegger hoped to show the dynamic, kinetic character of being in the transcendental conditions of *Dasein*.

But Husserlian intentionality alone was not enough to provide a genuinely phenomenological indication for a "being-directed" understanding of meaning. It was Wilhelm Dilthey who played a crucial role in helping Heidegger to perceive the significance of concrete factical-historical existence for the problem of meaning in twentieth-century German thought. At the age of seventy, Dilthey enthusiastically read the *Logical Investigations* and admired Husserl's attempt to provide a "universally valid theory of knowledge" for the natural and human sciences. But where Husserl sought to achieve "absolute impartiality" for transcendental consciousness, Dilthey refused to abandon the historicity and facticity of life. "*Life* is the fundamental fact that must form the starting point for philosophy," Dilthey insisted. "It is that which is known from within, that behind which one cannot go. Life cannot be brought before the judgment seat of reason. Life is historical insofar as it is grasped in its moving forth in time and in the nexus of actions that arise therefrom."[136] By thematizing "life" as the fundamental topic of philosophy and grasping it as a *temporal* movement whose meaning lay not in worldless subjectivity but in the nexus of historical relations, Dilthey opened up to Heidegger a horizon from which to rethink the Neo-Kantian problematic of epistemology and history.

vii. Greek Ontology and Christian *Kairos*: Heidegger's
Destruktion of the Metaphysics of Presence

Heidegger had read Dilthey as early as 1914 and was affected by his penetrating critique of Neo-Kantian value-philosophy.[137] Many of his early lectures from 1919 to 1925 include important references to

---

[136] Wilhelm Dilthey, *Gesammelte Schriften*, vol. 7 (Stuttgart: Teubner, 1973), 261. For Husserl on absolute impartiality, see *Cartesianische Meditationen* (The Hague: Martinus Nijhoff, 1950), 74.
[137] See Sheehan, "Heidegger's *Lehrjahre*."

Dilthey's work, and section 77 of *Being and Time* is explicitly devoted to the connection of "the problem of historicity with the researches of Wilhelm Dilthey."[138] Heidegger found in Dilthey a way of historicizing the lifeless, worldless sphere of transcendental subjectivity and making historicity itself the transcendental condition for the possibility of human understanding. Rickert's attempts to make judgments (*Urteile*) the very ground of meaning were rendered meaningless by Dilthey's hermeneutic grasp of life as experience. In effect, Rickert's and Windelband's taxonomy of the sciences had, according to Heidegger, "trivialized" and "twisted" Dilthey's basic problems beyond recognition.[139] Against Rickert's universally valid theory of the sciences, Dilthey saw clearly that it was the historicity of life, not the validity of historical science, which provided the genuine meaning of history. As Heidegger put it in his lectures on "The History of the Concept of Time," "Dilthey's scientific work sought to secure that way of regarding human beings which, contrary to scientific psychology, does not take them for its objects as things of nature, explaining and construing them by means of other universal laws of 'events' but instead *understands* them as *living persons actively involved in history* and *describes* and *analyzes* them in this understanding."[140]

Rickert's epistemological mode of questioning had completely bypassed this living, historical process of understanding and had focused energy instead on the "object of knowledge" (*der Gegenstand der Erkenntnis*) for philosophy. The basis of Rickert's approach was an inquiry into the constitution of the object by the transcendental subject, an approach associated with the founder of nineteenth-century value-philosophy, Rudolf Lotze. In his lectures "Logic: The Question concerning the Truth" in the winter semester of 1925/26, Heidegger had identified Lotze's thinking as a modern strain of Platonism, an axiological theory of modern forms. Rejecting all types of correspondence theory, Lotze argued that truth is nothing other than the valid affirmation of propositions; it is "the permanent, enduring object of inner intuition," that which is "ever identical with itself and invariable [*beständig*]."[141] Lotze interpreted Plato's theory of forms as nothing other than "the validity of truths" and maintained that where Plato spoke of the being of the forms, he really intended a kind of

---

[138] Heidegger, *Being and Time*, 449; *Sein und Zeit*, 397.
[139] Heidegger, *History of the Concept of Time*, 17; *GA* 20: 20.
[140] Heidegger, *History of the Concept of Time*, 117; *GA* 20: 161.
[141] Heidegger, *GA* 21: 70–90.

theory of validity. But, Lotze argued, because the Greeks lacked a concept for validity, Plato spoke of form as *ousia*, which Lotze then linked to the concept of "hypostasis," a kind of being-present (*Vorhandensein*) for things and substances. Heidegger seized on these terminological distinctions to offer a formidable critique of the whole Neo-Kantian tradition rooted in the etymology of concepts. By returning to the original meanings of philosophical terms in the Greek language, Heidegger hoped to show how the standard lexicon of academic philosophy had become far removed from any living context. Specifically, Heidegger interrogated the Neo-Kantian notion of an object, or *Gegen-stand*, which literally meant that which "stands over against" (the subject). In this notion of "standing," "standing over against," and "standing there," Heidegger derived a reading of Neo-Kantian epistemology as a metaphysics of standing presence (*Anwesenheit*).

Lotze's notion of "hypostasis" yielded a curious meaning if grasped etymologically. *Hypo*, the Greek prefix (under), and *stasis*, the Greek noun (standing), together denote a "standing under," translated into Latin as *substantia* (*sub*, "under," plus *stare*, "to stand," or *substare*, "to be present"), the Latin equivalent of *ousia*.[142] The German word *Substanz* has a similar etymology. The interpretation of *ousia* as "real being," in contrast to "appearance," depends on this characteristic insistence on its "substance" or its "standing under." But Heidegger wanted to provide a *Destruktion* of the substance-concept (*ousia*, *substantia*) by showing that it is based on the same ontico-logical principles as all Neo-Kantian epistemology, namely, as a form of knowledge which grasps entities as "standing (there) before" a subject (*episteme*, from the Greek *ephistanai*, originally *epi* plus *histanai*, "to stand before").[143] Rickert's project of the "constitution of an object (*Gegenstand*) by a transcendental subject" rests on these same epistemological foundations; even the operative term *constitution* betrays a hidden preference for metaphors of "standing": the Latin verb *constituere* means "to set up, to set together," and *statuere* "to set, place"; both come from *stare*, "to stand," related to the Greek *statos*, "placed, standing," and *histanai*, "to cause to stand."[144]

In Heidegger's reading, the whole Western tradition of metaphysi-

---

[142] *Webster's New World Dictionary of the American Language* (New York: World Publishing, 1970), 1420; and F. P. Leverett, ed., *Freund's Lexicon of the Latin Language* (Philadelphia: Lippincott, 1900), 859.

[143] *Webster's*, 471; Liddell and Scott, *Greek-English Lexicon*, 745.

[144] *Webster's*, 304, 1392; Leverett, *Freund's Lexicon*, 846.

cal thinking back to Plato could be understood in terms of these same ontological inscriptions. The Neo-Kantian thematization of *Gegenstand* was only the most recent. Rickert's exclusive emphasis on the "standing object" led him to define ontology as that branch of philosophy dealing with objects, sub-stances, and things separate from the subject. He maintained that ontology could not account for the Kantian problematic of how these objects were constituted as forms of knowledge for the natural and human sciences. Heidegger wished to show, however, that ontology is not merely one discipline among others, a category dealing solely with a theory of objects, but is itself the basis of all epistemological distinctions, including any possible theory of value or logic of the sciences. The fundamental question of *Being and Time*—"the question of the meaning of being"—retrieves the concealed meaning of ancient Greek ontology and repeats its underlying theme of *ousia* (in the sense of the constancy of presence) as a way of disclosing the ontological prejudices of Neo-Kantian epistemology. Heidegger, in the introduction to *Being and Time*, saw in this question about the meaning of being a way of interpreting the unity of the Western metaphysical tradition.

According to Heidegger's narrative, for the Greeks (even as far back as Parmenides), the manner of approaching the problem of being was always tied to the way beings revealed themselves to human logos; in *Being and Time* Heidegger wrote:

> As the ontological clue gets progressively worked out—namely, in the 'hermeneutic' of the logos—it becomes increasingly possible to grasp the problem of being in a more radical fashion. . . . *Legein* itself—or rather *noein*, that simple awareness of something present-at-hand in its sheer presence-at-hand [*Vorhandenheit*], which Parmenides had already taken to guide him in his own interpretation of being—has the temporal structure of a pure "making-present" [*Gegenwärtigen*] of something. Those beings which show themselves *in* this and *for* it, and which are understood as beings in the most authentic sense, thus get interpreted with regard to the present [*Gegen-wart*]; that is, they are conceived as presence (*ousia*) [*Anwesenheit*].[145]

The Greek inscription of beings within the structure of "being-present" or "standing before" defined them as substances or objects "there" for a subject. Yet the hidden presupposition behind this notion of *ousia* as "standing presence" was an unacknowledged notion

---

[145] Heidegger, *Being and Time*, 47–48 (translation modified); *Sein und Zeit*, 25–26.

of time. For this way of grasping beings led to "the treatment of the meaning of being as *parousia* or *ousia*, which signifies, in ontologico-temporal terms, 'presence.' Beings are grasped in their being as 'presence'; this means they are understood with regard to a definite mode of time—the 'present.'"[146]

In his remarkable reading of ancient Greek ontology as a "metaphysics of presence," Heidegger came to grasp the unity of the Western philosophical tradition as a projection on beings of a unidimensional concept of time, namely, the time of the "now," the eternal present. As Heidegger saw it, metaphysics functions as a kind of ontological glaciation—a freezing of the lived experience of the present into the *nunc stans*, or "standing now," of eternity.[147] But as always in Heidegger's thinking, the reading of ancient ontology was conceived within the horizon of early Christian theology. If Plato and Aristotle, following Parmenides, understood being as *ousia*, or permanent presence, then the Pauline epistles revealed a different understanding of being as *parousia*, not merely presence as a "being-with" (in Greek, *ousia*, "being," plus *para*, "beside, by the side of" when followed by a noun in the dative case) but also in the sense of a "being-toward" (as *para*, with the accusative, indicates "motion to, toward").[148] Heidegger recognized in Paul's experience of Christ's "coming" an ecstatic experience of time which overturned the glacial ontology of the Greeks. For in Heidegger's account of Paul's epistles, the *parousia* is neither a second coming that one waits for or anticipates nor the futural being-present-with Christ of the early Christian community. It is neither a future "present" nor an event that is to be calculated or re-presented in advance. The genuine meaning of the *parousia* is an experience of being as pure temporality; that is, it cannot be grasped as incremental units of mathematical and calendrical time but as the "time of deci-

---

[146] Heidegger, *Being and Time*, 47; *Sein und Zeit*, 25; for related passages on presence and temporality see Martin Heidegger, *Grundprobleme der Phänomenologie, Gesamtausgabe* 24 (Frankfurt: Klostermann, 1989), 153, 367, 433; translated by Albert Hofstadter as *The Basic Problems of Phenomenology* (Bloomington: Indiana University Press, 1982), 109, 260, 305.

[147] This reading of the *nunc stans* can be found, for example, in Heidegger, *Sein und Zeit*, 427 n. 13 (*Being and Time*, 499 n. xiii) and in *Kant und das Problem der Metaphysik* (Frankfurt: Klostermann, 1973), 233, which was translated by Richard Taft as *Kant and the Problem of Metaphysics* (Bloomington: Indiana University Press, 1990), 164.

[148] For different ways of translating *parousia*, see W. E. Vine, *An Expository Dictionary of the New Testament* (Old Tappan, N.J.: F. H. Revell, 1966), 208; Arndt and Gingrich, *Greek-English Lexicon of the New Testament*, 635; and Alois Vanicek, *Griechisch-Lateinisches Etymologisches Wörterbuch* (Leipzig: Teubner, 1877), 73. Benseler, *Griechisch-Deutsches Wörterbuch*, 686, translates *parousia* as both *Anwesenheit* and *Gegenwart*.

sion," "the time of care," the "time of a 'situation,'" captured in the Greek term *kairos* (which Heidegger translates as *Augenblick*).[149]

The original Christian meaning of the *parousia* revealed to Heidegger the genuine experience of being as time, as a factical experience of life within the historical situation of a "coming." The consequences for Heidegger's own reading of the Greek metaphysical tradition were enormous. For Heidegger began to see that the reality of time is not something measurable, quantifiable, thingly, or present-at-hand but involves one within a horizon of possibility and caring that marks the phenomenon of existence. Existence (from the Latin *sistere*, "to stand," plus *ex*, "out, out from," derived from Greek *stasis* and related to the word *ekstasis*) is now defined as a "standing out from" the present-at-hand world of beings into the openness and possibility of being itself.[150] With this understanding of time as a nexus of possibilities or a unity of horizons (that is, an ecstatic phenomenon), Heidegger made a fundamental break with the ontological tradition of standing presence, a move that had fateful consequences for his interpretation of historicism. Here Heidegger de-structured the traditional historicist concept of time as a succession of fixed "now" points to reveal a kinetic movement of temporal possibilities within a unified horizon—a unity that, in the lexicon of a glacial metaphysics of time, had been sundered and designated by the separate names of "past," "present," and "future."

Kierkegaard had already anticipated Heidegger in this break. For Kierkegaard, time is not an abstract or static "now" but a movement of past and future into the present whereby the past persists as a possibility contemporaneous with the present situation. In one's own attitude to the past one could, Kierkegaard claimed, "understand at a distance" or "understand in contemporaneity" the difference being one's resolve in either grasping the temporality of time or in falling back into the static consciousness of time as a succession of instants. What determined this difference, according to Kierkegaard, was the Christian insight into the momentous quality of every moment as a choice or decision where all eternity hangs in the balance.[151] In "the

[149] Sheehan's "Heidegger's 'Introduction'" is especially good on this point. See also van Buren, *Young Heidegger*, chap. 5, and Hans-Georg Gadamer, "The Religious Dimension in Heidegger," in Alan Olson, ed., *Transcendence and the Sacred* (South Bend, Ind.: University of Notre Dame Press, 1981), 193–207.

[150] Heidegger, *GA* 24: 377–378; *Basic Problems of Phenomenology*, 267.

[151] Søren Kierkegaard, *The Concept of Anxiety* (Princeton, N.J.: Princeton University Press, 1980), 87–90; and Caputo, *Radical Hermeneutics*, 15–21.

moment" (Danish, *Oiblikket*; German, *Augenblick*), one sees the present situation in a way that is radically different from the objective time concept in the natural sciences; as Kierkegaard put it in *The Concept of Anxiety*, "Time has no significance at all for nature."[152] Repeating Kierkegaard's own reading of human temporality as a kind of Christian decision about the moment, Heidegger found in Paul's notion of the *parousia* a way to overcome the Neo-Kantian logic of the natural and historical sciences based on a unidimensional model of time. Heidegger believed that by tracing the Greek and Latin roots of epistemological and metaphysical concepts, he could work through the impasse in contemporary philosophy.

The historical translation of Greek terms like *ousia* and *parousia* into Latin as *praeesse* (*prae*, "before" plus *esse*, "to be," whence "essence") and *praesens* had the effect, Heidegger maintained, of covering over and concealing the very temporality of time, thus rendering it as an objectively present entity "there" for observation.[153] Heidegger hoped to find an indication for another way to think about being than as the Graeco-Latin idea of "standing presence," an indication that might provide a new, nonmetaphysical beginning for Western thought. If Paul and Kierkegaard had provided him with hints for this new beginning by helping him understand the *futural* character of temporality, then one could argue that it was Dilthey who convinced him about the meaning of the *past* and of historicity. In Dilthey's project of understanding the historicity of life, Heidegger found the source for his fundamental ontology of *Dasein*: an *experience* of being, marked by temporality. By following his reading of Dilthey, we will come to see how Heidegger's own critical relationship to Dilthey's work helped to reveal the basic aporia of historicism.

viii. Dilthey's *Fragestellung* and Heidegger's Question concerning the Meaning of History

In Chapter 4, in discussing Dilthey's "Critique of Historical Reason," I attempted to show that Dilthey's emphasis on life experience and historical understanding presented a powerful alternative to the axiological interpretation of history advanced by the Neo-Kantians. Clearly, Dilthey had a decisive effect on an entire generation of Ger-

---

[152] Kierkegaard, *Concept of Anxiety*, 89.
[153] On *praeesse* and *praesens*, see *Webster's*, 1124, and Leverett, *Freund's Lexicon*, 692.

man thinkers who tried to find a path between the rigorous demands of *Wissenschaft* and the cultural aesthetics of *Weltanschauung*. But Heidegger found something else of significance in Dilthey's work which prompted him to claim that "Dilthey was the first to understand 'the aims of phenomenology.'"[154] What Dilthey brought to his study of "life" was a keen interest in the contextualized relations and temporal continuity that make up the experience of living—its processual character as well as its structural coherence. Where Rickert saw the discrete facts of historical and natural-scientific observation, Dilthey embraced a hermeneutic approach to life in which every part is understood in relation to a whole. In Dilthey's hermeneutics, connections between phenomena were not linked to sense-impressions of nature but to the primordial unity of historical life granted in experience. Again, if for Rickert the separation between history and nature lay in the realm of transcendental values, for Dilthey it had primarily to do with their different notions of time.

"In time," Dilthey argued, "life exists in the relation of parts to a whole, that is, as a context—there [*da*]."[155] And yet the time concept of natural science was very different. It defined *time* as an abstract series of equi-valent intervals wholly indifferent to the cluster of human designs. Dilthey insisted, however, that human beings experience life temporally; he even went so far as to claim that "the basic categorial determination of life is temporality which serves as the foundation for all the others."[156] In the experiencing of factical life, past and future form a synchronic whole with the present, a continuity that is not a succession of moments but a living, vital unity. By moving away from the empty, a priori conception of Kantian time, Dilthey believed he had cleared the path for a new approach to the fundamental reality that lay at the root of the human sciences.

Heidegger was deeply affected by Dilthey's understanding of life in terms of temporality, especially his tendency to understand the past as an ongoing, effective process vital to lived experience rather than as an already determined "fact" of history. In *Being and Time*, Heidegger gave rare praise to Dilthey by suggesting that he was "on his way towards [*unterwegs*] the question of life" and that his "real

[154] Heidegger, *History of the Concept of Time*, 118; *GA* 20: 163.
[155] Wilhelm Dilthey, *Gesammelte Schriften*, 7: 229; "The Construction of the Historical World in the Human Studies," in H. P. Rickman, ed., *Dilthey: Selected Writings*, trans., Rickman (Cambridge: Cambridge University Press, 1976), 237.
[156] Dilthey, "Construction of the Historical World in the Human Studies," 209; *GS* 7: 192.

philosophical tendencies were aimed at an ontology of 'life.'"[157] Moreover, Heidegger believed that Dilthey brought to the debate about the
crisis of the sciences and the crisis of historicism a way "to see historical reality in its authentic reality," namely, as a meaningful form of
being for human beings and not as a taxonomic exercise in epistemological concept-formation.[158] In his unpublished Kassel lectures of
1925, "Wilhelm Dilthey's Researches and the Struggle for a Historical
World-View," Heidegger offered an extensive treatment of Dilthey's
hermeneutical inquiry, clearly admiring his interpretation of historical
reality as a "phenomenon" rather than as a mere object of research. In
Dilthey's claims that "the nexus [of life] is always already there and
not first constructed out of elements" and that "life is originally given
in its totality," Heidegger found an indication for a phenomenological
approach to the problem of facticity which later, in *Being and Time*,
developed into a fundamental ontological analysis of *Dasein*.[159]

In his Summer Semester 1923 lectures, "Ontology: Hermeneutics of
Facticity," Heidegger defined facticity as "one's own *Dasein* questioned in its being-character . . . [where] one's own *Dasein* is what it is
only in its *temporally particular* [*jeweiligen*] 'there' [*Da*]."[160] Heidegger
went on to say that the fundamental phenomenon of facticity could
only be clarified in and as temporality. Later, in the Kassel lectures, he
raised this issue again and tried to show how far Dilthey's researches
had come in relating factical life experience to the problem of temporality. Dilthey had begun to understand the authentic meaning of
history as a question concerning *Dasein*'s experience as a "historical
being" rather than as a question of empirical research or of an overarching epochal process called "world history." But, even as he ex-
plored the meaning of historical reality, he never asked the question
concerning historicity itself—"the question concerning the meaning
of being and the being of beings."[161] Dilthey never really possessed
the means with which to pose this question, Heidegger claimed, because he remained tied to a fundamentally Cartesian problematic and
focused his attention on a theory of science and an epistemological
grounding of the human sciences. Even his hermeneutical questioning was always dominated by this methodological ideal.

[157] Heidegger, *Being and Time*, 72, 494; *Sein und Zeit*, 46, 249.
[158] Heidegger, "KV," 8.
[159] Ibid., 10.
[160] Heidegger, *GA* 63: 29.
[161] Heidegger, "KV," 12.

And yet Heidegger found in Dilthey a way to understand the past not as a prior happening or mere cultural possession but as a form of experience with ontological consequences; in this passage from Heidegger's Aristotle lectures, one can hear Diltheyan echoes: "The nexus of life [*Lebenszusammenhang*] *is* in factical life; the facticity of life, *Dasein*, is in itself historical and, as historical, has a relation (as comportment) to the objective historical world and time that precedes it. The question concerning the meaning and right of tradition—itself a phenomenon in the basic phenomenon of the historical—is taken back into the problematic of the historical itself, which is meaningfully rooted in the facticity of factical life itself."[162] When speaking of history, Heidegger always returned to Dilthey's fundamental insight about the facticity of historical life. Despite his Cartesian roots, Dilthey understood that experience (*Erlebnis*, or what the early Heidegger called "factical life") is not an isolated fact of science but a part of a whole life process or nexus whose meaning is located in the dynamic center of immediate reflexive awareness (*Innewerden*) where self and world come together.[163] The meaning of a whole life could be opened up in just such an experience, revealing that this meaning is not "in" the past or "in" the future but happens as a kind of phenomenality of process or as temporality. Aristotle had defined time as "the quantification of motion in respect to 'before' and 'after'"; Kant conceived it as a continuity of now sequences. But neither had begun "to understand time as the reality of our own selves," that is, as authentic temporality.[164] Dilthey had begun to see the unity of temporality in *Innewerden* and provided the tradition with the possibility of a new beginning. Heidegger seized on that possibility in *Being and Time* as he retrieved Dilthey's notion of historicity for his own ontological project.

But Dilthey also affected Heidegger in a much more profound, if less obvious, way. Almost all Dilthey's works, from his *Introduction to the Human Sciences* to his various studies on the development of hermeneutics, involved a reading of the history of philosophy as a unified and coherent tradition. Whether he was tracing the influence of Greek metaphysics on Augustine or the impact of Luther on Schleier-

---

[162] Heidegger, *GA* 61: 76.
[163] Wilhelm Dilthey, *Gesammelte Schriften*, vol. 19 (Göttingen: Vandenhoeck & Ruprecht, 1982), 177; *Introduction to the Human Sciences*, trans. Rudolf Makkreel and Frithjof Rodi (Princeton, N.J.: Princeton University Press, 1984), 358.
[164] Heidegger, "KV," 26.

macher, Dilthey always conceived of Western philosophy historically. Even as he tried to work against the metaphysical imperatives within the tradition, Dilthey defined them *as* a tradition. For him, questions of temporality, experience, hermeneutical reflection, and historicity all belonged to his lifelong dialogue with the history of philosophy. To the very end of his life, Heidegger, too, continued to think of philosophy historically—as part of the history of being, thought as the history of the oblivion of being. The historical movement from the Pre-Socratics to Nietzsche revealed to him the nihilistic character of the metaphysics of presence with its instrumentalist strategies for dominion over beings. Even his notion of the "end of philosophy" was grounded in the unspoken acceptance of a unified tradition, "beginning" with the Greeks and "ending" with Nietzsche.

Heidegger transformed Dilthey's notion of history, however, by rethinking the meaning of *crisis*, which for him referred not only to the academic crisis of historicism but also to a crisis in the Western tradition itself, understood as the history of nihilism. Dilthey could still conceive of history as a movement of progress and meaning, but Heidegger, in the wake of his own religious upheaval and the cultural pessimism of Weimar, did not take the meaning of history as something itself historical. Rather, he followed a phenomenological path that approached the problem of history not in the narrow sense of *Historie* as historical science but as the authentic happening of *Dasein* engaged in its own search for new ways and possibilities of being. As Heidegger put it: "History as *Geschichte* signifies a happening [*Geschehen*] that we ourselves are, where we are there present. . . . We *are* history, that is, our own past. Our future lives out of its past. We are carried by the past."[165]

Traditional historicists characterized history as something unique and unrepeatable that proceeded according to an inner principle of development. In this sense they understood history principally as the realm of values and freedom in contrast to the value-neutral and law-governed world of nature. Moreover, historicists believed that to truly "understand" the alien past, one had to escape one's own time by immersing oneself in the documentary historical evidence. Heidegger questioned the basic tenets of the historicist tradition, however, and dismissed its approach as superficial and lacking in original insight.[166]

---

[165] Ibid., 27.
[166] Heidegger, *Begriff der Zeit*, 25.

He challenged the long-held view that the crucial difference between nature and history lay in the realm of values, seeing this as another manifestation of a subject/object metaphysics based on the Cartesian duality of body-nature/res extensa and mind-spirit/res cogitans. Rather than seeing historicism as a break with naturalist metaphysics or the theory of natural law (an argument put forward by such contemporaries as Troeltsch, Meinecke, and Spengler), Heidegger identified it as another example of the metaphysics spawned by the early modern sciences of nature. By defining the crisis of historicism as a battle between relativism and objectivism or *Weltanschauung* and *Wissenschaft*, his contemporaries were reinforcing the same metaphysical principles that had defined the Cartesian-Kantian tradition as a metaphysics of presence. Heidegger maintained, however, that history is not and could never be a science or something capable of scientific explanation, because it involves one in an original relation to time which cannot be reduced to the status of "fact." In his "Remarks on Karl Jaspers's *Psychology of World-Views*" (1919–1921), Heidegger wrote: "The historical is not only something from which one gets information and about which there are books; it is much more what we ourselves are, that which we bear."[167]

By defining history as something "past," held there for contemplation by the researcher, historians and epistemologists had forgotten the original meaning of history as a form of temporality. Moreover, in deciding on the epistemological status of historical research, they had in the process also forgotten the historical roots of their own scientific inquiry. In Heidegger's view, the sciences of nature and history were not themselves primordial forms of inquiry dealing with originary phenomena called "nature" or "history." They were, rather, historically defined "fields" of research, ontic possibilities of *Dasein* constituted within the given structures of university faculties and research practices, practices that were themselves defined by the accepted division of the sciences in Cartesian and Baconian metaphysics.

Heidegger wanted to push conventional epistemological distinctions to their limits—in *Being and Time* he stresses that "even nature is historical"—to reveal history and nature *before* their scientific elaboration, in an "original relationship to the topics themselves."[168] Heidegger's topic, however, was not a "place" (*topos*) in the usual sense but a

[167] Heidegger, *GA* 9: 33–34.
[168] Heidegger, *Being and Time*, 440; *Sein und Zeit*, 388; and *History of the Concept of Time*, 4–5; *GA* 20: 6–7.

mode of comportment or way of being which Heidegger grasped as a "phenomenon." As phenomena, history and nature are temporal processes or, rather, are experienced temporally by human beings. This original mode of experiencing precedes all explicitly scientific thematization of nature or history as "objects" and makes such thematization first possible. Heidegger sought to get back behind these given definitions of historical and natural science to the underlying unity of experience in order "to see history in its historicity," a theme to which he explicitly turned in *Being and Time*.[169]

ix. Historicity and History in *Being and Time*

In the second division, chapter 5 of *Being and Time*, Heidegger offered a penetrating analysis of the problem of historicity, an analysis that went a long way toward undermining the epistemological foundations of historicism advanced by his contemporaries. In Heidegger's interpretation, historicity was not an explicitly "historical" mode of being in the sense of belonging to a field of research entitled *Historie*. Instead, historicity, or *Geschichtlichkeit*, has an original relationship to *Geschichte* (etymologically drawn from Middle High German *geschiht* and new High German *Geschehen*, or "happening") in the sense of *Ereignis*: not *a* specific historical event (e.g., Napoléon's campaign at Waterloo) but the phenomenality or disclosure of that which happens prior to any specific scholarly inquiry.[170] In this way, nature, too, as an experience for human beings, is marked by historicity. Historicity signified for Heidegger the explicitly *ontological* understanding of the existential-temporal conditions of the "happening" that we ourselves are. Heidegger structured this happening in terms of three temporal moments: the past (understood as *Gewesenheit* or mode of "having been"), present (or *Gegen-wart* as a "waiting-toward"), and future (or *Zu-kunft* as a "coming-toward"), a unity whose ground he located in the phenomenon of care.[171]

Heidegger rejected the explicitly backward-looking, antiquarian element within historical thinking and emphasized that as a mode of temporality, history, or *Geschichte*, is not past-oriented but essentially

[169] Heidegger, *History of the Concept of Time*, 1; GA 20: 2.
[170] For an etymological history, see Pfeifer, *Etymologisches Wörterbuch des Deutschen*, 2:553. Heidegger plays on the difference between *Geschichte*, *Geschichtlichkeit*, and *Geschehen* in *Being and Time*, 41–42; *Sein und Zeit*, 19–20.
[171] Heidegger, *Being and Time*, 372–378; *Sein und Zeit*, 325–329.

futual. In his discussion of "temporality as the ontological meaning of care" in section 65 of *Being and Time*, he explained that "only in so far as Dasein *is* (as the *having-been* [*bin-gewesen*] of an 'I' that *is*) can it come towards [*zukünftig*] itself futurally in such a way that it comes *back* to itself. Dasein *is*, as an authentically *having-been*, an authentically futural anticipation of one's utmost and ownmost possibility coming back, in an understanding way, to one's ownmost *having-been*. Dasein can only *be* what it has been insofar as it is futural. One's already *having-been* arises, in a certain way, from the future."[172]

Classical historicists denied this futural dimension of historical experience, preferring to explore the epistemological questions of verification and access. Ranke, for example, spoke of history as an objectively valid realm "there" for the historian to research—in the form of diplomatic correspondence, papal proclamations, material artifacts, and the like—so that one could "know" it *wie es eigentlich gewesen ist*, or "as it actually happened." The only way to bring about a radical *Destruktion* of Rankean historicism was, according to Heidegger, to follow up on Graf Yorck's criticism of Dilthey's research, which provided him with a way of asking "the question of historicity [as] an *ontological* question concerning the constitution of the being of historical beings."[173] Yorck had understood that "the germinal point of historicity is the fact that the entire psycho-physical datum *lives* rather than *is*," a point that Heidegger interpreted to mean that genuine historicity involves an experience of temporality (which lives) and is not the same as the mere present-at-hand being of nature (which is). In Yorck's view, Dilthey had not been sensitive enough to the significance of these distinctions in his epistemological critique of the human sciences. In fact, in his extensive correspondence, Yorck went on to say that Dilthey's researches "stressed too little the generic difference between the ontical [*Ontischem*] and the historical [*Historischem*]."[174] For Heidegger, the whole misunderstanding about the so-called crisis of historicism derived from a fundamental inability to grasp Yorck's careful distinction. The essence of history is not anything "historical" in the sense of historiography or historical research but lies in the realm of what it means to *be* (or, in Dilthey's lexicon, to *live*). The ways of being for human beings are, in Heidegger's view, radically temporal, in the sense that their unity lies within the tempo-

---

[172] Heidegger, *Being and Time*, 373 (translation modified); *Sein und Zeit*, 326.
[173] Heidegger, *Being and Time*, 455 and 453; *Sein und Zeit*, 403 and 401.
[174] Heidegger, *Being and Time*, 451; *Sein und Zeit*, 399.

ral horizons of expectation (future), retrieval (past), and making present (*gegenwärtigen*). No experience within the world can bracket out or prescind this temporality of being, because being itself is historical and belongs to a lived context of relations. Ontological neutrality thus becomes impossible, for being itself is always structured as temporality within the phenomenon of care (*Sorge*). Simply put, for Heidegger, we are never in a position to judge objectively about the meaning of the past because our relations to ourselves and other beings are always mediated by our existential cares and concerns.

Ironically, in their great haste to preserve and reconstruct the meaning of the past on its own terms, historicists (such as Ranke and Droysen and their followers) had isolated the very historicity of human being which made history possible. In his ontological analysis of ontic/historical research, Heidegger tried to show that most historicists presented inauthentic accounts of history rooted either in the aesthetics of empathy or the pseudoscientific positivism of fact-collecting. Heidegger rejected aestheticism as another shallow example of *Weltanschauungsphilosophie*; he similarly dismissed historical positivism for its indiscriminate acceptance of rational judgment and theory as the proper method by which to study the past. *Being and Time* offered an extensive critique of *ratio*, *logos*, and *theoria* as "the" authentic means of scientific inquiry; Heidegger made it clear that logos, in the sense of scientific reason, is only one mode of human comportment in the world among the many moods and states of mind that characterize *Dasein*.[175] Thus, if instrumentalist theory and reason served to reify the dynamic of historical life, the method of *Verstehen* was hardly better. "*Verstehen* too," Heidegger claimed, "always has its mood" and cannot be genuinely understood as an operation of consciousness; it is much more "*Dasein*'s projection of its being upon possibilities," or, more fundamentally, a form of interpretation.[176]

Historicism had set up the classic aporia for the metaphysical tradition—it attempted to "understand" the unique, unrepeatable experience of historical life within the frame of a "science" of history. But Heidegger doubted whether one could provide Cartesian certitude for the dynamic and fluid processes of understanding and interpretation. The historicist project, he believed, was misconceived from its foundations, ensnared as it was in the contradictory goals of find-

---

[175] Heidegger, *Being and Time*, 55–59, 249; *Sein und Zeit*, 32–34, 205.
[176] Heidegger, *Being and Time*, 182, 188; *Sein und Zeit*, 143, 148.

ing an objective science for subjective life experience. For Heidegger, understanding is not a method or a theory but the original mode of being for human beings, the very basis of historicity and historical meaning. Rankeans sought meaning "in" the past itself as an objective process, purposeful and with direction; Rickert located it, conversely, in the transcendental operations of consciousness which related specific meanings to logical meaning itself. Attempting to overcome the spurious polarities of both these positions, Dilthey focused his attention on the historical and hermeneutical aspects of human meaning rather than on any objective or ideal characteristics. But Heidegger sought to uncover the ontological character of human meaning as a form of temporal projection, which lay not in beings themselves but in the way beings are taken up and appropriated by human beings. In this sense, the genuine character of history was not its unique, unrepeatable singularity but its ability to be repeated or retrieved (*wieder-holt*) for future possibilities of *Dasein*.

In Heidegger's interpretation, historical inquiry becomes something other than a movement backward in time; it discloses the possibilities of what *Dasein* can be futurally on the basis of what has already been. As he explained in *Being and Time*:

> If historical science, which arises from authentic historicity, reveals through retrieval the *Dasein* that has-been-there in its possibility, then it has already made manifest the universal in the singular. The question of whether historical science has as its object merely the succession of singular and "individual" events or "laws" is mistaken at its root. The theme of historical science is neither a singular happening nor something universal floating above but the factically existent possibility that has been. This possibility is not retrieved as such (that is, understood in an authentically historical sense) if it gets perverted by the pallor of a supratemporal model. Only factically authentic historicity can disclose past history as a resolute fate that, through retrieval, strikes home the force of what is possible in factical existence—that is, in its futurity that comes toward [*zu-kommt*] existence. Historical science, then . . . does not take its departure from the present . . . but discloses itself temporally in terms of the future.[177]

Heidegger's peculiar language, with its neologistic phrases, word-play, and endless etymologizing, sometimes strikes the modern

[177] Heidegger, *Sein und Zeit*, 395. The translation that I have provided here is fundamentally different from the Macquarrie and Robinson version; cf. *Being and Time*, 446–447.

reader as turgid and overwrought. Admittedly, the semantic and grammatical complexities of Heidegger's style—especially the scholastic idiom of *Being and Time*—only add to charges that phenomenological ontology is a science of arcana. In his own mind, Heidegger envisioned this new discourse as a way of breaking out of the language and style of traditional metaphysics with its grammar of being, logic of argument, subject-predicate relations, and philological taxonomies. The placement of the question of history in *Being and Time* must be understood within this general assault on the language of traditional metaphysics. If Yorck could still speak of the difference between the ontical and historical, accusing historians and philosophers of often conflating the two, Heidegger found it necessary to radicalize Yorck's language and mode of questioning by seeking "a more primordial unity" at the root of objective, ontic nature and subjective, historical spirit. This new ontological understanding of history had to focus on the historicity of human being as well as on the scientific foundations of historiography. Ultimately, however, any interpretation of *Dasein*, or of science, had to be reconceived in terms of the history of thought and its grammatical-linguistic structures.

If Heidegger worked toward a "destruction/de-structuring of the history of ontology," this was not his only intention; he also proposed a *Destruktion* of metaphysical language which would reveal "the primordial sources" of historical being. By choosing the romantic trope of "source," or *Quelle*, as his theme, Heidegger played on its double meaning as both metaphysical origin and as documentary material for scientific research. Phenomenology's task was to offer a new kind of research, or *Forschung*, which would re-search, in the sense of searching after or retrieving, that which was hidden in and by metaphysics: "As research work, phenomenology is precisely the work of laying open and letting be seen, understood as the methodologically directed dismantling (*Abbau*) of concealments."[178] What would be re-searched, however, were not facts, in Ranke's sense, but phenomena; that is, temporal happenings of human beings, which are not the same as mere occurrences in physics. Heidegger recognized that direct access to our historicity was blocked by the very research practices of the human sciences which took history as their theme. To thematize historicity in a genuine way demanded that one first dismantle the history of historical research in order to get to the roots of

<hr/>

[178] Heidegger, *History of the Concept of Time*, 86; *GA* 20: 118.

historical scholarship in temporal-ecstatic experience. Fundamentally, Heidegger's critique of historicism was essentially a working out of this process in the form of a dismantling and retrieval.

Dilthey and Yorck had provided Heidegger with a set of questions about the science of history. They had shown how both the Neo-Kantians and historicists, by focusing on methodological issues, had succeeded only in alienating history from its life-origins. Dilthey especially had revealed that the problem of history could not be explained through a direct analysis of historical happenings but only through a hermeneutic reflection back onto the foundations of life. Heidegger transformed Dilthey's insights, however, shedding their anthropological assumptions and methodological focus and laying bare the ontological structures of *Dasein*. In seizing on Yorck's critical distinction between the ontical and historical, he managed to de-structure the epistemological implications of Dilthey's work and retrieve the notion of historicity in its genuinely hermeneutic sense, as an interpretation of factical-historical existence rather than as a method of research. But he also broke with the long-standing historicist notion, which even Dilthey shared, that historical meaning is the product of an objective, world-historical pattern of development, "telling the sequence of events like the beads of a rosary."[179] The meaning of history, for Heidegger, was always connected to the question of being itself, understood as a disclosure of time. But historical being could never be revealed in the abstract world-historical time of Rankean *Weltgeschichte*; it could be disclosed only through the temporality of *Dasein*. All the careful historicist distinctions between nature and history or explanation and understanding were based on an interpretation of time in only one of its modes: the standing presence of the present. But Heidegger grasped time as temporality, as a mode of finite projection unified in the three ecstases of existence (future), facticity (past), and fallenness (present). Despite their penetrating insights, both Dilthey and Yorck had failed to grasp the essential temporality of human being as the key to the aporias of historicism. It was, above all, Nietzsche who helped to direct Heidegger on a path of questioning which opened up the genuine meaning of history not as a science of research but as a crisis for existence: a decision about the "use and abuse of history for life."

[179] I borrow this metaphor from the essay by Walter Benjamin, "Theses on the Philosophy of History," in *Illuminations* (New York: Schocken, 1969), 263.

x. Historicity, Crisis, and Decision: Heidegger's Retrieval of
   Nietzsche

By the time Heidegger published *Being and Time* in 1927, the German academic scene had become inundated by both a literature and a rhetoric of "crisis." Part of my effort has been to situate Heidegger's work within this narrative, with an eye toward understanding the Weimar crisis of historicism as part of a generational leitmotif. What makes Heidegger's writings so important in this context is their attempt to de-construct the idea of crisis itself, transforming the narrow scholarly debate about historicism into a philosophical confrontation with the entire Western tradition. Heidegger understood this confrontation, in its most fundamental sense, as an *Aus-einander-setzung*, or "setting asunder," and heard in the term an underlying relation to the original Greek word *krisis*.[180] In this sense the crisis of historicism signified for Heidegger a confrontation with the history of Western metaphysics, marked as it was by the fundamental aporia of temporal movement (the rosary bead sequentiality of progress) and ontological stasis (the metaphysics of presence). The superficial language that predominated at the universities, however, was inadequate to the task of presenting the generational crisis as a genuine *Auseinandersetzung*; as Heidegger caustically wrote in one of his early lectures: "*Today*: the position of the sciences and the university has become something ever more questionable. What happens? Nothing. One writes brochures about the crisis of the sciences and science as a vocation. One person says to another: 'one says, as one hears, science is done for.' Today there's even a special literature dealing with the question as, of course, must be. Otherwise, nothing happens."[181]

In this same lecture, Heidegger conjoined the superficiality of "today" with "the cultural consciousness [*Bildungsbewußtsein*] of the age and the palaver of the average, public mind; today: modern 'intellectuality.'" So as to leave no doubt in the minds of his listeners about the targets of his attack, Heidegger specifically referred to the superficiality of "historical consciousness" and "philosophical consciousness" as prominent examples of this contemporary malaise. In a significant way, Heidegger understood crisis in an almost medical sense as an index to the health of a culture, a generation, a tradition. At the

---

[180] Pfeifer, *Etymologisches Wörterbuch des Deutschen*, 2:934 and 3:1623–1624.
[181] Heidegger, *GA* 63:32–33.

beginning of *Being and Time* he wrote: "The level which a science has reached is determined by how far it is *capable* of a crisis in its fundamental concepts. In such immanent crises of science the relationship of positive, investigative questioning to the topics [*Sachen*] questioned itself starts to totter."[182] In Heidegger's reading, crisis opens up the question of questioning itself either as something genuine (that is, as a question concerning the meaning of being) or as something superficial ("modern intellectuality," "the university," the world of average, public curiosity). It confronts us with the possibility of a decision: whether to accept the deadening stasis of theory or to stand against it by returning to the factical-historical praxis of life. Heidegger's whole confrontation with the historicist tradition brings this matter to question by asking to what extent history and the human sciences are capable of withstanding a crisis in their fundamental concepts. Consequently, when Heidegger spoke of "the emergence of a problem of 'historicism'" as the symptom of *Dasein*'s inauthentic relationship to history, he meant to present it as a decision regarding an "authentic" or "inauthentic" way of being.[183]

Inauthentically, *Dasein* understands the past as something temporally distant, a fact "there" for research or merely to be forgotten within the horizon of "today," but always as something present. Authentic *Dasein*, on the other hand, grasps history as temporality, "as the moment of vision [*Augenblick*] of anticipatory resolution."[184] Heidegger was careful to point out, however, that a decision between authentic or inauthentic existence could never be settled permanently; genuine decision making was something tied to the temporal movement of *Dasein* itself, a movement stretched out between possibility and retrieval. Rankean historicism renounced this moment of decision and disputed its meaning for history. Instead, it defined the true character of historical science in terms of an epistemological imperative to suspend one's own judgment, thus indulging its objectivist tendencies toward self-extinguishment. In a fundamental way, historicism had denied the importance of temporal happening for understanding history by clinging to the stasis of "temporal distance" and the ocularism of Rankean fact-collecting.

But as Heidegger ventured to work through the problems of historicism, he found few indications of an original approach to historical

---

[182] Heidegger, *Being and Time*, 29 (translation modified); *Sein und Zeit*, 9.
[183] Heidegger, *Being and Time*, 448; *Sein und Zeit*, 396.
[184] Heidegger, *Being and Time*, 443–444; *Sein und Zeit*, 391.

Forschung among his predecessors. In his view, the only figure in the tradition to understand clearly the primacy of time for historical thinking was Nietzsche, who "recognized what was essential concerning 'the Use and Abuse of History for Life' in the second of his *Untimely Meditations* (1874) and said it unequivocally and with force." Where Nietzsche spoke of "monumental," "antiquarian," and "critical" forms of history, Heidegger tried to think beyond the historiographical implications of these categories to "the necessity of this triad and the ground of its unity . . . in the historicity of *Dasein*." Although Nietzsche never explicitly articulated the meaning of this unity, Heidegger claimed, he "understood more than he set forth in his publication." That is, he perceived the essential meaning of history to be an experience circumscribed by the horizons of temporality, an experience that could not be measured by the practices of a scholarly discipline or the glories of a world-historical pageant. Nietzsche warranted that "when it is authentically historical, monumental-antiquarian history is, necessarily, a critique of the 'present'" and is grounded in the unity of three modes of time: past-present-future.[185] But Nietzsche also recognized that each mode of history could constitute either a use or abuse of life; in any case, one could never understand them as innocent or neutral practices of research. What determines the outcome of one's relation to history, Nietzsche claimed, is a fundamental decision regarding the meaning of the past within the horizon of one's own life. In this sense, the past is like a Greek oracle, standing before us as a riddle in need of interpretation, offering neither certitude nor objectivity but only the possibility of an open future. Consequently, Nietzsche's hermeneutics of the oracular demanded not so much knowledge of the past as knowledge of oneself and of the unity of one's own temporal horizons.

To overcome the sterility of Rankean self-extinguishment, Nietzsche conceived his second *Untimely Meditation* as an attack on "the modern privilege of theoretical man," turning instead to the ancient Greeks before Socrates for a healthy example of the *bios theoretikos*. The entire essay is framed as a confrontation with the tradition, struggling to find historical sources for a critique of history, turning theory against itself and laying bare the artifice and pretense of modern academic life. At the same time, it provided a diagnosis of nineteenth-century German culture, which Nietzsche saw as part of an overall crisis in

---

[185] Heidegger, *Being and Time*, 448 (translation modified); *Sein und Zeit*, 396.

Western thought. In abandoning the neutered objectivity of theoretical life, Nietzsche demanded that we make a decision about the meaning of history for our own existence, a topic that Heidegger took up again, in a reconstituted form, in *Being and Time*.

What Heidegger drew from Nietzsche was a way of grasping the fundamental aporias of the historicist tradition, aporias that derived not from the research practices of historians but from the history of Western metaphysics. For Nietzsche, this history was characterized by a fundamental confrontation between the healthy corporeality of the Greeks and the pathogenic asceticism of Christianity. In Nietzsche's genealogy of Western values, the modern era of science culminated in a nihilistic movement of culture—"the history of an error."[186] But the narrative of this history always ended, for Nietzsche, in a decision regarding the meaning of the narrative for life. Later, in his lectures in the 1930s on Nietzsche, Heidegger explicitly formulated this Nietzschean narrative as a decision between beings and being in the history of the West and interpreted this history as nihilism: "The highest decision that can be made and that becomes the ground of all history is that between the predominance of beings and the rule of being. Whenever and however beings as a whole are thought expressly, thinking stands within the dangerous zone of this decision . . . Nietzsche is an essential thinker because he thinks ahead in a decisive sense, not evading the decision."[187] Heidegger then proceeded to identify Nietzsche as "the *last metaphysician* of the West" and connected his thought to the history of Western metaphysics, a history whose inner movement is nihilistic, for "nihilism *is* history" and "nihilism determines the historicity of Western history." As Heidegger explained: "The age whose consummation unfolds in his thought, the modern age, is a final age. This means an age in which at some point and in some way the historical decision arises as to whether this final age is the conclusion of Western history or the counterpart to another beginning. To go the length of Nietzsche's path of thought to the will to power means to catch sight of this historical decision."[188]

In his Nietzsche lectures, Heidegger presented the meaning of this "final age" as a crisis for Western thinking, a crisis that would gen-

[186] Friedrich Nietzsche, *The Twilight of the Idols*, trans. R. J. Hollingdale (New York: Penguin, 1968).

[187] Martin Heidegger, *Nietzsche*, trans. David F. Krell, 4 vols. (New York: Harper and Row, 1979–1987), 3: 5–8; German edition: *Nietzsche*, 2 vols. (Pfullingen: Neske, 1961), I: 476–480.

[188] Heidegger, *Nietzsche*, 3: 8; *Nietzsche*, I: 480.

erate a confrontation between Greek and Christian thought, culminating in a decision. But whereas Nietzsche defined this crisis as a struggle over values and power, Heidegger interpreted it as a confrontation between "the predominance of beings and the rule of being." Throughout these lectures the name "Nietzsche" came to signify for Heidegger a reading of history *as* crisis: as a struggle within the history of metaphysics for a controlling definition of being as pure presence within the temporal mode of the present. But the emergence of a crisis-consciousness in these lectures should not be understood solely in terms of the European political situation after 1933 or Heidegger's affiliation with National Socialism. Even during the early twenties Heidegger developed an elaborate interpretation of crisis as an epochal *Auseinandersetzung*. Within this context, the "crisis" of historicism became important because it offered Heidegger a real opportunity both to question the appearance of a contemporary crisis and to de-structure the underlying metaphysical assumptions that defined its fundamental meaning.

What Heidegger retrieved from Nietzsche, especially the early Nietzsche, was an understanding of historical time as horizonal. As Nietzsche wrote, "This is a universal law: every living being can be healthy, strong and productive only within a horizon; if it is unable to draw a horizon around itself . . . it will feebly waste away or hasten to a timely decline."[189] The horizon offers a limit or threshold within which to situate one's own being, a boundary against which possibilities and resolutions can be projected, measured, and ultimately decided. What made Nietzsche's reading of horizonality unique, however, was that he moved beyond the traditional understanding of horizon as the static frame of the present and tried to express the unity of all three temporal modes in the dynamic possibilities of openness and interpretation. Heidegger pursued the hermeneutic implications of this reading for his own project, especially as it related to the problem of time. He found in Nietzsche's understanding of horizon an indication for a new beginning in thinking, a beginning marked by the openness of temporality against the closure of an eternal "now." The Nietzschean idea of horizon connoted for Heidegger a phenomenological opening or place within which beings show themselves. Horizon becomes, in this phenomenological sense, a place of

---

[189] Friedrich Nietzsche, *Untimely Meditations*, trans. R. J. Hollingdale (Cambridge: Cambridge University Press, 1983), 63; *Unzeitgemässe Betrachtungen* (Leipzig: Kröner, 1930), 105.

disclosure—"the open expanse"—rather than a limit, boundary, or container.[190] Within this structure, time is grasped as the unity of horizons that mark the very being of *Dasein*. As Heidegger explained in the Kassel lectures: "*Dasein* is nothing other than the being of time [*Zeit-Sein*]. Time is nothing that one meets with in the world outside but is what I myself am. . . . Time determines the totality of *Dasein*. Not only in a temporally particular moment is *Dasein* there, but it is itself only as a being stretched along between its possibilities and its past." And Heidegger always understood these possibilities to be horizonal.[191]

Any genuine approach to history, especially the history of philosophy, had to take into account this horizonal structure of the past which was not merely a *factum brutum* standing there against the researcher but an authentic possibility for future existence. Nietzsche's un-timely essay revealed the significance of time for the understanding of history; Heidegger transformed this insight into a judgment about the meaning of the Western tradition itself. In a sense, Heidegger's judgment was really a decision about whether to follow Nietzsche or Dilthey for a genuine understanding of human historicity.[192] Were beings to be located within the field of scientific research and described in terms of a scientific practice of history? Were they to be thought of as permanently "there," present for consciousness, enclosed, self-evident, or certain? Or were they, to speak in terms of Greek *aletheia*, to offer a place for disclosure and the openness of historical appropriation? Ultimately, as Heidegger moved away from the "crisis of the sciences" in *Being and Time* to the topic of a "turning" (*Kehre*) in/to "the event of being" (*Ereignis*) the decision became clearer and unmistakable. One need only read his extensive lecture notes on Nietzsche, where neither the name nor the topic of Dilthey appears, to get a sense of the turning in Heidegger's conception of history.

[190] Heidegger discussed the problem of the "ecstatical horizon" in *Sein und Zeit*, 365 (*Being and Time*, 416) and in *GA* 24: 378 (*Basic Problems of Phenomenology*, 267).
[191] Heidegger, "KV," 22.
[192] Of course, the meaning of Heidegger's decision changed during the 1930s. In the period before 1927, Dilthey played a significant role in the crisis of historical thinking, a crisis that Heidegger carefully addressed in *Sein und Zeit*. But as Heidegger's understanding of crisis changed, he began to conceive of history more broadly as a history of ontology or, rather, of different ways of approaching ontology. Ultimately, Heidegger began to see the limitations in Dilthey's overly scientific and methodological approach to lived experience. He then began to see Nietzsche as the genuine prophet of crisis, someone who understood the need for "another beginning" in Western thought. Heidegger's relation to Nietzsche can hardly be appreciated outside of this context.

xi. The Danger of Thinking in a "Time of Need"

Heidegger's encounter with the "problem" of historicism had important consequences for his own reading of the history of the West, even if during the 1930s they sometimes appeared ominous and fraught with danger. Like most of the other mandarins of his generation, Heidegger's experience of the Great War was profound and genuinely decisive. Although he did serve as a weatherman in the Ardennes, Heidegger never really saw action at the front, despite his valorization of the *Fronterlebnis* and his later claims to having endured "combat in the trenches in Verdun."[193] And yet the war exercised an immediate and powerful influence on his thought. Around late 1917, after his break with Catholicism and before the war emergency semester of 1919, he took up a new topic: finding an originary language for the phenomenological disclosure of "worlding" (*es weltet*), an early indication for the question of the meaning of being. But his question was never posed in an intellectual vacuum—it was always framed by the crisis-mentality of a specific historical situation: a Germany confronted by economic chaos, political turmoil, class warfare, and the devastation of the prewar vision of order and stability.

Like Nietzsche's *Untimely Meditations*, written just after the Franco-Prussian War, Heidegger's work of the early twenties is marked by a distinctive postwar consciousness. Each thinker, in his own way, found the feverish public response to victory or defeat to be an indication of the ills plaguing German public consciousness. Whereas Nietzsche began his assault on the literary blandishments of David Friedrich Strauss, Heidegger remonstrated against the fashionable *Kulturpessimismus* of Spengler. Both captured perfectly in their work the mood of the day: the chauvinistic bombast of Bismarck's newly configured *Reich* and the crisis-mentality of troubled Weimar. In the wake of catastrophe, Heidegger initiated a radical critique of the present, one grounded in a consciousness of history. In a letter to Karl Löwith from 1923, Heidegger spoke of "a radical dismantling [*Abbau*] and disintegration, a *Destruktion*" of the old Europe which, in the face of the idle chatter and bustle of clever and enterprising men of learning, demanded a concentration on "the one thing that matters": a decision concerning "the existential limit of one's ownmost historical facticity." Heidegger's path of inquiry was, however, free of the

---

[193] Sheehan, "Heidegger's *Lehrjahre*," 21; Ott, *Martin Heidegger*, 104.

old choices of the *Weltanschauung* variety: "whether from this destruction a new culture will emerge or there will be an acceleration of decline."[194] Instead, Heidegger chose to grasp this crisis of destruction not as decline (*Untergang*) but as a time of transition (*Übergang*). Later, in his lectures of Winter Semester 1937–1938, Heidegger spoke of both Nietzsche and Hölderlin as thinkers of the end and as thinkers of transition, because they proclaimed "the end of the first beginning of the history of Western philosophy."[195] In this time of transition, which Heidegger understood as a "turning," he accentuated the significance of both end and beginning: "we stand before the *decision between the end* (which may perhaps run on for centuries yet) *and the other beginning* which can only be a moment of vision whose preparation will require a certain patience which the 'optimists' just as little as the 'pessimists' will hardly measure up to."[196]

The crisis of the postwar generation offered to Heidegger a new topic for his thought: the task of rethinking history not as a process of sequential development or historicoscientific observation (*historischer Betrachtung*) but as a meditation on the temporal-historical happening that we ourselves are (*geschichtlicher Besinnung*).[197] If he understood this crisis, in a phenomenological sense, as a *Krisis*, or "turning" (in the sense of a *Kehre* to another beginning), he did so on the basis of a new reading of temporality, one that rejected the linear, diachronic consciousness of Ranke for the horizonal temporality of Nietzsche. In terms reminiscent of the second *Untimely Meditation*, Heidegger explained that "the historical does not refer to a kind of comprehension or investigation but to temporal happening [*Geschehen*] itself. The historical is not the past, also not the present, but the future–that which is to come is the origin of history."[198] As he began to consider the generational crisis of postwar science and culture, Heidegger came to understand history (*Geschichte*), in a new sense as something many-layered (*vielschichtig*) and fateful (*geschicklich*), not as a historicist collection of facts hermetically enclosed in the museum of the past.

If the crisis of historicism were to have any essential meaning for an understanding of history, Heidegger believed, then Weimar historians would have to abandon their superficial rhetoric of "pessim-

---

[194] Löwith, *Mein Leben*, 28, 31.
[195] Martin Heidegger, *Grundfragen der Philosophie: Ausgewählte "Probleme" der "Logik," Gesamtausgabe* 45 (Frankfurt: Klostermann, 1984), 133–134.
[196] Ibid., 124.
[197] Ibid., 40.
[198] Ibid.

ism," "catastrophe," and "decline" for a language of disclosure and revelation. Initially, Heidegger found the model for such language in Paul's epistles, Luther's sermons, the phenomenological interpretations of Aristotle, and the ethical ironies of Kierkegaard. As he began to formulate his own vision of history in *Being and Time*, however, a new language emerged. Now Heidegger referred to crisis itself as a form of destruction which would initiate a return to the sources of history in the history of ontology. This new form of destruction revealed the radical aporia at the heart of the historicist debate: the fundamental incompatibility of the Greek idea of being and the Christian experience of time. By interpreting crisis in both ontological and historicotemporal terms and dismantling the traditional *Fragestellung* of his contemporaries, Heidegger transformed both the style and the meaning of the historicist debate. In this sense we can speak of *Being and Time* as a work that offers a solution to the crisis of historicism by way of a radical dissolution of those metaphysical categories that first made historicism possible.

As Heidegger moved toward a fuller encounter with Nietzsche (and Hölderlin) in the 1930s, the implications of these earlier ideas became more explicit. Especially in the *Beiträge*, his pivotal work, Heidegger interpreted crisis not as a momentary historical event in Weimar but as "the event of being" which reveals itself as the possibility of a turning in Western history from the end of metaphysics to a new beginning for thought. In a peculiar kind of archaeology, Heidegger sought to destroy or de-construct the edifice of Western philosophy down to its structural roots in Greek *arche*. But in Heidegger's scheme of destruction, the beginning (*arche*) lies in the end (*eschaton*), and the end, in the beginning. Both moments are gathered together in a confrontation with the history of being, a history implicated in a decision about the meaning of history itself. In the *Beiträge*, Heidegger played with the different meanings of history as both *Historie* and *Geschichte* and framed his understanding of decision in and against these double meanings. Extending his critique of historicism in *Being and Time*, Heidegger argued that "the essence of *Historie* is grounded in the subject-object relation; it is objective because it is subjective and insofar as it is the one, it must be the other. Consequently, any 'opposition' between 'subjective' and 'objective' *Historie* has no meaning. All *Historie* ends in anthropological-psychological biographism."[199] Heidegger interpreted *Geschichte*, on the other hand, as the history of

[199] Martin Heidegger, *Beiträge zur Philosophie*, *Gesamtausgabe* 65 (Frankfurt: Klostermann, 1989), 494.

be-ing (*die Geschichte des Seyns*), where being is another name for *Ereignis*.[200]

Heidegger intended that this re-inscription of history as the history of be-ing would retrieve the authentic ontological sense of history as a crisis of the futural—a decision about what is to come. If the *Historie* of Ranke and Droysen offered objective truth at a temporal distance, Heidegger's own interpretation of *Geschichte* offered an either/or choice about the meaning of the entire Western tradition judged by one thought alone: the event of being. The traditional historicist understanding of history as "crisis" could now be thought of as a *Kehre* in the history of being, as a "turning" in and to the metaphysical epoch of technological nihilism. Like Nietzsche before him, Heidegger introduced the topic of history for the purpose of rethinking the basic meaning of Western thought, calling into question its preference for theoretical metaphysics by confronting a practical decision: whether it was genuinely possible "to think in primordial reflection toward an overcoming of the metaphysics of the will to power—that is to say, to begin a confrontation with Western thought by returning to its beginning."[201] Again in the *Beiträge*, Heidegger spoke of the *Kehre* as a "decision concerning a decision" and of the "need" or "necessity" (*Not*) of future philosophy to allow its possibilities to be open. But in the same breath he cautioned against an anthropocentric understanding of "decision" which would focus solely on the process of subjective reflection (*Reflexion*) and would miss the deeper sense of the turning. As Heidegger put it, the essence of this decision, which can be characterized as the either/or of being/not-being, is "the opening up of a cleft in be-ing itself, grasped within the history of being, and not as a moral-anthropological decision."[202] With this turn away from anthropocentrism, the dissolution of historicism begins, both in the sense of its dominance as a prevailing *Weltanschauung* and as a tenable category for articulating the "crisis" of modernity.

---

[200] *Ereignis* is a fundamental term in the lexicon of the later Heidegger. A notoriously difficult word to translate, it is often rendered into English as "occurrence," "event," "event of being," "appropriation," or even as "en-owning." Heidegger himself admitted that "it can no more be translated than the Greek word *logos* or the Chinese word *Tao*." *Identität und Differenz* (Pfullingen: Neske, 1957), 25; *Identity and Difference*, trans. Joan Stambaugh (New York: Harper and Row, 1969), 36.

[201] Martin Heidegger, "The Rectorate, 1933–34: Facts and Thoughts," trans. Karsten Harries, *Review of Metaphysics* 38 (March 1985): 485 (translation altered); and *Die Selbstbehauptung der deutschen Universität: Das Rektorat, 1933/34* (Frankfurt: Klostermann, 1983), 25. Although Heidegger employs the term *Überwindung*, or "overcoming," here, one might also think in terms of the later Heidegger's preference for the term *Verwindung*, or "recovery." See Gianni Vattimo, *The Transparent Society* (Baltimore: Johns Hopkins University Press, 1992).

[202] Heidegger, *GA* 65: 103.

Heidegger's work of dissolution and destruction did not, however, end with his critique of historical temporality and historicity in *Being and Time*. Over the next decade he repeated his efforts to transform the occlusions (*aporias*) of historicism into the openness (*euporia*) and unconcealment of *Seinsgeschichte*. Although the focus of his lectures changed as he engaged the work of Hölderlin, Nietzsche, and Schelling, his fundamental themes remained the same. Thus, despite the appearance of a break with his work of the twenties, Heidegger's student Hans-Georg Gadamer maintains that "Heidegger's *Kehre* is an attempt and a series of attempts to elude the problems of historicism."[203] As Heidegger radicalized these "attempts" to elude historicism—by abandoning moral-anthropological decision making for the "saving power" of Hölderlin's poetic word—he also exposed the limits of his own thinking. As we examine his turn to political questions in the thirties, we need to weigh the consequences of his "destruction" of historicism and reflect on its dangers. Did Heidegger's narrative of a "turning in the history of being" provide a more terrible form of destruction than the academic mandarinate of Weimar could comprehend? If the objectivism of Ranke's priests of research (those whom Nietzsche called "the eunuchs in the harem of history") led to a peculiar kind of impotence—an inability to *decide* politically—then what are we to make of Heidegger's own political decision making after 1933? Certainly, the mythopoeic vision of a Germanic *Volk*, the nature mysticism of a Hölderlinian brotherhood, and the irremediable *Heimweh* ("homesickness") for the stillness of Todtnauberg offered Heidegger an "other" path away from the technological nihilism of the atomic age. And yet where did the path lead? Of what did the "danger" consist? The act of destroying the old Europe and its cultural museum of the past had far-reaching consequences. Heidegger always understood this. Even a cursory look at the language of the *Rektoratsrede*, with its paramilitary rhetoric of *Kampf* (struggle) and *Wehrdienst* (armed service), cannot fail to uncover the ominous possibilities of a too forceful destruction of the Western tradition, "when the spiritual strength of the West fails and the joints of the world no longer hold, when this moribund semblance of a culture caves in and drags all that remains strong into confusion and lets it suffocate in madness."[204]

[203] Hans-Georg Gadamer, letter to the author, February 26, 1990.
[204] Martin Heidegger, "The Self-Assertion of the German University," trans. Karsten Harries, *Review of Metaphysics* 38 (March 1985): 479–480; *Die Selbstbehauptung der deutschen Universität*, 19.

Obviously, Heidegger's complicity in the world-historical drive of National Socialism was not an incidental sideline but was fundamentally related to his own understanding of the particular historical situation in Weimar as one of "crisis." Within this crisis-narrative, Heidegger conceived of the destruction of historicism as part of a larger narrative of Western history guided by a movement of nihilism which was unrelenting in its dominion over the world of beings. His attraction to National Socialism was clear: it provided the hope of a new beginning in a planetary-political sense. More concretely, it initiated a movement within the university itself which abandoned both the tepid liberalism of the *Vernunftrepublikaner* and the sterile connoisseurship of the scholar-collector for a more active, dynamic involvement in shaping the "essence" of the university. In this sense, it provided an urgent critique of the spiritual mission of the university, in much the same way as had Heidegger's earlier lectures on Paul's epistle to the Thessalonians. As absurd as it might sound, both early Christianity and National Socialism furnished Heidegger, albeit in different ways, with concrete possibilities for rethinking the past in terms of the future and for overturning the complacent scientism of university education so that professors and students alike might get to the roots of factical life "in the here and now . . . in this place, in this lecture hall," as he declared in 1922.[205]

Ultimately, Heidegger's work of the twenties and thirties can be characterized as bold and ambitious. In uncompromising terms it set forth a powerful reading of modernity as an age of transition shaped by the idea of crisis. In the fragmentation, dissolution, and exhaustion of the modern world, Heidegger saw not the failure of various world views but a fundamental epochal shift: an age of *Übergang* rather than *Untergang*. But even in his attempt to understand this transition as a "turning," Heidegger became preoccupied, like many others of his generation, with thoughts of an end—of apocalyptic, millenarian, and eschatological yearnings that often obscured economic, social, and political problems that plagued the post-Versailles world. Heidegger tried, of course, to envision a path of transition away from this end, what in 1946 he called "the eschatology of being," by going back to the "first beginning" of Greek thought, the *arche* or ruling origin of Western history.[206] But in returning to the philosophical/poetic origin

---

[205] Heidegger, *GA* 61: 63.
[206] Heidegger, *Early Greek Thinking*, 18; *Holzwege*, 302.

Heidegger's *Destruktion* of Historicism   261

—whether as Heraclitean *logos* or as Hölderlinian *Heimkehr*—there is a danger that one might forget the origin of philosophy and poetry in the world of the polis.

Heidegger often spoke in tragic terms about the history of the West, finding ancient analogues to the modern situation in the plights of Oedipus and Antigone. In *An Introduction to Metaphysics* (1935), he spoke about Europe's imminent ruin and intimated that:

> The spiritual decline of the earth is so far advanced that nations [*Völker*] are threatened with losing the last spiritual power which makes it possible (taken in relation to the destiny of "being") to see the decline and to appraise it as such. This simple observation has nothing to do with *Kultur-pessimismus* nor with any sort of optimism. The darkening of the world, the flight of the gods, the destruction of the earth, the transformation of human beings into "mass man," the hatred and suspicion of everything free and creative, have assumed such proportions throughout the earth that such childish categories as pessimism and optimism have long since become ludicrous.[207]

Later in these lectures Heidegger spoke of Oedipus's blindness and the conflicts of Antigone, themes that became for him encrypted messages about the blindness of the philosopher and the nihilistic conflicts within technological will to power. In his discussion of *Antigone*, for example, Heidegger translated the entire text of Sophocles' first choral ode concerning the loss of home and the condition of the uncanny (*das Unheimliche*; in Greek, *to deinon*). The term *uncanny*—that which casts us out of the home (*Heim*)—became for Heidegger a symbol of the extreme limits of the human being, indicating both its wonderful powers at controlling the elemental forces of nature *and* pointing to its violent, destructive, and "strange" (*unheimlich*) capacity for overpowering all limits. Heidegger believed that Sophocles' description of the human being as "the uncanniest"—a creature both "wonderful" and "terrible" (*to deinon*)—pointed to an awareness about the conflicting forces at the source of human experience. For Heidegger, however, these conflicts expressed an underlying unity within being itself, a unity that he understood, paradoxically, as a fundamental abyss. Most human beings, Heidegger claimed, retreated from this insight concerning the wonderful/terrible source(s) of experience into the safe, secure familiarity of the everyday world. But there were

---

[207] Martin Heidegger, *An Introduction to Metaphysics*, trans. Ralph Manheim (Garden City, N.Y.: Anchor, 1961), 31; *Einleitung in die Metaphysik* (Tübingen: Niemeyer, 1953), 24.

others who experienced this abyss in a creative way, seeing its wonder and terror as the source of *historical* existence itself which helped to lay the foundation of the polis. Rejecting the conventional translation of *polis* as "city" or "city-state," Heidegger maintained that "polis means the place, the there [*Da*] *in* which, *out of* which, and *for* which history happens." Within the polis there are preeminent (*hypsipolis*) creators and rulers who experience the polis both as the *ground* of history and as the *abyss* that leaves one city-less (*apolis*). Heidegger explained, however, that even as these citizens become preeminent in the polis, "In this place where history happens, they become at the same time *apolis*, without city and place, alone, uncanny and without a home, without issue in the midst of being as a whole, at the same time without statute and limit, without structure and order because *as* creators they must first ground this all."[208]

These creators, such as Oedipus, Antigone, and Heraclitus (and Heidegger himself), experience the tension between being *apolis* and *hypsipolis* as the very source of their questioning. Their thoughts focus on beginnings and on the strange power of language, which sometimes appears foreign and incomprehensible to the other members of the polis. In his Heraclitus lectures, Heidegger explained that such figures often seem apolitical because they do not busy themselves with questions of immediate public concern.[209] Yet, he claimed, these solitary founders penetrate beneath the surface of political activity to the ground of the polis itself as the site of human existence. Thus, despite the public appearance of forsaking the political world, in their strange attunement to the question of being, they engender the most authentic and original political act. Out of the crisis of the Greek polis, these thinkers unleash the poetic word of being and the revelatory power of the logos.

Heidegger understood that the crisis of the polis, like the poetic texts of Sophocles, the oracular sayings of Heraclitus, and the brilliantly luminous temples and statues hewn from the rocks of the deathless Attic earth, might disclose the truth of the ancient world in a new sense. And yet even as he valorized the polis as the *topos*, or "site," of the revelation of being—the place, the there [*Da*], wherein and as which *Da-sein* is historical—he, too, was struck by the same unyielding tension between the preeminence of the hypsipolis (the

[208] Heidegger, *Introduction to Metaphysics*, 128 (translation modified); *Einleitung in die Metaphysik*, 117.
[209] Martin Heidegger, *Heraklit*, *Gesamtausgabe* 55 (Frankfurt: Klostermann, 1979), 11–13.

rector, the thinker, the world-renowned author of *Being and Time*) and the homelessness of the apolis.[210] In his turn in the thirties to a Hölderlinian folk religion of nature, Heidegger completed the Sophoclean cycle of tragic blindness and evasion: caught in the irony of seeing deeply into the mysteries of the word of being and yet not being able to see the very political consequences of his own thinking. The greater irony here is that Heidegger, the preeminent prophet of crisis, should have missed the truly foundational crisis of our times, an event, or *Ereignis*, that revealed the nihilism of the death of God in all too murderous images and yet withdrew into the silence of the unspoken. Though open to the possibilities of history and to "the cleft in being," Heidegger failed to comprehend the horrible consequences of his own hypsipolis/apolis evasions. Blinded by his own Oedipal filiation to "the one thing that mattered"—the question of being—Heidegger failed to see the "event" of Auschwitz. In his perceptive work *Heidegger, Art and Politics*, Philippe Lacoue-Labarthe writes about the conjoining of *Ereignis* and Auschwitz in Heidegger: "All I can say is that Auschwitz belongs to a sphere beyond tragedy, at once more and less than tragedy: more, because the infinite separation is absolutely hyperbolic: less, because no (re)presentation of it is possible. . . . That is, unfortunately, what Heidegger, who knew a good deal about the caesura (what else, after all, is the *Ereignis*?) and Heidegger alone can enable us to understand, he who obstinately refused, however, to acknowledge Auschwitz as the caesura of our times."[211]

In 1935 Heidegger could still write in blatantly chauvinistic terms about the German nation "as the most metaphysical *Volk*" and suggest that it "must move itself beyond the center of its futural happening into the originary realm of the powers of being." He then added, "If the great decision concerning Europe is not to lead to annihilation, then it can only be made through the unfolding of new historical-*spiritual* forces from out of the center."[212] Obviously, these new "spiritual" (*geistige*) forces would also carry the double sense of a "ghostly" burden, as Derrida has pointed out.[213] The Germanocentric vision of history, inspired by the poetic word of Hölderlin, would lead Heideg-

---

[210] Heidegger, *An Introduction to Metaphysics*, 128; *Einleitung in die Metaphysik*, 117.

[211] Philippe Lacoue-Labarthe, *Heidegger, Art, and Politics*, trans. Chris Turner (Oxford: Blackwell, 1990), 46.

[212] Heidegger, *An Introduction to Metaphysics*, 32 (translation modified); *Einleitung in die Metaphysik*, 29.

[213] Jacques Derrida, *Of Spirit*, trans. Geoffrey Bennington and Rachel Bowlby (Chicago: University of Chicago Press, 1989).

ger back to Pre-Socratic origins for a way out of the crisis of the modern spirit. But could the promise of a "new beginning" in National Socialism bring to completion the "first beginning" of Greek thought?

Perhaps, in the end, what a critical reading of Heidegger provides is another way of thinking about beginnings than as Heraclitean archai according to Heidegger's own epochal scheme of the history of philosophy. For if we take his work seriously, we are offered the possibility of reading Heidegger against himself, remembering all the while his own abiding preference for the word of Aristotle: *to on legetai pollachos*.[214] Being *is* said in many ways; it can take the form of a system expressed with enduring clarity, or it can withdraw into a silence more powerful than the sayings of philosophers, a silence of absence, and an absent other named only by the name of Auschwitz. It would be unfair to judge Heidegger's work solely by his own silence on this "topic" for thought, and yet, in some fundamental way, any meaningful approach to his work must grasp this event of history as a pivotal influence on his reading of the history of philosophy and the history of the West.

Heidegger's philosophical project, if project it was, destroyed the very foundations of historicism which lay at the root of history, uncovering its hidden metaphysical sources and its endless pretenses to "scientific" (re)presentation and self-extinguishment. But in this act of destruction, Heidegger's decision about being/beings became entangled in the dangerous historicity of his own National Socialist roots. What Heidegger's work offers, even in its alarming political rhetoric, is a vision of crisis that renders the nineteenth-century "crisis of the sciences" trivial and supererogatory. For Heidegger properly grasped *Krisis* as a turning, as a critical event not merely in the history of historical writing but in history itself as an aletheic process of disclosure and concealment. What lies concealed, however, is not something capable of revelation in the usual sense but only an apocalypse of the hidden dangers in being, dangers to which Heidegger, too, was subject.

If it makes sense to situate the crisis of modernity within the tradition of historicism, as I have tried to do, then Heidegger's work occupies a central position within this frame of questioning. The move from an epistemological foundation for the human sciences to an es-

---

[214] Martin Heidegger, *What Is Philosophy?* bilingual ed., trans. Jean T. Wilde and William Kluback (New Haven, Conn.: College and University Press, 1956), 96–97.

chatology of being demonstrated just how troubling the question of history became for the generation of German thinkers after 1880. Yet if Heidegger found no "solution" to the crisis, he did at least hold out the possibility of its dissolution. Modernity itself, as the struggle to define and understand this dissolution, makes no sense without the idea of crisis. Responding to the situation as a thinker "in a time of need," Heidegger reframed the question of history (*Geschichte*) by setting it within the larger context of what he termed a *fate* or *destiny* (*Geschick*) sent from being. At the conclusion of his essay "What Are Poets For?" (1946), he alluded to "the coming world era," an era that, he argued, "is neither a decay nor a downfall" but "a destiny which rests in being and lays claim to human being."[215] Rejecting the "historical" (*geschichtlich*) narrative of the modern epoch for a "fateful" (*geschicklich*) and posthistorical reading of an age to come, Heidegger demonstrated how far he had moved from the Neo-Kantian attempt to "resolve" the crisis of historicism. By thinking "history" and "crisis" together as points of intersection for understanding the modern epoch, Heidegger called into question modernity itself. As a self-styled "thinker in a destitute time," he challenged the German tradition of historical thinking from Ranke to Meinecke and exposed its metaphysical foundations through his work of *Destruktion*. But his poetic, "fateful" thinking set forth dangers of its own, marked as it was by a political commitment to another kind of crisis. By setting philosophy against politics and politics against history, Heidegger revealed the tensions at the heart of a long tradition, tensions that could hardly be resolved in strictly "historical" terms. In the end, by rejecting the metaphysics of *Weltgeschichte* for "the destiny of the world's night," he affirmed his commitment to "destiny," even if he always understood destiny as a question about history.[216] The history of modernity as a narrative in the form of a question is still to be decided. Heidegger's destructive reading helped to frame the question, leaving it ever more questionable and opening up the possibility of a different kind of historical reflection on the crisis of modernity.

[215] Martin Heidegger, "What Are Poets For?" trans. Albert Hofstadter, in *Poetry, Language, and Thought* (New York: Harper and Row, 1971), 142 (translation altered); *Holzwege*, 295.
[216] Heidegger, "What Are Poets For?" 142; *Holzwege*, 295.

Postscript

Historiography is a narcotic averting us from history.
—Martin Heidegger, *Basic Questions of Philosophy*

Heidegger's role within the tradition of historicism has been neglected, overlooked, marginalized, and dismissed by many commentators—on the genealogy of historicism and on Heidegger's work. My argument throughout this book has focused on the need to locate Heidegger's thought within the tradition of historicist thinking and, conversely, to situate the historicist mode of questioning within Heidegger's thought. I have tried to think through this mutually determined relation by centering my discussion on the notion of crisis and crisis-thinking. It seems to me that Heidegger's understanding of modernity situates the heritage of Cartesian and Enlightenment thinking within a narrative of technological domination and will to power. I believe that such an approach grows out of Heidegger's own attempts to account for the meaning of history (*Geschichte*) in terms of a new understanding of human temporality. This way of grasping history focuses not on the epistemological-methodological reconstruction of "what actually happened" but tries to approach history as something that still awaits us—as something futural rather than as something past.

As Heidegger began to move out of the constricted sphere of *Being and Time*, with its anthropocentric language of care, mood, conscience, and guilt, he tried to rethink the problems of history, historicity, and historiography which preoccupied him in that work. For the Heidegger of the thirties, questions about history no longer concern the tradition of historicism. In the summer semester of 1920, Heidegger still claimed that he no longer took "the ghosts of historicism and relativism seriously"; seven years later, in *Being and Time*, he indicated how the problem of historicism reveals a fundamental alienation of *Dasein* from its own historicity.[1] And yet for the Heidegger of the thirties, questions about history are no longer embedded within the historicist discourse but have been violently transformed into a new language of oracular pronouncement, a political discourse about a "secret" Germany: the Germany of a Hölderlinian brotherhood born of a new poetical-philosophical language and a postmetaphysical understanding of history and temporality.

The mantic language of the rectoral address signaled a new approach to history and the historical. There, in his appeal to the young students of Freiburg, Heidegger effectively destroyed the romantic appeal for a historicist narrative of history. Instead, he called for a resolute commitment "to recover the greatness of the beginning" prepared in Greek philosophy.[2] But this "first" beginning, he reminded his listeners, was not a historical event that could be established, known, and represented by Rankean methodology or the scientific study of history. It involved a posthistoricist understanding of temporality in which that which has been (*das Gewesene*) is not tied to the pastness of the past but returns back as a future (*Zu-kunft*) that comes toward us, opening up possibilities in the present (*Gegenwart*). In this sense, for Heidegger, "History is the arrival of what has been."[3] Throughout his later career Heidegger maintained that this posthistorical, postmetaphysical understanding of temporality expressed the "essence of history."[4] In the rectoral address, for example, Heidegger insisted that "the beginning still *is*. It does not lie *behind* us as something that was long ago, but stands *before* us. . . . The beginning has invaded our future."[5] Two years later, in the *Introduction to Meta-*

[1] Martin Heidegger, "Phänomenologie der Anschauung und des Ausdrucks," Nachschrift from F. J. Brecht, University of Freiburg July 19, 1920.
[2] Martin Heidegger, *Die Selbstbehauptung der deutschen Universität: Das Rektorat, 1933/34* (Frankfurt: Klostermann: 1990), 13.
[3] Martin Heidegger, "Grundsätze des Denkens," *Jahrbuch für Psychologie und Psychotherapie* 6 (1958): 35.
[4] Ibid.
[5] Heidegger, *Selbstbehauptung*, 12–13.

physics, Heidegger repeated his injunction that "the beginning be begun again in a more originary way"; again he wanted "to retrieve the beginning of [Germany's] historical-spiritual *Dasein* in order to transform it into an other beginning."[6] "This is possible" he claimed—and indeed it became something he continually worked on right through 1944 in his lectures on Nietzsche, Hölderlin, Parmenides, and Heraclitus.

Traditional German historicism as far back as Herder, Ranke, and Hegel understood history as a meaningful process of progressive development which handed down the power of tradition to the present as it shaped the future. But Heidegger understood history as an *Ereignis*, as a reciprocal appropriation of human beings and the history of being, an event whose beginning marked the belonging together of being and humanity and whose end threatened to annihilate the very possibility of history. Being's path of revelation had, in Heidegger's account, concealed its own *dynamis*, its own movement into presence, even as it withdrew back into absence. This way of understanding being as historical, as an aletheic process of what Thomas Sheehan has called "pres-ab-sence," finally broke with the German tradition of historicism and its metaphysical narrative of history as something always "present," something always "there" waiting to be revealed.[7]

And yet, didn't Heidegger's version of the history of being offer another metaphysical *grand récit* of the totalizing power of Western thinking—understood within the anthropocentric horizon of human being? Heidegger's willingness to take up the topic of history was never simple. In his works after 1933 one notices an essential tension in his thinking between a postmodern, aesthetic-ecological Heidegger, who warned of the "danger" of technological will to power, and a reactionary, political-ideological Heidegger, who entreated the German *Volk* to accept the challenge of "fulfilling its historical mission."[8] In this sense one is tempted to speak of at least two Heideggers: the Heidegger of paramilitary service "to the destiny [*Geschick*] of the state" and the Heidegger of *Gelassenheit*, of a circumspect attunement to the alternating cadences of being's poetic song, its matins and its

[6] Martin Heidegger, *Einleitung in die Metaphysik* (Tübingen: Niemeyer, 1976), 29 (translation mine); cf. *Introduction to Metaphysics*, trans. Ralph Manheim (Garden City, N.Y.: Anchor, 1961), 39.
[7] Thomas Sheehan, "On Movement and the Destruction of Ontology," *Monist* 64, no. 4 (October 1981): 537.
[8] Heidegger, *Selbstbehauptung*, 13.

vespers. No matter how we read Heidegger—as fascist apologist, as shepherd of being—we might better understand his thought if we acknowledge how decisively it was shaped by his understanding of modernity as an epoch of crisis: a turning in Western thinking both *onto* and *away from* the path of "ruinous blindness," "technological frenzy," and nihilistic will to power which dominates the twentieth century and whose echoes we hear in the names Passchendaele, Auschwitz, Hiroshima, Sarajevo.[9]

Heidegger's own commitments to National Socialism and to the openness of *aletheia* and *Ereignis* were never essentially at odds—at least in his own mind. They each reflected a preoccupation with crisis-thinking and with the *Destruktion* of the comfortable, reassuring orthodoxy of historicism. Heidegger wanted to break with conventional history so that he might retrieve the "first" beginning of Greek thought in the Pre-Socratics. He always understood the history of the West as a history of forgetting and of having forgotten this primordial Greek beginning, the *arche*, or "ruling origin," of Western thinking. He was utterly convinced that neither historicist scholarship nor nostalgic poetry could reclaim the force of that first beginning in any meaningful way. It could be appropriated only by finding hints, pointers, or "formal indications" within the Western tradition (Eckhart, Heraclitus, Hölderlin, Nietzsche) which still carried the force of this first beginning. Hence, when Heidegger writes in the winter semester of 1937/38 that "that which is to come is the origin of history; but the most futural coming is the great beginning," he is simply restating the message of the rectoral address and of *Being and Time*— namely, that the history of being is not an analogue to the history of philosophy or the history of historical writing.[10] Rather, it is an *anarchic* play of creative/destructive forces, without cause or ground— a play between arche and eschaton that denies the closure provided by archaeology and eschatology.

And yet this "play" within and of the history of being is not without its dangers. On the one hand, Heidegger's own playful engagements in "the *Geschick* of the state" reveal the dynamics of destruction involved in the German mission (*Auftrag*) of retrieving the Greek beginning.[11] On the other hand, by dismantling the metaphysical lan-

---

[9] Heidegger, *Introduction to Metaphysics*, 37; *Einleitung*, 28.

[10] Martin Heidegger, *Grundfragen der Philosophie, Gesamtausgabe* 45 (Frankfurt: Klostermann, 1984), 40.

[11] Heidegger, *Selbstbehauptung*, 16.

guage and structure of historicist thinking, Heidegger offered a different way of thinking about "history"—a posthistorical, playful, and anarchic attitude about the past which understood it as futural, as something that comes toward us rather than something that recedes from view. Such a view of history inevitably involves ambiguity. There is no single metaphysical arche or first principle that might rule or govern the diverse meanings laid out in the history that is still *unterwegs*, still on the path of unfolding its hidden folds. Heidegger's interpretation of history opens a space for the postmodern understanding of time as acausal, discontinuous, nonrepresentational. On this reading, history becomes polyvocal, disseminated in many ways and in a multiplicity of contexts, not speaking one language or privileging one path of truth but attuned to the plurality of dissonance, consonance, assonance, and resonance which reveals the myriad possibilities of *Ereignis*, the reciprocal appropriation of human beings and the history of being. For Heidegger, it is as if history were to lay claim to us rather than we to it.

Because Heidegger's thought is marked by both openness and closedness, by antimodernity and postmodernity, any claims put forward for a definitive reading of his work must always remain problematic. He himself did not provide a road map for the notorious windings on the path of thinking. We are left to be our own cartographers or rather to understand how the very desire for a cartography of being would vitiate the playful excursions and epochal sendings that the *Geschick* of being entails. If Heidegger's thought path was too powerfully marked by the insight into the "truth of the *Volk* as the openness of being," a truth that, being German and Greek, elided any Hebraic influences and found its roots in the lower-middle-class cultural politics of a Hölderlinian folk religion, then perhaps we should also notice its grave dangers. Perhaps we should raise the critical question of whether Heidegger's own provincial hierarchy of *Volk* and *Heimat* occluded the path of an "other" arche, an other beginning, against Heidegger's own pronouncements. If we do raise this question in a thoughtful way, then we are left with the possibility of reading Heidegger against himself, contrary to the exclusionary politics of his own historical situation. We might then begin to interpret Heidegger and his privileging of the *Heimat* in a way that is *unheimlich*, that allows for the possibility of all that is strange and uncanny, even against the strangeness that is so esteemed in Heidegger's own thinking.

Part of the effort of this book has been to read Heidegger in his context. But what would that mean given the problematizing contexts of reading that Heidegger's own work reveals? It can certainly not mean that we read him as only one among many German academics involved in a generational dispute about the crisis of historicism or the crisis of the sciences. His work is far too elusive, far too enigmatic to be reduced to any single register. And yet perhaps we need to take Heidegger's historical situation more seriously than we have thus far.

If the history of Heidegger's reception has been indifferent and even hostile to history itself, then a measure of the blame clearly lies with Heidegger. As he began preparing the edition of his complete works, he gave mixed signals about providing a historical-critical apparatus, footnotes, indexes, introductions, and so on.[12] Many of his followers have repeated the hybris of the master by writing in a language and style that is forbidding, arcane, and sometimes pretentious. By situating Heidegger within the tradition of historicism, I have sought to uncover at least one of the many contexts within which he can be read. What such a reading enables, I believe, is a way of getting at Heidegger's genuine "topic": the mysterious play of presence and absence, sendings and withdrawals, inaugurations and retrievals which resists any definitive name, whether *Sein*, *Seyn*, *Ereignis*, *aletheia*, or *Wesung*. This play emerges out of a reading of Western history as a narrative of crisis whose own beginning needs to be retrieved in order to find a pathway out of the crisis. But there is, properly speaking, not "a" pathway out; Heidegger's lifework involved the preparation of many pathways. If he sometimes found himself on a *Holzweg* (that is, a false path), as he did in 1933, that does not mean that we should follow. It falls to us to offer some resistance to the historicizing tendencies in Heidegger's own thinking.

The postmodern understanding of history does not have its roots in Heidegger's political mythology. And yet the very idea of being *post-histoire*, of being at the "end of history," grows out of the unspoken narrative of historical crisis which permeates Heidegger's writings. Heidegger understood the modern epoch as an era of decline, disintegration, and destruction. And yet unlike the cultural pessimists of Weimar who located the sources for the collapse of modernity in the

---

[12] Theodore Kisiel, "Edition und Übersetzung: Unterwegs von Tatsachen zu Gedanken, von Werken zu Wegen" in *Zur Philosophischen Aktualität Heideggers* vol. 3, *Im Spiegel der Welt: Sprache, Übersetzung, Auseinandersetzung*, ed. Dietrich Papenfuss und Otto Pöggeler (Frankfurt: Klostermann), 89–107.

postwar situation, Heidegger always traced his sources back to the very beginnings of Western history in Greek metaphysics. "Every decline remains hidden in the beginning," he wrote to a friend in December 1944.[13] But this was not a new theme for him; in "Europe and German Philosophy," a lecture given in Rome in April 1936, he had already announced his mission: "Insofar as we once again raise the *fundamental* question of Western philosophy from a *more originary* beginning, we stand in the service [*Dienst*] of a task that we can designate as the rescue of the West."[14]

As an antimodern who held forth the possibility of "rescue" from the "darkness of the world night," Heidegger revealed his fundamental rootedness in crisis-thinking. By deconstructing the narrative of linear temporality, metaphysical meaning, and ontological presence which framed the historicist understanding of modernity, Heidegger opened up the possibility of reconceiving the history of the West back to another beginning, another arche whose historical roots could never be recovered since they never existed.

Heidegger understood the history of modernity as a time of danger, as an *Aufbruch*, or "eruption," of fundamental crisis: the West would have to decide about the path of its own history in a way that opened up the possibility of its future. But we are left with a different kind of decision: whether to read Heidegger as part of a narrative of exclusion or as part of a revolutionary *Aufbruch* which does not speak of historical forces in national or racial terms but which allows them to bear their own force and to allow for the possibility of an other beginning, a beginning whose genealogy does not lead from Athens to Todtnauberg but allows for an arche governed by an anarchy born of tolerance. If we can read Heidegger tolerantly, then perhaps we can find our way onto other thought paths that Heidegger himself did not have the patience to follow.

[13] Georg Picht, "Die Macht des Denkens" in *Erinnerung an Martin Heidegger*, ed. Günter Neske (Pfullingen: Neske, 1977), 204–205.
[14] Martin Heidegger, "Europa und die deutsche Philosophie," in *Europa und die Philosophie*, ed. Hans-Helmut Gander (Frankfurt: Kostermann, 1993), 40.

Bibliography

Apel, Karl-Otto. "Scientistics, Hermeneutics, Critique of Ideology: An Outline of a Theory of Science from an Epistemological-Anthropological Point of View." In *The Hermeneutics Reader: Texts of the German Tradition from the Enlightenment to the Present*, 320–345. New York: Continuum, 1984.

Bambach, Charles. "Phenomenological Research as *Destruktion*: The Early Heidegger's Reading of Dilthey." *Philosophy Today* 37 (1993): 115–132.

Barash, Jeffrey. *Heidegger and the Problem of Historical Meaning*. Dordrecht: Martinus Nijhoff, 1988.

Barbiero, Daniel. "A Weakness for Heidegger: The German Root of *Il Pensiero Debole*." *New German Critique* 55 (1992): 159–172.

Bauer, Gerhard. *Geschichtlichkeit*. Berlin: Walter de Gruyter, 1963.

Baumgartner, Hans-Michael. "Wissenschaft." In *Handbuch philosophischer Grundbegriffe*, vol. 6, ed. Hermann Krings and H.-M. Baumgartner, 1740–1764. Munich: Kösel, 1974.

Benjamin, Walter. "Theses on the Philosophy of History." In *Illuminations*, trans. Harry Zohn, 253–264. New York: Schocken, 1969.

Berger, Johannes. "Gegenstandskonstitution und geschichtliche Welt." Diss., University of Munich, 1967.

Bernstein, Richard. *Beyond Objectivism and Relativism*. Philadelphia: University of Pennsylvania Press, 1983.

Besson, Waldemar. "Historismus." In *Das Fischer Lexikon: Geschichte*, 102–116. Frankfurt: Fischer, 1961.

Biemel, Walter, ed. "Der Briefwechsel Dilthey und Husserl." *Man and World* 1 (1968): 428–446.

——. "The Dilthey-Husserl Correspondence." In *Husserl: Shorter Works*, ed. Peter McCormick and Frederick Elliston, 203–209. South Bend: University of Notre Dame Press, 1981.

Blanke, Horst Walter, and Jörn Rüsen, eds. *Von der Aufklärung zum Historismus*. Paderborn: Schöningh, 1984.

Bodammer, Theodor. *Philosophie der Geisteswissenschaften*. Freiburg: Alber, 1987.

Bödeker, Hans-Erich, Georg Iggers, Jonathan Knudsen, and Peter Reill, eds., *Aufklärung und Geschichte*. Göttingen: Vandenhoeck & Ruprecht, 1986.

Boeder, Heribert. "Dilthey 'und' Heidegger: Zur Geschichtlichkeit des Menschen." In *Dilthey und der Wandel des Philosophiebegriffs*, ed. E. W. Orth, 161–177. Freiburg: Alber, 1984.

Brush, Stephen G. *The History of Modern Science: A Guide to the Second Scientific Revolution*. Ames: Iowa State University Press, 1988.

Bubner, Rüdiger. "Das Faktum der Wissenschaft und Paradigmenwechsel." *Studia Leibnitiana*, Sonderheft 6 (1974): 78–94.

Bulhof, Ilse. *Wilhem Dilthey: A Hermeneutic Approach to the Study of History and Culture*. The Hague: Martinus Nijhoff, 1980.

Burckhardt, Jacob. *Force and Freedom*. Trans. James Nichols. New York: Pantheon, 1943.

Burger, Thomas. *Max Weber's Theory of Concept Formation*. Durham, N.C.: Duke University Press, 1976.

Caputo, John. *Demythologizing Heidegger*. Bloomington: Indiana University Press, 1993.

——. *Radical Hermeneutics*. Bloomington: Indiana University Press, 1987.

Castoriadis, Cornelius. *Crossroads in the Labyrinth*. Cambridge: MIT Press, 1984.

Derrida, Jacques. *Of Spirit*. Trans. Geoffrey Bennington and Rachel Bowlby. Chicago: University of Chicago Press, 1989.

——. *The Other Heading*. Trans. Michael Naas and Pascale-Ann Brault. Bloomington: Indiana University Press, 1992.

——. *Positions*. Trans. Alan Bass. Chicago: University of Chicago Press, 1971.

Dilthey, Wilhelm. *Briefwechsel zwischen Wilhelm Dilthey und dem Grafen Paul Yorck von Wartenburg, 1877–1897*, ed. Sigrid von der Schulenburg. Halle: Niemeyer, 1923.

——. "The Dream." In *The Philosophy of History in Our Time*, ed. Hans Mayerhoff, 40. Garden City, N.Y.: Doubleday, 1959.

——. *The Essence of Philosophy*. Trans. Stephen A. Emery and William Emery. Chapel Hill: University of North Carolina Press, 1961.

——. *Gesammelte Schriften*. 20 vols. Göttingen: Vandenhoeck & Ruprecht, 1958–1990.

——. *Grundriß der Logik und des Systems der philosophischen Wissenschaften*. Berlin: Mittler, 1865.

——. *Introduction to the Human Sciences*. Ed. Rudolf Makkreel and Frithjof Rodi. Princeton, N.J.: Princeton University Press, 1989.

——. *Pattern and Meaning in History: Thoughts on History and Society*. Ed. H. P. Rickman. New York: Harper and Row, 1962.

——. *Wilhelm Dilthey: Selected Writings*. Ed. H. P. Rickman. Cambridge: Cambridge University Press, 1976.

——. *Wilhelm Dilthey: Texte zur Kritik der historischen Vernunft*. Ed. Hans-Ulrich Lessing. Göttingen: Vandenhoeck & Ruprecht, 1983.

Droysen, Johan Gustav. *Historik*. Darmstadt: Wissenschaftliche Buchgesellschaft, 1977.

Engelhardt, Dietrich von. *Historisches Bewußtsein in der Naturwissenschaft: Von der Aufklärung bis zum Positivismus*. Freiburg: Alber, 1979.

Ermarth, Elizabeth Deeds. *Sequel to History: Postmodernism and the Crisis of Representational Time*. Princeton, N.J.: Princeton University Press, 1992.

Ermarth, Michael. "Historical Understanding in the Thought of Wilhelm Dilthey." *History and Theory* 20, no. 3 (1981): 323–334.

——. "Objectivity and Relativity in Dilthey's Theory of Understanding." In *Dilthey and Phenomenology*, ed. Rudolf Makkreel and John Scanlon, 73–94. Washington, D.C.: University Press of America, 1987.

——. *William Dilthey: The Critique of Historical Reason*. Chicago: University of Chicago Press, 1978.

Forman, Paul. "Weimar Culture, Causality, and Quantum Theory." *Historical Studies in the Physical Sciences* 3 (1971): 1–116.

Fukuyama, Francis. *The End of History and the Last Man*. New York: Free Press, 1992.

Gadamer, Hans-Georg. "Das Faktum der Wissenschaft." In *Das Erbe Europas*, 87–105. Frankfurt: Suhrkamp, 1989.

——. "Dilthey nach 150 Jahren: Zwischen Romantik und Positivismus." In *Dilthey und die Philosophie der Gegenwart*, ed. E. W. Orth, 157–182. Freiburg: Alber, 1985.

——. "Geschichtlichkeit." In *Religion in Geschichte und Gesellschaft*, 2:1496–1498. Tübingen: Mohr, 1959.

——. "Historismus." In *Religion in Geschichte und Gesellschaft*, 3:369–370. Tübingen: Mohr, 1959.

——. "Neo-Kantianism." In *Philosophisches Lesebuch*, 3:215–218. Frankfurt: Fischer, 1988.

——. *Kleine Schriften*. 4 vols. Tübingen: Mohr, 1967–1970.

——. *Reason in the Age of Science*. Trans. Frederick G. Lawrence. Cambridge: MIT Press, 1981.

——. "Selbstdarstellung." *Gesammelte Werke*, 2: 479–508. Tübingen: Mohr, 1986.

——. *Truth and Method*. Translation revised by Joel Weinsheimer and Donald G. Marshall. New York: Crossroad, 1989.

——. *Wahrheit und Methode*. Tübingen: Mohr, 1960.

Gander, Hans-Helmuth. *Positivismus als Metaphysik: Voraussetzungen und Grundstrukturen von Diltheys Grundlegung der Geisteswissenschaften.* Freiburg: Alber, 1988.

Gedo, Andras. *Crisis Consciousness in Contemporary Philosophy.* Trans. Salomea Genin. Minneapolis: Marxist Educational Press, 1982.

Gillespie, Michael. *Hegel, Heidegger, and the Ground of History.* Chicago: University of Chicago Press, 1984.

Grondin, Jean. *Einführung in die philosophische Hermeneutik.* Darmstadt: Wissenschaftliche Buchgesellschaft, 1991.

Habermas, Jürgen. *Knowledge and Human Interests.* Trans. Jeremy Shapiro. Boston: Beacon Press, 1971.

Halsey, Charles S. *Etymology of Latin and Greek.* New Rochelle, N.Y.: Caratzas, 1983.

Hardtwig, Wolfgang. *Geschichtsschreibung zwischen Alteuropa und moderner Welt: Jacob Burckhardt in seiner Zeit.* Göttingen: Vandenhoeck & Ruprecht, 1974.

Heidegger, Martin. *The Basic Problems of Phenomenology.* Trans. Albert Hofstadter. Bloomington: Indiana University Press, 1982.

———. *Basic Writings.* Ed. David Krell. New York: Harper and Row, 1977.

———. *Der Begriff der Zeit.* Tübingen: Niemeyer, 1989.

———. *Being and Time.* Trans. John Macquarrie and Edward Robinson. New York: Harper and Row, 1962.

———. *The Concept of Time.* Trans. William McNeill. Oxford: Blackwell, 1992.

———. *Discourse on Thinking.* Trans. John Anderson and E. Hans Freund. New York: Harper and Row, 1966.

———. *Early Greek Thinking.* Trans. David F. Krell. New York: Harper and Row, 1984.

———. *Gelassenheit.* Pfullingen: Neske, 1959.

———. *Gesamtausgabe.* Vol. 1, *Frühe Schriften.* Frankfurt: Klostermann, 1978.

———. *Gesamtausgabe.* Vol. 2, *Sein und Zeit.* Frankfurt: Klostermann, 1977.

———. *Gesamtausgabe.* Vol. 5, *Holzwege.* Frankfurt: Klostermann, 1971.

———. *Gesamtausgabe.* Vol. 9, *Wegmarken.* Frankfurt: Klostermann, 1976.

———. *Gesamtausgabe.* Vol. 20, *Prolegomena zur Geschichte des Zeitbegriffs.* Frankfurt: Klostermann, 1988.

———. *Gesamtausgabe.* Vol. 21, *Logik: Die Frage nach der Wahrheit.* Frankfurt: Klostermann, 1976.

———. *Gesamtausgabe.* Vol. 24, *Grundprobleme der Phänomenologie.* Frankfurt: Klostermann, 1989.

———. *Gesamtausgabe.* Vol. 32, *Hegels Phänomenologie des Geistes.* Frankfurt: Klostermann, 1980.

———. *Gesamtausgabe.* Vol. 40, *Einführung in die Metaphysik.* Frankfurt: Klostermann, 1983.

———. *Gesamtausgabe.* Vol. 45, *Grundfragen der Philosophie: Ausgewählte "Probleme" der "Logik."* Frankfurt: Klostermann, 1984.

——. *Gesamtausgabe.* Vol. 56/57, *Zur Bestimmung der Philosophie.* Frankfurt: Klostermann, 1987.

——. *Gesamtausgabe.* Vol. 61, *Phänomenologische Interpretationen zu Aristoteles: Einführung in die phänomenologische Forschung.* Frankfurt: Klostermann, 1985.

——. *Gesamtausgabe.* Vol. 63, *Ontologie: Hermeneutik der Faktizität.* Frankfurt: Klostermann, 1987.

——. *Gesamtausgabe.* Vol. 65, *Beiträge zur Philosophie.* Frankfurt: Klostermann, 1989.

——. *History of the Concept of Time.* Trans. Theodore Kisiel. Bloomington: Indiana University Press, 1985.

——. *An Introduction to Metaphysics.* Trans. Ralph Mannheim. Garden City, N.Y.: Anchor, 1961.

——. *Nietzsche.* 4 vols. Trans. David F. Krell. New York: Harper and Row, 1979–1987.

——. *Nietzsche.* 2 vols. Pfullingen: Neske, 1961.

——. *On Time and Being.* Trans. Joan Stambaugh. New York: Harper and Row, 1972.

——. "Phänomenologische Interpretationen zu Aristoteles." Ed. Hans-Ulrich Lessing. *Dilthey-Jahrbuch* 6 (1989): 235–274.

——. *Poetry, Language, Thought.* Trans. Albert Hofstadter. New York: Harper and Row, 1971.

——. "The Rectorate, 1933–34: Facts and Thoughts." Trans. Karsten Harries. *Review of Metaphysics* 38 (March 1985): 481–502.

——. *Sein und Zeit.* Tübingen: Niemeyer, 1976.

——. *Die Selbstbehauptung der deutschen Universität: Das Rektorat, 1933/34.* Frankfurt: Klostermann, 1990.

——. "The Self-Assertion of the German University." Trans. Karsten Harries. *Review of Metaphysics* 38 (March 1985): 470–480.

Heidegger, Martin, and Elisabeth Blochmann. *Briefwechsel, 1918–1969.* Ed. Joachim W. Storck. Marbach: Deutsche Schillergesellschaft, 1989.

Heidegger, Martin, and Karl Jaspers. *Briefwechsel, 1920–1963.* Eds. Walter Biemel and Hans Saner. Frankfurt: Klostermann, 1990.

Herzberg, Guntolf. "Historismus: Wort, Begriff, Problem, und die philosophische Begründung durch Wilhelm Dilthey." *Jahrbuch für Geschichte* 25 (1982): 259–304.

——. "Wilhelm Dilthey und das Problem des Historismus." Diss., Humboldt University of Berlin, 1976.

Heussi, Karl. *Die Krisis des Historismus.* Tübingen: Mohr, 1932.

Hinske, Norbert. "Kants Begriff der Antinomie und die Etappen seiner Ausarbeitung." *Kant Studien* 56 (1965): 485–496.

Hoy, David. "History, Historicity, and Historiography." In *Heidegger and Modern Philosophy*, ed. Michael Murray, 329–353. New Haven, Conn.: Yale University Press, 1978.

Hünermann, Peter. *Der Durchbruch geschichtlichen Denkens im 19. Jahrhundert: Johann Gustav Droysen, Wilhelm Dilthey, Graf Paul Yorck von Wartenburg.* Freiburg: Herder, 1967.

Husserl, Edmund. *The Crisis of the European Sciences.* Trans. David Carr. Evanston, Ill.: Northwestern University Press, 1970.

——. *Phenomenology and the Crisis of Philosophy.* Trans. Quentin Lauer. New York: Harper Torchbooks, 1965.

——. "Philosophie als eine strenge Wissenschaft." *Logos* 1 (1911): 289–341.

Iggers, Georg. *The German Conception of History.* Middletown, Conn.: Wesleyan University Press, 1968.

——. "Historicism." In *The Dictionary of the History of Ideas,* 456–464. New York: Scribners, 1973.

——. "Review of *Von der Aufklärung zum Historismus.*" *History and Theory* 26, 1 (1987): 114–121.

——. "The University of Göttingen, 1760–1800, and the Transformation of Historical Scholarship." *Storia della Storiografia* 2 (1982): 11–37.

Iggers, Georg, and James Powell, eds. *Leopold von Ranke and the Shaping of the Historical Discipline.* Syracuse, N.Y.: Syracuse University Press, 1990.

Jaeger, Friedrich, and Jörn Rüsen. *Geschichte des Historismus.* Munich: Beck, 1992.

Jaspers, Karl. *Man in the Modern Age.* Trans. Eden Paul and Cedar Paul. Garden City, N.Y.: Doubleday, 1957.

Jensen, Bernard Eric. "The Role of Intellectual History in Dilthey's *Kritik der historischen Vernunft.*" *Dilthey-Jahrbuch* 2 (1984): 65–91.

Kahler, Erich. *Beruf der Wissenschaft.* Berlin: Bondi, 1920.

Kant, Immanuel. *Critique of Pure Reason.* Trans. Norman Kemp Smith. London: Macmillan, 1929.

——. *Gesammelte Schriften* 29 vols. Berlin: Walter de Gruyter, 1983.

Kisiel, Theodore. "Edition und Übersetzung: Unterwegs von Tatsachen zu Denken, von Werken zu Wegen." In *Zur philosophischen Aktualität Heideggers.* Vol. 3, *Im Spiegel der Welt: Sprache, Übersetzung, Auseinandersetzung,* ed. Dietrich Papenfuss and Otto Pöggeler, 89–107. Frankfurt: Klostermann, 1992.

——. "Das Entstehen des Begriffsfeldes 'Faktizität' im Frühwerk Heideggers." *Dilthey-Jahrbuch für Philosophie und Geschichte der Geisteswissenschaften* 4 (1986–87): 91–120.

——. *The Genesis of Heidegger's "Being and Time."* Berkeley: University of California Press, 1993.

——. "Heidegger (1907–1927): The Transformation of the Categorial." In *Continental Philosophy in America,* ed. H. J. Silverman, John Sallis, and T. M. Seebohm, 165–185. Pittsburgh: Duquesne University Press, 1983.

——. "Heidegger's Apology: Biography as Philosophy and Ideology." *Graduate Faculty Philosophy Journal* 14, no. 2–15, no. 1 (1991): 363–404.

——. "Das Kriegsnotsemester 1919: Heideggers Durchbruch zur hermeneutischen Phänomenologie." *Philosophisches Jahrbuch* 99, no. 1 (1992): 105–123.

——. "The Missing Link in the Early Heidegger." In *Hermeneutic Phenomenology: Lectures and Essays*, ed. Joseph J. Kockelmans, 1–40. Washington D.C.: University Press of America, 1988.

——. "On the Way to Being and Time: Introduction to the Translation of Heidegger's *Prolegomena zur Geschichte des Zeitbegriffs*." *Research in Phenomenology* 15 (1985): 193–226.

——. "War der frühe Heidegger tatsächlich ein 'christlicher Theologe'?" In *Philosophie und Poesie: Otto Pöggeler zum 60. Geburtstag*, ed. Anne Gethmann-Siefert, 2:59–75. Stuttgart: Fromann-Holzboog, 1988.

Köhnke, Klaus Christian. *Entstehung und Aufstieg des Neukantianismus: Die deutsche Universitätsphilosophie zwischen Idealismus und Positivismus*. Frankfurt: Suhrkamp, 1986.

Koselleck, Reinhart. "Geschichte, Historie." In *Geschichtliche Grundbegriffe*. Vol. 4. Ed. Otto Brunner, Werner Conze, and Reinhart Koselleck. Stuttgart: Klett, 1975.

Kovacs, George. "Philosophy as Primordial Science (*Urwissenschaft*) in the Early Heidegger." *Journal of the British Society for Phenomenology* 21 (1990): 121–135.

Krell, David. *Intimations of Mortality*. University Park: Pennsylvania State University Press, 1986.

Kuhn, Thomas. *The Structure of Scientific Revolutions*. Chicago: University of Chicago Press, 1962.

Lacoue-Labarthe, Philippe. *Heidegger, Art and Politics*. Trans. Chris Turner. Oxford: Blackwell, 1990.

Landgrebe, Ludwig. *Major Problems in Contemporary European Philosophy*. Trans. Kurt Reinhardt. New York: Ungar, 1966.

Lessing, Hans-Ulrich. *Die Idee einer Kritik der historischen Vernunft*. Freiburg: Alber: 1984.

Lessing, Hans-Ulrich and Frithjof Rodi, eds. *Materialien zur Philosophie Wilhelm Diltheys*. Frankfurt: Suhrkamp, 1984.

Liebert, Arthur. *Die Geistige Krisis der Gegenwart*. Berlin: Pan-Verlag Rolf Heise, 1924.

Linge, David. "Historicity and Hermeneutic." Ph.D. diss., Vanderbilt University, 1969.

Löwith, Karl. *Mein Leben in Deutschland vor und nach 1933: Ein Bericht*. Stuttgart: Metzler, 1986.

——. "Wahrheit und Geschichtlichkeit." In *Truth and Historicity*, ed. Hans-Georg Gadamer, 9–21. The Hague: Martinus Nijhoff, 1972.

Luther, Martin. "Heidelberg Disputation." In *Luther's Works*, ed. H. T. Lehmann. Vol. 31, *Career of the Reformer*, ed. Harold I. Grimm, part I. Philadelphia: Muhlenberg, 1957.

Lyotard, Jean-François. *The Postmodern Condition*. Trans. Geoff Bennington. Minneapolis: University of Minnesota Press, 1984.

Makkreel, Rudolf. *Dilthey: Philosopher of the Human Studies*. Princeton, N.J.: Princeton University Press, 1975.

——. "The Genesis of Heidegger's Phenomenological Hermeneutics and the Rediscovered 'Aristotle Introduction' of 1922." *Man and World* 23 (1990): 305–320.

Makkreel, Rudolf, and John Scanlon, eds. *Dilthey and Phenomenology*. Washington, D.C.: University Press of America, 1987.

Mandelbaum, Maurice. *The Problem of Historical Knowledge: An Answer to Relativism*. New York: Liveright, 1967.

Megill, Allan. *Prophets of Extremity: Nietzsche, Heidegger, Foucault, Derrida*. Berkeley: University of California Press, 1985.

Meinecke, Friedrich. *Die Entstehung des Historismus*. Munich: Oldenbourg, 1965.

——. "Geschichte und Gegenwart." In *Zur Theorie und Philosophie der Geschichte*. Stuttgart: Koehler, 1959.

——. *Historism*. Trans. J. E. Anderson. London: Routledge, 1972.

——. "Values and Causality in History." In *Varieties of History*, ed. Fritz Stern, 267–288. New York: World, 1972.

——. *Zur Theorie und Philosophie der Geschichte*. Stuttgart: Koehler, 1959.

Merleau-Ponty, Maurice. *The Visible and the Invisible*. Trans. Alphonso Lingis. Evanston, Ill.: Northwestern University Press, 1968.

Misch, Clara, ed. *Der junge Dilthey*. Göttingen: Vandenhoeck & Ruprecht, 1960.

Morris, Wesley. *Towards a New Historicism*. Princeton, N.J.: Princeton University Press, 1972.

Müller-Lauter, Wolfgang. "Die Konsequenzen des Historismus in der Philosophie der Gegenwart." *Zeitschrift für Theologie und Kirche* 59 (1962): 226–255.

Nabrings, Arie. "Historismus als Paralyse der Geschichte." *Archiv für Kulturgeschichte* 65 (1983): 157–212.

Niethammer, Lutz. *Posthistoire*. Trans. Patrick Camiller. London: Verso, 1992.

Nietzsche, Friedrich. *The Twilight of the Idols*. Trans. R. J. Hollingdale. New York: Penguin, 1968.

——. *Untimely Meditations*. Trans. R. J. Hollingdale. Cambridge: Cambridge University Press, 1983.

——. *Unzeitgemässe Betrachtungen*. Leipzig: Kröner, 1930.

——. *Werke. Kritische Gesamtausgabe*. Berlin: Walter de Gruyter, 1967–1988.

——. *The Will to Power*. Trans. Walter Kaufmann and R. J. Hollingdale. New York: Random House, 1968.

Oakes, Guy. *Weber and Rickert: Concept Formation in the Cultural Sciences*. Cambridge: MIT Press, 1988.

Oexle, Otto G. "Die Geschichtswissenschaft im Zeichen des Historismus." *Historische Zeitschrift* 238 (1984): 17–55.

——. "'Historismus': Überlegungen zur Geschichte des Phänomens und des Begriffs." *Jahrbuch der Braunschweigischen Wissenschaftlichen Gesellschaft* (1986): 119–155.

Orth, Ernst Wolfgang, ed. *Dilthey und der Wandel des Philosophiebegriffs seit dem 19. Jahrhundert.* Freiburg: Alber, 1984.

Ott, Hugo. *Martin Heidegger: Unterwegs zu seiner Biographie.* Frankfurt: Campus, 1988.

Otto, Stefan. "Dilthey und der Begriff des empirischen Apriori." *Philosophisches Jahrbuch* 91, no. 2 (1984): 376–382.

——. *Rekonstruktion der Geschichte: Zur Kritik der historischen Vernunft.* Munich: Fink, 1982.

Palmer, Richard. *Hermeneutics.* Evanston, Ill.: Northwestern University Press, 1969.

Pannwitz, Rudolf. *Die Krisis der Europäischen Kultur.* Nuremberg: H. Carl, 1917.

Pöggeler, Otto. "Historicity in Heidegger's Late Work." *Southwestern Journal of Philosophy* 4 (1973): 53–73.

——. *Martin Heidegger's Path of Thinking.* Trans. Daniel Magurshak and Sigmund Barber. Atlantic Highlands, N.J.: Humanities Press, 1987.

Popper, Karl. *The Poverty of Historicism.* London: Routledge, 1957.

Rand, Calvin. "Two Meanings of Historicism in the Work of Dilthey, Troeltsch, and Meinecke." *Journal of the History of Ideas* 25 (1964): 503–518.

Ranke, Leopold von. *The Secret of World History.* Trans. Roger Wines. New York: Fordham University Press, 1981.

——. *The Theory and Practice of History.* Ed. Konrad Moltke and Georg Iggers. New York: Bobbs-Merrill, 1973.

Redner, Harry. *The Ends of Philosophy.* Totowa, N.J.: Rowan and Allanheld, 1986.

——. *The Ends of Science.* Boulder, Colo.: Westview, 1987.

Reill, Peter. *The German Enlightenment and the Rise of Historicism.* Berkeley: University of California Press, 1975.

——. "Die Geschichtswissenschaft um die Mitte des 18. Jahrhunderts." In *Wissenschaften im Zeitalter der Aufklärung,* ed. Rudolf Vierhaus, 163–193. Göttingen: Vandenhoeck & Ruprecht, 1985.

——. "Narration and Structure in Late Eighteenth-Century Historical Thought." *History and Theory* 25 (1986): 286–298.

Renthe-Fink, Leonhard. "Geschichtlichkeit." In *Historisches Wörterbuch der Philosophie,* vol. 3, 404–408. Basel: Schwabe, 1971.

——. *Geschichtlichkeit: Ihr terminologischer und begrifflicher Ursprung bei Hegel, Haym, Dilthey, und Yorck.* Göttingen: Vandenhoeck & Ruprecht, 1964.

——. "Zur Herkunft des Wortes 'Geschichtlichkeit.'" *Archiv für Begriffsgeschichte* 15 (1971): 306–312.

Richardson, William. *Heidegger: Through Phenomenology to Thought*. The Hague: Martinus Nijhoff, 1963.

Rickert, Heinrich. "Einführung in die Erkenntnistheorie und Metaphysik." Ms. 59. Heidelberg: Heidelberg Universitätsbibliothek.

———. *Der Gegenstand der Erkenntnis: Einführung in die Transzendentalphilosophie*. Tübingen: Mohr, 1928.

———. "Geschichtsphilosophie." *Die Philosophie im Beginn des zwanzigsten Jahrhunderts*. Ed. Wilhelm Windelband. Festschrift for Kuno Fischer. Heidelberg: C. Winter, 1907.

———. *Die Grenzen der naturwissenschaftlichen Begriffsbildung: Eine logische Einleitung in die historischen Wissenschaften*. Tübingen: Mohr, 1929.

———. *Grundprobleme der Philosophie*. Tübingen: Mohr, 1934.

———. *Die Heidelberger Tradition in der deutschen Philosophie*. Tübingen: Mohr, 1931.

———. *Kant als Philosoph der modernen Kultur*. Tübingen: Mohr, 1924.

———. *Kulturwissenschaft und Naturwissenschaft*. Tübingen: Mohr, 1926.

———. "Lebenswerte und Kulturwerte." *Logos* 2 (1911–12): 131–167.

———. *The Limits of Concept Formation in Natural Science: A Logical Introduction to the Historical Sciences*. Trans. Guy Oakes. Cambridge: Cambridge University Press, 1986.

———. "Max Weber und seine Stellung zur Wissenschaft." *Logos* 15 (1926): 222–261.

———. *Die Philosophie des Lebens: Darstellung und Kritik der philosophischen Modeströmungen unserer Zeit*. Tübingen: Mohr, 1922.

———. *Die Probleme der Geschichtsphilosophie*. Heidelberg: Winter, 1924.

———. "Psychologie der Weltanschauung und Philosophie der Werte." *Logos* 10 (1920): 1–42.

———. *Science and History: A Critique of Positivist Epistemology*. Trans. George Reisman. Princeton, N.J.: Van Nostrand, 1962.

———. *System der Philosophie*. Tübingen: Mohr, 1921.

———. "Thesen zum System der Philosophie." *Logos* 21 (1932): 97–103.

———. "Vom System der Werte." *Logos* 4 (1913): 295–327.

———. "Wissenschaftliche Philosophie und Weltanschauung." *Logos* 22 (1933): 37–99.

———. "Zur Theorie der naturwissenschaftlichen Begriffsbildung." *Vierteljahrschrift für wissenschaftliche Philosophie* 18 (1894): 277–319.

Riedel, Manfred. *Für eine zweite Philosophie*. Frankfurt: Suhrkamp, 1988.

———. *Verstehen oder Erklären?: Zur Theorie und Geschichte der hermeneutischen Wissenschaften*. Stuttgart: Klett-Cotta, 1978.

Ringer, Fritz. *The Decline of the German Mandarins*. Cambridge: Harvard University Press, 1969.

Ritter, Harry. "Historicism, Historism." In *Dictionary of Concepts in History*, 183–187. Westport, Conn.: Greenwood, 1986.

Rodi, Frithjof. "Die Bedeutung Diltheys für die Konzeption von *Sein und Zeit*: Zum Umfeld von Heideggers Kasseler Vorträgen." *Dilthey-Jahrbuch* 4 (1986–87): 161–177.

———. "Dilthey, Gadamer, and Traditional Hermeneutics." *Reports on Philosophy* 7 (1983): 3–14.

———. *Erkenntnis des Erkannten*. Frankfurt: Suhrkamp, 1990.

Rorty, Richard. *Philosophy and the Mirror of Nature*. Princeton, N.J.: 1979.

Roth, Michael S. *Knowing and History*. Ithaca, N.Y.: Cornell University Press, 1988.

Rothacker, Erich. "Das Wort Historismus." *Zeitschrift für deutsche Wortforschung* 16 (1960): 3–6.

Rouse, Joseph. *Knowledge and Power: Toward a Political Philosophy of Science*. Ithaca, N.Y.: Cornell University Press, 1987.

Rüsen, Jörn. "Theorien im Historismus." *Theorien in der Geschichtswissenschaft*, ed. Jörn Rüsen and Hans Süssmuth. Düsseldorf: Schwann, 1980.

Sallis, John, ed. *Reading Heidegger: Commemorations*. Bloomington: Indiana University Press, 1993.

Schalow, Frank. *The Renewal of the Kant-Heidegger Dialogue*. Albany: State University of New York Press, 1992.

Schleier, Hans. "Leistungen und Grenzen des idealistischen deutschen Historismus." *Zeitschrift für Geschichtswissenschaft* 35 (1987): 955–970.

Schnädelbach, Herbert. *Die Geschichtsphilosophie nach Hegel*. Freiburg: Alber, 1974.

———. *Philosophy in Germany, 1831–1933*. Cambridge: Cambridge University Press, 1984.

———. *Vernunft und Geschichte*. Frankfurt: Suhrkamp, 1987.

Scholz, Gunter. "Historismus." In *Historisches Wörterbuch der Philosophie*, 3:1141–1147. Basel: Schwabe, 1974.

Schrimpf, Gangolf. "Zum Begriff der geschichtlichen Tatsache." *Dilthey-Jahrbuch für Philosophie und Geschichte der Geisteswissenschaften* 5 (1988): 100–140.

Schulz, Walter. *Philosophie in der veränderten Welt*. Pfullingen: Neske, 1972.

Sheehan, Thomas. "Heidegger's Early Years: Fragments for a Philosophical Biography." In *Heidegger: The Man and the Thinker*, ed. Thomas Sheehan, 3–19. Chicago: Precedent, 1981.

———. "Heidegger's 'Introduction to the Phenomenology of Religion,' 1920–21." *Personalist* 55 (1979–80): 312–324.

———. "Heidegger's *Lehrjahre*." In *The Collegium Phaenomenologicum: The First Ten Years*, ed. John Sallis, Giuseppe Moneta, and Jacques Taminiaux, 77–137. Dordrecht: Kluwer, 1988.

———. "On the Way to *Ereignis*: Heidegger's Interpretation of *Physis*." In *Continental Philosophy in America*, ed. Hugh J. Silverman, John Sallis, and Thomas M. Seebohm, 121–164. Pittsburgh: Duquesne University Press, 1983.

——. "Reading a Life: Heidegger and Hard Times." In *The Cambridge Companion to Heidegger*, ed. Charles Guignon, 70–96. Cambridge: Cambridge University Press, 1993.

——. "'Time and Being,' 1925–1927." In *Thinking about Being: Aspects of Heidegger's Thought*, ed. Robert W. Shahan and J. N. Mohanty, 177–219. Norman: University of Oklahoma Press, 1984.

Simmel, Georg. *Problems of the Philosophy of History*. New York: Free Press, 1977.

Spengler, Oswald. *The Decline of the West*. Trans. C. F. Atkinson. New York: Knopf, 1926.

Steenblock, Volker. *Transformationen des Historismus*. Munich: Wilhelm Fink, 1991.

Stegmaier, Werner. *Philosophie der Fluktuanz: Dilthey und Nietzsche*. Göttingen: Vandenhoeck & Ruprecht, 1992.

Steiner, George. "Heidegger, Again." *Salmagundi* 82–83 (1989): 3–23.

Stern, Alfred. *Philosophy of History and the Problem of Values*. Berkeley: University of California Press, 1962.

Sullivan, Robert. *Political Hermeneutics*. University Park: Pennsylvania State University Press, 1989.

Thomä, Dieter. *Die Zeit des Selbst und die Zeit danach: Zur Kritik der Textgeschichte Martin Heideggers*. Frankfurt: Suhrkamp, 1990.

Thomas, Brook. *The New Historicism*. Princeton, N.J.: Princeton University Press, 1991.

Tice, Terrence, and Thomas Slavens. *Research Guide to Philosophy*. Chicago: American Library Association, 1983.

Troeltsch, Ernst. "Die Geisteswissenschaften und der Streit um Rickert." *Schmoellers Jahrbuch* 46 (1922): 35–64.

——. *Der Historismus und seine Probleme*. Tübingen: Mohr, 1922.

——. *Der Historismus und seine Überwindung*. Berlin: Heise, 1924.

——. "Die Krisis des Historismus." *Die Neue Rundschau* 33 (June 1922): 572–590.

van Buren, John. "Heidegger's Autobiographies." *Journal of the British Society for Phenomenology* 23, no. 3 (1993): 201–221.

——. *The Young Heidegger*. Bloomington: Indiana University Press, 1994.

Vanicek, Alois. *Griechisch-Lateinisches Etymologisches Wörterbuch*. Leipzig: Teubner, 1887.

Vattimo, Gianni. "The End of History." *Chicago Review* 35 (1987): 25.

——. *The End of Modernity*. Trans. Jon Snyder. Baltimore: Johns Hopkins University Press, 1988.

——. *Essere, storia, e linguaggio in Heidegger*. Genoa: Marietti, 1989.

——. "Optimistic Nihilism." *Common Knowledge* 1, no. 3 (1992): 37–44.

Weber, Max. "Wissenschaft als Beruf." *Gesammelte Aufsätze zur Wissenschaftslehre*. Tübingen: Mohr, 1922.

Welsch, Wolfgang. *Unsere Postmoderne Moderne*. Weinheim: VCH, Acta Humaniora, 1991.

Windelband, Wilhelm. *Einleitung in die Philosophie*. Tübingen: Mohr, 1923.

——. *Geschichte der abendländischen Philosophie im Altertum*. 4th ed. Munich: Beck, 1923.

——. *Die Geschichte der neueren Philosophie in ihrem Zusammenhange mit der allgemeinen Kultur und den besonderen Wissenschaften*. 5th ed. 2 vols. Leipzig: Breitkopf and Härtel, 1911.

——. "History and Natural Science." Trans. Guy Oakes. *History and Theory* 19, no. 2 (1980): 165–185.

——. *A History of Philosophy*. Trans. James Tufts. New York: Macmillan, 1919.

——. *An Introduction to Philosophy*. Trans. Joseph McCabe. London: Unwin, 1921.

——. "Kulturphilosophie und transzendentaler Idealismus." *Logos* 1 (1910–11): 186–197.

——. *Lehrbuch der Geschichte der Philosophie*. Tübingen: Mohr. 1949.

——. *Die Philosophie im deutschen Geistesleben der Gegenwart*. Tübingen: Mohr, 1927.

——. *Präludien*. 2 vols. Tübingen: Mohr, 1924.

——. *Theories in Logic*. New York: Philosophical Library, 1961.

Wolin, Richard, ed. *The Heidegger Controversy: A Critical Reader*. New York: Columbia University Press, 1991.

——. *The Politics of Being: The Political Thought of Martin Heidegger*. New York: Columbia University Press, 1990.

Zimmerman, Michael. *Heidegger's Confrontation with Modernity*. Bloomington: Indiana University Press, 1990.

Index

Dilthey, Wilhelm (*cont.*)
  Weltanschauung, 30, 39–41, 130, 135,
    173, 176, 178, 184, 200, 204, 238
Droysen Johann G., 12, 16, 18, 43, 58,
    68, 69, 83, 136, 189, 223, 246, 259
Dühring, Eugen, 67

Eckhart, Meister, 200, 270
Eco, Umberto, 21
Einstein, Albert, 41, 50
ekstasis, 237
empiricism, 109, 137–139, 142, 150
enactment-meaning (*Vollzugssinn*), 231
end of history, 2, 3, 8, 9, 272
end of metaphysics, 137, 258
end of philosophy, 3, 54, 184, 242
Engelhardt, Dietrich von, 43
Engels, Friedrich, 67
Enlightenment, 10, 12, 42, 51, 59, 175,
    181, 267
ent-deutet ("de-signified"), 198, 227
ent-geschichtlicht ("dehistoricized"), 198
Ent-lebnis ("de-living"), 227
environing world, 208, 227
episteme, 234
epistemological certitude, 16, 34, 170,
    181
Erdmann, Johann, 62
Ereignis, 75, 207, 244, 255, 258, 259, 264,
    269–272
Erfahrungswissenschaften, 44
Erlebnis. (*See* Dilthey, Wilhelm: *Erlebnis*)
Ermarth, Michael, 12, 129, 131, 134, 137,
    148, 154–156, 162, 169, 174, 176, 179
Ernesti, Johann, 163
Ernst, Paul, 4, 23, 37, 38, 43, 57, 59, 62,
    85, 88, 118, 128, 132, 155, 171, 188
es er-eignet ("eventing"), 207, 228
es weltet ("it worlds"), 207, 256
eschatology, 10, 214, 262, 266, 270
eschaton, 258, 270
Eucken, Rudolf, 57
eventing (*es er-eignet*), 228
existential analytic of Dasein, 204, 229,
    231
existentialism, 87, 176, 199

Fachwissenschaft, 11, 15
factical life, 196, 199, 203, 204, 207–209,
    211, 212, 217, 239–241, 261
facticity, 31, 46, 199, 200, 204–206, 210–
    212, 216, 220, 224, 232, 240, 241,
    249, 256
Faktum der Erkenntnis, 121
Faktum der Wissenschaft, 34, 61, 213
fallenness, 31, 220, 249
falling, 201, 237

fate (*Geschick*), 43, 188, 247, 266
Fechner, Gustav, 67, 77
Fichte, Johann G., 24, 89, 133
Fischer, Kuno, 4, 24, 38, 62, 140, 143
fore-structure, 221, 222
formal indication (*formale Anzeige*), 199,
    200
formalism, 41, 117–119, 123, 201
Forman, Paul, 14, 41, 47
Forschung ("research"), 24, 129, 156,
    211, 248, 251
Frischeisen-Köhler, Max, 104
Fronterlebnis, 256

Gadamer, Hans-Georg, 1, 4, 17, 23, 29,
    34, 38, 47, 121, 142, 143, 151, 154,
    167, 176–178, 190, 236, 260
Galen, 6
Galileo Galilei, 49, 50, 67, 91, 104, 143
Garve, Christian von, 177
Gegenstände, 114, 230
Gegenständlichkeit, 120
Gegenwart, 23, 38, 39, 60, 70, 101, 128,
    136, 155, 167, 171, 172, 176, 185,
    201, 236
Gegenwärtigen ("making present"), 129,
    245
Gehaltssinn ("content meaning"), 231
Geist, 13, 21, 30, 37, 71, 80, 81, 99, 102,
    103, 114, 119, 128, 129, 143, 149,
    157, 161, 162, 164
Geistesgeschichte, 176, 211
Geisteswissenschaften, 7, 25, 42, 43, 69–
    73, 78, 79, 90, 93, 94, 99, 102, 104,
    118, 119, 123, 128, 129, 132–135,
    139, 148–150, 154, 156, 160, 162,
    167, 168, 172, 176, 200, 204
George, Stefan, 37, 40
Geschehen ("happening"), 125, 244, 251
Geschichte, 4, 5, 12, 15–18, 26, 35, 41–43,
    59, 60, 62, 63, 70, 109, 112, 123, 124,
    130, 136, 143, 151, 154, 167, 169,
    171, 185, 200, 204, 215, 220, 242,
    244, 257–259, 266, 267
  des Seyns, 259
Geschichtsphilosophie, 2, 59, 60, 75, 81,
    84–86, 99, 102, 103, 115, 141, 171,
    172
Geschichtstheologie, 13, 59
Geschichtswissenschaft, 12, 24, 42, 43,
    102, 172
Geschick, 257, 266, 270, 271
Gesetzeswissenschaften, 44
Gewesenheit, 244
Gogarten, Friedrich, 187, 191, 192, 195,
    202
Göttingen school, 42

Grimm, Jakob, 139, 197
Groethuysen, Bernhard, 131
Grundwissenschaft, 78, 87, 168

Habermas, Jürgen, 22, 27
Haeckel, Ernst, 87
happening (*Geschehen*), 15, 125, 213, 220, 240, 242, 244, 247, 251, 257, 264
Harnack, Adolf von, 189, 190
Haym, Rudolf, 17, 24, 166, 167
Hegel, G. W. F., 6, 17, 22, 23, 42, 43, 53, 67, 75, 85, 103, 128, 131, 133, 134, 136–138, 141, 162, 166, 167, 172, 177, 269
   Enzyklopaedie der Wissenschaften, 71
Heidegger, Martin, 1–3, 5, 9–11, 13–19, 23–26, 30, 31, 33–37, 41, 44, 46, 51–55, 58, 83, 109, 122–125, 142, 154, 167, 176, 177, 181–185, 187, 192–273
   an/other beginning (*anderer Anfang*), 2, 55, 253, 255, 257, 269, 271, 273
   Being and Time, 15, 21, 30, 31, 34, 122, 123, 143, 167, 197, 202, 204, 205, 209, 212, 215, 217, 219, 223, 228–230, 232, 235, 236, 239–241, 243–248, 250, 251, 253, 255, 258, 260, 264, 268, 270
   Beiträge, 24, 258, 259
   "The Concept of Time," 15, 34, 35, 41, 123, 215, 217, 218, 221, 224, 226, 227, 229, 231, 233, 239, 243, 244, 248
   crisis, 1, 184, 185, 188–195, 200–205, 210, 214–218, 222, 223, 225, 226, 228, 229, 239, 242, 243, 245, 249–261, 263–267, 270, 272, 273
   Destruktion, 31, 33, 46, 54, 55, 109, 124, 187, 197–199, 201, 210–212, 223, 224, 232, 234, 245, 248, 256, 266, 270
   eschatology of being, 262, 266
   event of being (*see also Ereignis*), 255, 258, 259
   everydayness (*Alltäglichkeit*), 201
   first beginning, 257, 262, 265, 270
   Geschichtlichkeit ("historicity"), 15, 17, 166, 167, 173, 220, 244
   Heraklit, 263
   hermeneutic phenomenology, 31
   historicity, 203, 204, 212, 219–221, 223, 232, 233, 238, 240–242, 244–249, 252, 253, 255, 260, 265, 268
   History of the Concept of Time, 34, 35, 41, 123, 215, 217, 218, 227, 229, 231, 233, 239, 243, 244, 248

"The Idea of Philosophy and the Problem of the World-view," 26
   intentionality, 196, 204, 208, 212, 221, 222, 227, 229, 231, 232
   Introduction to Metaphysics, 262, 264, 269, 270
   Kassel lectures, 200, 240, 255
   Kehre, 202, 203, 255, 257, 259, 260
   new beginning, 31, 190, 192, 200, 203, 215, 238, 241, 254, 258, 261, 265
   Nietzsche, 1, 2, 15, 143, 175, 181, 182, 253–255
   Phänomenologische Interpretationen zu Aristoteles, 196, 204
   "Phenomenology and Transcendental Value-Philosophy," 58, 224
   "The Self-Assertion of the German University," 261, 268–270
   Seinsgeschichte, 260
   temporal "*ecstases*," 220
   understanding (*Verstehen*), 190, 195–197, 199, 201, 202, 207, 212, 216–220, 222, 223, 230–233, 236–239, 244–246, 248–251, 254, 255, 257–259, 261, 266–273
   Weltanschauung, 200, 204, 205, 211, 217, 238, 243, 256, 260
   Wiederholung ("retrieval"), 211
   Zur Bestimmung der Philosophie, 26, 58, 194
Heidelberg, 23, 79, 84, 87, 122, 183, 197, 202, 211
Heimweh, 260
Heisenberg, Werner, 51
Helmholz, Hermann, 77
Herder, Johann G., 193, 222, 269
hermeneutic turn, 25, 131, 132
hermeneutics, 15, 16, 21, 28, 30, 43, 47, 50, 51, 55, 67, 108, 128–133, 150, 154, 155, 160, 163, 164, 167, 168, 170, 175–177, 180, 197, 199, 201, 203, 204, 210–212, 216, 221, 237, 239–241, 252
Hippocrates, 6
historia rerum gestarum, 16
historical being, 86, 109, 118, 124, 140, 146, 150, 151, 165, 173, 184, 219, 240, 248, 249
historical consciousness, 1, 2, 13, 14, 42, 43, 53, 121, 140, 141, 154, 155, 165, 169, 175–178, 180, 183, 195, 199, 200, 222, 250
historical development, 13, 62, 68, 85, 104, 112, 119, 120, 133, 162, 173, 189, 204
historical logic, 80, 81, 90, 103, 109, 123
historical objectivity, 9, 58, 85, 104, 107–109

historical reason. (*See* Dilthey, Wilhelm: historical reason)

Historical School, 68, 77, 104, 136, 137, 139–143, 148, 178, 180

historical science, 5, 12, 42, 44, 77, 83, 97, 100, 101, 104, 119, 122, 150, 151, 164, 168, 173, 217, 219, 220, 223, 226, 227, 233, 242, 247, 251

historicity (*see also* Dilthey, Wilhelm: historicity; Heidegger, Martin: historicity), 13–18, 21, 31, 33–35, 43, 45, 46, 51, 60, 77–79, 106, 109, 120–123, 125, 137, 140, 141, 147, 150, 151, 159, 160, 165–170, 173, 176, 178–181, 183, 184, 203, 204, 212, 219–221, 223, 232, 233, 238, 240–242, 244–249, 252, 253, 255, 260, 265, 268
of life, 17, 168, 203, 233, 238
of the object, 17, 168, 180
of the subject, 17, 180

historicization, 24, 25, 42, 43, 45, 213

Historie, 15, 16, 42, 167, 220, 242, 244, 245, 251, 258, 259

Historik, 12, 16, 125, 178

history of being, 202, 203, 242, 258–260, 269–271

history of ontology, 5, 18, 31, 217, 248, 255, 258

Hölderlin, Friedrich, 128, 257, 258, 260, 265, 269, 270

homogeneous continuum, 98

horizon, 5, 34, 121, 122, 124, 161, 232, 236, 237, 251, 252, 254, 255, 269

human sciences (*see also* Dilthey, Wilhelm: *Geisteswissenschaften*; *Geisteswissenschaften*), 5, 13, 17, 21, 24, 25, 27, 33, 41–44, 49, 60, 61, 69, 70, 74, 77, 79, 102, 103, 123, 128–130, 132–141, 146, 147, 151–156, 159–164, 166, 169, 172, 173, 178, 180, 181, 183, 213, 217, 218, 223, 226, 227, 232, 235, 239–241, 245, 248, 251, 266

Humanität, 111

Humboldt, Wilhelm von, 12, 43, 58, 60, 69, 83, 171, 204, 222

Husserl, Edmund, 25, 28, 39, 40, 44, 156, 173, 176, 194, 196, 198, 199, 204, 213, 221–223, 231, 232
Crisis of the European Sciences, 6, 28, 39
"Philosophy as Rigorous Science," 40

idiographic, 75–77, 81, 94, 99, 100, 217, 224, 225

Iggers, Georg, 4, 12, 18, 43, 47, 124, 172, 176

individuality, 86, 98, 100, 102–105, 120, 147, 174, 225, 226

indubitability, 31, 32, 217

intuitionism, 41

"it worlds" (*es weltet*), 207, 256

Jaeger, Werner, 12, 18, 59

Kahler, Erich, 37

kairos, 212, 214, 219, 232, 236

Kampf, 200, 209, 210, 260

Kant, Immanuel, 24, 28–32, 34, 43, 44, 59–65, 67–69, 72, 73, 76, 81, 84, 89–93, 98, 99, 103, 130, 133, 142–148, 150, 158, 165, 177, 178, 181–183, 219, 231, 236, 241
Critique of Judgement, 63
Critique of Practical Reason, 32, 44, 63, 64, 67, 72, 73, 81, 90, 91, 94, 145, 177
Critique of Pure Reason, 32, 44, 63–64, 67, 72, 73, 81, 90, 91, 94, 145, 177
Prolegomena to any Future Metaphysics, 92

Kathederphilosophie, 158, 198, 205, 210

Kepler, Johannes, 49, 67, 104, 143

Kierkegaard, Søren, 87, 89, 190, 199–202, 211, 229, 237, 238, 258

Kiwi language, 60

Klages, Ludwig, 40

Koselleck, Reinhart, 42

Krebs, Engelbert, 193, 194, 203

krisis (*see also* crisis), 4, 37–39, 41, 48, 49, 85, 190, 191, 195, 200, 202, 214, 250, 257, 265

Kuhn, Thomas, 47, 50, 51

Kultur, 38, 84, 102, 188

Kulturpessimismus, 256, 262

Lamprecht, Karl, 18

Landgrebe, Ludwig, 121, 123

Larvanz ("masking"), 201

Lask, Emil, 200

Lebensphilosophie, 26, 28, 39, 40, 54, 88, 90, 109, 145, 149, 171, 176, 222

Lessing, Theodor, 7, 83

Liebert, Arthur, 38, 39, 48

Litt, Theodor, 26, 37

Locke, John, 71, 91, 138, 146

logos, 40, 87, 129, 136, 173, 188, 201, 214, 226, 235, 246, 259, 262, 263

Lotze, Hermann, 62, 233

Löwith, Karl, 199, 200, 205, 214, 256

Luther, Martin, 161, 190, 191, 193, 195–
197, 199, 200, 204, 209–211, 223,
241
Lyotard, Jean-François, 9, 10

Marx, Karl, 67
materialism, 27, 76
Materialismusstreit, 22
Megill, Alan, 14, 52
Meinecke, Friedrich, 4, 12, 14, 37, 86,
104, 109–113, 116, 118–122, 140,
172, 185, 223, 243, 266
Merleau-Ponty, Maurice, 46
metaphysical faith, 13
metaphysics
euthanasia of, 137
Greek, 15, 203, 241, 273
of presence, 232, 236, 242, 243, 250
of time, 6, 221, 237
Methodenstreit, 57, 68
methodological objectivity, 13, 183
Michaelis, Johann, 163
middle-voice, 228
Mill, John Stuart, 70, 71, 74, 99, 134,
137–139, 142
"On the Logic of the Moral Sciences," 74
modernity, 1–3, 5, 8–11, 26, 30, 31, 33,
37, 46, 49, 51–55, 125, 184, 185, 216,
217, 260, 261, 265–267, 270, 272,
273
Moleschott, Jacob, 22
Mommsen, Theodor, 42, 69, 139
moral sciences, 70, 74, 128, 137–139
Musil, Robert, 175

National Socialism, 215, 216, 254, 261,
265, 270
Natorp, Paul, 40, 57, 69, 143
Natur, 21, 30, 43, 71, 73, 79–81, 90, 93,
94, 99, 102–104, 114, 136, 143, 148
naturalism, 27, 61, 88, 96, 155
Naturphilosophie, 71
Neo-Aristotelianism, 25, 219
Neo-Fichteanism, 25, 219
Neo-Hegelianism, 25
Neo-Kantianism, 5, 11–18, 25, 28, 29,
33–36, 57–127, 142–151, 169, 170,
180, 195, 198, 206, 210, 217–238,
266
Neo-Kantian theory of values, 25, 84
Neo-Kantian tradition of historical
logic, 109
Neo-Kantians
Baden, 60
Marburg, 59, 61
Neo-Thomism, 25, 219

Newton, Sir Isaac, 49, 67, 104
Niebuhr, H. Richard, 12, 42, 69, 180,
181
Nietzsche, Friedrich, 1, 2, 7, 10, 15, 40,
52, 53, 57, 84, 87, 89, 90, 112, 117,
121, 122, 129, 143, 165, 175, 181,
190, 242, 249, 252–260, 269, 270
Untimely Meditations, 7, 112, 165, 252,
254, 256, 257
nihilism, 1, 8, 11, 14, 32, 48, 52, 53, 85,
113, 115, 202, 215, 242, 253, 259–
261, 264
nomothetic, 75–77, 81, 94, 99, 100, 217,
224, 225

objective mind, 162–164
objectivism, 16, 32, 33, 45, 46, 221, 243,
260
objectivity, 5, 9, 11, 13–16, 28, 34, 35,
43, 44, 50, 52, 53, 58, 59, 85, 104–
109, 111, 115, 117, 124, 160, 173–
175, 178–181, 183, 184, 200, 211,
221, 223, 252
objektgeschichtlich, 213
objektiver Geist, 162
oblivion of being (*Seinsvergessenheit*),
197, 242
Ochsner, Heinrich, 194
Otto, Rudolf, 5, 17, 28, 42, 43, 128, 154,
167, 171, 175, 177, 194, 199, 201,
211, 272

Pannwitz, Rudolf, 38
parousia, 212, 225, 235–238
part: whole relationship, 158, 164, 167,
168
Pascal, Blaise, 199, 200
Paul, Saint, 209–214, 224, 225, 236–238
watchfulness (*wachsam Sein*), 203
Paulsen, Friedrich, 26
Petri, Elfriede, 193
Petzold, Joseph, 41
phenomenology, 30, 31, 35, 40, 46, 58,
83, 101, 132, 155, 174, 176, 194,
196–199, 210, 212, 213, 219, 222–
224, 227, 229, 236, 237, 239, 248,
255
philosophical method, 30, 90
philosophical research, 211, 213
philosophy of nature, 22, 70, 181
philosophy of philosophy, 174
philosophy of spirit (*Philosophie des
Geistes*), 22, 71, 128, 136
Planck, Max, 50
Plato, 24, 31, 70, 216, 223, 233, 234, 236
pneumatology, 70
polis, 262–264